DB2 11 for z/OS

Developer Training and Reference Guide

Robert Wingate

ISBN 13: 978-1-7345847-0-7

Disclaimer

The contents of this book are based upon the author's understanding of and experience with the IBM DB2 product. Every attempt has been made to provide correct information. However, the author and publisher do not guarantee the accuracy of every detail, nor do they assume responsibility for information included in or omitted from it. All of the information in this book should be used at your own risk.

Copyright

Contents

Introduction

Welcome

Congratulations on your purchase of DB2 11 for z/OS Developer Training and Reference Guide! This text book will give you the essential information you need to know about DB2 11 so you can be productive as soon as possible. You'll receive instruction, examples and questions/answers to help you learn and to gauge your proficiency and readiness to join a DB2 development team.

Assumptions

While I do not assume that you know a great deal about DB2, I do assume that you've worked on an IBM mainframe and know your way around. Also I assume that you have a working knowledge of either the COBOL or the PLI programming language which we will use for all the embedded SQL examples. Finally, I assume you have some familiarity with Structured Query Language (SQL). All in all, I assume you have:

1. A working knowledge of ISPF and JCL
2. A working knowledge of COBOL or PLI.
3. A basic understanding of SQL
4. Access to a mainframe computer running z/OS and DB2

To maximize your chances of success as a DB2 11 developer on z/OS, I recommend that you have or acquire two things:

1. Knowledge of DB2 11.
2. Experience with DB2 11.

Knowledge of DB2 11

We'll cover the fundamentals, beginning with the z/OS methods for accessing DB2 data stores. Then we'll deal with the three "languages" associated with relational database management systems: Data Definition Language (DDL), Data Manipulation Language (DML) and Data Control Language (DCL). Next, we'll look at embedded SQL in application programming using COBOL and PLI. Later we'll look at data concurrency, something many programmers don't get much exposure to, but which is really important for system performance. Then we'll look at advanced DB2 entities such as stored procedures, user defined functions and triggers. Finally there is a special project to put these concepts together.

Experience with DB2 11

Unless your shop has already upgraded to DB2 11, you may not have any experience with it.

My suggestion is to practice with whatever version of DB2 you have, and then put some extra study effort on the new features of DB2 11 so you'll be prepared when your shop adopts DB2 11. Once you are in an environment that uses DB2 11, this effort will pay off.

If you do not have access to a mainframe system through your job, I can recommend Mathru Technologies. You can rent a mainframe account from them at a very affordable rate, and this includes access to DB2 (at this writing they offer DB2 version 10). Their environment supports COBOL and PLI as well. The URL to the Mathru web site is:

http://mathrutech.com/index.html

Knowledge and experience. Will that guarantee that you'll succeed as a DB2 application developer? Of course, nothing is guaranteed in life. But if you put sufficient effort into a well-rounded study and exercise plan that includes both of the above, I believe you have a very good chance of excelling on your team as a DB2 application developer.

Best of luck!

Robert Wingate

IBM Certified Application Developer – DB2 11 for z/OS

CHAPTER ONE: BASIC Z/OS TOOLS FOR DB2

Welcome to the DB2 11 for z/OS Developer Training and Reference Guide! Before we get into development activities, I want to introduce you to the environment we'll be working in. If you've used DB2 on the mainframe, you're almost certainly familiar with these tools and this will be a quick review. But if you have little or no exposure to DB2 on z/OS, we need to make sure you are familiar with how to access it and use the basic tools available.

DB2 Interactive

You'll do much of your DB2 work in DB2 Interactive which is now typically called the DB2 Primary Option Menu. Regardless of which shop you work in, there should be a menu option on the ISPF main menu to get to DB2. It may be called DB2 or some other name with DB2 in it. On my system, the option is called DB2 and the description is DB2 Primary Menu. Select whichever option is on your main menu for DB2.

```
   Menu  Utilities  Compilers  Options  Status  Help
─────────────────────────────────────────────────────────────────
                       ISPF Primary Option Menu
Option ===>

  0   Settings      Terminal and user parameters        User ID . : HRUSER
  1   View          Display source data or listings     Time. . . : 21:19
  2   Edit          Create or change source data        Terminal. : 3278
  3   Utilities     Perform utility functions           Screen. . : 1
  4   Foreground    Interactive language processing     Language. : ENGLISH
  5   Batch         Submit job for language processing  Appl ID . : ISR
  6   Command       Enter TSO or Workstation commands   TSO logon : MATPROC
  7   Dialog Test   Perform dialog testing              TSO prefix: HRUSER
  10  SCLM          SW Configuration Library Manager    System ID : MATE
  11  Workplace     ISPF Object/Action Workplace        MVS acct. : MT529
  12  DITTO         DITTO/ESA for MVS                   Release . : ISPF 6.0
  13  FMN           File Manager
  15  DB2           DB2 Primary Menu
  17  QMF           DB2 Query Management Facility
  S   SDSF          Spool Search and Display Facility

       Enter X to Terminate using log/list defaults
```

This is the DB2 main menu. Select the first option, which is SPUFI. SPUFI is an acronym for SQL Processing Using File Input.

```
                              DB2I PRIMARY OPTION MENU           SSID: DBAX
COMMAND ===>

Select one of the following DB2 functions and press ENTER.

    1   SPUFI                  (Process SQL statements)
    2   DCLGEN                 (Generate SQL and source language declarations)
    3   PROGRAM PREPARATION    (Prepare a DB2 application program to run)
    4   PRECOMPILE             (Invoke DB2 precompiler)
    5   BIND/REBIND/FREE       (BIND, REBIND, or FREE plans or packages)
    6   RUN                    (RUN an SQL program)
    7   DB2 COMMANDS           (Issue DB2 commands)
    8   UTILITIES              (Invoke DB2 utilities)
    D   DB2I DEFAULTS          (Set global parameters)
    Q   QMF                    (Query Management Facility)
    X   EXIT                   (Leave DB2I)




PRESS:                        END to exit      HELP for more information
```

You'll see the following screen.

```
                          SPUFI                            SSID: DBAX
===>

Enter the input data set name:       (Can be sequential or partitioned)
  1   DATA SET NAME ... ===> 'HRUSER.SPUFI.CNTL(EXECSQL)'
  2   VOLUME SERIAL ... ===>          (Enter if not cataloged)
  3   DATA SET PASSWORD ===>          (Enter if password protected)

Enter the output data set name:      (Must be a sequential data set)
  4   DATA SET NAME ... ===> 'HRUSER.SPUFI.OUT'

Specify processing options:
  5   CHANGE DEFAULTS   ===> NO       (Y/N - Display SPUFI defaults panel?)
  6   EDIT INPUT ...... ===> YES      (Y/N - Enter SQL statements?)
  7   EXECUTE ......... ===> YES      (Y/N - Execute SQL statements?)
  8   AUTOCOMMIT ...... ===> YES      (Y/N - Commit after successful run?)
  9   BROWSE OUTPUT ... ===> YES      (Y/N - Browse output data set?)

For remote SQL processing:
10   CONNECT LOCATION  ===>


PRESS:  ENTER to process    END to exit            HELP for more information
```

This is the place you can specify an input file which will contain the SQL, DDL, DML or DCL statements you wish to execute. We'll explain DDL, DML and DCL in future chapters. For now just think of it as the place you can run SQL.

You must also specify an output file to capture the results from your statements. If these files do not already exist you must allocate them.

I recommend that you specify the processing options shown below, i.e., NO for CHANGE DEFAULTS, and yes for EDIT INPUT, EXECUTE, AUTOMCOMMIT and BROWSE OUTPUT.

When you press ENTER your input dataset will open and you can type the statements that you want to execute. In the example below, I've coded a SELECT statement to retrieve all records from a sample table named EMPLOYEE.

```
   File  Edit  Edit_Settings  Menu  Utilities  Compilers  Test  Help

   EDIT       HRUSER.SPUFI.CNTL(EXECSQL) - 01.00          Columns 00001 00072
   Command ===>                                           Scroll ===> PAGE
   ****** ***************************** Top of Data ****************************
   000001 SELECT * FROM EMPLOYEE;
   ****** ************************** Bottom of Data **************************
```

When you press PF3, and then press ENTER again, the output dataset is shown with the results from the query.

```
      Menu  Utilities  Compilers  Help

   BROWSE    HRUSER.SPUFI.OUT                      Line 00000000 Col 001 080
   Command ===>                                            Scroll ===> PAGE
   ****************************** Top of Data ********************************
   ---------+---------+---------+---------+---------+---------+---------+---------+
   SELECT * FROM EMPLOYEE;
   ---------+---------+---------+---------+---------+---------+---------+---------+
        EMPNO   NAME
   ---------+---------+---------+---------+---------+---------+---------+---------+
         100   SMITH
         200   JONES
   DSNE610I NUMBER OF ROWS DISPLAYED IS 2
   DSNE616I STATEMENT EXECUTION WAS SUCCESSFUL, SQLCODE IS 100
   ---------+---------+---------+---------+---------+---------+---------+---------+
   ---------+---------+---------+---------+---------+---------+---------+---------+
   DSNE617I COMMIT PERFORMED, SQLCODE IS 0
   DSNE616I STATEMENT EXECUTION WAS SUCCESSFUL, SQLCODE IS 0
   ---------+---------+---------+---------+---------+---------+---------+---------+
   DSNE601I SQL STATEMENTS ASSUMED TO BE BETWEEN COLUMNS 1 AND 72
   DSNE620I NUMBER OF SQL STATEMENTS PROCESSED IS 1
   DSNE621I NUMBER OF INPUT RECORDS READ IS 2
   DSNE622I NUMBER OF OUTPUT RECORDS WRITTEN IS 18
   ****************************** Bottom of Data ****************************
```

You will use SPUFI very frequently unless your shop has adopted another tool such as Data Studio.

DCLGEN

DCLGEN is an IBM utility that generates SQL data structures (table definition and host variables) for a table or view. DCLGEN stores the structure in a PDS member and then the PDS member can be included in a PLI or COBOL program by issuing an EXEC SQL INCLUDE statement. Put another way, DCLGEN generates table declarations (hence the name DCLGEN). Don't worry if this doesn't make sense yet. We'll generate and use these DCLGEN structures when we start writing programs.

Here's an example of running a DCLGEN for a table. From the DB2 Primary Option menu, select option 2 for DCLGEN.

```
                              DB2I PRIMARY OPTION MENU          SSID: DBAX
COMMAND ===>
Select one of the following DB2 functions and press ENTER.

    1   SPUFI                 (Process SQL statements)
    2   DCLGEN                (Generate SQL and source language declarations)
    3   PROGRAM PREPARATION   (Prepare a DB2 application program to run)
    4   PRECOMPILE            (Invoke DB2 precompiler)
    5   BIND/REBIND/FREE      (BIND, REBIND, or FREE plans or packages)
    6   RUN                   (RUN an SQL program)
    7   DB2 COMMANDS          (Issue DB2 commands)
    8   UTILITIES             (Invoke DB2 utilities)
    D   DB2I DEFAULTS         (Set global parameters)
    Q   QMF                   (Query Management Facility
    X   EXIT                  (Leave DB2I)




    PRESS:                    END to exit     HELP for more information
```

Now enter the DB2 table name, owner and the partitioned data set and member name to place the DCLGEN output into. In the example below we have a table named EMP_PAY_CHECK owned by HRSCHEMA. We want the output of the DCLGEN to be placed in member EMPPAY-CK of partitioned dataset HRUSER.DCLGEN.COBOL.

Once you've entered the required information, press ENTER.

```
                        DCLGEN                              SSID: DBAX
  ===>

  Enter table name for which declarations are required:
   1  SOURCE TABLE NAME ===> EMP_PAY_CHECK

   2  TABLE OWNER ..... ===> HRSCHEMA

   3  AT LOCATION ..... ===>                             (Optional)
  Enter destination data set:      (Can be sequential or partitioned)
   4  DATA SET NAME ... ===> 'HRUSER.DCLGEN.COBOL(EMPPAYCK)'
   5  DATA SET PASSWORD ===>        (If password protected)
  Enter options as desired:
   6  ACTION ......... ===> ADD      (ADD new or REPLACE old declaration)
   7  COLUMN LABEL .... ===> NO       (Enter YES for column label)
   8  STRUCTURE NAME .. ===>                             (Optional)
   9  FIELD NAME PREFIX ===>                             (Optional)
  10  DELIMIT DBCS .... ===> YES      (Enter YES to delimit DBCS identifiers)
  11  COLUMN SUFFIX ... ===> NO       (Enter YES to append column name)
  12  INDICATOR VARS .. ===> NO       (Enter YES for indicator variables)
  13  ADDITIONAL OPTIONS===> NO       (Enter YES to change additional options


  PRESS: ENTER to process    END to exit      HELP for more information
```

Next, you will receive a message indicating the DCLGEN has succeeded.

```
   DSNE905I EXECUTION COMPLETE, MEMBER EMPPAYCK ADDED
   ***
```

Now you can browse the PDS member EMPPAYCK to see the resulting structures. The first structure will declare the DB2 table definition, and the other structure will declare COBOL host variables that correspond to the table definition.

```
   ******************************************************************
   * DCLGEN TABLE(HRSCHEMA.EMP_PAY_CHECK)                           *
   *        LIBRARY(HRSCHEMA.DCLGEN.COBOL(EMPPAYCK))                *
   *        LANGUAGE(COBOL)                                         *
   *        QUOTE                                                   *
   * ... IS THE DCLGEN COMMAND THAT MADE THE FOLLOWING STATEMENTS   *
   ******************************************************************
        EXEC SQL DECLARE HRSCHEMA.EMP_PAY_CHECK TABLE
        ( EMP_ID                      INTEGER NOT NULL,
          EMP_REGULAR_PAY             DECIMAL(8, 2) NOT NULL,
          EMP_SEMIMTH_PAY             DECIMAL(8, 2) NOT NULL
        ) END-EXEC.
   ******************************************************************
   * COBOL DECLARATION FOR TABLE HRSCHEMA.EMP_PAY_CHECK            *
   ******************************************************************
     01  DCLEMP-PAY-CHECK.
         10 EMP-ID              PIC S9(9) USAGE COMP.
```

19

```
      10 EMP-REGULAR-PAY       PIC S9(6)V9(2) USAGE COMP-3.
      10 EMP-SEMIMTH-PAY       PIC S9(6)V9(2) USAGE COMP-3.
  *****************************************************************
  * THE NUMBER OF COLUMNS DESCRIBED BY THIS DECLARATION IS 3      *
  *****************************************************************
```

Again, the above structure can be included in your application program by simply issuing:

```
      EXEC SQL
         INCLUDE EMPPAYCK
      END-EXEC
```

Once you've included the structure in your application program, you have host variables declared for every column in the table, so you don't need to code these variables yourself.

DB2I Defaults

Your shop should have standard settings for DB2I defaults. If you are studying on your own, I recommend setting some defaults. First select option D from the DB2 Primary Option menu:

```
                           DB2I PRIMARY OPTION MENU          SSID: DBAX
      COMMAND ===>

      Select one of the following DB2 functions and press ENTER.

        1   SPUFI               (Process SQL statements)
        2   DCLGEN              (Generate SQL and source language declarations)
        3   PROGRAM PREPARATION  (Prepare a DB2 application program to run)
        4   PRECOMPILE          (Invoke DB2 precompiler)
        5   BIND/REBIND/FREE    (BIND, REBIND, or FREE plans or packages)
        6   RUN                 (RUN an SQL program)
        7   DB2 COMMANDS        (Issue DB2 commands)
        8   UTILITIES           (Invoke DB2 utilities)
        D   DB2I DEFAULTS       (Set global parameters)
        Q   QMF                 (Query Management Facility
        X   EXIT                (Leave DB2I)




      PRESS:                   END to exit      HELP for more information
```

Select the following options, specifying your correct DB2 subsystem identifier as the DB2 Name (ask your system admin if you are not sure – I have used DB2X as mine and that represents the subsystem identifier on my system).

If you are developing in COBOL, specify IBMCOB as the application language. Otherwise specify PLI or whichever language you are using. Our programming examples will be in COBOL and PLI.

```
                        DB2I DEFAULTS PANEL 1
        COMMAND ===>

        Change defaults as desired:

           1   DB2 NAME ............. ===> DB2X      (Subsystem identifier)
           2   DB2 CONNECTION RETRIES ===> 0         (How many retries for DB2 connection)
           3   APPLICATION LANGUAGE   ===> IBMCOB    (ASM, C, CPP, IBMCOB, FORTRAN, PLI)
           4   LINES/PAGE OF LISTING  ===> 60        (A number from 5 to 999)
           5   MESSAGE LEVEL ........ ===> I         (Information, Warning, Error, Severe)
           6   SQL STRING DELIMITER   ===> DEFAULT   (DEFAULT, ' or ")
           7   DECIMAL POINT ........ ===> .         (. or ,)
           8   STOP IF RETURN CODE >= ===> 8         (Lowest terminating return code)
           9   NUMBER OF ROWS ....... ===> 20        (For ISPF Tables)
          10   AS USER                ===>           (Userid to associate with the trusted
                                                      connection)



        PRESS:  ENTER to process    END to cancel        HELP for more information
```

BATCH UTILITIES

DB2 provides some batch utility programs you can use. The two most useful of these are DSNTIAUL and DSNSTEP2 (and DSNSTEP4 if you have large numbers of rows to unload because it uses multi-row fetch). You can use these instead of SPUFI to operate on data (or issue other statements) in a batch mode.

DSNTIAUL

DSNTIAUL is a utility most often used to unload a DB2 table into a flat file. Here is a sample JCL to run it, and of course you must adjust file names to your own environment. In the SYSIN file you specify the name of a table to unload. In this example we will unload the EMP_PAY table (the HRSCHEMA is a schema qualifier – we will talk about that later).

```
//HRSCHEMAD JOB MSGLEVEL=(1,1),NOTIFY=&SYSUID
//*
//*   DSNTIAUL RUN JCL
//*
//STEP01    EXEC PGM=IKJEFT01,
//             DYNAMNBR=20,REGION=4096K
//STEPLIB  DD  DISP=SHR,DSN=DSNTST.DBAX.SDSNEXIT   ß YOUR SYSTEM LIBRARIES
//         DD  DISP=SHR,DSN=DSNTST.SDSNLOAD        ß YOUR SYSTEM LIBRARIES
//SYSPRINT DD  SYSOUT=*
//SYSTSPRT DD  SYSOUT=*
//SYSPUNCH DD  SYSOUT=*
//SYSUDUMP DD  SYSOUT=*
//SYSTSIN  DD  *
```

```
DSN SYSTEM (DBAX   )
  RUN PROGRAM   (DSNTIAUL) -
     PLAN       (DSNTIAUL) -
     LIBRARY    ('DSNTST.DBAX.RUNLIB.LOAD')   ß YOUR SYS LOAD LIBRARY
END
/*
//SYSIN    DD *
 HRSCHEMA.EMP_PAY
//SYSOUT   DD  SYSOUT=*
```

The above unloads the entire EMP_PAY table. Our second example allows you to use SQL to select the data you want to unload. Notice that it includes PARMS('SQL') as a RUN parameter. The SQL is coded in the SYSIN file:

```
//HRSCHEMAD JOB MSGLEVEL=(1,1),NOTIFY=&SYSUID
//*
//STEP01   EXEC PGM=IKJEFT01,
//            DYNAMNBR=20,REGION=4096K
//STEPLIB  DD  DISP=SHR,DSN=DSNTST.DBAX.SDSNEXIT
//         DD  DISP=SHR,DSN=DSNTST.SDSNLOAD
//SYSPRINT DD  SYSOUT=*
//SYSTSPRT DD  SYSOUT=*
//SYSPUNCH DD  SYSOUT=*
//SYSUDUMP DD  SYSOUT=*
//SYSTSIN  DD  *
DSN SYSTEM (DBAX   )
  RUN PROGRAM   (DSNTIAUL) -
     PLAN       (DSNTIAUL) -
   PARMS('SQL') -
     LIBRARY    ('DSNTST.DBAX.RUNLIB.LOAD')
END
/*
//SYSIN    DD *
 SELECT
 EMP_ID, EMP_LAST_NAME, EMP_FIRST_NAME
 FROM HRSCHEMA.EMPLOYEE
 WHERE EMP_SERVICE_YEARS > 1
//SYSOUT   DD  SYSOUT=*
```

The above example shows that you can specify which columns to include in your output, as well as selecting which rows to unload.

DSNTEP2

The DSNTEP2 sample program allows you to execute dynamic SQL to select or update data. The JCL looks like this, and the example is reading data from the EMP_PAY_CHECK table:

```
//HRSCHEMA2 JOB MSGLEVEL=(1,1),NOTIFY=&SYSUID
//*
//STEP01   EXEC PGM=IKJEFT01,
//            DYNAMNBR=20,REGION=4096K
//STEPLIB  DD  DISP=SHR,DSN=DSNTST.DBAX.SDSNEXIT
//         DD  DISP=SHR,DSN=DSNTST.SDSNLOAD
```

```
//          DD  DISP=SHR,DSN=DSNTST.DBAX.RUNLIB.LOAD
//SYSPRINT DD  SYSOUT=*
//SYSTSPRT DD  SYSOUT=*
//SYSPUNCH DD  SYSOUT=*
//SYSUDUMP DD  SYSOUT=*
//SYSTSIN  DD  *
DSN SYSTEM (DBAX   )
  RUN PROGRAM (DSNTEP2) PLAN (DSNTEP2)
END
/*
//SYSIN     DD *
 SELECT * FROM HRSCHEMA.EMP_PAY_CHECK
 ORDER BY EMP_ID
//SYSOUT   DD  SYSOUT=*
```

You could also run an update or delete action with DSNTEP2. Just change the SYSIN control file content. Here's an example:

```
UPDATE HRSCHEMA.EMPLOYEE
SET EMP_SERVICE_YEARS = EMP_SERVICE_YEARS + 1
```

If you are not already using these sample programs, I suggest you learn more about them and use them. They are great utilities and will save you some custom coding effort!

CHAPTER TWO: DATA DEFINITION LANGUAGE

Before rushing into programming it is a good idea to understand how to create and maintain the basic DB2 objects. We'll look at the properties of the various objects (tables, indexes, views). We'll look over the various data types that DB2 provides as well. Finally we'll look at the DB2 catalog and the information it provides.

A DB2 database is a collection of objects including tablespaces, tables, indexes, views, triggers, stored procedures and sequences. Generally a database is concerned with a single domain such as marketing, accounting, shipping and receiving, etc. Within the database there are objects such as tables, indexes, views, etc.

In many shops a DBA creates and maintains the database objects. I don't expect you to know every nuance of each database object, but you need to know the basic Data Definition Language. So let's step through how to create and maintain the basic database objects.

For purposes of this text book, we will be creating and maintaining a simple human relations system for a fictitious company. So we'll create objects with that in mind.

DATABASES

CREATE
You can create a database with the CREATE DATABASE statement and you can assign options such as bufferpool, index bufferpool, storage group and CCSID. The required syntax to create the database is:

```
CREATE DATABASE <database name>
```

However you would normally specify names for a storage group, bufferpool and index bufferpool. Here's an example:

```
CREATE DATABASE DB1
STOGROUP DS1
BUFFERPOOL BP1
INDEXBP BP2;
```

You may not have security access to create a DB2 database, even a test database. This depends on your shop and whether or not it allows application developers to create database objects. If not, then you can ask a DBA to create the objects for you.

For our purposes, let's assume that you do have security and we'll go ahead and create our

HR database. Let's name the database `DBHR` and we'll specify a bufferpool named `BPHR`, an index bufferpool named `IBPHR`, and a storage group called `SGHR`. Finally we need to choose a CCSID (conceptually this is similar to a codepage) from ASCII, EBCDIC or UNICODE. We'll talk more about CCSIDs in the subsection on tables. For now, let's go ahead and specify UNICODE as the CCSID for our database.

The DDL to create our HR database is as follows:

```
CREATE DATABASE DBHR
STOGROUP SGHR
BUFFERPOOL BPHR
INDEXBP IBPHR
CCSID UNICODE;
```

ALTER

If you need to change anything about the database in the future, you can use the ALTER statement. Suppose for example we want to change the default bufferpool. You could issue this DDL to change the default bufferpool in the `DBHR` database to `BPHR2`.

```
ALTER DATABASE DBHR
BUFFERPOOL BPHR2;
```

DROP

Most database objects can be removed/deleted by issuing the DROP command. The syntax to delete a database is very simple:

```
DROP DATABASE <databasename>
```

You could DROP the DBHR database by simply issuing this command:

```
DROP DATABASE DBHR;
```

We won't drop the DBHR database now because we are going to add some more objects to it in this chapter.

TABLESPACES

A tablespace is a layer between the physical containers that hold data and the logical database. In essence, a tablespace defines storage areas into which DB2 objects may be placed and maintained.

DB2 11 supports the following types of tables spaces:

- Universal
- Segmented
- Partitioned
- EA enabled
- Large Object (LOB)
- XML
- Simple (cannot be created in DB2 11 but still supported if already exists)

Universal table spaces
A universal table space is a combination of partitioned and segmented table space schemes.

EA-enabled table spaces/index spaces
Table spaces and index spaces that are enabled for extended addressability is EA-enabled.

Large object table spaces
LOB table spaces (also known as auxiliary table spaces) hold large object data, such as graphics, video, or large text strings. If your data does not fit entirely within a data page, you can define one or more columns as LOB columns.

XML table spaces
An XML table space stores an XML table.

Partitioned (non-universal) table spaces (deprecated)
A table space that is partitioned stores a single table. DB2 divides the table space into partitions.

Simple table spaces (deprecated)
A simple table space is neither partitioned nor segmented. The creation of new simple table spaces is not supported in DB2 11. However, DB2 can still use existing simple table spaces.

Segmented (non-universal) table spaces (deprecated)
A table space that is segmented is useful for storing more than one table, especially relatively small tables. The pages hold segments, and each segment holds records from only one table.

Let us create a universal tablespace for our HR database, and we'll name it TSHR (tablespace HR). We'll specify storage group SGHR, provide the primary and secondary space allocations as 50 and 20, do locking at the page level and use bufferpool BPHR2. Don't worry if these values do not make perfect sense. A DBA usually handles tablespace operations.

Meanwhile, we'll create and use our new tablespace TSHR throughout this text book as a container for tables and other objects. Here's the DDL:

```
CREATE TABLESPACE TSHR
IN DBHR
USING STOGROUP SGHR
PRIQTY 50
SECQTY 20
LOCKSIZE PAGE
BUFFERPOOL BPHR2;
```

One other operation we will perform before moving on to tables is to create a schema. A schema is a qualifier used for logically grouping and owning objects. In our case we will create a schema named HRSCHEMA and then use that to group our tables, indexes, views, etc. The schema must have an owner and let's assume we can have it owned by system authorized id DBA001 (you can substitute your own logon id).

```
CREATE SCHEMA HRSCHEMA
AUTHORIZATION DBA001; -- this should be your id
```

Now you can create database objects such as tables, view, indexes and sequences and specify schema HRSCHEMA as the qualifier. For example you could create an EMPLOYEE table as HRSCHEMA.EMPLOYEE. If you do not specify a schema, DB2 assumes a default or current schema which is often your logon-id. Obviously if you are working as part of a group, a common schema name is a better alternative.

TABLES

As I'm sure you are aware, a table is the basic structure and container for DB2 data. Let's summarize the different types of tables in DB2 11, and then we'll generate sample tables for discussion.

Table Types

The following are the DB2 table types.

Type	Description
Archive	An archive table is a table that stores data that was deleted from another table. The other table is called an archive-enabled table.
Auxiliary	An auxiliary table is used to store Large Object (LOB) data that is linked to another base table.
Base	A table structure which physically persists records.

28

Type	Description
Clone	A table that is structurally identical to a base table.
History	A table that is used to store historical versions of rows from the associated system-period temporal table.
Materialized Query	A materialized query table basically stores the result set of a query. It is typically used to store aggregate results from one or more other tables.
Result	A non-persistent table that contains a set of rows that DB2 selects or generates, directly or indirectly, from one or more base tables or views in response to an SQL statement.
Temporal	A temporal table is one that keeps track of "versions" of data over time and allows you to query data according to the time frame.
Temporary	A table that is created and exists only for the duration of a session.
XML	A special table that holds only XML data.

DDL for Tables

Now let's look at the basic DDL that is used to manipulate tables. As with other DB2 objects, we use the CREATE, ALTER and DROP statements to create, change and delete tables respectively.

CREATE

The basic syntax to create a DB2 table specifies the table name, column specifications and the tablespace into which the table is to be created.

```
CREATE TABLE <tablename>
(field specifications)
IN <tablespace>
```

For an example, let's create the first table for our HR application. Here are the columns and data types for our table which we will name EMPLOYEE.

Field Name	Type	Attributes
EMP_ID	INTEGER	NOT NULL, PRIMARY KEY
EMP_LAST_NAME	VARCHAR(30)	NOT NULL
EMP_FIRST_NAME	VARCHAR(20)	NOT NULL
EMP_SERVICE_YEARS	INTEGER	NOT NULL, DEFAULT IS ZERO
EMP_PROMOTION_DATE	DATE	

The table can be created with the following DDL:

```
CREATE TABLE HRSCHEMA.EMPLOYEE(
EMP_ID INT NOT NULL,
EMP_LAST_NAME VARCHAR(30) NOT NULL,
EMP_FIRST_NAME VARCHAR(20) NOT NULL,
EMP_SERVICE_YEARS INT NOT NULL WITH DEFAULT 0,
EMP_PROMOTION_DATE DATE,
PRIMARY KEY(EMP_ID))
IN TSHR;
```

While we haven't talked about indexes yet, we will need to create a unique index to support the primary key. Otherwise when we try to access the table, our SQL will fail. Let's create an index now and then we'll talk more about indexes in the next sub-section.

```
CREATE UNIQUE INDEX NDX_EMPLOYEE
ON EMPLOYEE (EMP_ID);
```

Before we move on, let's create a couple more tables that we will use later. Let's say we need an EMP_PAY table to store the employee's annual pay amount, and an EMP_PAY_CHECK table that will be used to cut pay checks on the first and fifteen of the month. Here's the DDL for these:

```
CREATE TABLE HRSCHEMA.EMP_PAY(
EMP_ID INT NOT NULL,
EMP_REGULAR_PAY DECIMAL (8,2) NOT NULL,
EMP_BONUS_PAY DECIMAL   (8,2))
IN TSHR;

CREATE TABLE HRSCHEMA.EMP_PAY_CHECK(
EMP_ID INT NOT NULL,
EMP_REGULAR_PAY  DECIMAL (8,2) NOT NULL,
EMP_SEMIMTH_PAY DECIMAL (8,2) NOT NULL)
IN TSHR;
```

ALTER

You can change various aspects of a table using the ALTER command. ALTER is often used to add an index or additional columns. Here is an example:

```
ALTER TABLE HRSCHEMA.EMPLOYEE
ADD COLUMN EMP_PROFILE XML;
```

At this point we won't run this DDL because we want to do these operations later after some explanation. For now, just be aware that the way to change a DB2 table is to use the ALTER statement.

DROP

You can remove a table by issuing the DROP command.

```
DROP TABLE <table name>
```

Note: You cannot drop a table for which a trigger is still defined. You must first drop the trigger.

Base Tables

The most common type of table in DB2 is a base table. This is your typical table created with the CREATE TABLE statement. A sample is our original DDL used for the EMPLOYEE table:

```
CREATE TABLE HRSCHEMA.EMPLOYEE(
EMP_ID INT NOT NULL,
EMP_LAST_NAME VARCHAR(30) NOT NULL,
EMP_FIRST_NAME VARCHAR(20) NOT NULL,
EMP_SERVICE_YEARS INT NOT NULL WITH DEFAULT 0,
EMP_PROMOTION_DATE DATE,
PRIMARY KEY(EMP_ID))
IN TSHR;
```

Result Tables

A result table is called that because it is the result set of a query. It is not persistent. To show an example let's first add a record to the EMPLOYEE table. We haven't reviewed DML yet, but let's go ahead and do an INSERT with the following:

```
INSERT INTO HRSCHEMA.EMPLOYEE
(EMP_ID,
 EMP_LAST_NAME,
 EMP_FIRST_NAME,
 EMP_SERVICE_YEARS,
 EMP_PROMOTION_DATE)
VALUES (3217,
'JOHNSON',
'EDWARD',
4,
'01/01/2017');
```

Now run the following query:

```
SELECT EMP_ID, EMP_LAST_NAME,
EMP_FIRST_NAME
FROM HRSCHEMA.EMPLOYEE
WHERE EMP_ID = 3217;
---------+---------+---------+---------+---------+---
   EMP_ID  EMP_LAST_NAME         EMP_FIRST_NAME
---------+---------+---------+---------+---------+---
     3217  JOHNSON               EDWARD
DSNE610I NUMBER OF ROWS DISPLAYED IS 1
```

The displayed data is a result table. After the query is run and the data is displayed, you cannot reference or change the result table, i.e., it is not persistent.

Clone Tables

In some situations you may need to work with a copy of a base table, and then at some point switch the copy for the original. A clone table is useful for this purpose. A clone table is structurally identical to the base table. It is created by ALTERING the original. To take an example, let's clone the EMPLOYEE table:

```
ALTER TABLE HRSCHEMA.EMPLOYEE
ADD CLONE HRSCHEMA.EMPLOYEE_CLONE;
```

Now you can load the clone table with data and manipulate it in whatever fashion you need to. Later you can switch the tables using the EXCHANGE command:

```
EXCHANGE DATA BETWEEN TABLE HRSCHEMA.EMPLOYEE
AND HRSCHEMA.EMPLOYEE_CLONE;
```

In actuality, no data is moved. Instead, the names on the physical tables are just switched behind the scenes. In the example, the original EMPLOYEE base table has now become EMPLOYEE_CLONE and the EMPLOYEE_CLONE table has become EMPLOYEE. To switch them back, issue the EXCHANGE command again.

```
EXCHANGE DATA
BETWEEN TABLE
HRSCHEMA.EMPLOYEE
AND
HRSCHEMA.EMPLOYEE_CLONE;
```

Note: You cannot clone a table unless that table exists in a universal table space (UTS).

Archive Tables

An archive table is a table that stores data that was deleted from another table called an archive-enabled table. When a row is deleted from the archive-enabled table, DB2 automatically adds the row to the archive table. When you query the archive-enabled table, you can specify whether or not to include archived records or not. We'll look at these features in an example.

Assume we want to delete some records from our EMPLOYEE table and we want to automatically archive the deleted records to a new table named EMPLOYEE_ARCHIVE. One way to set up and define the archive table with exactly the same column definitions as EMPLOYEE is to use the LIKE clause with the CREATE statement:

```
CREATE TABLE HRSCHEMA.EMPLOYEE_ARCHIVE
LIKE HRSCHEMA.EMPLOYEE
IN TSHR;
```

To enable archiving of deleted records from table EMPLOYEE to table EMPLOYEE_ARCHIVE, you would execute the following:

```
ALTER TABLE EMPLOYEE
ENABLE ARCHIVE
USE EMPLOYEE_ARCHIVE;
```

To automatically archive records, set the global variable SYSIBMADM.MOVE_TO_ARCHIVE to Y or E. This value indicates whether deleting a record from an archive-enabled table should store a copy of the deleted record in the archive table. The values are:

Y - store a copy of the deleted record, and also make any attempted insert/update operation against the archive table an error.

E - store a copy of the deleted record.

N- do not store a copy of the deleted record.

In the future when you query the EMPLOYEE table you can choose to include or exclude the archived records in a given session. To do this, your package must first be bound with the ARCHIVESENSITIVE(YES) bind option. Then the package/program should set the GET_ARCHIVE global variable to Y (the default is N). At this point, any query against the archive-enabled table during this session will automatically include data from the corresponding archive table. This is very handy for when you want to do historical research.

In our EMPLOYEE example, suppose we have a package EMP001 that is bound with ARCHIVESENSITIVE(YES). Suppose further that the program issues this SQL:

```
SET SYSIBMADM.GET_ARCHIVE = 'Y';
```

Now any query we issue during this session against the EMPLOYEE table will automatically return any qualifying rows from both the EMPLOYEE and EMPLOYEE_ARCHIVE tables. For example:

```
SELECT EMP_ID,
EMP_LAST_NAME,
EMPL_FIRST_NAME
FROM EMPLOYEE
ORDER BY EMP_ID;
```

If the package needs to revert to only picking up data from the EMPLOYEE table, it can simply issue the SQL:

```
SET SYSIBMADM.GET_ARCHIVE = 'N';
```

Some design advantages of an archive table are:

Your historical data is managed automatically. You don't need to manually or programmatically move older data to a separate table.

The scope of your query is controlled using a global variable. Consequently you can modify your query results to include or exclude the archive table data and you don't have to change the SQL statement (only the global variable value).

Older rows that are less often retrieved can be stored in a separate archive table which could potentially be located on a cheaper device.

Auxiliary Tables

An auxiliary table is used to store Large Object (LOB) data that is linked to another base table. The best way to understand this is by example. Suppose that we decide to add an employee photo column to the EMPLOYEE table.

Now let's add an employee photo column as a 5 megabyte BLOB. The DDL we would use is as follows:

```
ALTER TABLE EMPLOYEE
ADD EMP_PHOTO BLOB(5M);
```

Now we must create the auxiliary table to store the LOB data. It must be created in the new LOB tablespace, and our DDL must specify that it will store column EMP_PHOTO from table

EMPLOYEE. We also need a unique index on the auxiliary table.

If we do not already have an LOB table space, we can create one as follows:

```
CREATE LOB TABLESPACE
EMP_PHOTO_TS
IN DBHR LOG NO;
```

While not mandatory, it is good practice to avoid logging the LOB data, as this can slow performance considerably for large amounts of LOB data. Of course if the data is mission critical you may need to log it for recoverability purposes if no other recovery method exists.

Now we are ready to create the auxiliary table. The syntax for this type of table is:

```
CREATE AUX TABLE <table name>
IN <LOB table space>
STORES (the base table name>
COLUMN <column in the base table>;
```

Here's the DDL to create our new auxiliary table to support the EMP_PHOTO column:

```
CREATE AUX TABLE EMP_PHOTOS_TAB
IN EMP_PHOTO_TS
STORES EMPLOYEE
COLUMN (EMP_PHOTO);

CREATE UNIQUE INDEX XEMP_PHOTO
ON EMP_PHOTOS_TAB;
```

Now we would need to rerun the DCLGEN on the EMPLOYEE table. You'll notice that the DCLGEN now specifies the EMP_PHOTO as a BLOB type.

```
SQL TYPE IS BLOB (5M) EMP_PHOTO;
```

Our update program can now load the photo data by defining a host variable into which you load the binary photo data, and then you use that host variable in the SQL as follows (assume we have declared PHOTO-DATA as our host variable):

```
UPDATE EMPLOYEE
SET EMP_PHOTO =:PHOTO-DATA
WHERE EMP_ID = :EMP_ID;
```

Materialized Query Tables

A materialized query table basically stores the results of an SQL query. It holds the aggregate results from querying one or more other tables or views. MQTs are often used to improve performance for certain aggregation queries by providing pre-computed results. Consequently, MQTs are often used in analytic or data warehousing environments.

MQTs are either system-maintained or user maintained. For a system maintained table, the data must be updated using the REFRESH TABLE statement. A user-maintained MQT can be updated using the LOAD utility, and also the UPDATE, INSERT, and DELETE SQL statements.

Let's do an example of an MQT that summarizes monthly payroll. Assume we have a source table named EMP_PAY_HIST which will be a history of each employee's salary for each paycheck. The table requirements are summarized as follows:

Column Name	Definition
EMP_ID	Numeric
EMP_PAY_DATE	Date
EMP_PAY_AMT	Decimal(8,2)

The DDL for the table is as follows:

```
CREATE TABLE EMP_PAY_HIST(
EMP_ID        INT NOT NULL,
EMP_PAY_DATE  DATE NOT NULL,
EMP_PAY_AMT   DECIMAL (8,2) NOT NULL)
IN TSHR;
```

Before we can use the table for an MQT we need to add some records to it. Let's run the following DDL to do that:

```
INSERT INTO HRSCHEMA.EMP_PAY_HIST
VALUES (3217,'01/15/2017',2291.66);

INSERT INTO HRSCHEMA.EMP_PAY_HIST
VALUES (3217,'01/31/2017',2291.66);

INSERT INTO HRSCHEMA.EMP_PAY_HIST
VALUES (3217,'02/15/2017',2291.66);

INSERT INTO HRSCHEMA.EMP_PAY_HIST
VALUES (3217,'02/28/2017',2291.66);

INSERT INTO HRSCHEMA.EMP_PAY_HIST
VALUES (7459,'01/15/2017',3333.33);

INSERT INTO HRSCHEMA.EMP_PAY_HIST
```

```
VALUES (7459,'01/31/2017',3333.33);

INSERT INTO HRSCHEMA.EMP_PAY_HIST
VALUES (7459,'02/15/2017',3333.33);

INSERT INTO HRSCHEMA.EMP_PAY_HIST
VALUES (7459,'02/28/2017',3333.33);
```

Now let's select the data in the `EMP_PAY_HIST` table is as follows:

```
SELECT * FROM HRSCHEMA.EMP_PAY_HIST;
---------+---------+---------+---------+
    EMP_ID  EMP_PAY_DATE  EMP_PAY_AMT
---------+---------+---------+---------+
      3217  2017-01-15       2291.66
      3217  2017-01-31       2291.66
      3217  2017-02-15       2291.66
      3217  2017-02-28       2291.66
      7459  2017-01-15       3333.33
      7459  2017-01-31       3333.33
      7459  2017-02-15       3333.33
      7459  2017-02-28       3333.33
DSNE610I NUMBER OF ROWS DISPLAYED IS 8
```

Finally, let's assume we regularly need an aggregated total of each employee's year to date pay. We could do this with a materialized query table. Let's build the query that will summarize the employee pay from the beginning of the year to current date:

```
SELECT EMP_ID, SUM(EMP_PAY_AMT) AS EMP_PAY_YTD
FROM HRSCHEMA.EMP_PAY_HIST
GROUP BY EMP_ID
ORDER BY EMP_ID;
---------+---------+---------+---------+---------
    EMP_ID              EMP_PAY_YTD
---------+---------+---------+---------+---------
      3217                 9166.64
      7459                13333.32
```

Using the model query above, let's create the MQT using the following DDL, and we'll make it a system managed table:

```
CREATE TABLE EMP_PAY_TOT (EMP_ID, EMP_PAY_YTD) AS
(SELECT EMP_ID, SUM(EMP_PAY_AMT) AS EMP_PAY_YTD
FROM HRSCHEMA.EMP_PAY_HIST
GROUP BY EMP_ID)
DATA INITIALLY DEFERRED
REFRESH DEFERRED
MAINTAINED BY SYSTEM
ENABLE QUERY OPTIMIZATION;
```

We can now populate the table by issuing the REFRESH TABLE statement as follows:

```
REFRESH TABLE HRSCHEMA.EMP_PAY_TOT;
```

Finally we can query data from the MQT as follows:

```
SELECT * FROM HRSCHEMA.EMP_PAY_TOT;

---------+---------+---------+---------+---------+--------
    EMP_ID            EMP_PAY_YTD
---------+---------+---------+---------+---------+--------
      3217              9166.64
      7459             13333.32
DSNE610I NUMBER OF ROWS DISPLAYED IS 2
```

Again, the benefit of an MQT is that you can generate the query results once, and then the results can be queried many times by many users without the overhead of regenerating the results each time. Also, to update the table you need only issue the REFRESH command. These benefits may seem trivial for a small query, but it can save a great deal of time and CPU cycles for complex queries involving multiple tables and large amounts of aggregated data.

Temporal Tables

Temporal tables were introduced to DB2 z/OS in version 10. Briefly, a temporal table is one that keeps track of "versions" of data over time and allows you to query data according to the time frame. The following are the basic concepts.

Business Time

Business time concerns data that is valid in a business sense for some period of time. Let's go back to our employee application. An employee's pay typically changes over time. Besides wanting to know current salary, there are scenarios under which an HR department or supervisor might need to know what pay rate was in effect for an employee at some time in the past. We might also need to allow for cases where the employee terminated for some period of time and then returned. Or maybe they took a non-paid leave of absence.

This is the concept of business time and it can be fairly complex depending on the business rules required by the application. It basically means a period of time during which the data is accurate from a business standpoint or according to a business rule. You could think of the event or condition as having an effective date and discontinue date.

A table can only have one business time period. When a BUSINESS_TIME period is defined for a table, DB2 generates a check constraint in which the end column value must be greater

38

than the begin column value.

System Time

System time simply means the time during which a piece of data is in the database, i.e., when the data was added, changed or deleted. Sometimes it is important to know this information. For example a user might enter an employee's salary change on a certain date but the effective date of the salary change might be earlier or later than the date it was entered into the system. The system time simply records when the data was actually entered into the system, changed in the system, or deleted from the system. An audit trail application or table often has a time-stamp that can be considered system time.

Bitemporal Support

In some cases you may need to support both business and system time in the same table. DB2 supports this and it is called bi-temporal support.

History Table

A history table is used to store older versions of rows from the associated system-period temporal table. This is how you can determine the column values of a row at a particular point in time.

Temporary Table

Sometimes you may need the use of a table for the duration of a session but no longer than that. For example you may have a programming situation where it is convenient to load a temporary table for these operations:

1. To join the data in the temporary table with another table
2. To store intermediate results to be queried later in the program
3. To load data from a flat file into a relational format

In all cases, it is assumed that you only need a temporary table for the duration of a session (or iteration of a program) since temporary tables are dropped as soon as the session ends.

Temporary tables are created using either the CREATE statement or the DECLARE statement. We'll enumerate their differences below.

```
CREATE GLOBAL TEMPORARY TABLE
EMP_INFO(
EMP_ID     INT,
EMP_LNAME  VARCHAR(30),
EMP_FNAME  VARCHAR(30));
```

```
DECLARE GLOBAL TEMPORARY TABLE
EMP_INFO(
EMP_ID    INT,
EMP_LNAME  VARCHAR(30),
EMP_FNAME  VARCHAR(30));
```

CREATED Temporary Tables

Created temporary tables:

1. Have an entry in the system catalog (`SYSIBM.SYSTABLES`)
2. Cannot have indexes
3. Their columns cannot use default values (except NULL)
4. Cannot have constraints
5. Cannot be used with DB2 utilities
6. Cannot be used with the UPDATE statement
7. If DELETE is used at all, it will delete all rows from the table
8. Do not provide for locking or logging

DECLARED Temporary Tables

A declared temporary table offers some advantages over created temporary tables.

1. Can have indexes and check constraints
2. Can use the UPDATE statement
3. Can do positioned deletes

So declared temporary tables offer more flexibility than created temporary tables. However, when a session ends, DB2 will automatically delete the table definition. So if you want a table definition that persists in the DB2 catalog for future use, you would need to use a created temporary table.

Things to remember about temporary tables:

1. Use temporary tables when you need the data only for the duration of the session.

2. Created temporary tables can provide excellent performance because they do not use locking or logging.

3. Declared temporary tables can also be very efficient because you can choose not to log, and they only allow limited locking.

4. The schema for a temporary table is always `SESSION`.

5. If you create a temporary table and you wish to replace any existing temporary table that has the same name, use the `WITH REPLACE` clause.

6. If you create a temporary table from another table using the LIKE clause, the temporary table will NOT have any unique constraints, foreign key constraints, triggers, indexes, table partitioning keys, or distribution keys from the original table.

XML Table

An XML table is a special table that holds only XML data. When you create a table with an XML column, DB2 implicitly creates an XML table space and an XML table to store the XML data. Here's an example of adding an employee profile XML column to the employee table we created earlier:

```
ALTER TABLE HRSCHEMA.EMPLOYEE
ADD COLUMN EMP_PROFILE XML;
```

The preceding DDL automatically creates a table space and table for the XML column. DB2 creates the XML table space and table in the same database as the table that defined the XML column (the base table). The XML table space is in the Unicode UTF-8 encoding scheme.

INDEXES

Indexes are structures that provide a means of quickly locating a record in a table. One of the main reasons for having indexes is that they improve performance when accessing data randomly. There are other reasons as well which we'll explore now.

Benefits of Indexes

Indexes are beneficial in three ways:

1. Indexes improve performance in that it is typically faster to use the index row locator to navigate to a specific row than to do a table scan (except in cases of very small tables).
2. Unique indexes ensure uniqueness of record keys (either primary or secondary).
3. Clustered indexes enable data to be organized in the base table to optimize sequential access and processing.

Types of Indexes

The types of indexes available in DB2 11 are listed below. I'll give examples of the most common ones in the next section. Some of these indexes are more advanced and we won't deal with them in this basic training text.

Unique index

A unique index enforces the rule that every row must contain a unique value in the indexed column. For example, if a unique index is defined for a column containing an employee's social security number, then the value must be unique for each row in the table.

Primary index

A primary index is the primary key column of the table. A table can have only one primary index. If you define a primary key on a table, you must also create a unique index on the column that was chosen for the primary key (another way of saying this is that the primary key must be unique).

Clustering index

A clustering index physically groups data according to a sequence to make certain kinds of processing more efficient. For example, if you have customers who have orders that must be processed, you might prefer that orders for a particular customer be located close together in the table. You therefore might create a clustering index for the orders based on customer id.

Expression-based index

An index that is defined based on a general expression.

Secondary index

A secondary index is any index that is not a primary index. For example you might have an employee table for which the primary key is an EMPLOYEE_ID. However you might also have a social security number column for which you have created a unique index. The index on social security number is a secondary index.

XML index

An XML index uses an XML pattern expression to locate values in XML documents (specifically those XML document that are stored in a single column which s common).

Other Indexes

We won't be covering data partitioning in this text, so I'm omitting these types of indexes:

- Partitioned index
- Partitioning index (PI)
- Data partitioned secondary index (DPSI)

We'll cover these in a future book. Now let's look at some examples of indexes.

Examples of Indexes

Unique primary

We created a unique primary index a while ago for the EMPLOYEE. Recall that we defined the EMPLOYEE table with a primary key. Before you can use a table with a primary key, you must create a unique index on the column or columns being used for the primary key.

This is the table:

```
CREATE TABLE HRSCHEMA.EMPLOYEE(
EMP_ID INT NOT NULL,
EMP_LAST_NAME VARCHAR(30) NOT NULL,
EMP_FIRST_NAME VARCHAR(20) NOT NULL,
EMP_SERVICE_YEARS INT NOT NULL WITH DEFAULT 0,
EMP_PROMOTION_DATE DATE,
PRIMARY KEY(EMP_ID));
```

And this is the unique index we created to support the primary key.

```
CREATE UNIQUE INDEX
HRSCHEMA.NDX_EMPLOYEE
ON HRSCHEMA.EMPLOYEE (EMP_ID);
```

Unique

While a table can only have one primary key, it can have more than one unique index. Suppose that we added a social security column to the employee table. For data security reasons (and simply to reduce the possibility of keying errors), we might want to create a unique index on the social security number column.

The DDL to add the social security number column to the table and create a unique index on it is as follows:

```
ALTER TABLE HRSCHEMA.EMPLOYEE
ADD COLUMN EMP_SSN CHAR(09);

CREATE UNIQUE INDEX HRSCHEMA.NDX_SSN
ON HRSCHEMA.EMPLOYEE (EMP_SSN);
```

Now it will be impossible to add a second record with the same EMP_SSN value into the table. It will also be efficient to search by EMP_SSN because it is indexed.

Clustering

A clustering index forces data to be grouped and ordered according to index sequence. One case in which a clustering index is helpful is when sequential processing is called for. Suppose we create an electronic funds transfer system with a table called EMP_PAY_EFT. We will use the EMP_PAY_CHECK records to generate table entries for the EMP_PAY_EFT table on pay day.

Given the above, we might like to physically locate the data according to pay date so the records for a pay cycle will be close together (otherwise our pay check program may have to jump all over the table to get the needed records for the pay cycle).

Here's the DDL we used to create the EMP_PAY_EFT table.

```
CREATE TABLE HRSCHEMA.EMP_PAY_EFT(
EMP_ID INT NOT NULL,
EMP_PAY_DATE   DATE NOT NULL,
EMP_REGULAR_PAY  DECIMAL (8,2) NOT NULL,
EMP_SEMIMTH_PAY DECIMAL (8,2) NOT NULL)
IN TSHR;
```

We can ensure that the data is clustered as we want it by creating this index:

```
CREATE INDEX
NDX_EMP_EFT
ON EMP_PAY_EFT (EMP_PAY_DATE, EMP_ID)
CLUSTER;
```

Now DB2 will attempt to order all records in the EMP_PAY_EFT table by EMP_PAY_DATE and EMP_ID. This should minimize the physical I/O required to obtain the pay data into memory.

Note: A new feature in DB2 11 allows you to prevent the entry of NULL values in an index by including the clause EXCLUDE NULL KEYS when you create the index. If you do not specify that you want to exclude null keys, then DB2 will allow null values in the index (assuming the indexed field is not defined with NOT NULL).

DATA TYPES
DB2 supports the following data types. You should be familiar with all of these so that you can choose the best data type for your purpose.

NUMERIC DATA TYPES
DB2 supports several types of numeric data types, each of which has its own characteristics.

SMALLINT
A small integer is an integer value between the values of -32768 and +32767.

INTEGER

An integer is sometimes referred to as a "large integer". This data type can store values between -2147483648 and +2147483647.

BIGINT

A big integer can store values between -9223372036854775808 to +9223372036854775807.

DECIMAL or NUMERIC

The decimal type is stored in packed decimal format and it has an implied decimal point. You would use this for any data values that need this precision, such as money values. For example, a column defined as DECIMAL (7,2) means a total of 7 decimal position with two values to the right of the decimal point. For example this value could be stored in a DECIMAL (7,2) column:

```
10,377.45
```

DECFLOAT

A DECFLOAT type means "decimal floating-point". The position of the decimal is stored with the value itself.

REAL

The real data type is a single-precision floating-point number. Its value can be between -7.2E+75 and 7.2E+75.

DOUBLE

The double data type is a double-precision floating-point number. Its value can be between -7.2E+75 to 7.2E+75.

STRING DATA TYPES

DB2 supports several types of string data: character strings, graphic strings, and binary strings.

CHARACTER(n)

The character or CHAR data type stores fixed length character strings. You would use this for character data which is always the same length, such as state codes which are two bytes. The maximum length of a CHAR type is 255 bytes.

VARCHAR(n)

The VARCHAR type stores varying length character strings for which the maximum length is specified. For example VARCHAR(40) means between 1 and 40 bytes in length. A VARCHAR can be defined with a maximum of 32704 bytes. If you need more, see the CLOB data type below under LOB data types.

GRAPHIC(n)
The GRAPHIC data type stores fixed-length graphic strings of length n in double byte format. The n refers to the number of double byte characters. The maximum length is 128 double byte chars.

VARGRAPHIC(n)
The VARGRAPHIC type stores varying-length graphic strings in double byte format. The n refers to the maximum number of double byte characters. The maximum length is 16352 double byte characters.

BINARY(n)
The BINARY type stores binary strings. The n refers to the number of fixed length bytes. The maximum length is 255 bytes.

VARBINARY(n)
The VARBINARY type stores varying-length binary strings. The n refers to the maximum number of bytes, so the actual length is between 1 and n bytes. The maximum length of a VARBINARY column is 32704 bytes.

DATE, TIME, AND TIMESTAMP DATA TYPES

Date/Time Types

DATE
The DATE type represents a date in year, month and day format. It is 10 bytes long and the format depends on the date format specified when DB2 was installed. The following are two common formats:

```
MM/DD/YYYY (USA standard)

YYYY-MM-DD (ISO standard)
```

TIME
The TIME type stores a time of day in hours, minutes and second. For example, 10:34 am and 27 seconds is:

```
10:34:27
```

TIMESTAMP
The TIMESTAMP type stores a value that represents both a date and a time. It includes the year, month, date, hour, minute, seconds and microseconds. For example:

```
2017-04-17-02.17.54.142357
```

XML data type
The XML data type defines a column that will store a well formed XML document.

Large object data types
You can use large object data types to store text as well as multimedia files such audio, video, images, and other files that are larger than 32 KB and up to 2GB in size.

Character large objects (CLOBs)
The CLOB data type can be used to store text that uses a single character set. This could include reports that need to be archived or any other text that exceeds the 32K limit imposed by the VARCHAR type. The limit for a CLOB is 2 GB.

Double-byte character large objects (DBCLOBs)
The DBCLOB can be used when the data is formatted in a double byte character set.

Binary large objects (BLOBs)
The BLOB data type stored binary (noncharacter) data. You would use this for multimedia files such as images, audio and video files.

ROWID data type
The ROWID type uniquely identifies a row in a table, including the location of the row. Using ROWIDs enables you to navigate directly to the row without using an index.

Distinct types
A distinct type is a user-defined data type that is based on existing built-in DB2 data types. Here are a couple of examples:

```
CREATE DISTINCT TYPE
US_DOLLAR AS DECIMAL (9,2);

CREATE DISTINCT TYPE
CANADIAN_DOLLAR AS DECIMAL (9,2);
```

CONSTRAINTS

Types of constraints

There are basically four types of constraints, as follows:

1. Unique
2. Referential
3. Check
4. NULL

A UNIQUE constraint requires that the value in a particular field in a table be unique for each record.

A REFERENTIAL constraint enforces relationships between tables. For example you can define a referential constraint between an EMPLOYEE table and a DEPARTMENT table, such that a DEPT field in the EMPLOYEE table can only contain a value that matches a key value in the DEPARTMENT table.

A CHECK constraint establishes some condition on a field, such as the stored value must be >= 10.

A NOT NULL constraint on a column establishes that each record must have a non-null value for this column.

Unique Constraints

A unique constraint is a rule that the values of a key are valid only if they are unique in a table. In the case of the EMPLOYEE table we have been working with, you can create a unique index as follows:

```
CREATE UNIQUE INDEX
NDX_EMPLOYEE
ON EMPLOYEE (EMP_ID);
```

Trying to add a duplicate key value results in an error.

Check Constraints

A check constraint is a rule that specifies the values that are allowed in one or more columns of every row of a base table. It establishes some condition on a column, such as the stored value must be >= 10. The real worth of check constraints is that some business rules such as edits and validations can be stored in and performed by the database manager instead of by application programs.

When you try to INSERT or UPDATE a table record, the column values are evaluated against the check constraint rules (if any) for that table. If the data follows the rules, then the action is permitted; otherwise the action will fail with a constraint violation.

Let's define some check constraints on the EMP_DATA table such that the employee number must be between zero and 9999. Also the employee's age must be between 18 and 99. We'll create the table and then alter it to add the two constraints:

```
CREATE TABLE HRSCHEMA.EMP_DATA
(EMP_ID    INT,
EMP_LNAME  VARCHAR(30),
EMP_FNAME  VARCHAR(20),
EMP_AGE    INT) IN TSHR;
---------+---------+---------+---------+---------+--------
DSNE616I STATEMENT EXECUTION WAS SUCCESSFUL, SQLCODE IS 0
```

Now let's add the constraint on employee id.

```
ALTER TABLE HRSCHEMA.EMP_DATA ADD CONSTRAINT  X_EMPID
CHECK (EMP_ID BETWEEN 0 AND 9999);
---------+---------+---------+---------+---------+--------
DSNE616I STATEMENT EXECUTION WAS SUCCESSFUL, SQLCODE IS 0
```

Finally, we'll add the constraint on age.

```
ALTER TABLE HRSCHEMA.EMP_DATA ADD CONSTRAINT X_AGE
CHECK (EMP_AGE >= 18);
---------+---------+---------+---------+---------+--------
DSNE616I STATEMENT EXECUTION WAS SUCCESSFUL, SQLCODE IS 0
```

Now let's try this insert:

```
INSERT INTO HRSCHEMA.EMP_DATA
VALUES
(17888,
 'BROWN',
 'WILLIAM',
 17);
---------+---------+---------+---------+---------+---------+---------+-
DSNT408I SQLCODE = -545, ERROR:  THE REQUESTED OPERATION IS NOT ALLOWED
         BECAUSE A ROW DOES NOT SATISFY THE CHECK CONSTRAINT X_EMPID
```

It turns out that we mis-keyed the employee id. It should be 1788 instead of 17888. The value 17888 exceeds 9999 which is the maximum limit for employee id according to the check constraint. So DB2 prevented the insert action.

Let's fix the employee id and try again:

```
INSERT INTO HRSCHEMA.EMP_DATA
VALUES
(1788,
 'BROWN',
 'WILLIAM',
 17);
---------+---------+---------+---------+---------+---------+---------+--
DSNT408I SQLCODE = -545, ERROR:  THE REQUESTED OPERATION IS NOT ALLOWED
           BECAUSE A ROW DOES NOT SATISFY THE CHECK CONSTRAINT X_AGE
```

Now we have violated the age constraint. Obviously 17 is less than 18 which is the defined lower limit on the employee age. So let's fix the age and we can see the row is accepted now.

```
INSERT INTO HRSCHEMA.EMP_DATA
VALUES
(1788,
 'BROWN',
 'WILLIAM',
 18);
---------+---------+---------+---------+----
DSNE615I NUMBER OF ROWS AFFECTED IS 1
```

Check constraints can be a very powerful way of building and centralizing business logic into the database itself. No application programming is required to implement a constraint (other than trapping and handling errors generated by the DBMS). There is great consistency in using check constraints because you can't forget to code them in a program (or code them inconsistently across multiple programs). They are applied by the DBMS regardless of which program or ad hoc process attempts the data modification.

Referential Constraints

A referential constraint is the rule that the non-null values of a foreign key are valid only if they also appear as a key in a parent table. The table that contains the parent key is called the parent table of the referential constraint, and the table that contains the foreign key is a dependent of that table. Referential integrity ensures data integrity by using primary and foreign key relationships between tables.

In DB2 you define a referential constraint by specifying in the child table a column which references a column in a parent table. For example, in a company you could have a DEPARTMENT table with column DEPT_CODE, and the EMP_DATA table that includes a column DEPT that represents the department code an employee is assigned to. The rule would be that you cannot have a value in the DEPT column of the EMP_DATA table that does not have a corresponding DEPT_CODE value in the DEPARTMENT table. You can think of this as a parent and child relationship between the DEPARTMENT table and the EMP_DATA table. DEPARTMENT is the parent table and EMP_DATA is the child table.

Let's create the DEPARTMENT table and also add the DEPT column to the EMP_DATA table. We'll also add a row to the DEPARTMENT table and update the corresponding row(s) in the EMP_DATA table to match

```
CREATE TABLE HRSCHEMA.DEPARTMENT
(DEPT_CODE    CHAR(04) NOT NULL,
 DEPT_NAME    VARCHAR (20) NOT NULL,
 PRIMARY KEY(DEPT_CODE))
IN TSHR;

CREATE UNIQUE INDEX HRSCHEMA.NDX_DEPT_CODE
       ON HRSCHEMA.DEPARTMENT (DEPT_CODE);

INSERT INTO HRSCHEMA.DEPARTMENT
VALUES ('DPTA','DEPARTMENT A');


ALTER TABLE HRSCHEMA.EMP_DATA
ADD DEPT CHAR(04);

UPDATE HRSCHEMA.EMP_DATA
SET DEPT_CODE = 'DPTA';
```

Adding a Foreign Key Relationship

Now let's add the foreign key relationship by performing an ALTER on the child table. Here is the DDL for our example:

```
ALTER TABLE HRSCHEMA.EMP_DATA
   FOREIGN KEY FK_DEPT_EMP (DEPT)
      REFERENCES HRSCHEMA.DEPARTMENT(DEPT_CODE) ;

   ---------+---------+---------+---------+---------+---------+---------+-
   DSNT404I SQLCODE = 162, WARNING:  TABLE SPACE DBHR.TSHR HAS BEEN PLACED
            IN CHECK PENDING
```

The constraint was successfully built, but before you can continue you must deal with the CHECK PENDING status on your tablespace. The CHECK PENDING status means the table is possibly in an inconsistent state because of the new constraint, and it must be checked. To clear the CHECK PENDING status you must issue a CHECK DATA command. In our case, the command will be:

51

```
CHECK DATA TABLESPACE DBHR.TSHR;
```

Once the CHECK DATA finishes, your tablespace is taken out of check pending and you can continue, provided there were no errors.

Now if you try to update an EMP_DATA record with a DEPT value that does not have a DEPT_CODE with the same value as the DEPT value you are using, you'll get an SQL error -530 which means a violation of a foreign key.

```
UPDATE HRSCHEMA.EMP_DATA
SET DEPT = 'DPTB'

---------+---------+---------+---------+---------+---------+---------+-
DSNT408I SQLCODE = -530, ERROR:  THE INSERT OR UPDATE VALUE OF FOREIGN KEY
FK_DEPT_EMP IS INVALID
```

And here is the full explanation of the error.

```
-530
THE INSERT OR UPDATE VALUE OF FOREIGN KEY constraint-name IS INVALID

Explanation
An insert or update operation attempted to place a value in a foreign key
of the object table; however, this value was not equal to some value of the
parent key of the parent table.

When a row is inserted into a dependent table, the insert value of a foreign
key must be equal to the value of the parent key of some row of the parent
table in the associated relationship.

When the value of the foreign key is updated, the update value of a foreign
key must be equal to the value of the parent key of some row of the parent
table of the associated relationship.
```

We know now that the parent table DEPARTMENT does not have DEPT_CODE DPTB in it, and it must be added before the EMP_DATA record can be updated.

Deleting a Record from the Parent Table
Now let's talk about what happens if you want to delete a record from the parent table. Assuming no EMP_DATA records are linked to the DEPARTMENT record, deleting that record may be fine. But what if you are trying to delete a DEPARTMENT record whose DEPT_CODE is referenced by one or more records in the EMP_DATA table?

Let's look at a record in the table:

```
SELECT EMP_ID, DEPT
 FROM HRSCHEMA.EMP_DATA
WHERE EMP_ID = 1788;
--------+---------+------
    EMP_ID  DEPT
--------+---------+------
      1788  DPTA
```

Ok, we know that the DEPT_CODE in use is DPTA. Now let's try to delete DPTA from the DEPARTMENT table.

```
DELETE FROM HRSCHEMA.DEPARTMENT
 WHERE DEPT_CODE = 'DPTA';
---------+---------+---------+---------+---------+---------+---------+-
DSNT408I SQLCODE = -532, ERROR:  THE RELATIONSHIP FK_DEPT_EMP RESTRICTS
THE DELETION OF ROW WITH RID X'0000002201'
```

As you can see, when we try to remove the DEPT_CODE from the DEPARTMENT table, we will get a -532 SQLCODE telling us our SQL is in violation of the referential constraint. That's probably what we want, i.e., to have an error flagged. But there are some other options for handling the situation.

You can specify the action that will take place upon deleting a parent record by including an ON DELETE clause in the foreign key definition. If no ON DELETE clause is present, or if the ON DELETE RESTRICT clause is used, then the parent record cannot be deleted unless all child records referencing that parent record are first deleted (the child reference to that parent record can also be changed to some other existing parent record). RESTRICT is most commonly used with ON DELETE (or just omitting the ON DELETE clause which has the same effect). This is the case above.

Here are the two other options:

If ON DELETE CASCADE is specified, then any rows in the child table that correspond to the deleted parent record will also be deleted. Wow, that is probably not what we want! But there may be cases where this function is useful. Possibly if a certain product is discontinued then you might want to delete all pending SHIPPING table entries for it. I can't think of many other needs for this, but be aware that this option is available.

If ON DELETE SET NULL is specified, then the foreign key field will be set to NULL for corresponding child rows that reference the parent record that is being deleted.

Let's redefine our constraint to use this last option:

```
ALTER TABLE HRSCHEMA.EMP_DATA
DROP CONSTRAINT FK_DEPT_EMP;

COMMIT WORK;

ALTER TABLE HRSCHEMA.EMP_DATA
    FOREIGN KEY FK_DEPT_EMP (DEPT)
        REFERENCES HRSCHEMA.DEPARTMENT (DEPT_CODE)
            ON DELETE SET NULL;
---------+---------+---------+---------+---------+---------+---------+-
DSNT404I SQLCODE = 162, WARNING:  TABLE SPACE DBHR.TSHR HAS BEEN PLACED
         IN CHECK PENDING
```

Go ahead and run the CHECK DATA to clear the CHECK PENDING condition. Now try deleting the DPTA record from the DEPARTMENT table:

```
DELETE FROM DEPARTMENT
WHERE DEPT_CODE = 'DPTA';
---------+---------+---------+--------
DSNE615I NUMBER OF ROWS AFFECTED IS 1
```

We see the delete is successful. So now let's check and see if the DEPT value for the child record has been set to NULL.

```
SELECT EMP_ID, DEPT
FROM HRSCHEMA.EMP_DATA
WHERE EMP_ID = 1788;
---------+---------+---------+--------
    EMP_ID  DEPT
---------+---------+---------+--------
      1788  ----
DSNE610I NUMBER OF ROWS DISPLAYED IS 1
```

And in fact the DEPT column has been set to NULL.

Referential constraints are a very powerful and necessary function to ensure data integrity in a database. Be sure to keep this in mind when you design your systems.

Not Null Constraints

A NOT NULL constraint on a column requires that when you add or update a record, you must specify a non null value for that column. If you do not specify a non null value, you will get an error.

Let's take an example of trying to add an EMPLOYEE record without specifying a value for one of the columns. In this case, let's leave off the EMP_FIRST_NAME value which is defined in the table as NOT NULL.

```
INSERT INTO HRSCHEMA.EMPLOYEE
(EMP_ID,
 EMP_LAST_NAME,
 EMP_PROMOTION_DATE)

VALUES (7420,
'JACKSHIRT',
'09/01/2016')

---------+---------+---------+---------+---------+---------+---------+---
DSNT408I SQLCODE = -407, ERROR:  AN UPDATE, INSERT, OR SET VALUE IS NULL, BUT THE
OBJECT COLUMN EMP_FIRST_NAME CANNOT CONTAIN NULL VALUES
DSNT418I SQLSTATE   = 23502 SQLSTATE RETURN CODE
DSNT415I SQLERRP    = DSNXODM SQL PROCEDURE DETECTING ERROR
DSNT416I SQLERRD    = 12 0  0  -1  0  0 SQL DIAGNOSTIC INFORMATION
DSNT416I SQLERRD    = X'0000000C' X'00000000' X'00000000' X'FFFFFFFF'
           X'00000000' X'00000000' SQL DIAGNOSTIC INFORMATION
```

Defining a column with the NOT NULL attribute ensures that no record can be added to the table with a NULL value in this column. Defining this requirement in the table enforces the requirement no matter which application or user is processing the data. Consequently the rule is centralized and does not depend on program logic enforcing it.

SEQUENCIES and IDENTITIES

Some scenarios require an auto-generated sequence that can be used to uniquely identify a record. DB2 provides two methods of doing this: sequences and identity columns. Although both provide auto-generated numbers, they work differently. The main difference between an identity field and a sequence is that the former is a column contained in a specific table – it cannot be shared across objects. A sequence is itself a separate database object and can be used to generate numbers for multiple objects. Make sure you are clear on this difference!

We'll look at examples of both a sequence and an identity column on a table.

SEQUENCES

A sequence generates a sequential set of numbers. You define a sequence with a starting value and you increment it with the NEXTVAL function. You can also obtain the most recent previous value with the PREVVAL function.

The basic syntax for creating a sequence is:

```
CREATE SEQUENCE <name of sequence>
START WITH <start value>
INCREMENT BY <increment value>
NO CYCLE   <reuse old values?>
```

Now let's create a sequence for our employee table. Suppose we want to use this sequence to generate new employee numbers and that we want to start with employee number 1001. The following DDL would accomplish this:

```
CREATE SEQUENCE HRSCHEMA.EMPSEQ
START WITH 1001
INCREMENT BY 1
NO CYCLE;
```

The NO CYCLE means we will not reuse numbers when the maximum for the data type is reached. You could explicitly create the sequence as SMALLINT, INTEGER, BIGINT, or DEC-IMAL with a scale of zero. If you don't specify a data type, the default is INTEGER.

Now we could add a record to the EMPLOYEE table without specifying the employee number. Instead we would use the sequence number with the NEXTVAL option. Here's how we do it:

```
INSERT INTO HRSCHEMA.EMPLOYEE
  VALUES (NEXT VALUE FOR HRSCHEMA.EMPSEQ,
  'HENDERSON',
  'JOHN',
  1,
  '12/01/2016');
---------+---------+---------+---------+---------+---------+--
DSNE615I NUMBER OF ROWS AFFECTED IS 1
DSNE616I STATEMENT EXECUTION WAS SUCCESSFUL, SQLCODE IS 0
---------+---------+---------+---------+---------+---------+--
```

Now let's select the record with key 1001.

```
SELECT EMP_ID, EMP_LAST_NAME
FROM HRSCHEMA.EMPLOYEE
WHERE EMP_ID = 1001;
---------+---------+---------+---------+---------+---------+----
    EMP_ID  EMP_LAST_NAME
---------+---------+---------+---------+---------+---------+----
     1001  HENDERSON
DSNE610I NUMBER OF ROWS DISPLAYED IS 1
DSNE616I STATEMENT EXECUTION WAS SUCCESSFUL, SQLCODE IS 100
---------+---------+---------+---------+---------+---------+----
```

You can also change a sequence after it is created by using the ALTER statement. For example you could change the increment of the EMPSEQ sequence from 1 to 2 as follows:

```
ALTER SEQUENCE HRSCHEMA.EMPSEQ
INCREMENT BY 2;
```

You can delete a sequence by issuing the DROP command.

```
DROP SEQUENCE HRSCHEMA.EMPSEQ;
```

IDENTITY Columns

Now let's perform a similar setup with another table and this time we will use an identity column on the table. The identity column is so named because it allows you to uniquely identify a record. It provides a unique key. For this example we'll create a different table call EMPLOYE2.

```
CREATE TABLE HRSCHEMA.EMPLOYE2(
EMP_ID SMALLINT GENERATED ALWAYS AS IDENTITY
   (START WITH 1001,
    INCREMENT BY 1,
    NOCYCLE),
EMP_LAST_NAME VARCHAR(30) NOT NULL,
EMP_FIRST_NAME VARCHAR(20) NOT NULL,
EMP_SERVICE_YEARS INT
NOT NULL WITH DEFAULT 0,
EMP_PROMOTION_DATE DATE)
IN TSHR;
---------+---------+---------+---------+---------+---------+--
DSNE616I STATEMENT EXECUTION WAS SUCCESSFUL, SQLCODE IS 0
```

Now let's insert a row into the EMPLOYE2 table:

```
INSERT INTO HRSCHEMA.EMPLOYE2
  (EMP_LAST_NAME,
   EMP_FIRST_NAME,
   EMP_SERVICE_YEARS,
   EMP_PROMOTION_DATE)
VALUES
  ('JOHNSON',
   'BILL',
   1,
   '12/01/2016');
---------+---------+---------+---------+---------+--------
DSNE615I NUMBER OF ROWS AFFECTED IS 1
DSNE616I STATEMENT EXECUTION WAS SUCCESSFUL, SQLCODE IS 0
---------+---------+---------+---------+---------+--------
```

Notice that we did not specify any value for the EMP_ID. That is because it's an identity field and DB2 will generate the value. Now we can query the table and see the contents:

```
SELECT EMP_ID, EMP_LAST_NAME
FROM HRSCHEMA.EMPLOYE2;
```

```
---------+---------+---------+---------+-
EMP_ID   EMP_LAST_NAME
---------+---------+---------+---------+-
   1001  JOHNSON
DSNE610I NUMBER OF ROWS DISPLAYED IS 1
```

As you can see, we get the same results with the identity field that we got earlier using a sequence. The main difference is that an identity column takes care of generating the value without any prompting. Whereas with a sequence you must specify the sequence name and request the next value.

The other difference between sequences and identity columns is that sequences are a separate object in the database, i.e., they can be used for generating numbers independently of any table. But an identify column is always tied to a single table.

VIEWS

A view is a virtual table that is based on a SELECT query against a base table or another view. Views can include more than one table (or other view), which means they can include the results of a join.

DDL for Views
CREATE

The basic syntax to create a view is as follows:

```
CREATE VIEW <name of view>
AS
SELECT <columns>
FROM <table>
WHERE <condition>
```

You can use a view not only to select data, but also to insert new records into a base table. When you add or update records using a view, you have a choice of enforcing the view definition (meaning you can only those insert records that match the view definition), or you allow inserting of records that don't match the view definition. Using the WITH CHECK OPTION when creating the view ensures that a record inserted via a view is consistent with the view definition.

For example, let's go back to our EMPLOYE2 table. Let's say we want a view named EMP_SE-NIOR that shows us data from EMPLOYE2 only for senior employees, meaning employees with at least 5 years of service. We will also allow records to be inserted to the EMPLOYE2 table via the view. Here is the view definition:

58

```
CREATE VIEW HRSCHEMA.EMP_SENIOR AS
SELECT
EMP_ID,
EMP_LAST_NAME,
EMP_FIRST_NAME,
EMP_SERVICE_YEARS,
EMP_PROMOTION_DATE
FROM HRSCHEMA.EMPLOYE2
WHERE EMP_SERVICE_YEARS >= 5;
---------+---------+---------+---------+---------+---------
DSNE616I STATEMENT EXECUTION WAS SUCCESSFUL, SQLCODE IS 0
```

Now let's insert a couple of records using this view.

```
INSERT INTO HRSCHEMA.EMP_SENIOR
  (EMP_LAST_NAME,
   EMP_FIRST_NAME,
   EMP_SERVICE_YEARS,
   EMP_PROMOTION_DATE)
VALUES
  ('FORD',
   'JAMES',
   7,
   '10/01/2015');
---------+---------+---------+---------+---------+---------+---
DSNE615I NUMBER OF ROWS AFFECTED IS 1
DSNE616I STATEMENT EXECUTION WAS SUCCESSFUL, SQLCODE IS 0
```

This record is for an employee with 5 or more years of service. We got a successful insert which we can reconfirm by querying the table using the same view. Good.

```
SELECT EMP_ID,
EMP_LAST_NAME,
EMP_FIRST_NAME
FROM HRSCHEMA.EMP_SENIOR;


---------+---------+---------+---------+---------+---------+
EMP_ID  EMP_LAST_NAME        EMP_FIRST_NAME
---------+---------+---------+---------+---------+---------+
 1002  FORD                 JAMES
DSNE610I NUMBER OF ROWS DISPLAYED IS 1
```

Now let's insert a record that does not fit the view definition. In this case, let's add a record for which the employee has only 2 years service:

```
INSERT INTO HRSCHEMA.EMP_SENIOR
  (EMP_LAST_NAME,
   EMP_FIRST_NAME,
   EMP_SERVICE_YEARS,
```

```
        EMP_PROMOTION_DATE)
    VALUES
      ('BUFORD',
      'HOLLAND',
       2,
      '07/31/2016');
---------+---------+---------+---------+---------+-----
DSNE615I NUMBER OF ROWS AFFECTED IS 1
```

Interestingly, DB2 allowed the record to be added to the table via the view even though the data did not match the view definition. We cannot know that fact by querying the view because querying the view only shows us data which conforms to the view definition. Notice that only the record for the person with 5 or more years' service is returned by the view.

```
    SELECT EMP_ID,EMP_LAST_NAME,EMP_FIRST_NAME
    FROM HRSCHEMA.EMP_SENIOR;
---------+---------+---------+---------+------
EMP_ID  EMP_LAST_NAME      EMP_FIRST_NAME
---------+---------+---------+---------+------
  1002  FORD               JAMES
DSNE610I NUMBER OF ROWS DISPLAYED IS 1
```

But when we query the base table, we see the new record was in fact added:

```
EMP_ID  EMP_LAST_NAME      EMP_FIRST_NAME      EMP_SERVICE_YEARS
---------+---------+---------+---------+---------+---------+---------+-
  1001  JOHNSON            BILL                                1
  1002  FORD               JAMES                               7
  1003  BUFORD             HOLLAND                             2
DSNE610I NUMBER OF ROWS DISPLAYED IS 3
```

Maybe this is ok if it fits your overall business rules. However, if you want to prevent records that do not conform to the view definition from being inserted into the table using that view, you must define the view using the WITH CHECK OPTION clause. Let's drop the view and recreate it that way.

```
    DROP VIEW HRSCHEMA.EMP_SENIOR;
    COMMIT WORK;

    CREATE VIEW HRSCHEMA.EMP_SENIOR
    AS
    SELECT
    EMP_ID,
    EMP_LAST_NAME,
    EMP_FIRST_NAME,
    EMP_SERVICE_YEARS,
    EMP_PROMOTION_DATE
    FROM HRSCHEMA.EMPLOYE2
```

```
      WHERE EMP_SERVICE_YEARS >= 5
      WITH CHECK OPTION;
      ---------+---------+---------+---------+---------+---------
      DSNE616I STATEMENT EXECUTION WAS SUCCESSFUL, SQLCODE IS 0
```

Now let's try to insert two more records, first an employee with more 5 or more years of service.

```
      INSERT INTO HRSCHEMA.EMP_SENIOR
        (EMP_LAST_NAME,
         EMP_FIRST_NAME,
         EMP_SERVICE_YEARS,
         EMP_PROMOTION_DATE)

        VALUES
        ('JACKSON',
         'MARLO',
         8,
         '06/30/2015');
      ---------+---------+---------+---------
      DSNE615I NUMBER OF ROWS AFFECTED IS 1
```

This still works which is fine. Now let's try one with less than 5 years of service. In this case the insert fails as we can see:

```
      INSERT INTO HRSCHEMA.EMP_SENIOR
        (EMP_LAST_NAME,
         EMP_FIRST_NAME,
         EMP_SERVICE_YEARS,
         EMP_PROMOTION_DATE)
        VALUES
        ('TARKENTON',
         'QUINCY',
         3,
         '09/30/2015');
      ---------+---------+---------+---------+---------+---------+---------+-----
      DSNT408I SQLCODE = -161, ERROR:  THE INSERT OR UPDATE IS NOT ALLOWED BECAUSE
      A RESULTING ROW DOES NOT SATISFY THE VIEW DEFINITION
      DSNT418I SQLSTATE   = 44000 SQLSTATE RETURN CODE
      DSNT415I SQLERRP    = DSNXRSVW SQL PROCEDURE DETECTING ERROR
      DSNT416I SQLERRD    = -160 0   0   -1  0   0 SQL DIAGNOSTIC INFORMATION
      DSNT416I SQLERRD    = X'FFFFFF60'  X'00000000'  X'00000000'  X'FFFFFFFF'
               X'00000000'  X'00000000' SQL DIAGNOSTIC INFORMATION
      ---------+---------+---------+---------+---------+---------+---------+-----
```

So this is how to create a view that will disallow any insert or update that does not conform to the view definition.

ALTER

In general views cannot be changed. They must be dropped and recreated. One exception is that you can regenerate a view from the existing definition. The basic syntax to do this is:

```
ALTER VIEW <name of view> REGENERATE
```

Here's an example of regenerating the `EMPLOYEE_SENIOR` view.

```
ALTER VIEW
HRSCHEMA.EMP_SENIOR
REGENERATE;
```

DROP
Finally, you can delete a view by issuing the DROP command.

```
DROP VIEW <view name>
```

Read-Only Views
The following are some conditions under which a view is automatically read-only, meaning you cannot insert, update or delete any rows using a view that includes any of these conditions.

1. The first SELECT clause includes the keyword DISTINCT.
2. The first SELECT clause contains an aggregate function.
3. The first FROM clause identifies multiple tables or views.
4. The outer fullselect includes a GROUP BY clause.

Views for Security
A view is a classic way to restrict a subset of data columns to a specific set of users who are allowed to see or manipulate those columns. If you are going to use views for security you must make sure that users do not have direct access to the base tables, i.e. that they only access the data via view(s). Otherwise they could potentially circumvent access by view.

Let's look back at our employee table. Suppose we add a column for the employee's Social Security number. That is obviously a very private piece of information that not everyone should see. Our business rule will be that users HRUSER01, HRUSER02 and HRUSER99 are the only ones who should be able to view Social Security numbers. All other users and/or groups are not allowed to see the content of this column, but they can access all the other columns.

We can begin implementing this by adding the new column to the base table:

```
ALTER TABLE HRSCHEMA.EMPLOYEE
ADD COLUMN EMP_SSN CHAR(09);
```

Now let's update this column for employee 3217:

```
UPDATE HRSCHEMA.EMPLOYEE
SET EMP_SSN = '238297536'
WHERE EMP_ID = 3217;
```

Now let's create two views, one of which includes the EMP_SSN column, and the other of which does not:

```
CREATE VIEW HRSCHEMA.EMPLOYEE_ALL
AS SELECT
EMP_ID,
EMP_LAST_NAME,
EMP_FIRST_NAME,
EMP_SERVICE_YEARS,
EMP_PROMOTION_DATE,
EMP_PROFILE
FROM HRSCHEMA.EMPLOYEE;

CREATE VIEW HRSCHEMA.EMPLOYEE_HR
AS SELECT
EMP_ID,
EMP_LAST_NAME,
EMP_FIRST_NAME,
EMP_SERVICE_YEARS,
EMP_PROMOTION_DATE,
EMP_PROFILE,
EMP_SSN
FROM HRSCHEMA.EMPLOYEE;
```

Finally, issue the appropriate grants.

```
GRANT SELECT ON HRSCHEMA.EMPLOYEE_ALL TO PUBLIC;

GRANT SELECT on HRSCHEMA.EMPLOYEE_HR
TO HRUSER01, HRUSER02, HRUSER99;
```

At this point, assuming we are only accessing data through views, the three HR users are the only users able to access the EMP_SSN column. Other users cannot access the EMP_SSN column because it is not included in the EMPLOYEE_ALL view that they have access to. To prove this, let's run some queries:

```
SELECT EMP_ID, EMP_SSN
FROM HRSCHEMA.EMPLOYEE_ALL
WHERE EMP_ID = 3217;
---------+---------+---------+---------+---------+---------+---------+-----
DSNT408I SQLCODE = -206, ERROR:  EMP_SSN IS NOT VALID IN THE CONTEXT WHERE IT IS USED
```

If you are using the EMPLOYEE_ALL view, you do not have access to the SSN because it is not a column in that view. However, if you are one of the HR users, you will be able to access the

EMP_SSN column using the other view, EMPLOYEE_HR:

```
SELECT EMP_ID, EMP_SSN
FROM HRSCHEMA.EMPLOYEE_HR
WHERE EMP_ID = 3217;
---------+---------+------
    EMP_ID  EMP_SSN
---------+---------+------
      3217  238297536
```

Here are just a few more things you should remember about views. First, a view can reference another view. So we could create an EMPLOYEE_PAY view that includes a reference to the EMPLOYEE_ALL view.

Second, when a view gets deleted, then any dependent view will be marked inopertive. If you delete the EMPLOYEE_ALL view, the the EMPLOYEE_PAY view that references it will be marked inoperstive and you won't be able to use it.

Finally, if the column size increases on a base table, then any view which references that column will be automatically regenerated.

As we conclude the DDL chapter of this study guide, I strongly recommend that you remove all the objects we have created thus far. This will enable us to begin with a clean slate for the next chapter on Data Manipulation Language. The easiest way to remove all the objects is to simply drop the database and then recreate it.

```
DROP DATABASE DBHR;
```

Then recreate the database, tablespace and schema that we will use for the HR application. The following is the DDL to do that, and of course it must be customized to your physical environment.

```
CREATE DATABASE DBHR
STOGROUP SGHR
BUFFERPOOL BPHR
INDEXBP IBPHR
CCSID UNICODE;

CREATE TABLESPACE TSHR
IN DBHR
USING STOGROUP SGHR
PRIQTY 50
SECQTY 20
LOCKSIZE PAGE
BUFFERPOOL BPHR2;
```

```
CREATE SCHEMA HRSCHEMA
AUTHORIZATION DBA001;   <--   This should be your DB2 id, whatever it is.
```

The DB2 Catalog

The DB2 system catalog is a wealth of information for research and problem solving. The catalog consists of a set of tables containing information about the various objects in DB2 (tablespaces, tables, indexes, views, packages, etc). The schema for the system catalog is SYSIBM. If you have QMF you can browse a list of the tables by using the LIST command prompt and specifying SYSIBM as the schema.

Table and View Properties Stored in the System Catalog

I think it is good to mention here that you can discover various properties of tables, indexes and views by querying the system catalog. For example, if you want to know what type of tables you have associated with owner HRSCHEMA, you could query them this way:

```
SELECT NAME, TYPE, DBNAME, TSNAME
FROM SYSIBM.SYSTABLES
WHERE CREATOR = 'HRSCHEMA'
ORDER BY TYPE, NAME;


---------+---------+---------+---------+---------+---------+------
NAME                 TYPE  DBNAME              TSNAME
---------+---------+---------+---------+---------+---------+------
EMP_INFO             G     DSNDB06             SYSTSTAB
XEMPLOYEE            P     DBHR                XEMP0000
DEPARTMENT           T     DBHR                TSHR
DEPTMENT             T     DBHR                TSHR
EMPLOYEE             T     DBHR                TSHR
EMPLOYEE_NEW         T     DBHR                TSHR
EMPRECOG             T     DBHR                TSHR
EMP_DATA             T     DBHR                TSHR
EMP_DATA_X           T     DBHR                TSHR
EMP_PAY              T     DBHR                TSHR
EMP_PAY_CHECK        T     DBHR                TSHR
EMP_PAY_HIST         T     DBHR                TSHR
EMP_PAY_HST          T     DBHR                TSHR
EMP_PAY_X            T     DBHR                TSHR
PLAN_TABLE           T     DBHR                TSHR
EMPLOYEE_ALL         V     DBHR                TSHR
EMPLOYEE_HR          V     DBHR                TSHR
EMP_PROFILE_PAY      V     DBHR                TSHR
```

The meaning of the TYPE column is as follows:

A	Alias
C	Clone table
D	Accelerator-only table
G	Created global temporary table (note: declared global temporary is not in the catalog)
H	History table
M	Materialized query table
P	Table that was implicitly created for XML columns
R	Archive table
T	Table
V	View
X	Auxiliary table

You can also get information about views from the system catalog. For example, if you want to know what type of views you have, you could query the information this way:

```
SELECT NAME, TYPE
FROM SYSIBM.SYSVIEWS
WHERE CREATOR = 'HRSCHEMA'
ORDER BY TYPE, NAME
---------+---------+--------
NAME                     TYPE
---------+---------+--------
EMPLOYEE_ALL              V
EMPLOYEE_HR               V
EMP_PROFILE_PAY           V
```

Again, view types are as follows:

F	SQL function
M	Materialized query table
V	View

Chapter Two Questions

1. Which of the following is NOT a valid data type for use as an identity column?

    a. INTEGER
    b. REAL
    c. DECIMAL
    d. SMALLINT

2. You need to store numeric integer values of up to 5,000,000,000. What data type is appropriate for this?

    a. INTEGER
    b. BIGINT
    c. LARGEINT
    d. DOUBLE

3. Which of the following is NOT a LOB (Large Object) data type?

    a. CLOB
    b. BLOB
    c. DBCLOB
    d. DBBLOB

4. If you want to add an XML column VAR1 to table TBL1, which of the following would accomplish that?

    a. ALTER TABLE TBL1 ADD VAR1 XML
    b. ALTER TABLE TBL1 ADD COLUMN VAR1 XML
    c. ALTER TABLE TBL1 ADD COLUMN VAR1 (XML)
    d. ALTER TABLE TBL1 ADD XML COLUMN VAR1

5. If you want rows that have similar key values to be stored physically close to each other, what keyword should you specify when you create an index?

      a. UNIQUE
      b. ASC
      c. INCLUDE
      d. CLUSTER

6. To ensure all records inserted into a view of a table are consistent with the view definition, you would need to include which of the following keywords when defining the view?

      a. UNIQUE
      b. WITH CHECK OPTION
      c. VALUES
      d. ALIAS

7. If you want to determine various characteristics of a set of tables such as type (table or view), owner and status, which system catalog view would you query?

      a. SYSCAT.SYSTABLES
      b. SYSIBM.SYSTABLES
      c. SYSCAT.OBJECTS
      d. SYSIBM.OBJECTS

Chapter Two Exercises

1. Write a DDL statement to create a base table named `EMP_DEPENDENTS` owned by schema `HRSCHEMA` and in tablespace `TSHR`. The columns should be named as follows and have the specified attributes. There is no primary key.

Field Name	Type	Attributes
EMP_ID	INTEGER	NOT NULL
EMP_DEP_LAST_NAME	VARCHAR(30)	NOT NULL
EMP_DEP_FIRST_NAME	VARCHAR(20)	NOT NULL
EMP_RELATIONSHIP	VARCHAR(15)	NOT NULL

2. Create a statement to create a referential constraint on table `EMP_DEPENDENTS` such that only employee ids which exist on the `HRSCHEMA.EMPLOYEE` table can have an entry in `EMP_DEPENDENTS`. If there is an attempt to delete an `EMPLOYEE` record that has `EMP_DE-PENDENTS` records associated with it, then do not allow the delete to take place.

CHAPTER THREE: DATA MANIPULATION LANGUAGE

Overview

In this chapter we will explore DML (data Manipulation Language) which includes both SQL and several related topics.

Data Manipulation Language (DML) is used to add, change and delete data in a DB2 table. DML is one of the most basic and essential skills you must have as a DB2 professional. In this section we'll look at the five major DML statements: INSERT, UPDATE, DELETE, MERGE and SELECT.

XML data access and processing is another skill that you need to be familiar with. DB2 includes an XML data type and various functions for accessing and processing XML data. I'll assume you have a basic understanding of XML, but we'll do a quick review anyway. Then we'll look at some examples of creating an XML column, populating it, modifying it and manipulating it using XML functions such as XQuery.

Special registers allow you to access detailed information about the DB2 instance settings as well as certain session information. CURRENT DATE is an example of a special register. You can access special registers in SPUFI or in an application program and then use the information as needed.

Built-in functions can be used in SQL statements to return a result based on an argument. Think of these as productivity tools in that they can be used to replace custom coded functionality in an application program and thereby simplify development and maintenance. Whether your role is application developer, DBA or business services professional, the DB2 built-in functions can save you time if you know what they are and how to use them.

Database, Tablespace and Schema Conventions

Throughout this book we will be using a database called DBHR which is a database for a fictitious human relations department in a company. The main tablespace we will us is TSHR. Finally, our default schema will be HRSCHEMA. In some cases we will explicitly specify the schema in our DDL or SQL. If we don't explicitly specify a schema, it means we have defined the HRSCHEMA schema as the CURRENT SCHEMA so we don't need to specify it.

If you are following along and creating examples on your own system, you may of course use whatever database and schema is available to you on your system. If you want the basic DDL to create the objects named above, it is as follows:

```
CREATE DATABASE DBHR
STOGROUP SGHR
BUFFERPOOL BPHR
INDEXBP IBPHR
CCSID UNICODE;


CREATE TABLESPACE TSHR
IN DBHR
USING STOGROUP SGHR
PRIQTY 50
SECQTY 20
LOCKSIZE PAGE
BUFFERPOOL BPHR2;


CREATE SCHEMA HRSCHEMA
AUTHORIZATION DBA001;  <--  This should be your DB2 id, whatever it is.
```

DML SQL Statements

Data Manipulation Language (DML) is at the core of working with relational databases. You need to be very comfortable with DML statements: INSERT, UPDATE, DELETE, MERGE and SELECT. We'll cover the syntax and use of each of these. For purposes of this section, let's plan and create a very simple table. Here are the columns and data types for our table which we will name EMPLOYEE.

Field Name	Type	Attributes
EMP_ID	INTEGER	NOT NULL, PRIMARY KEY
EMP_LAST_NAME	VARCHAR(30)	NOT NULL
EMP_FIRST_NAME	VARCHAR(20)	NOT NULL
EMP_SERVICE_YEARS	INTEGER	NOT NULL, DEFAULT IS ZERO
EMP_PROMOTION_DATE	DATE	

The table can be created with the following DDL:

```
CREATE TABLE HRSCHEMA.EMPLOYEE(
EMP_ID INT NOT NULL,
EMP_LAST_NAME VARCHAR(30) NOT NULL,
EMP_FIRST_NAME VARCHAR(20) NOT NULL,
EMP_SERVICE_YEARS INT NOT NULL WITH DEFAULT 0,
EMP_PROMOTION_DATE DATE,
PRIMARY KEY(EMP_ID)) ;
```

We also need to create a unique index to support the primary key:

```
CREATE UNIQUE INDEX NDX_EMPLOYEE ON EMPLOYEE (EMP_ID);
```

INSERT Statement

The INSERT statement adds one or more rows to a table. There are three forms of the INSERT statement and you need to know the syntax of each of these.

1. Insert via Values
2. Insert via Select
3. Insert via FOR N ROWS

Insert Via Values

There are actually two sub-forms of the insert by values. One form explicitly names the target columns and the other does not. Generally when inserting a record you explicitly specify the target fields, followed by a VALUES clause that includes the actual values to apply to the new record. Let's use our EMPLOYEE table for this example:

```
INSERT INTO EMPLOYEE
(EMP_ID,
 EMP_LAST_NAME,
 EMP_FIRST_NAME,
 EMP_SERVICE_YEARS,
 EMP_PROMOTION_DATE)

VALUES (3217,
'JOHNSON',
'EDWARD',
4,
'01/01/2017');
```

Note that the values must be ordered in the same sequence that the columns are named in the INSERT query.

A second sub-form of the INSERT statement via values is to omit the target fields and simply provide the VALUES clause. You can do this only if your values clause includes values for ALL the columns in the correct positional order as defined in the table.

Here's an example of this second sub-form of insert via values:

```
INSERT INTO EMPLOYEE
VALUES (7459,
'STEWART',
'BETTY',
7,
'07/31/2016');
```

There are some options and rules for using default values as well as null values. For example, you can define a column as having a default value using the DEFAULT keyword with a value. If a column is defined with a DEFAULT value, and you want to assign that default value to the column, then you can simply specify DEFAULT for that column in your query. The default value will automatically be assigned.

When you define a column as NOT NULL, it must have a value assigned to it. You must either assign a specific value in the query, or if the column is defined with a default value, you can specify DEFAULT. If you do not assign a specific value or DEFAULT, you will get an error when you try to do the INSERT.

If a column is not defined as NOT NULL (or if it is explicitly defined as NULL meaning NULL-values are allowed), and you don't want to assign a value to that column, then you must specify NULL for the column in the values clause of your INSERT query.

Also notice that EMP_ID is defined as a primary key on the table. If you try inserting a row for which the primary key already exists, you will receive a -803 error SQL code (more on this later when we discuss table objects in detail).

Here's an example of specifying the DEFAULT value for the EMP_SERVICE_YEARS column, and the NULL value for the EMP_PROMOTION_DATE.

```
INSERT INTO EMPLOYEE
(EMP_ID,
EMP_LAST_NAME,
EMP_FIRST_NAME,
EMP_SERVICE_YEARS,
EMP_PROMOTION_DATE)

VALUES (9134,
'FRANKLIN',
'ROSEMARY',
DEFAULT,
NULL);
```

When you define a column using WITH DEFAULT, you do not necessarily have to specify the actual default value in your DDL. DB2 provides implicit default values for most data types and if you just specify WITH DEFAULT and no specific value, the implicit default value will be used.

In the EMPLOYEE table we specified WITH DEFAULT 0 for the employee's service years. However, the implicit default value here is also zero because the column is defined as INTEGER. So we could have simply specified WITH DEFAULT and it would have the same result as specifying WITH DEFAULT 0.

The following table denotes the default values for the various data types.

For columns of	Type	Default
Numbers	SMALLINT, INTEGER, BIGINT, DECIMAL, NUMERIC, REAL, DOUBLE, DECFLOAT, or FLOAT	0
Fixed-length strings	CHAR or GRAPHIC BINARY	Blanks Hexadecimal zeros
Varying-length strings	VARCHAR, CLOB, VARGRAPHIC, DBCLOB, VARBINARY, or BLOB	Empty string
Dates	DATE	CURRENT DATE
Times	TIME	CURRENT TIME
Timestamps	TIMESTAMP	CURRENT TIME-STAMP
ROWIDs	ROWID	DB2-generated

Before moving on to the Insert via Select option, let's take a look at the data we have in the table so far.

```
SELECT
EMP_ID,
EMP_LAST_NAME,
EMP_FIRST_NAME,
EMP_SERVICE_YEARS,
EMP_PROMOTION_DATE
FROM EMPLOYEE
ORDER BY EMP_ID;
-------+---------+---------+---------+---------+---------+---------+---------+-
   EMP_ID  EMP_LAST_NAME    EMP_FIRST_NAME   EMP_SERVICE_YEARS  EMP_PROMOTION_DATE
-------+---------+---------+---------+---------+---------+---------+---------+-
    3217  JOHNSON          EDWARD                          4   2017-01-01
    7459  STEWART          BETTY                           7   2016-01-01
    9134  FRANKLIN         ROSEMARY                        0   ---------

DSNE610I NUMBER OF ROWS DISPLAYED IS 3
```

Insert via Select

You can use a SELECT query to extract data from one table and load it to another. You can even include literals or built in functions in the SELECT query in lieu of column names (if you need them). Let's do an example.

Suppose you work in HR and you have an employee recognition request table named **EMPRECOG**. This table is used to generate/store recognition requests for employees who have been promoted during a certain time frame. Once the request is fulfilled, the date completed will be populated by HR in a separate process. The table specification is as follows:

Field Name	Type	Attributes
EMP_ID	INTEGER	NOT NULL
EMP_PROMOTION_DATE	DATE	NOT NULL
EMP_RECOG_RQST_DATE	DATE	NOT NULL WITH DEFAULT
EMP_RECOG_COMP_DATE	DATE	

The DDL to create the table is as follows:

```
CREATE TABLE EMPRECOG(
EMP_ID INT NOT NULL,
EMP_PROMOTION_DATE DATE NOT NULL,
EMP_RECOG_RQST_DATE DATE
NOT NULL WITH DEFAULT,
EMP_RECOG_COMP_DATE DATE)
IN TSHR;
```

Your objective is to load this table with data from the EMPLOYEE table for any employee whose promotion date occurs during the current month. The selection criteria could be expressed as:

```
SELECT
EMP_ID,
EMP_PROMOTION_DATE
FROM EMPLOYEE
WHERE MONTH(EMP_PROMOTION_DATE)
 = MONTH(CURRENT DATE)
```

To use this SQL in an INSERT statement on the EMPRECOG table, you would need to add another column for the request date (EMP_RECOG_RQST_DATE). Let's use the CURRENT DATE function to insert today's date. Now our select statement looks like this:

```
SELECT
EMP_ID, EMP_PROMOTION_DATE,CURRENT DATE AS RQST_DATE
FROM EMPLOYEE
WHERE MONTH(EMP_PROMOTION_DATE)
    = MONTH(CURRENT DATE)
```

Assuming we are running the SQL on January 10, 2017 we should get the following results:

```
---------+---------+---------+---------+---------+
    EMP_ID   EMP_PROMOTION_DATE   RQST_DATE
---------+---------+---------+---------+---------+
      3217   2017-01-01              2017-01-10
DSNE610I NUMBER OF ROWS DISPLAYED IS 1
```

Finally, let's create the INSERT statement for the EMPRECOG table. Since our query does not include the `EMP_RQST_COMP_DATE` (assume that the request complete column will be populated by another HR process when the request is complete), we must specify the target column names we are populating. Otherwise we will get a mismatch between the number of columns we are loading and the number in the table.

Professional Note: in circumstances where you have values for all the table's columns, you don't have to include the column names. You could just use the INSERT INTO and SELECT statement. But it is handy to include the target column names, even when you don't have to. It makes the DML more self-documenting and helpful for the next developer. This is a good habit to develop – thinking of the next person that will maintain your code.

Here is our SQL:

```
INSERT INTO EMPRECOG
(EMP_ID,
 EMP_PROMOTION_DATE,
 EMP_RECOG_RQST_DATE)
 SELECT
 EMP_ID,
 EMP_PROMOTION_DATE,
 CURRENT DATE AS RQST_DATE
 FROM EMPLOYEE
 WHERE MONTH(EMP_PROMOTION_DATE)
  = MONTH(CURRENT DATE)
```

If you are following along and running the examples, you may notice it doesn't work if the real date is not a January 2017 date. You can make this one work by specifying the comparison date as 1/1/2017. So your query would be:

```
INSERT INTO EMPRECOG
(EMP_ID,
 EMP_PROMOTION_DATE,
 EMP_RECOG_RQST_DATE)
 SELECT
 EMP_ID,
 EMP_PROMOTION_DATE,
 CURRENT DATE AS RQST_DATE
 FROM EMPLOYEE
 WHERE MONTH(EMP_PROMOTION_DATE)
  = MONTH('01/01/2017')
```

After you run the SQL, query the `EMPRECOG` table, and you can see the result:

```
SELECT * FROM EMPRECOG;
---------+---------+---------+---------+---------+---------+---------+---
    EMP_ID  EMP_PROMOTION_DATE  EMP_RECOG_RQST_DATE  EMP_RECOG_COMP_DATE
---------+---------+---------+---------+---------+---------+---------+---
      3217  2017-01-01          2017-01-10           ------------------
DSNE610I NUMBER OF ROWS DISPLAYED IS 1
```

77

The above is what we expect. Only one of the employees has a promotion date in January, 2017. This employee has been added to the EMPRECOG table with request date of January 10 and a NULL recognition completed date.

Insert via FOR N ROWS

The third form of the INSERT statement is used to insert multiple rows with a single statement. You can do this with an internal program table and host variables. We haven't talked yet about embedded SQL but we'll do a sample program now in COBOL along with a version in PLI, and I'll assume you know either the COBOL or PLI language.

We'll use our EMPLOYEE table and insert two new rows using the INSERT via FOR N ROWS. Note that we define our host variables with OCCURS 2 TIMES to create arrays, and then we load the arrays with data before we do the INSERT statement. Also notice the FOR 2 ROWS clause at the end of the SQL statement. You could also have an array with more than two rows. And the number of rows you insert using FOR X ROWS can be less than the actual array size.

```
       IDENTIFICATION DIVISION.
       PROGRAM-ID. COBEMP1.
      *******************************************************
      *      PROGRAM USING DB2 INSERT FOR MULTIPLE ROWS    *
      *******************************************************

       ENVIRONMENT DIVISION.
       DATA DIVISION.
       WORKING-STORAGE SECTION.

           EXEC SQL
             INCLUDE SQLCA
           END-EXEC.

           EXEC SQL
             INCLUDE EMPLOYEE
           END-EXEC.

           01 HV-EMP-VARIABLES.
           10   HV-ID            PIC S9(9) USAGE COMP OCCURS 2 TIMES.
           10   HV-LAST-NAME     PIC X(30) OCCURS 2 TIMES.
           10   HV-FIRST-NAME    PIC X(20) OCCURS 2 TIMES.
           10   HV-SERVICE-YEARS PIC S9(9) USAGE COMP OCCURS 2 TIMES.
           10   HV-PROMOTION-DATE PIC X(10) OCCURS 2 TIMES.

       PROCEDURE DIVISION.

       MAIN-PARA.
           DISPLAY "SAMPLE COBOL PROGRAM: MULTIPLE ROW INSERT".

      *   LOAD THE EMPLOYEE ARRAY

           MOVE +4720               TO HV-ID (1).
```

```
MOVE 'SCHULTZ'          TO HV-LAST-NAME(1).
MOVE 'TIM'              TO HV-FIRST-NAME(1).
MOVE +9                 TO HV-SERVICE-YEARS(1).
MOVE '01/01/2017'       TO HV-PROMOTION-DATE(1).

MOVE +6288              TO HV-ID (2).
MOVE 'WILLARD'          TO HV-LAST-NAME(2).
MOVE 'JOE'              TO HV-FIRST-NAME(2).
MOVE +6                 TO HV-SERVICE-YEARS(2).
MOVE '01/01/2016'       TO HV-PROMOTION-DATE(2).

*   LOAD THE EMPLOYEE TABLE

    EXEC SQL
        INSERT INTO HRSCHEMA.EMPLOYEE
        (EMP_ID,
         EMP_LAST_NAME,
         EMP_FIRST_NAME,
         EMP_SERVICE_YEARS,
         EMP_PROMOTION_DATE)

        VALUES
        (:HV-ID,
         :HV-LAST-NAME,
         :HV-FIRST-NAME,
         :HV-SERVICE-YEARS,
         :HV-PROMOTION-DATE)

        FOR 2 ROWS

    END-EXEC.

    STOP RUN.
```

An additional option for the multiple row INSERT is to specify `ATOMIC` or `NOT ATOMIC`. Specifying `ATOMIC` means that if any of the row operations fails, any successful row operations are rolled back. It's all or nothing. This may be what you want, but that will depend on your program design and how you plan to handle any failed rows.

```
    EXEC SQL
        INSERT INTO HRSCHEMA.EMPLOYEE
        (EMP_ID,
         EMP_LAST_NAME,
         EMP_FIRST_NAME,
         EMP_SERVICE_YEARS,
         EMP_PROMOTION_DATE)

        VALUES
        (:HV-ID,
         :HV-LAST-NAME,
         :HV-FIRST-NAME,
         :HV-SERVICE-YEARS,
         :HV-PROMOTION-DATE)

        FOR 2 ROWS
        ATOMIC
```

```
        END-EXEC.

        STOP RUN.
```

Before you can run this program, it must be pre-compiled, compiled, link-edited and bound. How you do this depends on the shop. Typically you will either submit a JCL from your own library, or you will use a set of online panels to run the steps automatically. Check with a fellow programmer or system admin in your environment for the details of how to do this.

If you are renting a mainframe id with Mathru Technologies, they will provide you with the JCL to compile, bind and run your program.

I'll provide you with the PLI version of the COBEMP1 program, but first you will need to run a DCLGEN for the PLI output structures. To specify PLI you will need to change the programming language default on the DB2I Defaults panel (remember during setup we initially set the application language to IBMCOB to specify the COBOL language). Here's the panel to change the APPLICATIONS LANGUAGE to PLI.

```
                          DB2I DEFAULTS PANEL 1
    COMMAND ===>

    Change defaults as desired:

        1   DB2 NAME ............. ===> DBAX       (Subsystem identifier)
        2   DB2 CONNECTION RETRIES ===> 0          (How many retries for DB2 connection)
        3   APPLICATION LANGUAGE   ===> PLI        (ASM, C, CPP, IBMCOB, FORTRAN, PLI)
        4   LINES/PAGE OF LISTING  ===> 60         (A number from 5 to 999)
        5   MESSAGE LEVEL ........ ===> I          (Information, Warning, Error, Severe)
        6   SQL STRING DELIMITER   ===> DEFAULT    (DEFAULT, ' or ")
        7   DECIMAL POINT ........ ===> .          (. or ,)
        8   STOP IF RETURN CODE >= ===> 8          (Lowest terminating return code)
        9   NUMBER OF ROWS ....... ===> 20         (For ISPF Tables)
       10   AS USER                ===>            (Userid to associate with the trusted
                                                    connection)




    PRESS:  ENTER to process    END to cancel         HELP for more information
```

Now run the DCLGEN on the EMPLOYEE table to create the PLI structures.

Finally, here is the PLI program code.

```
PLIEMP1: PROCEDURE OPTIONS(MAIN) REORDER;
/*******************************************************************
* PROGRAM NAME :   PLIEMP1 - PERFORM MULTI ROW INSERT TO DB2 TABLE *  ``
*******************************************************************/

/*******************************************************************
/*              W O R K I N G   S T O R A G E               *
*******************************************************************/

     DCL 01  HV_ID(2)              FIXED BIN(31);
     DCL 01  HV_LAST_NAME(2)       CHAR(30);
     DCL 01  HV_FIRST_NAME(2)      CHAR(20);
     DCL 01  HV_SERVICE_YEARS(2)   FIXED BIN(31);
     DCL 01  HV_PROMOTION_DATE(2)  CHAR(10);

  DCL RET_SQL_CODE               FIXED BIN(31) INIT(0);
  DCL RET_SQL_CODE_PIC           PIC 'S999999999' INIT (0);

  EXEC SQL
    INCLUDE SQLCA;

  EXEC SQL
    INCLUDE EMPLOYEE;

/*******************************************************************
/*              P R O G R A M   M A I N L I N E             *
*******************************************************************/

  PUT SKIP LIST ('SAMPLE PLI PROGRAM: MULTIPLE ROW INSERT');

  /* LOAD THE EMPLOYEE ARRAY */

     HV_ID(1)              = +4720;
     HV_LAST_NAME(1)       = 'SCHULTZ';
     HV_FIRST_NAME(1)      = 'TIM';
     HV_SERVICE_YEARS(1)   = +9;
     HV_PROMOTION_DATE(1)  = '01/01/2017';

     HV_ID(2)              = +6288;
     HV_LAST_NAME(2)       = 'WILLARD';
     HV_FIRST_NAME(2)      = 'JOE';
     HV_SERVICE_YEARS(2)   = +6;
     HV_PROMOTION_DATE(2)  = '01/01/2016';


     EXEC SQL
        INSERT INTO HRSCHEMA.EMPLOYEE
        (EMP_ID,
```

```
                    EMP_LAST_NAME,
                    EMP_FIRST_NAME,
                    EMP_SERVICE_YEARS,
                    EMP_PROMOTION_DATE)

                 VALUES
                 (:HV_ID,
                  :HV_LAST_NAME,
                  :HV_FIRST_NAME,
                  :HV_SERVICE_YEARS,
                  :HV_PROMOTION_DATE)

                 FOR 2 ROWS
                 NOT ATOMIC CONTINUE ON SQLEXCEPTION;

           IF SQLCODE = 0 THEN;
           ELSE
              DO;
                 EXEC SQL
                    GET DIAGNOSTICS CONDITION 1
                    :RET_SQL_CODE  = DB2_RETURNED_SQLCODE;

                 RET_SQL_CODE_PIC   = RET_SQL_CODE;
                 PUT SKIP LIST (RET_SQL_CODE_PIC);
              END;

        END PLIEMP1;
```

After you've pre-compiled, compiled, link-edited and bound your program, run it and now let's check out table contents:

```
SELECT
EMP_ID,
EMP_LAST_NAME,
EMP_FIRST_NAME,
EMP_SERVICE_YEARS,
EMP_PROMOTION_DATE
FROM EMPLOYEE
WHERE EMP_ID IN (3217, 4720, 6288, 7459, 9134)
ORDER BY EMP_ID;
---------+---------+---------+---------+---------+---------+---------+---------
    EMP_ID  EMP_LAST_NAME   EMP_FIRST_NAME   EMP_SERVICE_YEARS   EMP_PROMOTION_DATE
---------+---------+---------+---------+---------+---------+---------+---------
      3217  JOHNSON         EDWARD                          4   2017-01-01
      4720  SCHULTZ         TIM                             9   2017-01-01
      6288  WILLARD         JOE                             6   2016-01-01
      7459  STEWART         BETTY                           7   2016-01-01
      9134  FRANKLIN        ROSEMARY                        0   ----------
DSNE610I NUMBER OF ROWS DISPLAYED IS 5
```

Note: On the ATOMIC option, you have another choice which is to specify NOT ATOMIC CONTINUE ON SQLEXCEPTION. In this case any successful row operations are still applied to the table, and any unsuccessful ones are not. The unsuccessfully inserted rows are discarded. The key point here is that NOT ATOMIC means the unsuccessful inserts do not cause the entire query to fail. Make sure to remember this point!

Note: You can also INSERT to an underlying table via a view. The syntax is exactly the same as for inserting to a table. This topic will be considered in a later chapter.

UPDATE Statement

The UPDATE statement is pretty straightforward. It changes one or more records based on specified conditions. There are two forms of the UPDATE statement:

1. The Searched Update
2. The Positioned Update

Searched Update

The searched update is performed on records that meet a certain search criteria using a WHERE clause. The basic form and syntax you need to know for the searched update is:

```
UPDATE <TABLENAME>
SET FIELDNAME = <VALUE>
WHERE <CONDITION>
```

For example, recall that we left the promotion date for employee 9134 with a NULL value. Now let's say we want to update the promotion date to October 1, 2016. We could use this SQL to do that:

```
UPDATE EMPLOYEE
SET EMP_PROMOTION_DATE = '10/01/2016'
WHERE EMP_ID = 9134;
```

If you have more than one column to update, you must use a comma to separate the column names. For example, let's update both the promotion date and the first name of the employee. We'll make the first name Brianna and the promotion date 10/1/2016.

```
UPDATE EMPLOYEE
SET EMP_PROMOTION_DATE = '10/01/2016',
    EMP_FIRST_NAME = 'BRIANNA'
WHERE EMP_ID = 9134;
```

Another sub-form of the UPDATE statement to be aware of is UPDATE without a WHERE clause. For example, to set the EMP_RECOG_COMP_DATE field to January 31, 2017 for every row in the EMPRECOG table, you could use this statement:

```
UPDATE EMPRECOG
SET EMP_RECOG_COMP_DATE = '01/31/2017';
```

Obviously you should be very careful using this form of UPDATE, as it will set the column value(s) you specify for every row in the table. This is normally not what you want, but it could be useful in cases where you need to initialize one or more fields for all rows of a relatively small table.

Positioned Update

The positioned update is an update based on a cursor in an application program. Let's continue with our EMPLOYEE table examples by creating an update DB2 program that will generate a result set based on a cursor and then update a set of records.

We need to specially set up test data for our example, so if you are following along, execute the following query:

```
UPDATE EMPLOYEE
SET EMP_LAST_NAME = LOWER(EMP_LAST_NAME)
WHERE
EMP_LAST_NAME IN ('JOHNSON', 'STEWART', 'FRANKLIN');
```

Now here is the current content of our EMPLOYEE table:

```
SELECT EMP_ID, EMP_LAST_NAME, EMP_FIRST_NAME
FROM EMPLOYEE
ORDER BY EMP_ID;

---------+---------+---------+---------+---------+---------+----
    EMP_ID  EMP_LAST_NAME                    EMP_FIRST_NAME
---------+---------+---------+---------+---------+---------+----
      3217  johnson                          EDWARD
      4720  SCHULTZ                          TIM
      6288  WILLARD                          JOE
      7459  stewart                          BETTY
      9134  franklin                         BRIANNA
```

As you can see we have some last names that are in lower case. Further, assume that we have decided we want to store all names in upper case. So we have to correct the lowercase data. We want to check all records in the EMPLOYEE table and if the last name is in lower case, we want to change it to upper case. We also want to report the name (both before and after correction) of the corrected records.

To accomplish our objective we'll define and open a cursor on the EMPLOYEE table. We can

84

specify a WHERE clause that limits the result set to only those records where the `EMP_LAST_NAME` contains lower case characters. After we find them, we will change the case and replace the records.

To code a solution, first we need to identify the rows that include lower case letters in `EMP_LAST_NAME`. We can do this using the DB2 `UPPER` function. We'll compare the current contents of `EMP_LAST_NAME` to the value of `UPPER(EMP_LAST_NAME)` and if the results are not identical, we know that the row in question has lower case characters and needs to be changed. Our result set should include all rows where these two values are not identical. So our SQL would be:

```
SELECT EMP_ID, EMP_LAST_NAME
FROM HRSCHEMA.EMPLOYEE
WHERE EMP_LAST_NAME <> UPPER(EMP_LAST_NAME);
```

Once our FETCH statement has loaded the last name value into the host variable `EMP-LAST-NAME`, we can use the COBOL Upper-case function to convert it from lowercase to uppercase.

```
MOVE FUNCTION UPPER-CASE (EMP-LAST-NAME) TO EMP-LAST-NAME
```

With this approach in mind, we are now ready to write the complete COBOL program. We will define and open the cursor, cycle through the result set using FETCH, modify the data and then do the UPDATE action specifying the current record of the cursor. That is what is meant by a positioned update – the cursor is positioned on the record to be changed, hence you do not need to specify a more elaborate WHERE clause in the UPDATE. Only the `WHERE CURRENT OF <cursor name>` clause need be specified. Also we will include the FOR UPDATE clause in our cursor definition to tell DB2 that our intent is to update the data we retrieve.

The program code follows:

```
        IDENTIFICATION DIVISION.
        PROGRAM-ID. COBEMP2.

        ****************************************************
        *       PROGRAM USING DB2 CURSOR HANDLING          *
        ****************************************************

        ENVIRONMENT DIVISION.
        DATA DIVISION.
        WORKING-STORAGE SECTION.

            EXEC SQL
              INCLUDE SQLCA
            END-EXEC.
```

```
        EXEC SQL
          INCLUDE EMPLOYEE
        END-EXEC.


        EXEC SQL
            DECLARE EMP-CURSOR CURSOR FOR
            SELECT EMP_ID, EMP_LAST_NAME
            FROM EMPLOYEE
            WHERE EMP_LAST_NAME <> UPPER(EMP_LAST_NAME)
            FOR UPDATE OF EMP_LAST_NAME
        END-EXEC.


    PROCEDURE DIVISION.

    MAIN-PARA.
        DISPLAY "SAMPLE COBOL PROGRAM: UPDATE USING CURSOR".

        EXEC SQL
            OPEN EMP-CURSOR
        END-EXEC.

        DISPLAY 'OPEN CURSOR SQLCODE: ' SQLCODE.

        PERFORM FETCH-CURSOR
          UNTIL SQLCODE NOT EQUAL 0.

        EXEC SQL
            CLOSE EMP-CURSOR
        END-EXEC.

        DISPLAY 'CLOSE CURSOR SQLCODE: ' SQLCODE.

        STOP RUN.

    FETCH-CURSOR.

        EXEC SQL
            FETCH EMP-CURSOR INTO :EMP-ID, :EMP-LAST-NAME
        END-EXEC.

        IF SQLCODE = 0
           DISPLAY 'BEFORE CHANGE  ', EMP-LAST-NAME
           MOVE FUNCTION UPPER-CASE (EMP-LAST-NAME)
              TO EMP-LAST-NAME
           EXEC SQL
              UPDATE EMPLOYEE
              SET EMP_LAST_NAME = :EMP-LAST-NAME
              WHERE CURRENT OF EMP-CURSOR
           END-EXEC
        END-IF.

        IF SQLCODE = 0
           DISPLAY 'AFTER CHANGE   ', EMP-LAST-NAME
        END-IF.
```

To avoid redundancy, from this point I will assume that you will pre-compile, compile, link-edit and bind your programs using whatever procedures are used in your shop. I won't mention those steps again. I will just assume that you perform them before you run the program.

Here is the output from running our COBOL program:

```
SAMPLE COBOL PROGRAM: UPDATE USING CURSOR
OPEN CURSOR SQLCODE: 0000000000
BEFORE CHANGE    johnson
AFTER CHANGE     JOHNSON
BEFORE CHANGE    stewart
AFTER CHANGE     STEWART
BEFORE CHANGE    franklin
AFTER CHANGE     FRANKLIN
CLOSE CURSOR SQLCODE: 0000000000
```

If you are using PLI, here is the PLI version of the program, and notice there is an UPPER-CASE function in this language, too.

```
PLIEMP2: PROCEDURE OPTIONS(MAIN) REORDER;

/******************************************************************
* PROGRAM NAME :   PLIEMP2 - USE CURSOR TO UPDATE DB2 ROWS        *
******************************************************************/

/******************************************************************
/*                W O R K I N G   S T O R A G E                   *
******************************************************************/

    DCL RET_SQL_CODE          FIXED BIN(31) INIT(0);
    DCL RET_SQL_CODE_PIC      PIC 'S999999999' INIT (0);


    EXEC SQL
      INCLUDE SQLCA;

    EXEC SQL
      INCLUDE EMPLOYEE;

    EXEC SQL
      DECLARE EMP_CURSOR CURSOR FOR
      SELECT EMP_ID, EMP_LAST_NAME
      FROM HRSCHEMA.EMPLOYEE
      WHERE EMP_LAST_NAME <> UPPER(EMP_LAST_NAME)
      FOR UPDATE OF EMP_LAST_NAME;

/******************************************************************
/*              P R O G R A M   M A I N L I N E                   *
******************************************************************/

    PUT SKIP LIST ('SAMPLE PLI PROGRAM: CURSOR TO UPDATE ROWS');

    EXEC SQL OPEN EMP_CURSOR;

    PUT SKIP LIST ('OPEN CURSOR SQLCODE: ' || SQLCODE);
```

```
     IF SQLCODE = 0 THEN
        DO UNTIL (SQLCODE ¬= 0);
           CALL P0100_FETCH_CURSOR;
        END;

     EXEC SQL CLOSE EMP_CURSOR;

     PUT SKIP LIST ('CLOSE CURSOR SQLCODE: ' || SQLCODE);

     IF SQLCODE ¬= 0 THEN
        DO;
           EXEC SQL
              GET DIAGNOSTICS CONDITION 1
              :RET_SQL_CODE  = DB2_RETURNED_SQLCODE;

           RET_SQL_CODE_PIC  = RET_SQL_CODE;
           PUT SKIP LIST (RET_SQL_CODE_PIC);
        END;

  P0100_FETCH_CURSOR: PROC;

     EXEC SQL
        FETCH EMP_CURSOR INTO :EMP_ID, :EMP_LAST_NAME;

     IF SQLCODE = 0 THEN
        DO;
           PUT SKIP LIST ('BEFORE CHANGE  ' || EMP_LAST_NAME);
           EMP_LAST_NAME = UPPERCASE(EMP_LAST_NAME);
           EXEC SQL
              UPDATE HRSCHEMA.EMPLOYEE
              SET EMP_LAST_NAME = :EMP_LAST_NAME
              WHERE CURRENT OF EMP_CURSOR;
           IF SQLCODE = 0 THEN
              PUT SKIP LIST ('AFTER CHANGE   ' || EMP_LAST_NAME);
        END;


  END P0100_FETCH_CURSOR;

  END PLIEMP2;
```

And here is the modified table:

```
SELECT * FROM EMPLOYEE
ORDER BY EMP_ID;
---------+---------+---------+---------+---------+---------+----
    EMP_ID EMP_LAST_NAME                   EMP_FIRST_NAME
---------+---------+---------+---------+---------+---------+----
      3217 JOHNSON                         EDWARD
      4720 SCHULTZ                         TIM
      6288 WILLARD                         JOE
      7459 STEWART                         BETTY
      9134 FRANKLIN                        BRIANNA
```

This method of using a positioned cursor update is something you will use often, particularly when you do not know your result set beforehand, and anytime you need to examine the content of the record before you perform the update.

DELETE Statement

The DELETE statement is also pretty straightforward. It removes one or more records from the table based on specified conditions. As with the UPDATE statement, there are two forms of the DELETE statement:

1. The Searched Delete
2. The Positioned Delete

Searched DELETE

The searched delete is performed on records that meet a certain criteria, i.e., based on a WHERE clause. The basic form and syntax you need to remember for the searched DELETE is:

```
DELETE FROM <TABLENAME>
WHERE <CONDITION>
```

For example, we might want to remove the record for the employee with id 9134. We could use this SQL to do that:

```
DELETE FROM EMPLOYEE WHERE EMP_ID = 9134;
```

Another sub-form of the DELETE statement to be aware of is the DELETE without a WHERE clause. For example, to remove all records from the EMPRECOG table, use this statement:

```
DELETE FROM EMPRECOG;
```

Be very careful using this form of DELETE, as it will remove every record from the target table. This is normally not what you want, but it could be useful in cases where you need to initialize a relatively small table to empty.

Positioned Delete

The positioned DELETE is similar to the positioned UPDATE. It is a DELETE based on a cursor position in an application program. Let's create a DB2 program that will delete records based on a cursor. We'll have it delete any record where the employee has not received a promotion – don't feel bad for them, remember we're just using the example to illustrate a coding point!

Before we can proceed, we need to add a record to the EMPLOYEE table because currently we have no records that lack a promotion date. So we will add one.

```
INSERT INTO EMPLOYEE
VALUES (1122, 'JENKINS', 'DEBORAH', 5, NULL);
```

At this time, we have a single record in the table for which the promotion data is NULL, which is employee 1122, Deborah Jenkins:

```
SELECT
EMP_ID,
EMP_LAST_NAME,
EMP_FIRST_NAME,
EMP_PROMOTION_DATE
FROM EMPLOYEE
ORDER BY EMP_ID;
---------+---------+---------+---------+---------+---------+---------+---
    EMP_ID  EMP_LAST_NAME    EMP_FIRST_NAME      EMP_PROMOTION_DATE
---------+---------+---------+---------+---------+---------+---------+---
      1122  JENKINS          DEBORAH             ----------
      3217  JOHNSON          EDWARD              2017-01-01
      4720  SCHULTZ          TIM                 2017-01-01
      6288  WILLARD          JOE                 2016-01-01
      7459  STEWART          BETTY               2016-07-31
DSNE610I NUMBER OF ROWS DISPLAYED IS 5
```

The SQL for our cursor should look like this:

```
SELECT
EMP_ID,
FROM EMPLOYEE
WHERE EMP_PROMOTION_DATE IS NULL
FOR UPDATE;
```

We'll include the FOR UPDATE clause with our cursor to ensure DB2 knows our intention is to use the cursor to delete the records we retrieve. In case you are wondering, there is no FOR DELETE clause. The FOR UPDATE clause covers both updates and deletes.

Our program code will look like this:

```
IDENTIFICATION DIVISION.
PROGRAM-ID. COBEMP3.
*******************************************************
*       PROGRAM USING DB2 CURSOR HANDLING AND DELETE *
*******************************************************
ENVIRONMENT DIVISION.
DATA DIVISION.
WORKING-STORAGE SECTION.

    EXEC SQL
      INCLUDE SQLCA
```

90

```
          END-EXEC.

          EXEC SQL
            INCLUDE EMPLOYEE
          END-EXEC.

          EXEC SQL
              DECLARE EMP-CURSOR CURSOR FOR
              SELECT EMP_ID
              FROM HRSCHEMA.EMPLOYEE
              WHERE EMP_PROMOTION_DATE IS NULL
              FOR UPDATE
          END-EXEC.

      PROCEDURE DIVISION.

      MAIN-PARA.
          DISPLAY "SAMPLE COBOL PROGRAM: UPDATE USING CURSOR".

          EXEC SQL
              OPEN EMP-CURSOR
          END-EXEC.

          DISPLAY 'OPEN CURSOR SQLCODE: ' SQLCODE.

          PERFORM FETCH-CURSOR
            UNTIL SQLCODE NOT EQUAL 0.

          EXEC SQL
              CLOSE EMP-CURSOR
          END-EXEC.

          DISPLAY 'CLOSE CURSOR SQLCODE: ' SQLCODE.
          STOP RUN.

      FETCH-CURSOR.

          EXEC SQL
              FETCH EMP-CURSOR INTO :EMP-ID, :EMP-LAST-NAME
          END-EXEC.

          IF SQLCODE = 0
            EXEC SQL
                DELETE HRSCHEMA.EMPLOYEE
                WHERE CURRENT OF EMP-CURSOR
            END-EXEC
          END-IF.
          IF SQLCODE = 0
            DISPLAY 'DELETED EMPLOYEE ', EMP-ID
          END-IF.
```

The output from the program looks like this:

91

```
SAMPLE COBOL PROGRAM: DELETE USING CURSOR
OPEN CURSOR SQLCODE: 0000000000
DELETED EMPLOYEE 000001122
CLOSE CURSOR SQLCODE: 0000000000
```

The PLI version of the program is as follows.

```
PLIEMP3: PROCEDURE OPTIONS(MAIN) REORDER;

/***********************************************************************
* PROGRAM NAME :   PLIEMP3 - USE CURSOR TO DELETE DB2 ROWS          *
***********************************************************************/

/***********************************************************************
/*                 W O R K I N G   S T O R A G E               *
***********************************************************************/

   DCL RET_SQL_CODE              FIXED BIN(31) INIT(0);
   DCL RET_SQL_CODE_PIC          PIC 'S999999999' INIT (0);


   EXEC SQL
     INCLUDE SQLCA;

   EXEC SQL
     INCLUDE EMPLOYEE;

   EXEC SQL
     DECLARE EMP_CURSOR CURSOR FOR
     SELECT EMP_ID
     FROM HRSCHEMA.EMPLOYEE
     WHERE EMP_PROMOTION_DATE IS NULL
     FOR UPDATE;


/***********************************************************************
/*              P R O G R A M   M A I N L I N E                *
***********************************************************************/

   PUT SKIP LIST ('SAMPLE PLI PROGRAM: CURSOR TO DELETE ROWS');

   EXEC SQL OPEN EMP_CURSOR;

   PUT SKIP LIST ('OPEN CURSOR SQLCODE: ' || SQLCODE);

   IF SQLCODE = 0 THEN
      DO UNTIL (SQLCODE ¬= 0);
         CALL P0100_FETCH_CURSOR;
      END;

   EXEC SQL CLOSE EMP_CURSOR;
```

```
                    PUT SKIP LIST ('CLOSE CURSOR SQLCODE: ' || SQLCODE);

               IF SQLCODE ¬= 0 THEN
                  DO;
                     EXEC SQL
                        GET DIAGNOSTICS CONDITION 1
                         :RET_SQL_CODE  = DB2_RETURNED_SQLCODE;

                     RET_SQL_CODE_PIC  = RET_SQL_CODE;
                     PUT SKIP LIST (RET_SQL_CODE_PIC);
                  END;

          P0100_FETCH_CURSOR: PROC;

             DCLEMPLOYEE = '';

             EXEC SQL
                 FETCH EMP_CURSOR INTO :EMP_ID;

             IF SQLCODE = 0 THEN
                DO;
                   EXEC SQL
                      DELETE HRSCHEMA.EMPLOYEE
                      WHERE CURRENT OF EMP_CURSOR;
                   IF SQLCODE = 0 THEN
                      PUT SKIP LIST ('DELETED EMPLOYEE ' || EMP_ID);
                END;


          END P0100_FETCH_CURSOR;

          END PLIEMP3;
```

A single row was deleted from the table, as we can confirm by querying EMPLOYEE:

```
SELECT EMP_ID,
EMP_PROMOTION_DATE
FROM HRSCHEMA.EMPLOYEE
ORDER BY EMP_ID

---------+---------+---------+---------+---
    EMP_ID  EMP_PROMOTION_DATE
---------+---------+---------+---------+---
      3217  2017-01-01
      4720  2017-01-01
      6288  2016-01-01
      7459  2016-07-31
DSNE610I NUMBER OF ROWS DISPLAYED IS 4
```

As with the positioned update statement, the positioned delete is something you will use when you do not know your result set beforehand, or when you have to first examine the content of the record and then decide whether or not to delete it.

MERGE Statement

The MERGE statement updates a target table or view using specified input data. Rows that already exist in the target table are updated as specified by the input source, and rows that do not exist in the target are inserted using data from that same input source.

So what problem does the merge solve? It adds/updates records for a table from a data source when you don't know whether the row already exists in the table or not. An example could be if you are updating data in your table based on a flat file you receive from another system, department or even another company. Assuming the other system does not send you an action code (add, change or delete), you won't know whether to use the INSERT or UPDATE statement.

One way of handling this situation is to first try doing an INSERT and if you get a -803 SQL error code, then you know the record already exists. In that case you would then need to do an UPDATE instead. Or you could first try doing an UPDATE and then if you received an SQLCODE +100, you would know the record does not exist and you would need to do an INSERT. This solution works, but it inevitably wastes some DB2 calls and could potentially slow down performance.

A more elegant solution is the MERGE statement. We'll look at an example of this below. You'll notice the example is a pretty long SQL statement, but don't be put off by that. The SQL is only slightly longer than the combined INSERT and UPDATE statements you would have needed to use otherwise.

Single Row Merge Using Values

Let's go back to our EMPLOYEE table for this example. Let's say we have employee information for Deborah Jenkins whom we previously deleted, and now we want to apply her information back to the table. This information is being fed to us from another system which also supplied an EMP_ID, but we don't know whether that EMP_ID already exists in our EMPLOYEE table or not. So let's use the MERGE statement:

```
MERGE INTO EMPLOYEE AS T
USING
(VALUES (1122,
'JENKINS',
'DEBORAH',
5,
NULL))
AS S
(EMP_ID,
```

```
       EMP_LAST_NAME,
       EMP_FIRST_NAME,
       EMP_SERVICE_YEARS,
       EMP_PROMOTION_DATE)
ON S.EMP_ID = T.EMP_ID


WHEN MATCHED
   THEN UPDATE
      SET T.EMP_LAST_NAME       = S.EMP_LAST_NAME,
          T.EMP_FIRST_NAME      = S.EMP_FIRST_NAME,
          T.EMP_SERVICE_YEARS   = S.EMP_SERVICE_YEARS,
          T.EMP_PROMOTION_DATE  = S.EMP_PROMOTION_DATE

WHEN NOT MATCHED
   THEN INSERT
      VALUES (S.EMP_ID,
      S.EMP_LAST_NAME,
      S.EMP_FIRST_NAME,
      S.EMP_SERVICE_YEARS,
      S.EMP_PROMOTION_DATE);
```

Note that the existing EMPLOYEE table is given with a T qualifier and the new information is given with S as the qualifier (these qualifiers are arbitrary – you can use anything you want). We are matching the new information to the table based on employee id. When the specified employee id is matched to an employee id on the table, an update is performed using the S values, i.e., the new information. If it is not matched to an existing record, then an insert is performed – again based on the S values.

To see that our MERGE action was successful, let's take another look at our EMPLOYEE table.

```
SELECT
EMP_ID,
EMP_LAST_NAME,
EMP_FIRST_NAME,
EMP_PROMOTION_DATE
FROM EMPLOYEE
ORDER BY EMP_ID;

---------+---------+---------+---------+---------+---------+---------+------
    EMP_ID  EMP_LAST_NAME      EMP_FIRST_NAME      EMP_PROMOTION_DATE
---------+---------+---------+---------+---------+---------+---------+------
      1122  JENKINS            DEBORAH             ----------
      3217  JOHNSON            EDWARD              2017-01-01
      4720  SCHULTZ            TIM                 2017-01-01
      6288  WILLARD            JOE                 2016-01-01
      7459  STEWART            BETTY               2016-07-31
DSNE610I NUMBER OF ROWS DISPLAYED IS 5
```

Merge Using HOST Variables

You can also do a merge in an application program using host variables. For this example, let's create a new table and a new program. The table will be EMP_PAY and it will include the base and bonus pay for each employee identified by employee id. Here are the columns we need to define.

Field Name	Type	Attributes
EMP_ID	INTEGER	NOT NULL
EMP_REGULAR_PAY	DECIMAL	NOT NULL
EMP_BONUS	DECIMAL	

The DDL would look like this:

```
CREATE TABLE EMP_PAY(
EMP_ID INT NOT NULL,
EMP_REGULAR_PAY DECIMAL (8,2) NOT NULL,
EMP_BONUS_PAY DECIMAL   (8,2));
```

Next, let's add a few records:

```
INSERT INTO HRSCHEMA.EMP_PAY
VALUES (3217, 80000.00, 4000);

INSERT INTO HRSCHEMA.EMP_PAY
VALUES (7459, 80000.00, 4000);

INSERT INTO HRSCHEMA.EMP_PAY
VALUES (9134, 70000.00, NULL);
```

Now the current data in the table is as follows:

```
SELECT * FROM EMP_PAY;
---------+---------+---------+---------+----
    EMP_ID  EMP_REGULAR_PAY  EMP_BONUS_PAY
---------+---------+---------+---------+----
      3217        80000.00         4000.00
      7459        80000.00         4000.00
      9134        70000.00    -------------
```

Ok, let's create an update file for the employees where some of the data is for brand new employees and some is for updating existing employees. We'll have the program read the file and use the input data with a MERGE statement to update the table. Here's the content of the file with the three fields, EMP_ID, EMP_REGULAR_PAY and EMP_BONUS_PAY:

```
----+----1----+----2----+----3---
3217      65000.00  5500.00
7459      85000.00  4500.00
9134      75000.00  2500.00
4720      80000.00  2500.00
6288      70000.00  2000.00
```

Looking at these records we know we will need to update three records that are already on the table, and we need to add two that don't currently exist on the table.

Here is sample code for a MERGE program that is based on reading the above input file and applying the data to the EMP_PAY table. It differs from the single row insert example only in that we are using host variables for the update data rather than using hard coded values. The power of the MERGE statement should be getting clearer to you now.

```
       IDENTIFICATION DIVISION.
       PROGRAM-ID. COBEMP4.

      **********************************************************
      *      PROGRAM USING DB2 MERGE WITH HOST VARIABLES   *
      **********************************************************

       ENVIRONMENT DIVISION.
       INPUT-OUTPUT SECTION.

           FILE-CONTROL.
               SELECT EMPLOYEE-FILE    ASSIGN TO EMPFILE.

       DATA DIVISION.

       FILE SECTION.
       FD   EMPLOYEE-FILE
            RECORDING MODE IS F
            LABEL RECORDS ARE STANDARD
            RECORD CONTAINS 80 CHARACTERS
            BLOCK CONTAINS 0 RECORDS.

           01 EMPLOYEE-RECORD.
               05  E-ID        PIC X(04).
               05  FILLER      PIC X(76).


       WORKING-STORAGE SECTION.

           EXEC SQL
             INCLUDE SQLCA
           END-EXEC.

           EXEC SQL
             INCLUDE EMPPAY
           END-EXEC.

       01 WS-FLAGS.
           05  SW-END-OF-FILE-SWITCH   PIC X(1) VALUE 'N'.
               88  SW-END-OF-FILE             VALUE 'Y'.
               88  SW-NOT-END-OF-FILE         VALUE 'N'.

       01 IN-EMPLOYEE-RECORD.
           05  EMPLOYEE-ID   PIC X(04).
           05  FILLER        PIC X(05).
           05  REGULAR-PAY   PIC 99999.99.
           05  FILLER        PIC X(02).
```

```cobol
           05   BONUS-PAY       PIC 9999.99.
           05   FILLER          PIC X(54).


      PROCEDURE DIVISION.

       MAIN-PARA.
           DISPLAY "SAMPLE COBOL PROGRAM: UPDATE USING MERGE".

           OPEN INPUT EMPLOYEE-FILE.

      *  MAIN LOOP - READ THE INPUT FILE, LOAD HOST VARIABLES
      *              AND CALL THE MERGE ROUTINE.

           PERFORM UNTIL SW-END-OF-FILE

               READ EMPLOYEE-FILE INTO IN-EMPLOYEE-RECORD
                   AT END SET SW-END-OF-FILE TO TRUE
               END-READ

               IF SW-END-OF-FILE
                  CLOSE EMPLOYEE-FILE
               ELSE
                  MOVE EMPLOYEE-ID TO  EMP-ID
                  MOVE REGULAR-PAY TO  EMP-REGULAR-PAY
                  MOVE BONUS-PAY   TO  EMP-BONUS-PAY
                  PERFORM A1000-MERGE-RECORD
               END-IF

           END-PERFORM.

           STOP RUN.

       A1000-MERGE-RECORD.

           EXEC SQL

               MERGE INTO EMP_PAY AS TARGET
               USING (VALUES(:EMP-ID,
               :EMP-REGULAR-PAY,
               :EMP-BONUS-PAY))
               AS SOURCE(EMP_ID,
               EMP_REGULAR_PAY,
               EMP_BONUS_PAY)
               ON TARGET.EMP_ID = SOURCE.EMP_ID

               WHEN MATCHED THEN UPDATE
                  SET TARGET.EMP_REGULAR_PAY
                         = SOURCE.EMP_REGULAR_PAY,
                      TARGET.EMP_BONUS_PAY
                         = SOURCE.EMP_BONUS_PAY

               WHEN NOT MATCHED THEN INSERT
                 (EMP_ID,
                  EMP_REGULAR_PAY,
                  EMP_BONUS_PAY)
                  VALUES
                  (SOURCE.EMP_ID,
                   SOURCE.EMP_REGULAR_PAY,
                   SOURCE.EMP_BONUS_PAY)
```

```
   END-EXEC.

   IF SQLCODE = 0
      DISPLAY 'RECORD MERGED SUCCESSFULLY', EMP-ID
   ELSE
      DISPLAY 'ERROR - SQLCODE = ', SQLCODE, EMP-ID
   END-IF.
```

Here are the results from the program.

```
SAMPLE COBOL PROGRAM: UPDATE USING MERGE
RECORD MERGED SUCCESSFULLY   000003217
RECORD MERGED SUCCESSFULLY   000007459
RECORD MERGED SUCCESSFULLY   000009134
RECORD MERGED SUCCESSFULLY   000004720
RECORD MERGED SUCCESSFULLY   000006288
```

Finally, here is the PLI version of the program.

```
PLIEMP4: PROCEDURE OPTIONS(MAIN) REORDER;
/*******************************************************************
* PROGRAM NAME :   PLIEMP4 - USE DB2 MERGE WITH HOST VARIABLES.   *
*******************************************************************/

/*******************************************************************
*                    F I L E S
*******************************************************************/
   DCL EMPFILE   FILE RECORD SEQL INPUT;

/*******************************************************************
/*               W O R K I N G   S T O R A G E                    *
*******************************************************************/

   DCL SW_END_OF_FILE            STATIC BIT(01) INIT('0'B);

   DCL 01 IN_EMPLOYEE_RECORD,
         05  EMPLOYEE_ID    CHAR(04),
         05  FILLER1        CHAR(05),
         05  REGULAR_PAY    PIC '99999V.99',
         05  FILLER2        CHAR(02),
         05  BONUS_PAY      PIC '9999V.99',
         05  FILLER3        CHAR(54);

   DCL EMP_REGULAR_PAY_FD   FIXED DEC (8,2);
   DCL EMP_BONUS_PAY_FD     FIXED DEC (8,2);


   DCL RET_SQL_CODE             FIXED BIN(31) INIT(0);
   DCL RET_SQL_CODE_PIC         PIC 'SZZZZZ9999' INIT (0);

   EXEC SQL
```

99

```pli
      INCLUDE SQLCA;

   EXEC SQL
     INCLUDE EMPPAY;

/*********************************************************************
/*              O N   C O N D I T I O N S                           *
*********************************************************************/

   ON ENDFILE (EMPFILE) SW_END_OF_FILE =  '1'B;

/*********************************************************************
/*              P R O G R A M   M A I N L I N E                     *
*********************************************************************/

   PUT SKIP LIST ('SAMPLE PLI PROGRAM: UPDATE USING MERGE');


       OPEN FILE(EMPFILE);

       READ FILE (EMPFILE) INTO (IN_EMPLOYEE_RECORD);

     /* MAIN LOOP - READ THE INPUT FILE, LOAD HOST VARIABLES  */
     /*            AND CALL THE MERGE ROUTINE.                */

       DO WHILE (¬SW_END_OF_FILE);

           EMP_ID              = EMPLOYEE_ID;
           EMP_REGULAR_PAY_FD = REGULAR_PAY;
           EMP_BONUS_PAY_FD   = BONUS_PAY;
           EMP_REGULAR_PAY    = EMP_REGULAR_PAY_FD;
           EMP_BONUS_PAY      = EMP_BONUS_PAY_FD;
           CALL A1000_MERGE_RECORD;
           READ FILE (EMPFILE) INTO (IN_EMPLOYEE_RECORD);

       END; /* DO WHILE */

       CLOSE FILE(EMPFILE);


   A1000_MERGE_RECORD: PROC;

       EXEC SQL

         MERGE INTO EMP_PAY AS TARGET
         USING (VALUES(:EMP_ID,
         :EMP_REGULAR_PAY,
         :EMP_BONUS_PAY))
         AS SOURCE(EMP_ID,
         EMP_REGULAR_PAY,
         EMP_BONUS_PAY)
         ON TARGET.EMP_ID = SOURCE.EMP_ID
```

```
              WHEN MATCHED THEN UPDATE
                 SET TARGET.EMP_REGULAR_PAY
                         = SOURCE.EMP_REGULAR_PAY,
                    TARGET.EMP_BONUS_PAY
                         = SOURCE.EMP_BONUS_PAY

              WHEN NOT MATCHED THEN INSERT

                 (EMP_ID,
                  EMP_REGULAR_PAY,
                  EMP_BONUS_PAY)
                  VALUES
                  (SOURCE.EMP_ID,
                   SOURCE.EMP_REGULAR_PAY,
                   SOURCE.EMP_BONUS_PAY;

         IF SQLCODE = 0 THEN
            PUT SKIP LIST ('RECORD MERGED SUCCESSFULLY ' || EMP_ID);
         ELSE
            DO;
               PUT SKIP LIST ('*** SQL ERROR ***');
               EXEC SQL
                  GET DIAGNOSTICS CONDITION 1
                   :RET_SQL_CODE  = DB2_RETURNED_SQLCODE;

               RET_SQL_CODE_PIC   = RET_SQL_CODE;
               PUT SKIP LIST (RET_SQL_CODE_PIC);
            END;

      END A1000_MERGE_RECORD;

   END PLIEMP4;
```

And the output from the PLI version:

```
   SAMPLE PLI PROGRAM: UPDATE USING MERGE
   RECORD MERGED SUCCESSFULLY          3217
   RECORD MERGED SUCCESSFULLY          7459
   RECORD MERGED SUCCESSFULLY          9134
   RECORD MERGED SUCCESSFULLY          4720
   RECORD MERGED SUCCESSFULLY          6288
```

And now we can verify that the results were actually applied to the table.

```
   SELECT *
   FROM EMP_PAY;

   ---------+---------+---------+---------+-------
      EMP_ID  EMP_REGULAR_PAY  EMP_BONUS_PAY
   ---------+---------+---------+---------+-------
        3217         65000.00         5500.00
        7459         85000.00         4500.00
```

```
        9134            75000.00            2500.00
        4720            80000.00            2500.00
        6288            70000.00            2000.00
DSNE610I NUMBER OF ROWS DISPLAYED IS 5
```

Again the power of the MERGE statement is that you do not need to know whether a record already exists when you apply the data to the table. The program logic is simplified – there is no trial and error to determine whether or not the record exists.

SELECT Statement

SELECT is the main statement you will use to retrieve data from a table or view. The basic syntax for the select statement is:

```
SELECT              <column names>
FROM                <table or view name>
WHERE      <condition>
ORDER BY   <column name or number to sort by>
```

Let's return to our EMPLOYEE table for an example:

```
SELECT EMP_ID, EMP_LAST_NAME, EMP_FIRST_NAME
FROM HRSCHEMA.EMPLOYEE
WHERE EMP_ID = 3217;

---------+---------+---------+---------+---------+-----
    EMP_ID  EMP_LAST_NAME        EMP_FIRST_NAME
---------+---------+---------+---------+---------+-----
     3217  JOHNSON              EDWARD
DSNE610I NUMBER OF ROWS DISPLAYED IS 1
```

You can also change the column heading on the result set by specifying <column name> AS <literal>. For example:

```
SELECT EMP_ID AS "EMPLOYEE NUMBER",
EMP_LAST_NAME AS "EMPLOYEE LAST NAME",
EMP_FIRST_NAME AS "EMPLOYEE FIRST NAME"
FROM HRSCHEMA.EMPLOYEE
WHERE EMP_ID = 3217 ;
---------+---------+---------+---------+---------+---------+---
EMPLOYEE NUMBER  EMPLOYEE LAST NAME    EMPLOYEE FIRST NAME
---------+---------+---------+---------+---------+---------+---
         3217  JOHNSON              EDWARD
DSNE610I NUMBER OF ROWS DISPLAYED IS 1
```

Now let's look at some clauses that will further qualify the rows that are returned.

WHERE CONDITION

There are quite a lot of options for the WHERE condition. In fact, you can use multiple where conditions by specifying AND and OR clauses. Be aware of the equality operators which are:

```
=           Equal to
<>          Not equal to
>           Greater than
>=          Greater than or equal to
<           Less than
<=          Less than or equal to
```

Let's look at some various examples of WHERE conditions.

OR

```
SELECT EMP_ID, EMP_LAST_NAME, EMP_FIRST_NAME
FROM EMPLOYEE
WHERE EMP_ID = 3217 OR EMP_ID = 9134;
---------+---------+---------+---------+---------+---------
    EMP_ID  EMP_LAST_NAME       EMP_FIRST_NAME
---------+---------+---------+---------+---------+---------
    3217  JOHNSON             EDWARD
    9134  FRANKLIN            BRIANNA
DSNE610I NUMBER OF ROWS DISPLAYED IS 2
```

AND

```
SELECT EMP_ID,
EMP_LAST_NAME,
EMP_FIRST_NAME,
EMP_PROMOTION_DATE
FROM HRSCHEMA.EMPLOYEE
WHERE (EMP_SERVICE_YEARS > 1)
  AND (EMP_PROMOTION_DATE > '12/31/2016')

---------+---------+---------+---------+---------+---------+---------+---
    EMP_ID  EMP_LAST_NAME       EMP_FIRST_NAME       EMP_PROMOTION_DATE
---------+---------+---------+---------+---------+---------+---------+---
    3217  JOHNSON             EDWARD               2017-01-01
    4720  SCHULTZ             TIM                  2017-01-01
DSNE610I NUMBER OF ROWS DISPLAYED IS 2
```

IN

You can specify that the column value must be present in a specified collection of values, either those you code in the SQL explicitly or a collection that is a result of a query. Let's look at an example of specifying specific EMP_IDs.

```
SELECT EMP_ID,
EMP_LAST_NAME,
EMP_FIRST_NAME
FROM HRSCHEMA.EMPLOYEE
WHERE EMP_ID IN (3217, 9134);
```

```
---------+---------+---------+---------+---------+
    EMP_ID  EMP_LAST_NAME        EMP_FIRST_NAME
---------+---------+---------+---------+---------+
    3217  JOHNSON              EDWARD
    9134  FRANKLIN             BRIANNA
DSNE610I NUMBER OF ROWS DISPLAYED IS 2
```

Now let's provide a listing of employees who are in the EMPLOYEE table but are NOT in the EMP_PAY table yet. This example shows us two new techniques, use of the NOT keyword and use of a sub-select to create a collection result set. First, let's add a couple of records to the EMPLOYEE table:

```
INSERT INTO EMPLOYEE
(EMP_ID,
EMP_LAST_NAME,
EMP_FIRST_NAME,
EMP_SERVICE_YEARS,
EMP_PROMOTION_DATE)

VALUES (3333,
'FORD',
'JAMES',
7,
'10/01/2015');

INSERT INTO EMPLOYEE
(EMP_ID,
EMP_LAST_NAME,
EMP_FIRST_NAME,
EMP_SERVICE_YEARS,
EMP_PROMOTION_DATE)

VALUES (7777,
'HARRIS',
'ELISA',
2,
NULL);
```

Now let's run our mismatch query:

```
SELECT EMP_ID,
EMP_LAST_NAME,
EMP_FIRST_NAME
FROM EMPLOYEE
WHERE EMP_ID
NOT IN (SELECT EMP_ID FROM EMP_PAY);


---------+---------+---------+---------+---------+---------+-
    EMP_ID  EMP_LAST_NAME        EMP_FIRST_NAME
---------+---------+---------+---------+---------+---------+-
    3333  FORD                 JAMES
    7777  HARRIS               ELISA
DSNE610I NUMBER OF ROWS DISPLAYED IS 2
```

By the way you can also use the EXCEPT clause to identify rows in one table that have no counterpart in the other. For example, suppose we want the employee ids of any employee who has not received a paycheck. You could quickly identify them with this SQL:

```
        SELECT EMP_ID
        FROM EMPLOYEE
        EXCEPT (SELECT EMP_ID FROM EMP_PAY);
---------+---------+---------+---------+--------+---
     EMP_ID
---------+---------+---------+---------+--------+---
      3333
      7777
DSNE610I NUMBER OF ROWS DISPLAYED IS 2
```

One limitation of the EXCEPT clause is that the two queries have to match exactly, so you could not bring back a column from EMPLOYEE that does not also exist in the EMP_PAY table. Still the EXCEPT is useful in some cases, especially where you need to identify discrepancies between tables using a single column.

BETWEEN

The BETWEEN clause allows you to specify a range of values inclusive of the start and end value you provide. Here's an example where we want to retrieve the employee id and pay rate for all employees whose pay rate is between 60,000 and 85,000 annually.

```
      SELECT EMP_ID,
      EMP_REGULAR_PAY
      FROM EMP_PAY
      WHERE EMP_REGULAR_PAY
      BETWEEN 60000 AND 85000;
    ---------+---------+---------+---------+----
       EMP_ID  EMP_REGULAR_PAY
    ---------+---------+---------+---------+----
        3217          65000.00
        7459          85000.00
        9134          75000.00
        4720          80000.00
        6288          70000.00
DSNE610I NUMBER OF ROWS DISPLAYED IS 5
```

LIKE

You can use the LIKE predicate to select values that match a pattern. For example, let's choose all rows for which the last name begins with the letter B. The % character is used as a wild card for any string value or character. So in this case we are retrieving every record for which the EMP_FIRST_NAME starts with the letter B.

```
      SELECT EMP_ID,
      EMP_LAST_NAME,
      EMP_FIRST_NAME
      FROM HRSCHEMA.EMPLOYEE
```

```
      WHERE EMP_FIRST_NAME LIKE 'B%'

---------+---------+---------+---------+---------+---------
    EMP_ID   EMP_LAST_NAME         EMP_FIRST_NAME
---------+---------+---------+---------+---------+---------
      7459   STEWART               BETTY
      9134   FRANKLIN              BRIANNA
DSNE610I NUMBER OF ROWS DISPLAYED IS 2
```

DISTINCT

Use the DISTINCT operator when you want to eliminate duplicate values. To illustrate this, let's create a couple of new tables. The first is called EMP_PAY_CHECK and we will use to store a calculated bi-monthly pay amount for each employee based on their annual salary. The DDL to create EMP_PAY_CHECK is a s follows:

```
CREATE TABLE EMP_PAY_CHECK(
EMP_ID INT NOT NULL,
EMP_REGULAR_PAY  DECIMAL (8,2) NOT NULL,
EMP_SEMIMTH_PAY DECIMAL (8,2) NOT NULL) IN TSHR;
```

Now let's insert some data into the EMP_PAY_CHECK table by calculating a twice monthly pay check:

```
INSERT INTO EMP_PAY_CHECK
(SELECT EMP_ID, EMP_REGULAR_PAY, EMP_REGULAR_PAY / 24 FROM EMP_PAY);
```

Let's look at the results:

```
SELECT *
FROM HRSCHEMA.EMP_PAY_CHECK;

---------+---------+---------+---------+---------+--
    EMP_ID   EMP_REGULAR_PAY   EMP_SEMIMTH_PAY
---------+---------+---------+---------+---------+--
      3217        65000.00          2708.33
      7459        85000.00          3541.66
      9134        75000.00          3125.00
      4720        80000.00          3333.33
      6288        70000.00          2916.66
DSNE610I NUMBER OF ROWS DISPLAYED IS 5
```

We now know how much each employee should make in their pay check. The next step is to create a history table of each pay check the employee receives. First we'll create the table and then we'll load it with data.

```
CREATE TABLE EMP_PAY_HIST(
EMP_ID INT NOT NULL,
EMP_PAY_DATE  DATE NOT NULL,
EMP_PAY_AMT   DECIMAL (8,2) NOT NULL)IN TSHR;
```

We can load the history table by creating pay checks for the first four pay periods of the year like this:

```
INSERT INTO EMP_PAY_HIST
SELECT EMP_ID,
 '01/15/2017',
 EMP_SEMIMTH_PAY
 FROM EMP_PAY_CHECK;

INSERT INTO EMP_PAY_HIST
SELECT EMP_ID,
 '01/31/2017',
 EMP_SEMIMTH_PAY
 FROM EMP_PAY_CHECK;

INSERT INTO EMP_PAY_HIST
SELECT EMP_ID,
 '02/15/2017',
 EMP_SEMIMTH_PAY
 FROM EMP_PAY_CHECK;

INSERT INTO EMP_PAY_HIST
SELECT EMP_ID,
 '02/28/2017',
 EMP_SEMIMTH_PAY
 FROM EMP_PAY_CHECK;
```

Now we can look at the history table content which is as follows:

```
SELECT * from HRSCHEMA.EMP_PAY_HIST;
---------+---------+---------+---------+------
   EMP_ID  EMP_PAY_DATE  EMP_PAY_AMT
---------+---------+---------+---------+------
     3217  2017-01-15       2708.33
     7459  2017-01-15       3541.66
     9134  2017-01-15       3125.00
     4720  2017-01-15       3333.33
     6288  2017-01-15       2916.66
     3217  2017-01-31       2708.33
     7459  2017-01-31       3541.66
     9134  2017-01-31       3125.00
     4720  2017-01-31       3333.33
     6288  2017-01-31       2916.66
     3217  2017-02-15       2708.33
     7459  2017-02-15       3541.66
     9134  2017-02-15       3125.00
     4720  2017-02-15       3333.33
     6288  2017-02-15       2916.66
     3217  2017-02-28       2708.33
     7459  2017-02-28       3541.66
     9134  2017-02-28       3125.00
     4720  2017-02-28       3333.33
     6288  2017-02-28       2916.66
DSNE610I NUMBER OF ROWS DISPLAYED IS 20
```

If you want a list of all employees who got a paycheck during the month of February, you would need to eliminate the duplicate entries because there are two for each employee. You could accomplish that with this SQL:

```
SELECT DISTINCT EMP_ID
FROM HRSCHEMA.EMP_PAY_HIST
WHERE MONTH(EMP_PAY_DATE) = '02'

---------+---------+---------+---------+-----
   EMP_ID
---------+---------+---------+---------+-----
      3217
      4720
      6288
      7459
      9134
DSNE610I NUMBER OF ROWS DISPLAYED IS 5
```

The DISTINCT operator ensures that only unique records are selected based on the columns you are returning. This is important because if you included additional columns in the results, any value that makes the record unique will also make it NOT a duplicate.

Let's add the payment date to our query and see the results:

```
SELECT DISTINCT EMP_ID, EMP_PAY_DATE
FROM HRSCHEMA.EMP_PAY_HIST
WHERE MONTH(EMP_PAY_DATE) = '02'

---------+---------+---------+---------+----
   EMP_ID  EMP_PAY_DATE
---------+---------+---------+---------+----
      3217  2017-02-15
      3217  2017-02-28
      4720  2017-02-15
      4720  2017-02-28
      6288  2017-02-15
      6288  2017-02-28
      7459  2017-02-15
      7459  2017-02-28
      9134  2017-02-15
      9134  2017-02-28
DSNE610I NUMBER OF ROWS DISPLAYED IS 10
```

Since the combination of the employee id and payment date makes each record unique, you'll get multiple rows for each employee. So you must be careful in using DISTINCT to ensure that the structure of your query is really what you want.

FETCH FIRST X ROWS ONLY

You can limit your result set by using the FETCH FIRST X ROWS ONLY clause. For example, suppose you just want the employee id and names of the first four records from the employee

108

table. You can code it as follows:

```
SELECT EMP_ID,
EMP_LAST_NAME,
EMP_FIRST_NAME
FROM HRSCHEMA.EMPLOYEE
FETCH FIRST 4 ROWS ONLY
---------+---------+---------+---------+---------+-
    EMP_ID  EMP_LAST_NAME       EMP_FIRST_NAME
---------+---------+---------+---------+---------+-
      3217  JOHNSON             EDWARD
      7459  STEWART             BETTY
      9134  FRANKLIN            BRIANNA
      4720  SCHULTZ             TIM
DSNE610I NUMBER OF ROWS DISPLAYED IS 4
```

Keep in mind that when you order the results you may get different records. For example if you order by last name, you would get this result:

```
SELECT EMP_ID,
EMP_LAST_NAME,
EMP_FIRST_NAME
FROM HRSCHEMA.EMPLOYEE
ORDER BY EMP_LAST_NAME FETCH FIRST 4 ROWS ONLY;

---------+---------+---------+---------+---------+-
    EMP_ID  EMP_LAST_NAME       EMP_FIRST_NAME
---------+---------+---------+---------+---------+-
      3333  FORD                JAMES
      9134  FRANKLIN            BRIANNA
      7777  HARRIS              ELISA
      3217  JOHNSON             EDWARD
DSNE610I NUMBER OF ROWS DISPLAYED IS 4
```

SUBQUERY

A subquery is essentially a query within a query. Suppose for example we want to list the employee or employees who make the largest salary in the company. You can use a subquery to determine the maximum salary, and then use that value in the WHERE clause.

```
SELECT EMP_ID, EMP_REGULAR_PAY
FROM EMP_PAY
WHERE EMP_REGULAR_PAY = (SELECT MAX(EMP_REGULAR_PAY)
        FROM EMP_PAY);

---------+---------+---------+---------+----
    EMP_ID  EMP_REGULAR_PAY
---------+---------+---------+---------+----
      7459          85000.00
DSNE610I NUMBER OF ROWS DISPLAYED IS 1
```

What if there is more than one employee who makes the highest salary? Let's bump two people up to 85000 (and 4500 bonus) and see.

```
UPDATE EMP_PAY
SET EMP_REGULAR_PAY = 85000.00,
    EMP_BONUS_PAY = 4500
WHERE EMP_ID IN (4720,9134);
```

Here are the results:

```
    SELECT * FROM EMP_PAY;
---------+---------+---------+---------+----
   EMP_ID  EMP_REGULAR_PAY  EMP_BONUS_PAY
---------+---------+---------+---------+----
     3217         65000.00         5500.00
     7459         85000.00         4500.00
     9134         85000.00         4500.00
     4720         85000.00         4500.00
     6288         70000.00         2000.00
DSNE610I NUMBER OF ROWS DISPLAYED IS 5
```

Now let's see if our subquery still works:

```
    SELECT EMP_ID, EMP_REGULAR_PAY
    FROM EMP_PAY
    WHERE EMP_REGULAR_PAY
      = (SELECT MAX(EMP_REGULAR_PAY)
           FROM EMP_PAY);
---------+---------+---------+---------+----
   EMP_ID  EMP_REGULAR_PAY
---------+---------+---------+---------+----
     7459         85000.00
     9134         85000.00
     4720         85000.00
DSNE610I NUMBER OF ROWS DISPLAYED IS 3
```

The query pulls all three of the highest paid employees. Subqueries are very powerful in that any value you can produce via a subquery can be substituted into a main query as selection or exclusion criteria.

GROUP BY

You can summarize data using the GROUP BY clause. For example, let's determine how many distinct employee salary rates there are and how many employees are paid those amounts.

```
    SELECT EMP_REGULAR_PAY,
    COUNT(*) AS "HOW MANY"
    FROM EMP_PAY
    GROUP BY EMP_REGULAR_PAY

    ---------+---------+---------+---------+-
    EMP_REGULAR_PAY    HOW MANY
    ---------+---------+---------+---------+-
         65000.00              1
    .
```

110

```
        70000.00              1
        85000.00              3
DSNE610I NUMBER OF ROWS DISPLAYED IS 3
```

ORDER BY

You can sort the display into ascending or descending sequence using the ORDER BY clause. To take the query we were just using for the group-by, let's present the data in descending sequence:

```
SELECT EMP_REGULAR_PAY,
  COUNT(*) AS "HOW MANY"
  FROM EMP_PAY
  GROUP BY EMP_REGULAR_PAY
  ORDER BY EMP_REGULAR_PAY DESC;


---------+---------+---------+---------+-----
EMP_REGULAR_PAY     HOW MANY
---------+---------+---------+---------+-----
        85000.00              3
        70000.00              1
        65000.00              1
DSNE610I NUMBER OF ROWS DISPLAYED IS 3
```

HAVING

You could also use the GROUP BY with a HAVING clause that limits the results to only those groups that meet another condition. Let's specify that the group must have more than one employee in it to be included in the results.

```
SELECT EMP_REGULAR_PAY,
COUNT(*) AS "HOW MANY"
FROM EMP_PAY
GROUP BY EMP_REGULAR_PAY
HAVING COUNT(*) > 1
ORDER BY EMP_REGULAR_PAY DESC;


---------+---------+---------+---------+-
EMP_REGULAR_PAY     HOW MANY
---------+---------+---------+---------+-
        85000.00              3
DSNE610I NUMBER OF ROWS DISPLAYED IS 1
```

Or if you want pay rates that have only one employee you could specify the count 1.

```
SELECT EMP_REGULAR_PAY,
COUNT(*) AS "HOW MANY"
FROM EMP_PAY
GROUP BY EMP_REGULAR_PAY
HAVING COUNT(*) = 1
```

```
ORDER BY EMP_REGULAR_PAY DESC

---------+---------+---------+---------+------
EMP_REGULAR_PAY     HOW MANY
---------+---------+---------+---------+------
        70000.00            1
        65000.00            1
DSNE610I NUMBER OF ROWS DISPLAYED IS 2
```

Before we move on, let's reset our two employees to whom we gave a temporary raise. Otherwise our EMP_PAY and EMP_PAY_CHECK tables will not be in sync.

```
UPDATE EMP_PAY
SET EMP_REGULAR_PAY = 80000.00,
    EMP_BONUS_PAY = 2500
WHERE EMP_ID = 4720;

UPDATE EMP_PAY
SET EMP_REGULAR_PAY = 75000.00,
    EMP_BONUS_PAY = 2500
WHERE EMP_ID = 9134;
```

Now our EMP_PAY table is restored:

```
SELECT * FROM EMP_PAY;
---------+---------+---------+---------+--------
    EMP_ID  EMP_REGULAR_PAY  EMP_BONUS_PAY
---------+---------+---------+---------+--------
      3217         65000.00        5500.00
      7459         85000.00        4500.00
      9134         75000.00        2500.00
      4720         80000.00        2500.00
      6288         70000.00        2000.00
DSNE610I NUMBER OF ROWS DISPLAYED IS 5
```

CASE Expressions

In some situations you may need to code more complex conditional logic into your queries. Assume we have a requirement to report all employees according to seniority. We've invented the classifications ENTRY, ADVANCED and SENIOR. We want to report those who have less than a year service as ENTRY, employees who have a year or more service but less than 5 years as ADVANCED, and all employees with 5 years or more service as SENIOR. Here is a sample query that performs this using a CASE expression:

```
SELECT EMP_ID,
EMP_LAST_NAME,
EMP_FIRST_NAME,
CASE
   WHEN EMP_SERVICE_YEARS < 1 THEN 'ENTRY'
   WHEN EMP_SERVICE_YEARS < 5 THEN 'ADVANCED'
```

```
      ELSE 'SENIOR'
  END CASE
  FROM HRSCHEMA.EMPLOYEE;


---------+---------+---------+---------+---------+---------+------
    EMP_ID  EMP_LAST_NAME     EMP_FIRST_NAME      CASE
---------+---------+---------+---------+---------+---------+------
      3217  JOHNSON           EDWARD              SENIOR
      7459  STEWART           BETTY               SENIOR
      9134  FRANKLIN          BRIANNA             ENTRY
      4720  SCHULTZ           TIM                 SENIOR
      6288  WILLARD           JOE                 SENIOR
      3333  FORD              JAMEs               SENIOR
      7777  HARRIS            ELISA               ADVANCED
DSNE610I NUMBER OF ROWS DISPLAYED IS 7
```

You'll notice that the column heading for the case result is CASE. If you want to use a more meaningful column heading, then instead of closing the CASE statement with END CASE, close it with END AS <some literal>. So if we want to call the result of the CASE expression an employee's "LEVEL", code it this way:

```
  SELECT EMP_ID,
  EMP_LAST_NAME,
  EMP_FIRST_NAME,
  CASE
      WHEN EMP_SERVICE_YEARS  < 1 THEN 'ENTRY'
      WHEN EMP_SERVICE_YEARS  < 5 THEN 'ADVANCED'
      ELSE 'SENIOR'
  END AS LEVEL
  FROM HRSCHEMA.EMPLOYEE;


---------+---------+---------+---------+---------+---------+-------
    EMP_ID  EMP_LAST_NAME     EMP_FIRST_NAME      LEVEL
---------+---------+---------+---------+---------+---------+-------
      3217  JOHNSON           EDWARD              SENIOR
      7459  STEWART           BETTY               SENIOR
      9134  FRANKLIN          BRIANNA             ENTRY
      4720  SCHULTZ           TIM                 SENIOR
      6288  WILLARD           JOE                 SENIOR
      3333  FORD              JAMEs               SENIOR
      7777  HARRIS            ELISA               ADVANCED
DSNE610I NUMBER OF ROWS DISPLAYED IS 7
```

JOINS

Now let's look at some cases where we need to pull data from more than one table. To do this we can use a join. Before we start running queries I want to add one row to the EMP_PAY_CHECK table. This is needed to make some of the joins work later, so bear with me.

```
INSERT INTO EMP_PAY_CHECK
VALUES
(7033,
77000.00,
77000 / 24);
```

113

Now our `EMP_PAY_CHECK` table has these rows.

```
     SELECT * FROM EMP_PAY_CHECK;
---------+---------+---------+---------+------
     EMP_ID  EMP_REGULAR_PAY  EMP_SEMIMTH_PAY
---------+---------+---------+---------+------
        3217          65000.00             2708.33
        7459          85000.00             3541.66
        9134          75000.00             3125.00
        4720          80000.00             3333.33
        6288          70000.00             2916.66
        7033          77000.00             3208.00
DSNE610I NUMBER OF ROWS DISPLAYED IS 6
```

Inner joins

An inner join combines each row of one table with matching rows of the other table, keeping only the rows in which the join condition is true. You can join more than two tables but keep in mind that the more tables you join, the more record I/O is required and this could be a performance consideration. When I say a "performance consideration" I do not mean it is necessarily a problem. I mean it is one factor of many to keep in mind when designing an application process.

Let's do an example of a join. Assume we want a report that includes employee id, first and last names and pay rate for each employee. To accomplish this we need data from both the `EMPLOYEE` and the `EMP_PAY` tables. We can match the tables on `EMP_ID` which is the column they have in common.

We can perform our join either implicitly or with the JOIN verb (explicitly). In the first example will do the join implicitly by specifying we want to include rows for which the `EMP_ID` in the `EMPLOYEE` table matches the `EMP_ID` in the `EMP_PAY` table. The join is specified by the equality in the WHERE condition:

```
     WHERE A.EMP_ID = B.EMP_ID.
```

Here's the full query:

```
     SELECT A.EMP_ID,
     A.EMP_LAST_NAME,
     A.EMP_FIRST_NAME,
     B.EMP_REGULAR_PAY
     FROM HRSCHEMA.EMPLOYEE A, HRSCHEMA.EMP_PAY B
     WHERE A.EMP_ID = B.EMP_ID
     ORDER BY EMP_ID
```

```
---------+---------+---------+---------+---------+---------+---------+---
    EMP_ID  EMP_LAST_NAME      EMP_FIRST_NAME      EMP_REGULAR_PAY
---------+---------+---------+---------+---------+---------+---------+---
      3217  JOHNSON            EDWARD                     65000.00
      4720  SCHULTZ            TIM                        80000.00
      6288  WILLARD            JOE                        70000.00
      7459  STEWART            BETTY                      85000.00
      9134  FRANKLIN           BRIANNA                    75000.00
DSNE610I NUMBER OF ROWS DISPLAYED IS 5
```

Notice that in the SQL the column names are prefixed with a tag that is associated with the table being referenced. This is needed in all cases where the column being referenced exists in both tables (using the same column name). In this case, if you do not specify the qualifying tag, you will get an error that your column name reference is ambiguous, i.e., DB2 does not know which column from which table you are referencing.

Moving on, you can use an explicit join by specifying the JOIN or INNER JOIN verbs. This is actually a best practice because it helps keep the query clearer for those developers who follow you, especially as your queries get more complex.

```
SELECT A.EMP_ID,
A.EMP_LAST_NAME,
A.EMP_FIRST_NAME,
B.EMP_REGULAR_PAY
FROM HRSCHEMA.EMPLOYEE A
INNER JOIN
HRSCHEMA.EMP_PAY B
ON A.EMP_ID = B.EMP_ID
ORDER BY EMP_ID
---------+---------+---------+---------+---------+---------+---------+---
    EMP_ID  EMP_LAST_NAME      EMP_FIRST_NAME      EMP_REGULAR_PAY
---------+---------+---------+---------+---------+---------+---------+---
      3217  JOHNSON            EDWARD                     65000.00
      4720  SCHULTZ            TIM                        80000.00
      6288  WILLARD            JOE                        70000.00
      7459  STEWART            BETTY                      85000.00
      9134  FRANKLIN           BRIANNA                    75000.00
DSNE610I NUMBER OF ROWS DISPLAYED IS 5
```

Finally let's do a join with three tables just to extend the concepts. We'll join the EMPLOYEE, EMP_PAY and EMP_PAY_HIST tables for pay date February 15 as follows:

```
SELECT A.EMP_ID,
A.EMP_LAST_NAME,
B.EMP_REGULAR_PAY,
C.EMP_PAY_AMT
FROM HRSCHEMA.EMPLOYEE A
    INNER JOIN
      HRSCHEMA.EMP_PAY  B ON A.EMP_ID = B.EMP_ID
    INNER JOIN
      HRSCHEMA.EMP_PAY_HIST C ON B.EMP_ID = C.EMP_ID
WHERE C.EMP_PAY_DATE = '2/15/2017'
```

```
--------+---------+---------+---------+---------+---------+-----
    EMP_ID  EMP_LAST_NAME         EMP_REGULAR_PAY  EMP_PAY_AMT
--------+---------+---------+---------+---------+---------+-----
      3217  JOHNSON                      65000.00      2708.33
      7459  STEWART                      85000.00      3541.66
      9134  FRANKLIN                     75000.00      3125.00
      4720  SCHULTZ                      80000.00      3333.33
      6288  WILLARD                      70000.00      2916.66
DSNE610I NUMBER OF ROWS DISPLAYED IS 5
```

Now let's move on to outer joins. There are three types of outer joins. A left outer join includes matching rows from both tables plus any rows from the first table (the LEFT table) that were missing from the other table but that otherwise satisfied the WHERE condition. A right outer join includes matching rows from both tables plus any rows from the second (the RIGHT) table that were missing from the join but that otherwise satisfied the WHERE condition. A full outer join includes matching rows from both tables, plus those in either table that were not matched but which otherwise satisfied the WHERE condition. We'll look at examples of all three types of outer joins.

Left Outer Join

Let's try a left outer join to include matching rows from the EMPLOYEE and EMP_PAY tables, plus any rows in the EMPLOYEE table that might not be in the EMP_PAY table. In this case we are not using a WHERE clause because the table is very small and we want to see all the results. But keep in mind that we could use a WHERE clause.

```
SELECT A.EMP_ID,
A.EMP_LAST_NAME,
A.EMP_FIRST_NAME,
B.EMP_REGULAR_PAY
FROM HRSCHEMA.EMPLOYEE A
LEFT OUTER JOIN
HRSCHEMA.EMP_PAY B
ON A.EMP_ID = B.EMP_ID
ORDER BY EMP_ID;
```

```
--------+---------+---------+---------+---------+---------+---------+---
    EMP_ID  EMP_LAST_NAME    EMP_FIRST_NAME         EMP_REGULAR_PAY
--------+---------+---------+---------+---------+---------+---------+---
      3217  JOHNSON          EDWARD                        65000.00
      3333  FORD             JAMES                  ---------------
      4720  SCHULTZ          TIM                           80000.00
      6288  WILLARD          JOE                           70000.00
      7459  STEWART          BETTY                         85000.00
      7777  HARRIS           ELISA                  ---------------
      9134  FRANKLIN         BRIANNA                       75000.00
DSNE610I NUMBER OF ROWS DISPLAYED IS 7
```

As you can see, we've included two employees who have not been assigned an annual salary yet. James Ford and Elisa Harris have NULL as their regular pay. The LEFT JOIN says we want all records in the first (left) table that satisfy the query even if there is no matching record

116

in the right table. That's why the query results included the two unmatched records.

Let's do another left join, and this time we'll join the EMPLOYEE table with the EMP_PAY_CHECK table. Like before, we want all records from the EMPLOYEE and EMP_PAY_CHECK tables that match on EMP_ID, plus any EMPLOYEE records that could not be matched to EMP_PAY_CHECK.

```
SELECT A.EMP_ID,
A.EMP_LAST_NAME,
A.EMP_FIRST_NAME,
B.EMP_SEMIMTH_PAY
FROM HRSCHEMA.EMPLOYEE A
LEFT OUTER JOIN
HRSCHEMA.EMP_PAY_CHECK B
ON A.EMP_ID = B.EMP_ID
ORDER BY EMP_ID;
```

```
---------+---------+---------+---------+---------+---------+---------+---
    EMP_ID  EMP_LAST_NAME    EMP_FIRST_NAME      EMP_SEMIMTH_PAY
---------+---------+---------+---------+---------+---------+---------+---
      3217  JOHNSON          EDWARD                      2708.33
      3333  FORD             JAMEs               ---------------
      4720  SCHULTZ          TIM                         3333.33
      6288  WILLARD          JOE                         2916.66
      7459  STEWART          BETTY                       3541.66
      7777  HARRIS           ELISA               ---------------
      9134  FRANKLIN         BRIANNA                     3125.00
DSNE610I NUMBER OF ROWS DISPLAYED IS 7
```

Again we find two records in the EMPLOYEE table with no matching EMP_PAY_CHECK records. From a business standpoint that could be a problem unless the two are new hires who have not received their first pay check.

Right Outer Join

Meanwhile, now let us turn it around and do a right join. In this case we want all matching records in the EMPLOYEE and EMP_PAY_CHECK records plus any unmatched records in the EMP_PAY_CHECK table (the right hand table). We could also add a WHERE condition such that the EMP_SEMIMTH_PAY column has to be populated (cannot be NULL). Let's do that.

```
SELECT B.EMP_ID,
A.EMP_LAST_NAME,
A.EMP_FIRST_NAME,
B.EMP_SEMIMTH_PAY
FROM HRSCHEMA.EMPLOYEE A
   RIGHT OUTER JOIN
      HRSCHEMA.EMP_PAY_CHECK B
         ON A.EMP_ID = B.EMP_ID
WHERE EMP_SEMIMTH_PAY IS NOT NULL;
```

```
---------+---------+---------+---------+---------+---------+---------+---
    EMP_ID  EMP_LAST_NAME    EMP_FIRST_NAME      EMP_SEMIMTH_PAY
---------+---------+---------+---------+---------+---------+---------+---
      3217  JOHNSON          EDWARD                      2708.33
```

117

```
        4720    SCHULTZ              TIM                      3333.33
        6288    WILLARD              JOE                      2916.66
        7033    --------------------  --------------------    3208.00
        7459    STEWART              BETTY                    3541.66
        9134    FRANKLIN             BRIANNA                  3125.00
     DSNE610I NUMBER OF ROWS DISPLAYED IS 6
```

Now we have a case where there is a record in the EMP_PAY_CHECK table for employee 7033, but that same employee number is NOT in the EMPLOYEE table. That is absolutely something to research! It is important to find out why this condition exists (of course we know it exists because we intentionally added an unmatched record to set up the example).

But let's pause for a moment. You may be thinking that this is not a realistic example because any employee getting a paycheck would also have to be in the EMPLOYEE table, so this mismatch condition would never happen. I chose this example for a few reasons. One reason is to point out the importance of referential data integrity. The reason the above exception is even possible is because we haven't defined a referential integrity relationship between these two tables. For now just know that these things can and do happen when a system has not been designed with tight referential integrity in place.

A second reason I chose this example is to highlight outer joins as a useful tool in tracking down data discrepancies between tables (subqueries are another useful tool). Keep this example in mind when you are called on by your boss or your client to troubleshoot a data integrity problem in a high pressure, time sensitive situation. You need all the tools you can get.

The third reason for choosing this example is that it very clearly demonstrates what a right join is – it includes all records from both tables that can be matched and that satisfy the WHERE condition, plus any unmatched records in the "right" table that otherwise meet the WHERE condition (in this case that the EMP_SEMIMTH_PAY is populated).

Full Outer Join
Finally, let's do a full outer join to include both matched and unmatched records from both tables that meet the where condition. This will expose all the discrepancies we already uncovered, but now we'll do it with a single query.

```
SELECT A.EMP_ID,
   A.EMP_LAST_NAME,
   B.EMP_SEMIMTH_PAY
   FROM EMPLOYEE A
      FULL OUTER JOIN
         EMP_PAY_CHECK B
            ON A.EMP_ID = B.EMP_ID;
```

```
----------+---------+---------+---------+---------+--
    EMP_ID  EMP_LAST_NAME         EMP_SEMIMTH_PAY
----------+---------+---------+---------+---------+--
      3217  JOHNSON                      2708.33
      3333  FORD                  ---------------
      4720  SCHULTZ                      3333.33
      6288  WILLARD                      2916.66
-----------  --------------------        3208.00
      7459  STEWART                      3541.66
      7777  HARRIS                ---------------
      9134  FRANKLIN                     3125.00
DSNE610I NUMBER OF ROWS DISPLAYED IS 8
```

So with the FULL OUTER join we have identified the missing EMPLOYEE record, as well as the two EMP_PAY_CHECK records that may be missing. Again these examples are intended both to explain the difference between the join types, and also to lend support to trouble-shooting efforts where data integrity is involved.

One final comment. The outer join examples we've given so far point to potential issues with the data, and these joins are in fact helpful in diagnosing such problems. But there are many cases where an entry in one table does not necessarily imply an entry in another. For example, suppose we have an EMP_SPOUSE table that exists to administer company benefits. A person who is single has no spouse, so they would not have an entry in the EMP_SPOUSE table. When querying for all persons covered by company benefits, an inner join between EMPLOYEE and EMP_SPOUSE would incorrectly exclude any employee who doesn't have a spouse. So you'd need a LEFT JOIN using EMPLOYEE and EMP_SPOUSE to return all insured employees plus their spouses. Your data model will govern what types of joins are needed, so be familiar with it.

UNION and INTERSECT

Another way to combine the results from two or more tables (or in some complex cases, to combine different result sets from a single table) is to use the UNION and INTERSECT statements. In some cases this can be preferable to doing a join.

Union

The UNION predicate combines the result sets from sub-SELECT queries. To understand how this might be useful, let's look at three examples. First, let's say we have two companies that have merged to form a third company. We have two tables EMP_COMPA and EMP_COMPB that we have structured with an EMP_ID, EMP_LAST_NAME and EMP_FIRST_NAME. We are going to structure a third table which will create all new employee ids by generation using an identity column. The DDL for the new table looks like this:

```
CREATE TABLE HRSCHEMA.EMPLOYEE_NEW(
EMP_ID INT GENERATED ALWAYS AS IDENTITY,
```

```
EMP_OLD_ID INTEGER,
EMP_LAST_NAME VARCHAR(30) NOT NULL,
EMP_FIRST_NAME VARCHAR(20) NOT NULL) IN TSHR;
```

Now we can load the table using a UNION as follows:

```
INSERT INTO
HRSCHEMA.EMPLOYEE_NEW

SELECT EMP_ID,
EMP_LAST_NAME,
EMP_FIRST_NAME
FROM HRSCHEMA.EMP_COMPA

UNION

SELECT EMP_ID,
EMP_LAST_NAME,
EMP_FIRST_NAME
FROM HRSCHEMA.EMP_COMPB;
```

This will load the new table with data from both the old tables, and the new employee numbers will be auto-generated. Notice that by design we keep the old employee numbers for cross reference if needed.

When using a UNION, the column list must be identical in terms of the number of columns and data types, but the column names need not be the same. The UNION operation looks at the columns by position in the subqueries, not by name.

Let's look at two other examples of UNION queries. First, recall that earlier we used a full outer join to return all employee ids, including those that exist in one table but not the other.

```
SELECT A.EMP_ID,
B.EMP_ID,
A.EMP_LAST_NAME,
B.EMP_SEMIMTH_PAY
FROM HRSCHEMA.EMPLOYEE A
    FULL OUTER JOIN
        HRSCHEMA.EMP_PAY_CHECK B
            ON A.EMP_ID = B.EMP_ID;
```

If we just needed a unique list of employee id numbers from the EMPLOYEE and EMP_PAY_ CHECK tables, we could instead use this UNION SQL:

```
SELECT EMP_ID
FROM HRSCHEMA.EMPLOYEE
UNION
```

```
SELECT EMP_ID
FROM HRSCHEMA.EMP_PAY_CHECK;

---------+---------+---------+---------+-
    EMP_ID
---------+---------+---------+---------+-
      3217
      3333
      4720
      6288
      7033
      7459
      7777
      9134
DSNE610I NUMBER OF ROWS DISPLAYED IS 8
```

If you are wondering why we didn't get duplicate employee numbers in our list, it is because the UNION statement automatically eliminates duplicates. If for some reason you need to retain the duplicates, you would need to specify UNION ALL.

One final example will show how handy the UNION predicate is. Suppose that you want to query the EMPLOYEE table to get a list of all employee names for an upcoming company party. But you also have a contractor who (by business rules) cannot be in the EMPLOYEE table. You still want to include the contractor's name in the result set for whom to invite to the party. Let's say you want to identify the contractor with a pseudo-employee-id of 9999, and the contractor's name is Janet Ko.

You could code the query as follows:

```
SELECT EMP_ID,
EMP_LAST_NAME,
EMP_FIRST_NAME
FROM HRSCHEMA.EMPLOYEE
UNION
SELECT 9999,
'KO',
'JANET'
FROM SYSIBM.SYSDUMMY1;
---------+---------+---------+---------+-----
      3217  JOHNSON              EDWARD
      3333  FORD                 JAMES
      4720  SCHULTZ              TIM
      6288  WILLARD              JOE
      7459  STEWART              BETTY
      7777  HARRIS               ELISA
      9134  FRANKLIN             BRIANNA
      9999  KO                   JANET
DSNE610I NUMBER OF ROWS DISPLAYED IS 8
```

Now you have listed all the employees plus your contractor friend Janet on your query results. This is a useful technique when you have a "mostly" table driven system that also has some exceptions to the business rules. Sometimes a system has one off situations that simply don't justify full blown changes to the system design. UNION can help in these cases.

Intersect

The INTERSECT predicate returns a combined result set that consists of all of the matching rows (existing in both result sets). In one of the earlier UNION examples, we wanted all employee ids as long as they existed in either the EMPLOYEE table or the EMP_PAY_CHECK table.

```
SELECT EMP_ID
FROM HRSCHEMA.EMPLOYEE
UNION
SELECT EMP_ID
FROM HRSCHEMA.EMP_PAY_CHECK


---------+---------+---------
      EMP_ID
---------+---------+---------
        3217
        4720
        6288
        7033
        7459
        9134
```

Now let's say we only want a list of employee ids that appear in both tables. The INTERSECT will accomplish that for us and we only need to change that one word in the query:

```
SELECT EMP_ID
FROM HRSCHEMA.EMPLOYEE
INTERSECT
SELECT EMP_ID
FROM HRSCHEMA.EMP_PAY_CHECK


---------+---------+---------+---------+--------
      EMP_ID
---------+---------+---------+---------+--------
        3217
        4720
        6288
        7459
        9134
DSNE610I NUMBER OF ROWS DISPLAYED IS 5
```

Common Table Expression

A common table expression is a result set that you can create and then reference in a query as though it were a table. It sometimes makes coding easier. Take this as an example. Suppose we need to work with an aggregated year-to-date total pay for each employee. Recall that our table named `EMP_PAY_HIST` includes these fields:

```
(EMP_ID INTEGER NOT NULL,
EMP_PAY_DATE DATE NOT NULL,
EMP_PAY_AMT DECIMAL (8,2) NOT NULL);
```

Assume further that we have created the following SQL that includes aggregated totals for the employees' pay:

```
WITH EMP_PAY_SUM (EMP_ID, EMP_PAY_TOTAL) AS
(SELECT EMP_ID,
SUM(EMP_PAY_AMT)
AS EMP_PAY_TOTAL
FROM EMP_PAY_HIST
GROUP BY EMP_ID)

SELECT B.EMP_ID,
A.EMP_LAST_NAME,
A.EMP_FIRST_NAME,
B.EMP_PAY_TOTAL
FROM EMPLOYEE A
INNER JOIN
EMP_PAY_SUM B ON A.EMP_ID = B.EMP_ID;
```

What we've done is to create a temporary result set named `EMP_PAY_SUM` that can be queried by SQL as if it were a table. This helps break down the data requirement into two pieces, one of which summarizes the pay data and the other of which adds columns from other tables.

This example may not seem like much because you could have as easily combined the two SQLs into one. But as your data stores get more numerous, and your queries and joins grow more complex, you may find that common table expressions can simplify queries both for you and for the developer that follows you.

Here's the result of our common table expression and the query against it.

```
WITH EMP_PAY_SUM (EMP_ID, EMP_PAY_TOTAL) AS
(SELECT EMP_ID,
SUM(EMP_PAY_AMT)
AS EMP_PAY_TOTAL
FROM EMP_PAY_HIST
GROUP BY EMP_ID)

SELECT B.EMP_ID,
A.EMP_LAST_NAME,
A.EMP_FIRST_NAME,
B.EMP_PAY_TOTAL
FROM EMPLOYEE A
INNER JOIN
EMP_PAY_SUM B
ON A.EMP_ID = B.EMP_ID;
```

```
---------+---------+---------+---------+---------+---------+---------+---
    EMP_ID  EMP_LAST_NAME      EMP_FIRST_NAME              EMP_PAY_TOTAL
---------+---------+---------+---------+---------+---------+---------+---
      3217  JOHNSON            EDWARD                          10833.32
      4720  SCHULTZ            TIM                             13333.32
      6288  WILLARD            JOE                             11666.64
      7459  STEWART            BETTY                           14166.64
      9134  FRANKLIN           BRIANNA                         12500.00
DSNE610I NUMBER OF ROWS DISPLAYED IS 5
```

XML

XML is a highly used standard for exchanging self-describing data files or documents. Even if you work in a shop that does not use the DB2 XML data type or XML functions, it is good to know how to use these. A complete tutorial on XML is well beyond the scope of this book. We'll review some XML basics, but if you have little or no experience with XML, I strongly suggest that you purchase some books to acquire this knowledge. The following are a few that can help fill in the basics:

XML in a Nutshell, Third Edition 3rd Edition by Elliotte Rusty Harold (ISBN 978-0596007645)

XSLT 2.0 and XPath 2.0 Programmer's Reference by Michael Kay (ISBN: 978-0470192740)

XQuery: Search Across a Variety of XML Data by Priscilla Walmsley
(ISBN: ISBN-13: 978-1491915103)

Basic XML Concepts

You may know that XML stands for Extensible Markup Language. XML technology is cross-platform and independent of machine and software. It provides a structure that consists of both data and data element tags, and so it describes the data in both human readable and machine readable format. The tag names for the elements are defined by the developer/user of the data.

XML Structure

XML has a tree type structure that is required to begin with a root element and then it expands to the branches. To continue our discussion of the EMPLOYEE domain, let's take a simple XML example with an employee profile as the root. We'll include the employee id, the address and birth date. The XML document might look like this:

```
<?xml version="1.0" encoding="UTF-8"?>
<EMP_PROFILE>
       <EMP_ID>4175</EMP_ID>
       <EMP_ADDRESS>
<STREET>6161 MARGARET LANE</STREET>
<CITY>ERINDALE</CITY>
```

124

```
<STATE>AR</STATE>
<ZIP_CODE>72653</ZIP_CODE>
</EMP_ADDRESS>
<BIRTH_DATE>07/14/1991</BIRTH_DATE>
</EMP_PROFILE>
```

XML documents frequently begin with a declaration which includes the XML version and the encoding scheme of the document. In our example, we are using XML version 1.0 which is still very common. This declaration is optional but it's a best practice to include it.

Notice after the version specification that we continue with the tag name EMP_PROFILE enclosed by the <> symbols. The employee profile element ends with /EMP_PROFILE enclosed by the <> symbols. Similarly each sub-element is tagged and enclosed and the value (if any) appears between the opening and closing of the element.

XML documents must have a single root element, i.e., one element that is the root of all other elements. If you want more than one EMP_PROFILE in a document, then you would need a higher level element to contain the profiles. For example you could have a DEPARTMENT element that contains employee profiles, and a COMPANY element that contains DEPARTMENTs.

All elements must have a closing tag. Elements that are not populated can be represented by an opening and closing with nothing in between. For example, if an employee's birthday is not known, it can be represented by <BIRTH_DATE></BIRTH_DATE> or you can use the short hand form <BIRTH_DATE/>.

The example document includes elements such as the employee id, address and birth date. The address is broken down into a street name, city, state and zip code. Comments can be included in an XML document by following the following format:

```
<!-- This is a sample comment -->
```

By default, white space is preserved in XML documents.

Ok, so we've given you a drive-thru version of XML. We have almost enough information to move on to how to manipulate XML data in DB2. Before we get to that, let's briefly look at two XML-related technologies that we will need.

XML Related Technologies

XPath
The extensible path language (XPath) is used to locate and extract information from an XML

document using "path" expressions through the XML nodes. For example, in the case of the employee XML document we created earlier, you could locate and return a zip code value by specifying the path.

Recall this structure:

```
<EMP_PROFILE>
       <EMP_ID>4175</EMP_ID>
       <EMP_ADDRESS>
<STREET>6161 MARGARET LANE</STREET>
<CITY>ERINDALE</CITY>
<STATE>AR</STATE>
<ZIP_CODE>72653</ZIP_CODE>
</EMP_ADDRESS>
<BIRTH_DATE>07/14/1991</BIRTH_DATE>
</EMP_PROFILE>
```

In this example, the employee profile nodes with zip code 72653 can be identified using the following path:

```
/EMP_PROFILE/ADDRESS[ZIP_CODE=72653]
```

The XPath expression for all employees who live in Texas as follows:

```
/EMP_PROFILE/ADDRESS[STATE="TX"]
```

XQuery

XQuery enables us to query XML data using XPath expressions. It is similar to how we query relational data using SQL, but of course the syntax is different. Here's an example of pulling the employee id of every employee who lives at a zip code greater than 90000 from an XML document named employees.xml.

```
for $x in doc("employees.xml")employee/profile/address/zipcode
where $x/zipcode>90000
order by $x/zipcode
return $x/empid
```

In DB2 you run an XQuery using the built-in function XMLQUERY. We'll show you some examples using XMLQUERY shortly.

DB2 Support for XML

The pureXML technology provides support for XML under DB2 for z/OS. DB2 includes an XML data type and many built-in DB2 functions to validate, traverse and manipulate XML data. The DB2 XML data type can store well-formed XML documents in their hierarchical form and retrieve entire documents or portions of documents.

You can execute DML operations such as inserting, updating and deleting XML documents. You can index and create triggers on XML columns. Finally, you can extract data items from an XML document and then store those values in columns of relational tables using the SQL XMLTABLE built-in function.

XML Examples

XML for the EMPLOYEE table

Suppose that we need to implement a new interface with our employee benefits providers who use XML as the data exchange format. This could give us a reason to store our detailed employee information in an XML structure within the EMPLOYEE table. For our purposes, we will add a column named EMP_PROFILE to the EMPLOYEE table and make it an XML column. Here's the DDL:

```
ALTER TABLE HRSCHEMA.EMPLOYEE
ADD COLUMN EMP_PROFILE XML;
```

We could also establish an XML schema to validate our data structure, but for the moment we'll just deal with the basic SQL operations. As long as the XML is well formed, DB2 will accept it without a schema to validate against.

Let's assume we are going to add a record to the EMPLOYEE table for employee Fred Turnbull who has employee id 4175, has 1 year if service and was promoted on 12/1/2016.

Here's a sample XML document structure we want for storing the employee profile:

```
<EMP_PROFILE>
        <EMP_ID>4175</EMP_ID>
        <EMP_ADDRESS>
<STREET>6161 MARGARET LANE</STREET>
<CITY>ERINDALE</CITY>
<STATE>AR</STATE>
<ZIP_CODE>72653</ZIP_CODE>
</EMP_ADDRESS>
<BIRTH_DATE>07/14/1991</BIRTH_DATE>
</EMP_PROFILE>
```

INSERT With XML

Now we can insert the new record as follows:

```
INSERT INTO HRSCHEMA.EMPLOYEE
(EMP_ID,
 EMP_LAST_NAME,
```

```
EMP_FIRST_NAME,
EMP_SERVICE_YEARS,
EMP_PROMOTION_DATE,
EMP_PROFILE)
VALUES (4175,
'TURNBULL',
'FRED',
1,
'12/01/2016',
'
<EMP_PROFILE>
        <EMP_ID>4175</EMP_ID>
        <EMP_ADDRESS>
<STREET>6161 MARGARET LANE</STREET>
<CITY>ERINDALE</CITY>
<STATE>AR</STATE>
<ZIP_CODE>72653</ZIP_CODE>
</EMP_ADDRESS>
<BIRTH_DATE>07/14/1991</BIRTH_DATE>
</EMP_PROFILE>
');
```

SELECT With XML

You can do a SELECT on an XML column and depending on what query tool you are using, you can display the content of the record in fairly readable form. Since the XML data is stored as one long string, it may be difficult to read in its entirety without reformatting. We'll look at some options for that later. Let's select the column we just added using SPUFI.

```
SELECT EMP_ID, EMP_PROFILE FROM HRSCHEMA.EMPLOYEE
WHERE EMP_ID = 4175;
-------+---------+---------+---------+---------+---------+---------+---------+-----
   EMP_ID   EMP_PROFILE
-------+---------+---------+---------+---------+---------+---------+---------+-----
    4175   <?xml version="1.0" encoding="IBM037"?><EMP_PROFILE><EMP_ID>41
```

In SPUFI, you would need to scroll to the right to see the rest of the column contents.

UPDATE With XML

To update an XML column you can use standard SQL if you want to update the entire content of the column. Suppose we want to change the address. This SQL will do it:

```
UPDATE HRSCHEMA.EMPLOYEE
SET EMP_PROFILE
 = '<EMP_PROFILE>
            <EMP_ID>3217</EMP_ID>
            <EMP_ADDRESS>
            <STREET>2913 PATE DR</STREET>
            <CITY>FORT WORTH</CITY>
            <STATE>TX</STATE>
            <ZIP_CODE>76105</ZIP_CODE>
        </EMP_ADDRESS>
```

```
            <BIRTH_DATE>03/15/1952</BIRTH_DATE>
          </EMP_PROFILE>
          '
    WHERE EMP_ID = 3217;
```

DELETE With XML

If you wish to delete the entire EMP_PROFILE, you can set it to NULL as follows:

```
    UPDATE HRSCHEMA.EMPLOYEE
    SET EMP_PROFILE = NULL
    WHERE EMP_ID = 3217;

    SELECT EMP_ID, EMP_PROFILE FROM HRSCHEMA.EMPLOYEE
    WHERE EMP_ID = 3217;
    -------+--------+--------+--------+--------+--------+--------+-----
       EMP_ID  EMP_PROFILE
    -------+--------+--------+--------+--------+--------+--------+-----
         3217  -----------------------------------------------------
```

As you can see, the EMP_PROFILE column has been set to NULL. At this point, only one row in the EMPLOYEE table has the EMP_PROFILE populated.

```
    SELECT EMP_ID, EMP_PROFILE FROM HRSCHEMA.EMPLOYEE;

    -------+--------+--------+--------+--------+--------+--------+--------
       EMP_ID  EMP_PROFILE
    -------+--------+--------+--------+--------+--------+--------+--------
         3217  ---------------------------------------------------------
         7459  ---------------------------------------------------------
         9134  ---------------------------------------------------------
         4175  <?xml version="1.0" encoding="IBM037"?><EMP_PROFILE><EMP_ID>4175<
```

Let's go ahead and add the XML data back to this record so we can use it later for other XML queries.

```
    UPDATE HRSCHEMA.EMPLOYEE
    SET EMP_PROFILE
     = '<EMP_PROFILE>
              <EMP_ID>3217</EMP_ID>
              <EMP_ADDRESS>
              <STREET>2913 PATE DR</STREET>
              <CITY>FORT WORTH</CITY>
              <STATE>TX</STATE>
              <ZIP_CODE>76105</ZIP_CODE>
         </EMP_ADDRESS>
         <BIRTH_DATE>03/15/1952</BIRTH_DATE>
       </EMP_PROFILE>
         '
    WHERE EMP_ID = 3217;
```

Also, let's update one more record so we have a bit more data to work with.

```
UPDATE EMPLOYEE
SET EMP_PROFILE
 = '<EMP_PROFILE>
  <EMP_ID>7459</EMP_ID>
  <EMP_ADDRESS>
      <STREET>6742 OAK ST</STREET>
      <CITY>DALLAS</CITY>
      <STATE>TX</STATE>
      <ZIP_CODE>75277</ZIP_CODE>
    </EMP_ADDRESS>
    <BIRTH_DATE>09/22/1963</BIRTH_DATE>
   </EMP_PROFILE>
  '
WHERE EMP_ID = 7459;
```

XML BUILTIN FUNCTIONS

XMLQUERY

XMLQUERY is the DB2 built-in function that enables you to run XQuery. Here is an example of using XMLQUERY with the XQuery xmlcolumn function to retrieve an XML element from the EMP_PROFILE element. In this case we will select the zip code for employee 4175.

```
SELECT XMLQUERY
('for $info
in db2-fn:xmlcolumn("HRSCHEMA.EMPLOYEE.EMP_PROFILE")/EMP_PROFILE
return $info/EMP_ADDRESS/ZIP_CODE') AS ZIPCODE
from HRSCHEMA.EMPLOYEE
where EMP_ID = 4175


ZIPCODE
-------------------------
<ZIP_CODE>72653</ZIP_CODE>
```

Notice that the data is returned in XML format. If you don't want the data returned with its XML structure, simply add the XQuery text() function at the end of the return string, as below:

```
SELECT XMLQUERY
('for $info
in db2-fn:xmlcolumn("HRSCHEMA.EMPLOYEE.EMP_PROFILE")/EMP_PROFILE
return $info/EMP_ADDRESS/ZIP_CODE/text()') AS ZIPCODE
FROM HRSCHEMA.EMPLOYEE
WHERE EMP_ID = 4175;
```

The result of this query will not include the XML format.

```
ZIPCODE
-------
 72653
```

XMLEXISTS

The XMLEXISTS predicate specifies an XQuery expression. If the XQuery expression returns an empty sequence, the value of the XMLEXISTS predicate is false. Otherwise, XMLEXISTS returns true and those rows matching the XMLEXISTS value of true are returned.

XMLEXISTS enables us to specify rows based on the XML content which is often what you want to do. Suppose you want to return the first and last names of all employees who live in the state of Texas? This query with XMLEXISTS would accomplish it:

```
SELECT EMP_LAST_NAME, EMP_FIRST_NAME
FROM HRSCHEMA.EMPLOYEE
WHERE
XMLEXISTS('$info/EMP_PROFILE[EMP_ADDRESS/STATE/text()="TX"]'
PASSING EMP_PROFILE AS "info");


---------+---------+---------+---------+---------+---------+---------+---
EMP_LAST_NAME                      EMP_FIRST_NAME
---------+---------+---------+---------+---------+---------+---------+---
JOHNSON                            EDWARD
STEWART                            BETTY
```

You can also use XMLEXISTS with update and delete functions.

XMLSERIALIZE

The XMLSERIALIZE function returns a serialized XML value of the specified data type that is generated from the first argument. You can use this function to generate an XML structure from relational data. Here's an example.

```
SELECT E.EMP_ID,
XMLSERIALIZE(XMLELEMENT ( NAME "EMP_FULL_NAME",
   E.EMP_FIRST_NAME || ' ' || E.EMP_LAST_NAME)
             AS CLOB(100)) AS "RESULT"
    FROM HRSCHEMA.EMPLOYEE E;
---------+---------+---------+---------+---------+---------+-
    EMP_ID  RESULT
---------+---------+---------+---------+---------+---------+-
      3217  <EMP_FULL_NAME>EDWARD JOHNSON</EMP_FULL_NAME>
      7459  <EMP_FULL_NAME>BETTY STEWART</EMP_FULL_NAME>
      9134  <EMP_FULL_NAME>BRIANNA FRANKLIN</EMP_FULL_NAME>
      4175  <EMP_FULL_NAME>FRED TURNBULL</EMP_FULL_NAME>
      4720  <EMP_FULL_NAME>TIM SCHULTZ</EMP_FULL_NAME>
      6288  <EMP_FULL_NAME>JOE WILLARD</EMP_FULL_NAME>
      3333  <EMP_FULL_NAME>JAMEs FORD</EMP_FULL_NAME>
```

```
         7777   <EMP_FULL_NAME>ELISA HARRIS</EMP_FULL_NAME>
    DSNE610I NUMBER OF ROWS DISPLAYED IS 8
```

XMLTABLE

This function can be used to convert XML data to relational data. You can then use it for traditional SQL such as in joins. To use XMLTABLE you must specify the relational column names you want to use. Then you point these column names to the XML content using path expressions. For this example we'll pull address information from the profile:

```
SELECT X.*
FROM HRSCHEMA.EMPLOYEE,
XMLTABLE ('$x/EMP_PROFILE'
          PASSING EMP_PROFILE as "x"

    COLUMNS
        STREET   VARCHAR(20)  PATH 'EMP_ADDRESS/STREET',
        CITY     VARCHAR(20)  PATH 'EMP_ADDRESS/CITY',
        STATE    VARCHAR(02)  PATH 'EMP_ADDRESS/STATE',
        ZIP      VARCHAR(10)  PATH 'EMP_ADDRESS/ZIP_CODE')
        AS X;


---------+---------+---------+---------+---------+---------+-
STREET                     CITY               STATE  ZIP
---------+---------+---------+---------+---------+---------+-
2913 PATE DR               FORT WORTH          TX     76105
6742 OAK ST                DALLAS              TX     75277
6161 MARGARET LANE         ERINDALE            AR     72653
DSNE610I NUMBER OF ROWS DISPLAYED IS 3
```

XMLMODIFY

XMLMODIFY allows you to make changes within the XML document. There are three expressions available for XMLMODIFY: insert, delete and replace. Here is a sample of using the replace expression to change the ZIP_CODE element of the EMP_ADDRESS for employee 4175:

```
UPDATE HRSCHEMA.EMPLOYEE
SET EMP_PROFILE
= XMLMODIFY('replace value of node
HRSCHEMA.EMPLOYEE/EMP_PROFILE/EMP_ADDRESS/ZIP_CODE
with "72652" ')
WHERE EMP_ID = 4175;
```

Now let's verify that the statement worked successfully by finding the zip code on EMP_ID 4175.

```
SELECT XMLQUERY
('for $info
in db2-fn:xmlcolumn("HRSCHEMA.EMPLOYEE.EMP_PROFILE")/EMP_PROFILE
return $info/EMP_ADDRESS/ZIP_CODE/text()') AS ZIPCODE
from HRSCHEMA.EMPLOYEE
where EMP_ID = 4175;


------------------------------------------------
ZIPCODE
------------------------------------------------
  72652
```

Important: to use XMLMODIFY, you must have created the table in a universal table space (UTS). Otherwise you will receive this SQLCODE error when you try to use the XMLMODIFY function:

```
DSNT408I SQLCODE = -4730, ERROR:  INVALID SPECIFICATION OF XML COLUMN
EMPLOYEE.EMP_PROFILE IS NOT DEFINED IN THE XML VERSIONING
FORMAT,REASON 1
```

SPECIAL REGISTERS

Special registers allow you to access detailed information about the DB2 instance settings as well as certain session information. CURRENT DATE is an example of a special register that is often used in programming (see example below). The following are SQL examples of some commonly used special registers. I suggest that you focus on these.

CURRENT CLIENT_USERID

CURRENT CLIENT_USERID contains the value of the client user ID from the client information that is specified for the connection. In the following example, the TSO logon id of the user is HRSCHEMA.

```
SELECT CURRENT CLIENT_USERID
FROM SYSIBM.SYSDUMMY1;
--------+--------+---------
HRSCHEMA
```

CURRENT DATE

CURRENT DATE specifies a date that is based on a reading of the time-of-day clock when the SQL statement is executed at the current server. This is often used in application programs to establish the processing date.

```
SELECT CURRENT DATE
FROM SYSIBM.SYSDUMMY1;
--------+---------+--
```

```
---------+---------+--
2017-01-13
```

CURRENT DEGREE

CURRENT DEGREE specifies the degree of parallelism for the execution of queries that are dynamically prepared by the application process. A value of "ANY" enables parallel processing. A value of 1 prohibits parallel processing. You can query for the value of the CURRENT DEGREEE as follows:

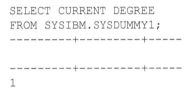

```
SELECT CURRENT DEGREE
FROM SYSIBM.SYSDUMMY1;
---------+---------+-----

---------+---------+-----
1
```

CURRENT MEMBER

CURRENT MEMBER specifies the member name of a current DB2 data sharing member on which a statement is executing. The value of CURRENT MEMBER is a character string. More information on data sharing is provided later.

CURRENT OPTIMIZATION HINT

CURRENT OPTIMIZATION HINT specifies the user-defined optimization hint that DB2 should use to generate the access path for dynamic statements.

CURRENT RULES

CURRENT RULES specifies whether certain SQL statements are executed in accordance with DB2 rules or the rules of the SQL standard.

```
SELECT CURRENT RULES
FROM SYSIBM.SYSDUMMY1;
---------+---------+----

---------+---------+----
DB2
```

CURRENT SCHEMA

CURRENT SCHEMA specifies the schema name used to qualify unqualified database object references in dynamically prepared SQL statements.

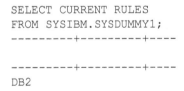

```
SELECT CURRENT SCHEMA
FROM SYSIBM.SYSDUMMY1;
---------+---------+---

HRSCHEMA
```

CURRENT SERVER

CURRENT SERVER specifies the location name of the current server.

```
SELECT CURRENT SERVER
FROM SYSIBM.SYSDUMMY1;
---------+---------+--------

---------+---------+--------
LOCRGNA
```

CURRENT SQLID

CURRENT SQLID specifies the SQL authorization ID of the process.

```
SELECT CURRENT SQLID
FROM SYSIBM.SYSDUMMY1;
---------+---------+----

HRSCHEMA
```

CURRENT TEMPORAL BUSINESS_TIME

The CURRENT TEMPORAL BUSINESS_TIME 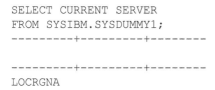 special register specifies a TIME-STAMP(12) value that is used in the default BUSINESS_TIME period specification for references to application-period temporal tables.

CURRENT TEMPORAL SYSTEM_TIME

The CURRENT TEMPORAL SYSTEM_TIME special register specifies a TIMESTAMP(12) value that is used in the default SYSTEM_TIME period specification for references to system-period temporal tables.

CURRENT TIME

The CURRENT TIME special register specifies a time that is based on a reading of the time-of-day clock when the SQL statement is executed at the current server.

```
SELECT CURRENT TIME
FROM SYSIBM.SYSDUMMY1;
---------+---------+----

10.12.12
```

CURRENT TIMESTAMP

The CURRENT TIMESTAMP special register specifies a timestamp based on the time-of-day clock at the current server.

```
SELECT CURRENT TIMESTAMP
FROM SYSIBM.SYSDUMMY1;
---------+---------+--------

---------+---------+--------
2017-01-13-10.12.51.778225
```

SESSION_USER

SESSION_USER specifies the primary authorization ID of the process.

```
SELECT SESSION_USER
FROM SYSIBM.SYSDUMMY1;
---------+---------+-----

---------+---------+-----
HRSCHEMA
```

NOTE: You can use all special registers in a user-defined function or a stored procedure. However, you can modify only some of the special registers. The following are the special registers that can be modified:

```
CURRENT APPLICATION COMPATIBILITY
CURRENT APPLICATION ENCODING SCHEME
CURRENT DEBUG MODE
CURRENT DECFLOAT ROUNDING MODE
CURRENT DEGREE
CURRENT EXPLAIN MODE
CURRENT GET_ACCEL_ARCHIVE
CURRENT LOCALE LC_CTYPE
CURRENT MAINTAINED TABLE TYPES FOR OPTIMIZATION
CURRENT OPTIMIZATION HINT
CURRENT PACKAGE PATH
CURRENT PACKAGESET
CURRENT PATH
CURRENT PRECISION
CURRENT QUERY ACCELERATION
CURRENT REFRESH AGE
CURRENT ROUTINE VERSION
CURRENT RULES
CURRENT SCHEMA
CURRENT SQLID1
CURRENT TEMPORAL BUSINESS_TIME
CURRENT TEMPORAL SYSTEM_TIME
ENCRYPTION PASSWORD
SESSION TIME ZONE
```

BUILT-IN FUNCTIONS

Built-in functions can be used in SQL statements to return a result based on an argument. These functions are great productivity tools because they can replace custom coded functionality in an application program. Whether your role is application developer, DBA or business services professional, the DB2 built-in functions can save you a great deal of time and effort if you know what they are and how to use them.

There are three types of builtin functions:

1. Aggregate
2. Scalar
3. Table

We'll look at examples of the first two types. The TABLE type is primarily of interest to DBAs instead of application developers.

AGGREGATE Functions

An aggregate function receives a set of values for each argument (such as the values of a column) and returns a single-value result for the set of input values. These are especially useful in data analytics. Here are some examples of commonly used aggregate functions.

AVERAGE

The average function returns the average of a set of numbers. Using our EMP_PAY table, you could get the average REGULAR_PAY for your employees like this:

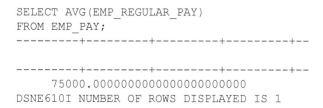

```
SELECT AVG(EMP_REGULAR_PAY)
FROM EMP_PAY;
---------+---------+---------+---------+--

---------+---------+---------+---------+--
    75000.0000000000000000000000
DSNE610I NUMBER OF ROWS DISPLAYED IS 1
```

COUNT

The COUNT function returns the number of rows or values in a set of rows or values. Suppose you want to know how many employees you have. You could use this SQL to find out:

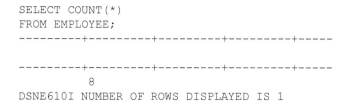

```
SELECT COUNT(*)
FROM EMPLOYEE;
---------+---------+---------+---------+-----

---------+---------+---------+---------+-----
        8
DSNE610I NUMBER OF ROWS DISPLAYED IS 1
```

MAX

The MAX function returns the maximum value in a set of values.

MIN

The MIN function returns the minimum value in a set of values.

In the next two examples, we use the MAX and MIN functions to determine the highest and lowest paid employees:

```
SELECT MAX(EMP_REGULAR_PAY)
FROM EMP_PAY;
---------+---------+--------

---------+---------+--------
   85000.00
```

Now if we want know which both the maximum salary and the employee who earns it, it is a bit more complex, but not much:

```
SELECT EMP_ID, EMP_REGULAR_PAY
FROM EMP_PAY
WHERE EMP_REGULAR_PAY =
(SELECT MAX(EMP_REGULAR_PAY) FROM EMP_PAY);

---------+---------+---------+---------+------
     EMP_ID  EMP_REGULAR_PAY
---------+---------+---------+---------+------
       7459          85000.00
```

Similarly, we can find the minimum using the MIN function.

```
SELECT MIN(EMP_REGULAR_PAY)
FROM EMP_PAY;

---------+---------+---------+-
   65000.00

SELECT EMP_ID, EMP_REGULAR_PAY
FROM EMP_PAY
WHERE EMP_REGULAR_PAY =
(SELECT MIN(EMP_REGULAR_PAY) FROM EMP_PAY);

---------+---------+---------+---------+---
     EMP_ID  EMP_REGULAR_PAY
---------+---------+---------+---------+---
       3217          65000.00
```

SUM

The SUM function returns the sum of a set of numbers. Suppose you need to know what your base payroll will be for the year. You could find out with this SQL:

```
SELECT SUM(EMP_REGULAR_PAY)
FROM EMP_PAY;
---------+---------+---------+---------

---------+---------+---------+---------
          375000.00
DSNE610I NUMBER OF ROWS DISPLAYED IS 1
```

SCALAR Functions

A scalar function can be used wherever an expression can be used. It is often used to calculate a value or to influence the result of a query. Again we'll provide some examples, and then a complete list of the scalar functions and what they do.

COALESCE

The COALESCE function returns the value of the first nonnull expression. It is normally used to assign some alternate value when a NULL value is encountered that would otherwise cause an entire record to be excluded from the results. For example, consider the EMP_PAY table with data as follows:

```
SELECT *
FROM EMP_PAY;
---------+---------+---------+---------+---------
   EMP_ID  EMP_REGULAR_PAY  EMP_BONUS_PAY
---------+---------+---------+---------+---------
     3217         65000.00         5500.00
     7459         85000.00         4500.00
     9134         75000.00         2500.00
     4720         80000.00         2500.00
     6288         70000.00         2000.00
DSNE610I NUMBER OF ROWS DISPLAYED IS 5
```

To demonstrate how COALESCE works, let's change the bonus pay amount for employee 9134 to NULL.

```
UPDATE EMP_PAY
SET EMP_BONUS_PAY = NULL
WHERE EMP_ID = 9134;
```

Now our data looks like this:

```
SELECT *
FROM EMP_PAY;
---------+---------+---------+---------+------
    EMP_ID   EMP_REGULAR_PAY   EMP_BONUS_PAY
---------+---------+---------+---------+------
      3217          65000.00         5500.00
      7459          85000.00         4500.00
      9134          75000.00     -------------
      4720          80000.00         2500.00
      6288          70000.00         2000.00
DSNE610I NUMBER OF ROWS DISPLAYED IS 5
```

Ok, here's the example. Let's find the average bonus pay in the EMP_PAY table.

```
SELECT AVG(EMP_BONUS_PAY)
AS AVERAGE_BONUS
FROM EMP_PAY;
---------+---------+---------+---------
                    AVERAGE_BONUS
---------+---------+---------+---------
    3625.000000000000000000000
```

There is a potential problem here! The problem is that the average bonus is not 3625, it is 2900 (total 14,500 divided by five employees). The problem here is that one of the employee records has NULL in the EMP_BONUS_PAY column. Consequently this record was excluded from the calculated average because NULL is not a numeric value and therefore cannot be included in a computation.

Assuming that you do want to include this record in your results to get the correct average, you will need to convert the NULL to numeric value zero. You can do this using the COALESCE function.

```
SELECT AVG(COALESCE(EMP_BONUS_PAY,0))
AS AVERAGE_BONUS
FROM EMP_PAY;
---------+---------+---------+---------+-----
                    AVERAGE_BONUS
---------+---------+---------+---------+-----
        2900.00000000000000000
DSNE610I NUMBER OF ROWS DISPLAYED IS 1
```

The above says calculate the average EMP_BONUS_PAY using the first non-null value of EMP_ BONUS_PAY or zero. Since employee 9134 has a NULL value in the EMP_BONUS_PAY field, DB2 substitutes a zero instead of the NULL. Zero is a numeric value, so this record can now be included in the computation of the average. This gives the correct average which is 2900.

Before we move on let's reset the bonus pay on our employee 9134 so that it can be used correctly for other queries later in the study guide.

```
UPDATE HRSCHEMA.EMP_PAY
SET EMP_BONUS_PAY = 2500.00
WHERE EMP_ID = 9134;
```

You can use COALESCE anytime you need to include a record that would otherwise be excluded due to a NULL value. Converting the NULL to a value will ensure the record can be included in the results.

CONCAT

The CONCAT function combines two or more strings. Suppose for example you want to list each employee's first and last names from the EMPLOYEE table. You could so it with this SQL:

```
SELECT
CONCAT(CONCAT(EMP_FIRST_NAME,' '),EMP_LAST_NAME)
AS EMP_FULL_NAME
FROM HRSCHEMA.EMPLOYEE;

---------+---------+---------+---------+---------+---
EMP_FULL_NAME
---------+---------+---------+---------+---------+---
EDWARD JOHNSON
BETTY STEWART
BRIANNA FRANKLIN
FRED TURNBULL
TIM SCHULTZ
JOE WILLARD
JAMEs FORD
ELISA HARRIS
DSNE610I NUMBER OF ROWS DISPLAYED IS 8
```

LCASE

The LCASE function returns a string in which all the characters are converted to lowercase characters. I can't think of many good applications for this, but here is an example of formatting the last name of each employee to lower case. Note: this function does not change any value on the table, it is only formatting the value for presentation.

```
SELECT EMP_ID, LCASE(EMP_LAST_NAME)
FROM HRSCHEMA.EMPLOYEE;
---------+---------+---------+---------+---
    EMP_ID
---------+---------+---------+---------+---
      3217  johnson
      7459  stewart
      9134  franklin
      4175  turnbull
```

```
                       4720   schultz
                       6288   willard
                       3333   ford
                       7777   harris
             DSNE610I NUMBER OF ROWS DISPLAYED IS 8
```

LEFT

The LEFT function returns a string that consists of the specified number of leftmost bytes of the specified string units. Suppose you have an application that needs the first four letters of the last name (my pharmacy does this as part of the automated prescription filling process). You could accomplish that with this SQL:

```
        SELECT EMP_ID, LEFT(EMP_LAST_NAME,4)
        FROM HRSCHEMA.EMPLOYEE;
      ---------+---------+---------+---------+-----
          EMP_ID
      ---------+---------+---------+---------+-----
            3217   JOHN
            7459   STEW
            9134   FRAN
            4175   TURN
            4720   SCHU
            6288   WILL
            3333   FORD
            7777   HARR
      DSNE610I NUMBER OF ROWS DISPLAYED IS 8
```

MAX

The MAX function returns the maximum value in a set of values. For example if we wanted to know the largest base pay for our EMP_PAY table, we could use this SQL:

```
        SELECT MAX(EMP_REGULAR_PAY)
        AS HIGHEST_PAY
        FROM HRSCHEMA.EMP_PAY;
        ---------+---------+-------
        HIGHEST_PAY
        ---------+---------+-------
           85000.00
```

MIN

The MIN scalar function returns the minimum value in a set of values. For example if we wanted to know the largest base pay for our EMP_PAY table, we could use this SQL:

```
        SELECT MIN(EMP_REGULAR_PAY)
        AS LOWEST_PAY
        FROM HRSCHEMA.EMP_PAY
```

```
---------+---------+-------
LOWEST_PAY
---------+---------+-------
   65000.00
```

MONTH

The MONTH function returns the month part of a date value. We used this one earlier to compare the month of the employee's promotion to the current month.

```
SELECT
EMP_ID,
EMP_PROMOTION_DATE,
CURRENT DATE AS RQST_DATE
FROM HRSCHEMA.EMPLOYEE
WHERE MONTH(EMP_PROMOTION_DATE)
 = MONTH(CURRENT DATE);


---------+---------+---------+---------+---------+----
    EMP_ID  EMP_PROMOTION_DATE  RQST_DATE
---------+---------+---------+---------+---------+----
      3217  2017-01-01          2017-01-19
      7459  2016-01-01          2017-01-19
      4720  2017-01-01          2017-01-19
      6288  2016-01-01          2017-01-19
DSNE610I NUMBER OF ROWS DISPLAYED IS 4
```

REPEAT

The REPEAT function returns a character string that is composed of an argument that is repeated a specified number of times. Suppose for example that you wanted to display 10 asterisks as a literal field on a report. You could specify it this way:

```
SELECT EMP_ID,
REPEAT('*',10) AS "FILLER LITERAL",
EMP_SERVICE_YEARS
FROM HRSCHEMA.EMPLOYEE;


---------+---------+---------+---------+---------+-
    EMP_ID  FILLER LITERAL  EMP_SERVICE_YEARS
---------+---------+---------+---------+---------+-
      3217  * * * * * * * *                  6
      7459  * * * * * * * *                  7
      9134  * * * * * * * *                  0
      4175  * * * * * * * *                  1
      4720  * * * * * * * *                  9
      6288  * * * * * * * *                  6
      3333  * * * * * * * *                  7
      7777  * * * * * * * *                  2
DSNE610I NUMBER OF ROWS DISPLAYED IS 8
```

SPACE

The SPACE function returns a character string that consists of the number of blanks that the argument specifies. You could use this in place of the quotation literals (especially when you want a lot of spaces). The example I'll give uses the SPACE function instead of having to concatenate an empty string using quotation marks.

```
SELECT
CONCAT(CONCAT(EMP_FIRST_NAME,SPACE(1)),
EMP_LAST_NAME)
AS EMP_FULL_NAME
FROM HRSCHEMA.EMPLOYEE;

---------+---------+---------+---------+----
EMP_FULL_NAME
---------+---------+---------+---------+----
EDWARD JOHNSON
BETTY STEWART
BRIANNA FRANKLIN
FRED TURNBULL
TIM SCHULTZ
JOE WILLARD
JAMEs FORD
ELISA HARRIS

DSNE610I NUMBER OF ROWS DISPLAYED IS 8
```

SUBSTR

The SUBSTR function returns a substring of a string. Let's use the earlier example of retrieving the first four letters of the last name via the LEFT function. You could also accomplish that with this SQL:

```
    SELECT EMP_ID, SUBSTR(EMP_LAST_NAME,1,4)
    FROM HRSCHEMA.EMPLOYEE;
---------+---------+---------+---------+---
    EMP_ID
---------+---------+---------+---------+---
      3217  JOHN
      7459  STEW
      9134  FRAN
      4175  TURN
      4720  SCHU
      6288  WILL
      3333  FORD
      7777  HARR
DSNE610I NUMBER OF ROWS DISPLAYED IS 8
```

The 1,4 means starting in position one for a length of four. Of course, you could use a different starting position. An example that might make more sense is reformatting the current date. For example:

144

```
SELECT CURRENT DATE,
SUBSTR(CHAR(CURRENT DATE),6,2)
|| '/'
||SUBSTR(CHAR(CURRENT DATE),9,2)
|| '/'
|| SUBSTR(CHAR(CURRENT DATE),1,4)
AS REFORMED_DATE
FROM SYSIBM.SYSDUMMY1;

---------+---------+---------+---
           REFORMED_DATE
---------+---------+---------+---
2017-01-12  01/12/2017
```

UCASE

The UCASE function returns a string in which all the characters are converted to uppercase characters. Here is an example of changing the last name of each employee to upper case. First we will have to covert the uppercase EMP_LAST_NAME values to lowercase. We can do that using the LOWER function. Let's do this for a single row:

```
UPDATE HRSCHEMA.EMPLOYEE
SET EMP_LAST_NAME
= LOWER(EMP_LAST_NAME)
WHERE EMP_ID = 3217;
```

We can verify that the data did in fact get changed to lower case.

```
SELECT EMP_LAST_NAME
FROM HRSCHEMA.EMPLOYEE
WHERE EMP_ID = 3217;

---------+---------+---------+---------
EMP_LAST_NAME
---------+---------+---------+---------
johnson
DSNE610I NUMBER OF ROWS DISPLAYED IS 1
```

Now let's use the UCASE function to have the EMP_LAST_NAME display as upper case.

```
SELECT EMP_ID, UCASE(EMP_LAST_NAME)
FROM HRSCHEMA.EMPLOYEE
WHERE EMP_ID = 3217;
---------+---------+---------+---------+---------
     EMP_ID
---------+---------+---------+---------+---------
     3217  JOHNSON
DSNE610I NUMBER OF ROWS DISPLAYED IS 1
```

Note that the SELECT query did not change any data on the table. We have simply reformatted the data for presentation. Now let's actually convert the data on the record back to upper case:

```
UPDATE HRSCHEMA.EMPLOYEE
SET EMP_LAST_NAME = UPPER(EMP_LAST_NAME)
WHERE EMP_ID = 3217;
```

And we'll verify that it reverted back to uppercase:

```
SELECT EMP_LAST_NAME
FROM HRSCHEMA.EMPLOYEE
WHERE EMP_ID = 3217;
---------+---------+---------+---------+---
EMP_LAST_NAME
---------+---------+---------+---------+---
JOHNSON
DSNE610I NUMBER OF ROWS DISPLAYED IS 1
```

YEAR

The YEAR function returns the year part of a value that is a character or graphic string. The value must be a valid string representation of a date or timestamp.

```
SELECT CURRENT DATE AS TODAYS_DATE,
YEAR(CURRENT DATE) AS CURRENT_YEAR
FROM SYSIBM.SYSDUMMY1;

---------+---------+---------+--------
TODAYS_DATE  CURRENT_YEAR
---------+---------+---------+--------
2017-01-12          2017
```

Chapter Three Questions

1. Assume you are doing a multi-row INSERT and have specified NOT ATOMIC CONTINUE ON SQLEXCEPTION. On the INSERT of one of the rows, a -803 is returned. What will the result be for this transaction?

   a. The row causing the -803 will not be inserted, and the other inserted rows will be backed out.
   b. The rows are all inserted but the row causing the -803 is also placed in an error table.
   c. The rows up until the -803 are all inserted but none after that and the program will continue with the next statement.
   d. The row causing the -803 will not be inserted but the other rows will be inserted.

2. Suppose you issue this INSERT statement:

```
UPDATE HRSCHEMA.EMPLOYEE
SET EMP_PROFILE
= (
'<?xml version="1.0"?>
<EMP_PROFILE>
<EMP_ID>4175</EMP_ID>
<EMP_ADDRESS>
<STREET>6161 MARGARET LANE</STREET>
<CITY>ERINDALE</CITY>
<STATE>AR</STATE>
<ZIP_CODE>72653</ZIP_CODE>
</EMP_ADDRESS>
<BIRTH_DATE>07/14/1991</BIRTH_DATE>
<EMP_PROFILE>
' )
WHERE EMP_ID = 4175;
```

What will the result be?

   a. An error – the specified XML version is incorrect
   b. An error – the document is not well formed
   c. The record will be inserted with a warning that it has not been validated
   d. The record will be inserted successfully

3. Which of the following is NOT a valid expression to use with the XMLMODIFY function?

    a. Insert expressions.
    b. Delete expressions.
    c. Update expressions.
    d. Replace expressions.

4. Which of the following is NOT a special register in DB2 11?

    a. CURRENT DEGREE
    b. CURRENT RULES
    c. CURRENT HINT
    d. All of the above are valid DB2 special registers.

5. Which built-in routine returns the value of the first non-null expression?

    a. COALESCE
    b. ABS
    c. CEILING
    d. MIN

6. If you want the aggregate total for a set of values, which function would you use?

    a. COUNT
    b. SUM
    c. ABS
    d. CEIL

7. If you want to return the first 3 characters of a 10-character column, which function would you use?

    a. SUBSTR
    b. LTRIM
    c. DIGITS
    d. ABS

8. Assuming all referenced objects are valid, what will the result of this statement be?

```
DELETE FROM EMPLOYEE;
```

    a. The statement will fail because there is no WHERE clause.
    b. The statement will fail because you must specify DELETE * .
    c. The statement will succeed and all rows in the table will be deleted.
    d. The statement will run but no rows in the table will be deleted.

Chapter Three Exercises

1. Write a query to display the last and first names of all employees in the EMPLOYEE table. Display the names in alphabetic order by EMP_LAST_NAME.

2. Write a query to change the first name of Edward Johnson (employee 3217) to Eddie.

3. Write a query to produce the number of employees in the EMPLOYEE table.

CHAPTER FOUR: DATA CONTROL LANGUAGE

You don't need to be an expert on DB2 security unless your company puts you in charge of security. However, it is important to understand the basics of how DB2 security works.

Authorities and privileges are the domain of DBAs and system administrators. As such I won't be going into these. However, as an application developer you may need to know the GRANT and REVOKE statements, as well as something about roles and trusted contexts.

Data Control Language Statements

Data Control Language (DCL) is used to grant and revoke privileges. A privilege enables its holder to perform a specific operation, usually on a specific object. Simple examples of privileges include SELECT, INSERT, UPDATE and DELETE on a particular table or view.

You basically just need to know the syntax of these DCL statements, plus a few options.

GRANT

The basic syntax of the GRANT statement is:

```
GRANT <PRIVILEGE> ON <OBJECT> TO <USER OR GROUP>
```

Let's look at some examples for table privileges. Suppose you want to grant the SELECT privilege on table EMPLOYEE to user USER01. You would issue the following DCL:

```
GRANT SELECT ON EMPLOYEE TO USER01;
```

If you wanted to grant multiple privileges (such as SELECT, INSERT, UPDATE, DELETE), you would use this DCL:

```
GRANT SELECT, INSERT, UPDATE, DELETE
ON EMPLOYEE TO USER01;
```

If you wanted to grant the SELECT privilege to all users, you would grant the privilege to PUBLIC:

```
GRANT SELECT ON EMPLOYEE TO PUBLIC;
```

Keep in mind that in a well secured environment, granting privileges to PUBLIC is usually not what you want, and it is not a best practice. Create appropriate profiles and/or roles, and grant access based on those.

If you want to grant all table privileges to a user or group, use this syntax:

```
GRANT ALL ON EMPLOYEE TO USER01;
```

Finally, if you want the recipient of the grant to be able to grant the same privilege to others, use the WITH GRANT OPTION clause:

```
GRANT SELECT ON EMPLOYEE
TO USER01
WITH GRANT OPTION;
```

Although the basic structure of a GRANT is the same for most objects, the privileges and keywords are somewhat different. We'll show an example of each of these after we look at the REVOKE statement.

Collection
Database
Distinct type
Function or stored procedure
Package
Plan
Schema
Sequence
System
Table or view
Distinct type, array type, or JAR file
Variable
Use

REVOKE

The revoke statement removes a privilege from a user or role. There are basically two forms of the REVOKE. One removes the specified privilege only from the specified user or role. However if REVOKE is used with the BY <userid/role> and the INCLUDING DEPENDENT PRIVILEGES clause, then in addition to revoking the access from the user/role specified in the FROM clause, all access that was explicitly granted to other users by the specified user/ role will also be automatically revoked.

The basic syntax of the REVOKE statement is:

```
REVOKE <PRIVILEGE> FROM <user/role>
BY <GRANTING USER OR GROUP>
<NOT><INCLUDING DEPENDENT PRIVILEGES>
<RESTRICT>
```

`RESTRICT` prevents the named privilege from being revoked under some circumstances.

DCL Examples

COLLECTION

Syntax is:

```
GRANT CREATE ON COLLECTION <collection-id> TO <USER/ROLE>

GRANT PACKADM ON COLLECTION <collection-id> TO <USER/ROLE>
```

Example:

```
GRANT CREATE ON COLLECTION HRDATA TO HRUSER01
```

DATABASE

Syntax is:

```
GRANT [authority or privilege] ON DATABASE <database name>
TO <USER/ROLE>
```

Example:

```
GRANT CREATETAB ON DATABASE DBHR TO HRUSER01
```

FUNCTION/STORED PROCEDURE

Syntax is:

```
GRANT EXECUTE ON FUNCTION  <FUNCTION>  TO <USER/ROLE>

GRANT EXECUTE ON PROCEDURE <PROCEDURE> TO <USER/ROLE>
```

Examples:

```
GRANT EXECUTE ON FUNCTION EMP_SALARY TO HRUSER09;

GRANT EXECUTE ON PROCEDURE GET_EMP_INFO TO ROLE HRUSERS;
```

PACKAGE

Syntax is:

```
GRANT <privilege> ON PACKAGE <package name> TO <USER/ROLE>
```

Example:

```
GRANT EXECUTE ON PACKAGE COBEMP1 TO ROLE HRUSERS;
```

PLAN

Syntax is:

```
GRANT <privilege> ON PLAN <plan name> TO <USER/ROLE>
```

Example:

```
GRANT EXECUTE ON PLAN COBEMP1 TO ROLE HRUSERS;

GRANT BIND,EXECUTE ON PLAN COBEMP4 TO DBA001;
```

SCHEMA

Syntax is:

```
GRANT <privilege> ON SCHEMA <schema name> TO <USER/ROLE>
```

Example:

```
GRANT CREATEIN ON SCHEMA HRDATA TO ROLE HR_DEVELOPERS;
```

SEQUENCE

Syntax is:

```
GRANT <privilege> ON SEQUENCE <sequence name> TO <USER/ROLE>
```

Example:

```
GRANT USAGE ON SEQUENCE EMPL_ID__SEQ TO PUBLIC;
```

TABLE OR VIEW

Syntax is:

```
GRANT <privilege> ON TABLE/VIEW <table/view name> TO <USER/ROLE>
```

Example:

```
GRANT ALTER ON TABLE EMPLOYEE TO DBA001

GRANT SELECT,INSERT,UPDATE,DELETE ON EMPLOYEE TO USER01
```

USE

Syntax is:

```
GRANT USAGE ON OBJECT <Object name> TO <USER/ROLE>
```

Example:

```
GRANT USAGE ON SEQUENCE EMPL_ID__SEQ TO PUBLIC;
```

VIEWS

A view is a classic way to restrict a subset of data columns to a specific set of users who are allowed to see or manipulate those columns. If you are going to use views for security you must make sure that users do not have direct access to the base tables, i.e. that they can only access the data via view(s). Otherwise they could circumvent the restrictions of the view by accessing the base table.

Let's look back at our employee table. Suppose we add a column for the employee's Social Security number. That is obviously a very private piece of information that not everyone should see. Our business rule will be that users HRUSER01, HRUSER02 and HRUSER99 are the only ones who should be able to view Social Security numbers. All other users and/or groups are not allowed to see the content of this column, but they can access all the other columns.

We might implement this as follows:

```
ALTER TABLE HRSCHEMA.EMPLOYEE
ADD COLUMN EMP_SSN CHAR(09);
```

Now let's update the value of this column for employee 3217:

155

```
UPDATE HRSCHEMA.EMPLOYEE
SET EMP_SSN = '238297536'
WHERE EMP_ID = 3217;
```

Now let's create two views, one of which includes the EMP_SSN column, and the other of which does not:

```
CREATE VIEW HRSCHEMA.EMPLOYEE_ALL
AS SELECT
EMP_ID,
EMP_LAST_NAME,
EMP_FIRST_NAME,
EMP_SERVICE_YEARS,
EMP_PROMOTION_DATE,
EMP_PROFILE
FROM HRSCHEMA.EMPLOYEE;


CREATE VIEW HRSCHEMA.EMPLOYEE_HR
AS SELECT
EMP_ID,
EMP_LAST_NAME,
EMP_FIRST_NAME,
EMP_SERVICE_YEARS,
EMP_PROMOTION_DATE,
EMP_PROFILE,
EMP_SSN
FROM HRSCHEMA.EMPLOYEE;
```

Finally, issue the appropriate grants.

```
GRANT SELECT ON HRSCHEMA.EMPLOYEE_ALL TO PUBLIC.

GRANT SELECT on HRSCHEMA.EMPLOYEE_HR
TO HRUSER01, HRUSER02, HRUSER99.
```

At this point, assuming we are only accessing data through views, the three HR users are the only users able to access the EMP_SSN column. Other users cannot access the EMP_SSN column because it is not included in the EMPLOYEE_ALL view that they have access to. To prove this:

```
SELECT EMP_ID, EMP_SSN
FROM HRSCHEMA.EMPLOYEE_ALL
WHERE EMP_ID = 3217;
---------+---------+---------+---------+---------+---------+---------+---
DSNT408I SQLCODE = -206, ERROR:  EMP_SSN IS NOT VALID IN THE CONTEXT WHERE IT IS USED
```

If you are one of the HR users, you will be able to access the EMP_SSN column via the other view, EMPLOYEE_HR:

```
SELECT EMP_ID, EMP_SSN
FROM HRSCHEMA.EMPLOYEE_HR
WHERE EMP_ID = 3217;
---------+---------+------
   EMP_ID   EMP_SSN
---------+---------+------
     3217   238297536
```

ROLES

A role is a database object upon which database privileges can be granted and revoked. Often roles are created to simplify maintenance of privileges for a group of people (users, developers, administrators, etc).

Let's do an example. Assume we want to create a role HRUSER to which we can assign system users as needed, and we will also grant the privileges to the role as needed. Here's how to create the HRUSER role:

```
CREATE ROLE HRUSER;
```

That's it. Very simple. Next let's grant SELECT access on our special view EMPLOYEE_HR to the HRUSER role that we just created.

```
GRANT SELECT ON HRSCHEMA.EMPLOYEE_HR TO HRUSER;
```

Finally, we can grant the HRUSER role to specific userids for the HR personnel:

```
GRANT ROLE HRUSER TO HRUSER01, HRUSER02, HRUSER99;
```

Now everyone in the HRUSER group has access to the EMPLOYEE_HR view. Powerfully, we can add or revoke other privileges for the HRUSER role at any time and the change takes place immediately for all users who have been granted that role.

Next we will explore the use of roles with trusted contexts.

TRUSTED CONTEXTS

A trusted context is a database object that defines a secure connection based on a system authorization id and connection attributes such as an IP address. Trusted contexts are typically used to establish a trust relationship between DB2 and some middleware product such as a web service or an application. A trusted context is associated with a single system authorization ID.

The point of a trusted context is to enable an entity such as a web service to establish a connection to the database that can be used by that service without the service users themselves having to logon to the DB2 server. It also prevents the connection from being used from any location except the specified IP address. Finally, the authorized id can be granted appropriate privileges to operate on the database via use of a role or roles.

Now that we understand the basics, let's do an example. Earlier we created a role named HRUSER that allowed user ids assigned that role to view the Social Security numbers of employees. We can further require that the HRUSER access DB2 using a trusted context from a work location. Let's say we want the users to logon via a service application. Assume that the work server IP for the application is 202.033.178.267, and that we have a DB2 authorization id HRADM to be used by our service.

To define and implement our trusted context, we need to grant the role HRUSER to the system authorization id that the service app will be using to login to DB2 with, specifically HRADM. We can do that with this GRANT statement:

```
GRANT ROLE HRUSER TO HRADM;
```

Now we can grant create the trusted context for our application, specifying the IP address, authorization logon id and a default role of HRUSER.

```
CREATE TRUSTED CONTEXT HRCTXT
BASED UPON CONNECTION USING SYSTEM AUTHID HRADM
ATTRIBUTES (ADDRESS '202.033.178.267')
DEFAULT ROLE HRUSER
ENABLE
```

At this point, the service application can logon to DB2 with the HRADM id and use the privileges granted to the role HRUSER, provided that the connection is made from the specified server (IP address or domain name) defined in the trusted context, which is 202.033.178.267.

Other examples:

```
CREATE TRUSTED CONTEXT GGX1
        BASED UPON CONNECTION USING SYSTEM AUTHID DBA001
        ATTRIBUTES (ADDRESS '10.41.667.389',
                    ENCRYPTION 'LOW')
        DEFAULT ROLE GGXROLE
        ENABLE
        WITH USE FOR BILL, ROBERT ROLE ROLE1 WITH AUTHENTICATION;

CREATE TRUSTED CONTEXT CTX2
        BASED UPON CONNECTION USING SYSTEM AUTHID DBA002
```

```
ATTRIBUTES (JOBNAME 'ABCPROD')
DEFAULT ROLE ABCROLE WITH ROLE AS OBJECT OWNER AND QUALIFIER
ENABLE
WITH USE FOR SALLY;
```

Chapter Four Questions

1. Assume a table where certain columns contain sensitive data and you don't want all users to see these columns. Some other columns in the table must be made accessible to all users. What type of object could you create to solve this problem?

    a. INDEX
    b. SEQUENCE
    c. VIEW
    d. TRIGGER

2. To grant a privilege to all users of the database, grant the privilege to whom?

    a. ALL
    b. PUBLIC
    c. ANY
    d. DOMAIN

3. Tara wants to grant CONTROL of table TBL1 to Bill, and also allow Bill to grant the same privilege to other users. What clause should Tara use on the GRANT statement?

    a. WITH CONTROL OPTION
    b. WITH GRANT OPTION
    c. WITH USE OPTION
    d. WITH REVOKE OPTION

4. Assume USER01 was granted the UPDATE privilege on table TABLE01 and it was issued WITH GRANT OPTION. If you want to revoke user USER01's UPDATE access on TABLE01, and you also want to revoke the UPDATE access of any other users that were granted this permission by USER01, what clause would you include in the REVOKE statement?

    a. CASCADE
    b. EXTEND
    c. ALL GRANTED
    d. No other clause is required, DB2 automatically revokes the access from all users that received their grant from the designated user specified on the REVOKE command.

Chapter Four Exercises

1. Write a DCL statement to grant SELECT access on table `HRSCHEMA.EMPLOYEE` to users `HR001` and `HR002`.

2. Write a DCL statement to revoke SELECT access on table `HRSCHEMA.EMPLOYEE` from user `HR002`.

3. Write a DCL statement to grant SELECT, INSERT, UPDATE and DELETE access on table `HRSCHEMA.EMP_PAY` to user `HRMGR01`.

CHAPTER FIVE: Using DB2 In Application Programs

CURSORS

A cursor is a pointer to a record in a result set returned in an application program or stored procedure. If you do programming in DB2 with result sets, you will need to understand cursors. First let's talk about the types of cursors and the rules governing them. That will give you a good idea of what type of cursor to select for your processing. Then we'll provide a programming example of using a cursor.

Types of Cursors

Cursors are scrollable or nonscrollable, sensitive or insensitive, static or dynamic. A non-scrollable cursor moves sequentially through a result set. A scrollable cursor can move where you want it to move within the result set. Scrollable cursors can be sensitive or insensitive. A sensitive cursor can be static or dynamic.

To declare a cursor as scrollable, you use the SCROLL keyword. In addition, a scrollable cursor is either sensitive or insensitive, and you specify this with the SENSITIVE and INSENSITIVE keywords. Finally to specify a sensitive cursors as static or dynamic, use the STATIC or DYNAMIC keyword.

INSENSITIVE SCROLL

If you declare a cursor as INSENSITIVE SCROLL, it means that the result set is static. Neither the size nor the ordering of the rows can be changed. Also you cannot change any data values of the rows. Finally, if any rows change in the underlying table or view after you open the cursor, those changes will not be visible to the cursor (and the changes will not be reflected in the result set).

SENSITIVE STATIC SCROLL

If you declare a cursor as SENSITIVE STATIC SCROLL, it means that the result set is static. Neither the size nor the ordering of the rows can be changed. If any rows change in the underlying table or view after you open the cursor, those changes will not be visible to the cursor (and the changes will not be reflected in the result set). An exception to this is if you specify SENSITIVE on the FETCH statement

You can change the rows in the rowset and the changes will be reflected in the result set. Also, if you change a row such that it no longer satisfies the query upon which the cursor is based, that row disappears from the result set. Additionally, if a row in a result set is deleted from the underlying table, the row will disappear from the result set.

SENSITIVE DYNAMIC SCROLL

If you declare a cursor as SENSITIVE DYNAMIC SCROLL, it means that the size of the result set and the ordering can change each time you do a fetch. The rowset would change if there are any changes to the underlying table after the cursor is opened.

Any rows in the rowset can be changed and deleted, and the changes will be reflected in the result set. If you change a row such that it no longer satisfies the query upon which the cursor is based, that row disappears from the result set. Additionally, if a row in a result set is deleted from the underlying table, the row will disappear from the result set.

Additional Cursor Options

A cursor can specify WITHOUT HOLD or WITH HOLD, the main difference being whether or not the cursor is closed on a COMMIT. Specifying WITHOUT HOLD allows a cursor to be closed when a COMMIT operation occurs. Specifying WITH HOLD prevents the cursor from being closed when a COMMIT takes place.

A cursor can specify WITHOUT RETURN or WITH RETURN, the difference being whether the result set is intended to be returned to a calling program or procedure. Specifying WITH RETURN means that the result set is meant to be returned from the procedure it is generated in. Specifying WITHOUT RETURN means that the cursor's result set is not intended to be returned from the procedure it is generated in.

A cursor can also specify WITH ROWSET POSITIONING or WITHOUT ROWSET POSITIONING. If you specify WITH ROWSET POSITIONING, then your cursor can return either a single row or rowset (multiple rows) with a single FETCH statement. If WITHOUT ROWSET POSITIONING is specified, it means the cursor can only return a single row with a FETCH statement.

Sample Program

To use cursors in a program, you must:

1. Declare the cursor
2. Open the Cursor
3. Fetch the cursor (one or more times)
4. Close the cursor

I suggest you memorize the sequence above.

Here is a basic program that uses a cursor to retrieve and update records. We showed this program earlier in the DML chapter to demonstrate the positioned UPDATE operation. If you haven't used cursors much, I suggest getting very familiar with the structure of this program.

Let's say that we want to check all records in the EMPLOYEE table and if the last name is in lower case, we want to change it to upper case and display the employee number of the corrected record. Let's first set up some test data:

```
UPDATE HRSCHEMA.EMPLOYEE
SET EMP_LAST_NAME = LOWER(EMP_LAST_NAME)
WHERE
EMP_LAST_NAME IN ('JOHNSON', 'STEWART', 'FRANKLIN');
```

After you execute this SQL, here's the current content of the EMPLOYEE table:

```
SELECT EMP_ID, EMP_LAST_NAME, EMP_FIRST_NAME
FROM HRSCHEMA.EMPLOYEE;
---------+---------+---------+---------+---------+-----
    EMP_ID  EMP_LAST_NAME          EMP_FIRST_NAME
---------+---------+---------+---------+---------+-----
      3217  johnson                EDWARD
      7459  stewart                BETTY
      9134  franklin               BRIANNA
      4720  SCHULTZ                TIM
      6288  WILLARD                JOE
      1122  JENKINS                DEBBIE
      4175  TURNBULL               FREDERICK
      1001  HENDERSON              JOHN
DSNE610I NUMBER OF ROWS DISPLAYED IS 8
```

To accomplish our objective we'll define and open a cursor on the EMPLOYEE table. We can specify a WHERE clause that limits the result set to only those records that contain lower case characters. After we find them, we will change the case to upper and replace the records.

First we need to identify the rows that include lower case letters in column EMP_LAST_NAME. We can do this using the UPPER function. We'll compare the current contents of the EMP_LAST_NAME to the value of UPPER(EMP_LAST_NAME) and if the results are not identical, the row in question has lower case and needs to be changed. Our result set should include all rows where these two values are not identical. So our SQL would be:

```
SELECT EMP_ID, EMP_LAST_NAME
FROM EMPLOYEE
WHERE EMP_LAST_NAME <> UPPER(EMP_LAST_NAME)
```

Once we've placed the last name value in the host variable EMP_LAST_NAME, we can use the COBOL Upper-case function to convert lowercase to uppercase.

```
MOVE FUNCTION UPPER-CASE (EMP-LAST-NAME) TO EMP-LAST-NAME
```

Now we are ready to write the program. So we define and open the cursor, cycle through the result set using FETCH, modify the data and then do the UPDATE action specifying the current record of the cursor. That is what is meant by a positioned update – the cursor is positioned on the record to be changed, hence you do not need to specify a more elaborate WHERE clause in the UPDATE. Only the `WHERE CURRENT OF <cursor name>` clause need be specified. Also we will include the FOR UPDATE clause in our cursor definition to ensure DB2 knows our intent is to update the data we retrieve.

The program code follows:

```
IDENTIFICATION DIVISION.
PROGRAM-ID. COBEMP2.

**************************************************
*        PROGRAM USING DB2 CURSOR HANDLING       *
**************************************************

ENVIRONMENT DIVISION.
DATA DIVISION.
WORKING-STORAGE SECTION.

    EXEC SQL
      INCLUDE SQLCA
    END-EXEC.


    EXEC SQL
      INCLUDE EMPLOYEE
    END-EXEC.

    EXEC SQL
        DECLARE EMP-CURSOR CURSOR FOR
        SELECT EMP_ID, EMP_LAST_NAME
        FROM EMPLOYEE
        WHERE EMP_LAST_NAME <> UPPER(EMP_LAST_NAME)
        FOR UPDATE OF EMP_LAST_NAME
    END-EXEC.


PROCEDURE DIVISION.

MAIN-PARA.
    DISPLAY "SAMPLE COBOL PROGRAM: UPDATE USING CURSOR".

    EXEC SQL
        OPEN EMP-CURSOR
    END-EXEC.
```

```
            DISPLAY 'OPEN CURSOR SQLCODE: ' SQLCODE.

            PERFORM FETCH-CURSOR
              UNTIL SQLCODE NOT EQUAL 0.

            EXEC SQL
                CLOSE EMP-CURSOR
            END-EXEC.

            DISPLAY 'CLOSE CURSOR SQLCODE: ' SQLCODE.

            STOP RUN.

        FETCH-CURSOR.

            EXEC SQL
                FETCH EMP-CURSOR INTO :EMP-ID, :EMP-LAST-NAME
            END-EXEC.

            IF SQLCODE = 0
               DISPLAY 'BEFORE CHANGE   ', EMP-LAST-NAME
               MOVE FUNCTION UPPER-CASE (EMP-LAST-NAME)
                  TO EMP-LAST-NAME
               EXEC SQL
                  UPDATE EMPLOYEE
                  SET EMP_LAST_NAME = :EMP-LAST-NAME
                  WHERE CURRENT OF EMP-CURSOR
               END-EXEC

            END-IF.

            IF SQLCODE = 0
               DISPLAY 'AFTER CHANGE    ', EMP-LAST-NAME
            END-IF.
```

Here is the output from running the program:

```
SAMPLE COBOL PROGRAM: UPDATE USING CURSOR
OPEN CURSOR SQLCODE: 0000000000
BEFORE CHANGE    johnson
AFTER CHANGE     JOHNSON
BEFORE CHANGE    stewart
AFTER CHANGE     STEWART
BEFORE CHANGE    franklin
AFTER CHANGE     FRANKLIN
CLOSE CURSOR SQLCODE: 0000000000
```

Here is the PLI version of the program.

```
PLIEMP2: PROCEDURE OPTIONS(MAIN) REORDER;
/********************************************************************
* PROGRAM NAME :   PLIEMP2 - USE CURSOR TO UPDATE DB2 ROWS         *
********************************************************************/


/********************************************************************
/*                W O R K I N G   S T O R A G E                    *
********************************************************************/
   DCL RET_SQL_CODE              FIXED BIN(31) INIT(0);
   DCL RET_SQL_CODE_PIC          PIC 'S999999999' INIT (0);


   EXEC SQL
     INCLUDE SQLCA;

   EXEC SQL
     INCLUDE EMPLOYEE;

   EXEC SQL
      DECLARE EMP_CURSOR CURSOR FOR
      SELECT EMP_ID, EMP_LAST_NAME
      FROM HRSCHEMA.EMPLOYEE
      WHERE EMP_LAST_NAME <> UPPER(EMP_LAST_NAME)
      FOR UPDATE OF EMP_LAST_NAME;

/********************************************************************
/*               P R O G R A M   M A I N L I N E                   *
********************************************************************/

   PUT SKIP LIST ('SAMPLE PLI PROGRAM: CURSOR TO UPDATE ROWS');

   EXEC SQL OPEN EMP_CURSOR;

   PUT SKIP LIST ('OPEN CURSOR SQLCODE: ' || SQLCODE);

   IF SQLCODE = 0 THEN
      DO UNTIL (SQLCODE ¬= 0);
         CALL P0100_FETCH_CURSOR;
      END;

   EXEC SQL CLOSE EMP_CURSOR;

   PUT SKIP LIST ('CLOSE CURSOR SQLCODE: ' || SQLCODE);

   IF SQLCODE ¬= 0 THEN
      DO;
         EXEC SQL
            GET DIAGNOSTICS CONDITION 1
            :RET_SQL_CODE  = DB2_RETURNED_SQLCODE;

         RET_SQL_CODE_PIC  = RET_SQL_CODE;
         PUT SKIP LIST (RET_SQL_CODE_PIC);
      END;
```

```
P0100_FETCH_CURSOR: PROC;

    EXEC SQL
        FETCH EMP_CURSOR INTO :EMP_ID, :EMP_LAST_NAME;

    IF SQLCODE = 0 THEN
        DO;
            PUT SKIP LIST ('BEFORE CHANGE  ' || EMP_LAST_NAME);
            EMP_LAST_NAME = UPPERCASE(EMP_LAST_NAME);
            EXEC SQL
                UPDATE HRSCHEMA.EMPLOYEE
                SET EMP_LAST_NAME = :EMP_LAST_NAME
                WHERE CURRENT OF EMP_CURSOR;
            IF SQLCODE = 0 THEN
                PUT SKIP LIST ('AFTER CHANGE  ' || EMP_LAST_NAME);
        END;


    END P0100_FETCH_CURSOR;

    END PLIEMP2;
```

And here is the modified table:

```
    SELECT EMP_ID,
    EMP_LAST_NAME,
    EMP_FIRST_NAME
    FROM HRSCHEMA.EMPLOYEE;
---------+---------+---------+---------+---------+-----
    EMP_ID  EMP_LAST_NAME        EMP_FIRST_NAME
---------+---------+---------+---------+---------+-----
      3217  JOHNSON              EDWARD
      7459  STEWART              BETTY
      9134  FRANKLIN             BRIANNA
      4720  SCHULTZ              TIM
      6288  WILLARD              JOE
      1122  JENKINS              DEBBIE
      4175  TURNBULL             FREDERICK
      1001  HENDERSON            JOHN
DSNE610I NUMBER OF ROWS DISPLAYED IS 8
```

This method of using a positioned cursor update is something you will use often, particularly when you do not know your result set beforehand, or anytime you need to examine the content of the record before you perform the update.

ERROR HANDLING

In over three decades of experience with DB2, I believe one of the most neglected areas in programmer training is error resolution. I'm not sure why this is, but I'd like to provide some standards that may help save time and make programmers more effective. First, let's look at SQLCODE processing, and then we'll look at standardizing an error reporting routine.

SQLCODES

When using embedded SQL with DB2 you include a SQLCA structure which includes an SQLCODE variable. DB2 sets the SQLCODE after each SQL statement. The SQLCODE should be interrogated to determine the success or failure of the SQL statement.
The value of the SQLCODE can be interpreted generally as follows:

- If SQLCODE = 0, execution was successful.
- If SQLCODE > 0, execution was successful with a warning.
- If SQLCODE < 0, execution was not successful.
- SQLCODE = 100, "no data" was found.

Here's an example of an SQL error message when a query is executed via SPUFI. In this case, the last name column is incorrectly spelled (it should be EMP_LAST_NAME) so DB2 does not recognize it. The -206 is accompanied by an explanation. A more complete explanation and recommendations for action to take is available if you look up the SQLCODE on the IBM product documentation web site.

```
   SELECT EMP_ID, EMP_LASTNAME
   FROM HRSCHEMA.EMPLOYEE;
---------+---------+---------+---------+---------+---------+---------+---
DSNT408I SQLCODE = -206, ERROR:  EMP_LASTNAME IS NOT VALID IN THE CONTEXT
         WHERE IT IS USED
DSNT418I SQLSTATE   = 42703 SQLSTATE RETURN CODE
DSNT415I SQLERRP    = DSNXORSO SQL PROCEDURE DETECTING ERROR
DSNT416I SQLERRD    = -100 0   0  -1   0   0 SQL DIAGNOSTIC INFORMATION
DSNT416I SQLERRD    = X'FFFFFF9C'  X'00000000'  X'00000000'  X'FFFFFFFF'
         X'00000000'  X'00000000' SQL DIAGNOSTIC INFORMATION
```

There are far too many SQL codes to memorize! I suggest concentrating on the codes listed below. Most developers have run into these at one time or another. They tend to be pretty common. If you run into one that's not on this list, you can search it in the IBM product documentation.

Common Error SQLCODES

Code	Meaning
-117	THE NUMBER OF VALUES ASSIGNED IS NOT THE SAME AS THE NUMBER OF SPECIFIED OR IMPLIED COLUMNS
-180	THE DATE, TIME, OR TIMESTAMP VALUE value IS INVALID

Code	Meaning
-181	THE STRING REPRESENTATION OF A DATETIME VALUE IS NOT A VALID DATETIME VALUE
-203	A REFERENCE TO COLUMN column-name IS AMBIGUOUS
-206	Object-name IS NOT VALID IN THE CONTEXT WHERE IT IS USED
-305	THE NULL VALUE CANNOT BE ASSIGNED TO OUTPUT HOST VARIABLE NUMBER position-number BECAUSE NO INDICATOR VARIABLE IS SPECIFIED
-501	THE CURSOR IDENTIFIED IN A FETCH OR CLOSE STATEMENT IS NOT OPEN
-502	THE CURSOR IDENTIFIED IN AN OPEN STATEMENT IS ALREADY OPEN
-803	AN INSERTED OR UPDATED VALUE IS INVALID BECAUSE THE INDEX IN INDEX SPACE indexspace-name CONSTRAINS COLUMNS OF THE TABLE SO NO TWO ROWS CAN CONTAIN DUPLICATE VALUES IN THOSE COLUMNS. RID OF EXISTING ROW IS X record-id
-805	DBRM OR PACKAGE NAME location-name.collection-id.dbrm-name.consistency-token NOT FOUND IN PLAN plan-name. REASON reason-code
-811	THE RESULT OF AN EMBEDDED SELECT STATEMENT OR A SUBSELECT IN THE SET CLAUSE OF AN UPDATE STATEMENT IS A TABLE OF MORE THAN ONE ROW, OR THE RESULT OF A SUBQUERY OF A BASIC PREDICATE IS MORE THAN ONE VALUE
-818	THE PRECOMPILER-GENERATED TIMESTAMP x IN THE LOAD MODULE IS DIFFERENT FROM THE BIND TIMESTAMP y BUILT FROM THE DBRM z
-904	UNSUCCESSFUL EXECUTION CAUSED BY AN UNAVAILABLE RESOURCE. REASON reason-code, TYPE OF RESOURCE resource-type, AND RESOURCE NAME resource-name.
-911	THE CURRENT UNIT OF WORK HAS BEEN ROLLED BACK DUE TO DEADLOCK OR TIMEOUT. REASON reason-code, TYPE OF RESOURCE resource-type, AND RESOURCE NAME resource-name
-913	UNSUCCESSFUL EXECUTION CAUSED BY DEADLOCK OR TIMEOUT. REASON CODE reason-code, TYPE OF RESOURCE resource-type, AND RESOURCE NAME resource-name.
-922	AUTHORIZATION FAILURE: error-type ERROR. REASON reason-code.

Standardizing an Error Routine

For optimal use of the SQLCODEs returned from DB2, I suggest you create and use a standard error routine in all your embedded SQL programs. I'll provide a model you can use, but first let's create a simple program and force an error to demonstrate the kind of problem resolution information that would be useful.

In this case, let's select a value into a host variable using a fullselect query. But we will make sure the fullselect query encounters more than one row. That will cause a -811 SQLCODE error which we will trap.

```
IDENTIFICATION DIVISION.
PROGRAM-ID. COBEMP5.

*********************************************************
*       PROGRAM USING DB2 SELECT WITH ERROR TO          *
*       DEMONSTRATE COMMON ERROR ROUTINE                *
*********************************************************

ENVIRONMENT DIVISION.
DATA DIVISION.
WORKING-STORAGE SECTION.

01 HV-EMP-VARIABLES.
    10  HV-ID               PIC S9(9) USAGE COMP.
    10  HV-LAST-NAME        PIC X(30).
    10  HV-FIRST-NAME       PIC X(20).
    10  HV-SERVICE-YEARS    PIC S9(9) USAGE COMP.
    10  HV-PROMOTION-DATE   PIC X(10).

77 ERR-CNT                  PIC S9(9) USAGE COMP.
77 RET-SQL-CODE             PIC -9(4).


    EXEC SQL
      INCLUDE SQLCA
    END-EXEC.

    EXEC SQL
      INCLUDE EMPLOYEE
    END-EXEC.

PROCEDURE DIVISION.

MAIN-PARA.
    DISPLAY "SAMPLE COBOL PROGRAM: COMMON ERROR ROUTINE".

*   LOAD THE EMPLOYEE ARRAY

    EXEC SQL
```

172

```
            SELECT EMP_ID
            INTO :HV-ID
            FROM HRSCHEMA.EMPLOYEE
            WHERE EMP_ID >= 3217

        END-EXEC.

        IF SQLCODE NOT EQUAL 0

            MOVE SQLCODE TO RET-SQL-CODE
            DISPLAY 'ERROR - SQL CODE = ' RET-SQL-CODE.


        STOP RUN.
```

This would generate the following output to SYSPRINT:

```
    SAMPLE COBOL PROGRAM: COMMON ERROR ROUTINE
    ERROR - SQL CODE = -0811
```

Ok, it's good that we trapped the error SQLCODE. But it would be better if DB2 returned the full error description. We can do that if we call a utility program named DSNTIAR. So let's create a common DB2 error subroutine with DSNTIAR so that we can use it in all our DB2 programs.

First, create these working storage variables.

```
    77 ERR-TXT-LGTH          PIC S9(9) USAGE COMP VALUE +72.

    01 ERR-MSG.
       05 ERR-MSG-LGTH        PIC S9(4) COMP VALUE +960.
       05 ERR-MSG-TXT         PIC X(72) OCCURS 12 TIMES
                                        INDEXED BY ERR-NDX.
```

The message and text length variables as well as the SQLCA structure will be passed to DSNTIAR.

Next, create two subroutines as follows. Combined, these subroutines will call DSNTIAR and display the returned output from that utility.

```
    P9999-SQL-ERROR.

        DISPLAY ERR-REC.

        CALL 'DSNTIAR' USING SQLCA,
                       ERR-MSG,
                       ERR-TXT-LGTH.
```

```
        IF RETURN-CODE IS EQUAL TO ZERO

            PERFORM P9999-DISP-ERR
                VARYING ERR-NDX FROM 1 BY 1
                UNTIL ERR-NDX > 12

        ELSE
            DISPLAY 'DSNTIAR ERROR CODE = ' RETURN-CODE
            STOP RUN.


    P9999-DISP-ERR.

        DISPLAY ERR-MSG-TXT(ERR-NDX).

    P9999-DISP-ERR-EXIT.
```

Finally we can modify our code to call the error routine anytime a bad SQL code is returned.

```
    EXEC SQL
        SELECT EMP_ID
        INTO :HV-ID
        FROM HRSCHEMA.EMPLOYEE
        WHERE EMP_ID >= 3217

    END-EXEC.

    IF SQLCODE IS NOT EQUAL TO ZERO
        MOVE SQLCODE TO SQLCODE-VIEW
        MOVE 'EMPLOYEE' TO ERR-TAB
        MOVE 'MAIN'     TO ERR-PARA
        MOVE EMP-ID     TO ERR-DETAIL
        PERFORM P9999-SQL-ERROR.
```

Now when we recompile, bind and rerun the program, the outlook looks like this:

```
    SAMPLE COBOL PROGRAM: COMMON ERROR ROUTINE
    SQLCODE = -811      EMPLOYEE        MAIN            000000000
     DSNT408I SQLCODE = -811, ERROR:  THE RESULT OF AN EMBEDDED SELECT
              STATEMENT OR A SUBSELECT IN THE SET CLAUSE OF AN UPDATE
              STATEMENT IS A TABLE OF MORE THAN ONE ROW, OR THE RESULT OF A
              SUBQUERY OF A BASIC PREDICATE IS MORE THAN ONE VALUE
     DSNT418I SQLSTATE   = 21000 SQLSTATE RETURN CODE
     DSNT415I SQLERRP    = DSNXREMS SQL PROCEDURE DETECTING ERROR
     DSNT416I SQLERRD    = -140  0  0  -1  0  0 SQL DIAGNOSTIC INFORMATION
     DSNT416I SQLERRD    = X'FFFFFF74'  X'00000000'  X'00000000'
              X'FFFFFFFF'  X'00000000'  X'00000000' SQL DIAGNOSTIC
              INFORMATION
```

The SQLCODE details, along with the other information we printed in the ERR-REC (such as the table name and paragraph name) are now displayed to SYSPRINT. This information is more helpful for debugging than just having the SQL code. Moreover, you can create these declarations and routines as copybooks and include them in all your DB2 programs. When used, they ensure standardization throughout your shop. They also will save a lot of time by making useful error-related information available on a consistent basis. I strongly recommend that you implement this standard in your shop!

Here is the entire program listing:

```
       IDENTIFICATION DIVISION.
       PROGRAM-ID. COBEMP5.

      ***************************************************
      *      PROGRAM USING DB2 SELECT WITH ERROR TO      *
      *      DEMONSTRATE COMMON ERROR ROUTINE            *
      ***************************************************

       ENVIRONMENT DIVISION.
       DATA DIVISION.
       WORKING-STORAGE SECTION.

       01 HV-EMP-VARIABLES.
          10   HV-ID              PIC S9(9) USAGE COMP.
          10   HV-LAST-NAME       PIC X(30).
          10   HV-FIRST-NAME      PIC X(20).
          10   HV-SERVICE-YEARS   PIC S9(9) USAGE COMP.
          10   HV-PROMOTION-DATE  PIC X(10).

       01 ERR-REC.
          05 FILLER               PIC X(10) VALUE 'SQLCODE = '.
          05 SQLCODE-VIEW         PIC -999.
          05 FILLER               PIC X(005) VALUE SPACES.
          05 ERR-TAB              PIC X(016).
          05 ERR-PARA             PIC X(015).
          05 ERR-DETAIL           PIC X(040).

       77 ERR-TXT-LGTH            PIC S9(9) USAGE COMP VALUE +72.

       01 ERR-MSG.
          05 ERR-MSG-LGTH         PIC S9(04) COMP VALUE +864.
          05 ERR-MSG-TXT          PIC X(072) OCCURS 12 TIMES
                                             INDEXED BY ERR-NDX.

           EXEC SQL
             INCLUDE SQLCA
           END-EXEC.

           EXEC SQL
             INCLUDE EMPLOYEE
           END-EXEC.

       PROCEDURE DIVISION.

       MAIN-PARA.
           DISPLAY "SAMPLE COBOL PROGRAM: COMMON ERROR ROUTINE".
```

```
*  SELECT AN EMPLOYEE

    EXEC SQL
       SELECT EMP_ID
       INTO :HV-ID
       FROM HRSCHEMA.EMPLOYEE
       WHERE EMP_ID >= 3217

    END-EXEC.

    IF SQLCODE IS NOT EQUAL TO ZERO

       MOVE SQLCODE TO SQLCODE-VIEW
       MOVE 'EMPLOYEE' TO ERR-TAB
       MOVE 'MAIN'     TO ERR-PARA
       MOVE EMP-ID     TO ERR-DETAIL
       PERFORM P9999-SQL-ERROR.

    STOP RUN.

P9999-SQL-ERROR.

    DISPLAY ERR-REC.

    CALL 'DSNTIAR' USING SQLCA,
                   ERR-MSG,
                   ERR-TXT-LGTH.

    IF RETURN-CODE IS EQUAL TO ZERO

       PERFORM P9999-DISP-ERR
          VARYING ERR-NDX FROM 1 BY 1
          UNTIL ERR-NDX > 12

    ELSE
       DISPLAY 'DSNTIAR ERROR CODE = ' RETURN-CODE
       STOP RUN.

P9999-DISP-ERR.

    DISPLAY ERR-MSG-TXT(ERR-NDX).

P9999-DISP-ERR-EXIT.
```

The PLI version of this program is here.

```
PLIEMP5: PROCEDURE OPTIONS(MAIN) REORDER;
/********************************************************************
* PROGRAM NAME :  PLIEMP5 - PROGRAM USING DB2 SELECT WITH ERROR    *
*                           TO DEMONSTRATE COMMON ERROR ROUTINE.   *
********************************************************************/


/********************************************************************
*                E X T E R N A L   E N T R I E S                   *
********************************************************************/

   DCL DSNTIAR ENTRY OPTIONS(ASM INTER RETCODE);
```

```
/********************************************************************
*               W O R K I N G   S T O R A G E                      *
********************************************************************/

  DCL HV_ID            FIXED BIN (31) INIT (0);
  DCL HV_LAST_NAME     CHAR(30) INIT (' ');
  DCL HV_FIRST_NAME    CHAR(20) INIT (' ');
  DCL HV_SERVICE_YEARS FIXED BIN (31) INIT (0);
  DCL HV_PROMOTION_DATE CHAR(10) INIT (' ');

  DCL 01 ERR_REC,
        05 FILLER1           CHAR(10) INIT ('SQLCODE = '),
        05 SQLCODE_VIEW      PIC '-999',
        05 ERR_EMPID         FIXED BIN (31) INIT (0),
        05 FILLER2           CHAR(01) INIT (' '),
        05 ERR_TAB           CHAR(08) INIT (' '),
        05 ERR_PARA          CHAR(15) INIT (' ');

  DCL 01 ERR_MSG AUTOMATIC,
        05 ERR_LGTH          FIXED BIN (31) INIT (864),
        05 ERR_TXT(10)       CHAR(72);

  DCL ERR_TXT_LGTH           FIXED BIN (15) INIT (72);
  DCL ERR_NDX                FIXED BIN (31) INIT (0);


  EXEC SQL
    INCLUDE SQLCA;

  EXEC SQL
    INCLUDE EMPLOYEE;


/********************************************************************
/*              P R O G R A M   M A I N L I N E                     *
********************************************************************/

  PUT SKIP LIST ('SAMPLE PLI PROGRAM: COMMON ERROR ROUTINE');

        DCLEMPLOYEE = '';

    /* SELECT AN EMPLOYEE */

        EXEC SQL
           SELECT EMP_ID
           INTO :HV_ID
           FROM HRSCHEMA.EMPLOYEE
           WHERE EMP_ID >= 3217;


        IF SQLCODE ¬= 0 THEN
           DO;
              SQLCODE_VIEW = SQLCODE;
              ERR_TAB = 'EMPLOYEE';
              ERR_PARA = 'MAIN';
              ERR_EMPID = HV_ID;
              CALL P9999_SQL_ERROR;
           END;
```

```
P9999_SQL_ERROR: PROC;

    PUT SKIP LIST (ERR_REC);

    CALL DSNTIAR (SQLCA, ERR_MSG, ERR_TXT_LGTH);

    IF RETCODE = 0 THEN
        DO ERR_NDX = 1 TO 10;
            PUT SKIP DATA (ERR_TXT(ERR_NDX));
        END; /* DO */
    ELSE
        PUT SKIP LIST ('DSNTIAR ERROR CODE = ' || RETCODE);

    END P9999_SQL_ERROR;

    END PLIEMP5;
```

And here is the output:

```
SAMPLE PLI PROGRAM: COMMON ERROR ROUTINE
SQLCODE =              -811                              4175
MAIN
SQLCODE = -811    EMPLOYEE      MAIN            000000000
 DSNT408I SQLCODE = -811, ERROR:  THE RESULT OF AN EMBEDDED SELECT
          STATEMENT OR A SUBSELECT IN THE SET CLAUSE OF AN UPDATE
          STATEMENT IS A TABLE OF MORE THAN ONE ROW, OR THE RESULT OF A
          SUBQUERY OF A BASIC PREDICATE IS MORE THAN ONE VALUE
 DSNT418I SQLSTATE   = 21000 SQLSTATE RETURN CODE
 DSNT415I SQLERRP    = DSNXREMS SQL PROCEDURE DETECTING ERROR
 DSNT416I SQLERRD    = -140  0  0  -1  0  0 SQL DIAGNOSTIC INFORMATION
 DSNT416I SQLERRD    = X'FFFFFF74'  X'00000000'  X'00000000'
          X'FFFFFFFF'  X'00000000'  X'00000000' SQL DIAGNOSTIC
          INFORMATION
```

Dynamic versus Static SQL

Static SQL

Static SQL statements are embedded within an application program that is written in a traditional programming language such as COBOL or PL/I. The statement is prepared before the program is executed, and the executable statement persists after the program ends. You can use static SQL when you know before run time what SQL statements your application needs to use.

As a practical matter, when you use static SQL you cannot change the form of SQL statements unless you make changes to the program and recompile and bind it. However, you can increase the flexibility of those statements by using host variables. So for example you could write an SQL that retrieves employee information for all employees with X years of service where the X becomes a host variable that you load at run time. Using static SQL and host variables is more secure than using dynamic SQL.

178

Dynamic SQL

Unlike static SQL which is prepared before the program runs, with dynamic SQL DB2 prepares and executes the SQL statements at run time as part of the program's execution. Dynamic SQL is a good choice when you do not know the format of an SQL statement before you write or run a program. An example might be a user interface that allows a web application to submit SQL statements to a background COBOL program for execution. In this case, you wouldn't know the structure of the statement the client submits until run time.

Applications that use dynamic SQL create an SQL statement in the form of a character string. A typical dynamic SQL application takes the following steps:

1. Translates the input data into an SQL statement.
2. Prepares the SQL statement to execute and acquires a description of the result table (if any).
3. Obtains, for SELECT statements, enough main storage to contain retrieved data.
4. Executes the statement or fetches the rows of data.
5. Processes the returned information.
6. Handles SQL return codes.

Performance Comparison of Static versus Dynamic SQL

Ordinarily static SQL is more efficient than dynamic because the former is prepared and optimized before the program executes. For static SQL statements DB2 typically determines the access path when you bind the plan or package - the exception being if you code REOPT(ALWAYS) in your bind statement. If you code REOPT(ALWAYS) on a package that has static SQL, DB2 will determine the access path when you bind the plan or package and again at run time using the values of host variables and parameter markers (if included).

For dynamic SQL statements, DB2 determines the access path at run time, when the statement is prepared. The cost of preparing a dynamic statement many times can lead to less than optimal performance. If you encounter this, you can try caching dynamic statements. Ask the system admin to set the subsystem parameter CACHEDYN=YES. Another way of accomplishing this is to bind your package with REOPT(ALWAYS) so that you always re-optimize a statement at execution time.

To conclude this section, you generally want to use static SQL when you know the structure of your SQL statement and when performance is a significant goal. Use dynamic SQL when you need the flexibility of not knowing the structure of your SQL until run time.

Program Preparation

Before a DB2 program can be run, it must be prepared. Depending on what type of application it is, the programs may need to be pre-compiled, compiled, link-edited and bound. Let's consider each of these steps.

Precompile

Embedded SQL programs (those for which the SQL is embedded in an application program such as COBOL or PL/I) must be precompiled using either the DB2 precompiler or the DB2 coprocessor. The reason is the language compilers such as COBOL do not recognize SQL statements. The precompiler does two things:

1. It translates the SQL statements into something that can be compiled.
2. It outputs a DBRM (database request module) which is a file that includes all the SQL statements and is used to communicate with DB2.

Compile, link-edit

The program must also be compiled and link-edited to produce an executable load module. DB2 keeps track of the timestamp on the executable module and the timestamp on the DBRM module and these must match or you will receive a -805 SQL error.

Bind

After the precompile, the DBRM must be bound to a package. A package is a compiled version of a DBRM and so it includes the executable versions of SQL statements. You can also specify a collection name when you bind a package. A collection is a group of related packages. Here is a sample BIND PACKAGE statement:

```
BIND PACKAGE(LOCRGNA.HRSCHEMA) -
MEMBER(COBEMP6)        -
OWNER(HRSCHEMA)         -
QUALIFIER(HRSCHEMA)     -
ACTION(REPLACE)        -
CURRENTDATA(NO)        -
EXPLAIN(NO)            -
ISOLATION(CS)          -
VALIDATE  (BIND)       -
RELEASE   (COMMIT)
```

Packages themselves are not executable without being added to a DB2 plan. Here is a sample BIND PLAN statement:

```
BIND   PLAN       (COBEMP6 ) -
       PKLIST     (HRSCHEMA.COBEMP6 ) -
       ACTION     (REP)        -
       ISOLATION  (CS)         -
       EXPLAIN    (YES)        -
       VALIDATE   (BIND)       -
       RELEASE    (COMMIT)     -
       OWNER      (HRSCHEMA)   -
       QUALIFIER  (HRSCHEMA)
```

Non-Embedded SQL Applications

Some application types do not require the precompile, compile/link-edit and bind steps.

1. REXX procedures are interpreted (not compiled) so they do not need to be precompiled, compiled/link-edited and bound.

2. ODBC applications use dynamic SQL only, so they do not require precompile.

3. Java applications containing only JDBC do not need precompile or binding. However Java applications using the SQLJ interface use embedded SQL and they need precompile and bind steps.

Chapter Five Questions

1. Assume you are doing a multi-row INSERT and have specified `NOT ATOMIC CONTINUE ON SQLEXCEPTION`. On the INSERT of one of the rows, a -803 is returned. What will the result be for this transaction?

    a. The row causing the -803 will not be inserted, and the other inserted rows will be backed out.

    b. The rows are all inserted but the row causing the -803 is also placed in an error table.

    c. The rows up until the -803 are all inserted but none after that and the program will continue with the next statement.

    d. The row causing the -803 will not be inserted but the other rows will be inserted.

2. Which of the following will generate DB2 SQL data structures for a table or view that can be used in a PLI or COBOL program?

    a. DECLARE

    b. INCLUDE

    c. DCLGEN

    d. None of the above.

3. As part of the program preparation process, SQL in a program must be pre-processed. Which of the following CANNOT be used to accomplish the SQL pre-processing to prepare a program for execution?

    a. DB2 Precompiler.

    b. DB2 Bind Package.

    c. DB2 Coprocessor.

    d. All of the above are valid for doing SQL preprocessing of an application program.

4. Assuming you are using a DB2 precompiler, which of the following orders the DB2 program preparation steps correctly?

    a. Precompile SQL, Bind Package, Bind Plan.

    b. Precompile SQL, Bind Plan, Bind Package.

    c. Bind Package, Precompile SQL, Bind Plan.

    d. Bind Plan, Precompile SQL, Bind Package.

5. Assume you have a COBOL DB2 program and you have defined an error message area as follows:

```
ERR-MSG.
02  ERR-LEN    PIC S9(4)  COMP VALUE +1320.
ERR-TEXT  PIC X(132) OCCURS 10 TIMES
INDEXED BY ERR-INDEX.
77  ERR-TEXT-LEN     PIC S9(9)  COMP VALUE +132.
```

What is the correct syntax to use DSNTIAR to retrieve an error message after an SQL statement?

    a. CALL 'DSNTIAR' USING ERR-MSG ERR-TEXT-LEN SQLCA.

    b. CALL 'DSNTIAR' USING SQLCA ERR-TEXT-LEN ERR-MSG.

    c. CALL 'DSNTIAR' USING SQLCA ERR-MSG ERR-TEXT-LEN.

    d. All of the above are invalid and will fail.

6. If you want to still reference data using a cursor after you issue a COMMIT, which clause would you use when you declare the cursor?

    a. WITH HOLD

    b. WITH RETAIN

    c. WITH STAY

    d. WITH REOPEN

Chapter Five Exercises

1. Write a program that creates a cursor to select all employees who have 5 years or more of service from the HRSCHEMA.EMPLOYEE table. Include logic to fetch any rows that are returned. Display the employee number, last name and first name of these employees.

2. Write a program that tries to insert a record that already exists into the HRSCHEMA.EMPLOYEE table. Your program should capture the error, and your error routine should detail the cause of the error.

CHAPTER SIX: DATA CONCURRENCY

Isolation Levels & Bind Release Options

Isolation level means the degree to which a DB2 application's activities are isolated from the operations of other DB2 applications. The isolation level for a package is specified when the package is bound, although you can override the package isolation level in an SQL statement. There are four isolation levels: Repeatable Read, Read Stability, Cursor Stability and Uncommitted Read.

ISOLATIONS LEVELS

Repeatable Read (RR)
Repeatable Read ensures that a query issued multiple times within the same unit of work will produce the exact same results. It does this by locking all rows that could affect the result. It does not permit any adds/changes/deletes to the table that could affect the result.

Read Stability (RS)
Read Stability locks for the duration of the transaction those rows that are returned by a query, but it allows additional rows to be added to the table.

Cursor Stability (CS)
Cursor Stability only locks the row that the cursor is placed on (and any rows it has updated during the unit of work). This is the default isolation level if no other is specified.

Uncommitted Read (UR)
Uncommitted Read permits reading of uncommitted changes which may never be applied to the database. It does not lock any rows at all unless the row(s) is updated during the unit of work.

An IBM recommended best practice prefers isolation levels in this order:

1. Cursor stability (CS)
2. Uncommitted read (UR)
3. Read stability (RS)
4. Repeatable read (RR)

Of course the chosen isolation level depends on the scenario. We'll look at specific scenarios now.

Isolation Levels for Specific Situations

When your environment is basically read-only (such as with data warehouse environments), use UR (UNCOMMITTED READ) because it incurs the least overhead.

If you want to maximize data concurrency without seeing uncommitted data, use the CS (CURSOR STABILITY) isolation level. CS only locks the row where the cursor is placed (and any other rows which have been changed since the last commit point), thus maximizing concurrency compared to RR or RS.

If you want no existing rows that were retrieved to be changed by other processes during your unit of work, but you don't mind if new rows are inserted, use RS (READ STABILITY).

Finally if you must lock all rows that satisfy the query and also not permit any new rows to be added that could change the result of the query, use RR (REPEATABLE READ).

Based on the above, if we wanted to order the isolation levels from most to least impact on performance, the order would be:

1. REPEATABLE READ (RR)
2. READ STABILITY (RS)
3. CURSOR STABILITY (CS)
4. UNCOMMITTED READ (UR)

Finally, in DB2 11 there is a SKIP LOCKED DATA clause for the SELECT statement that allows it to bypass any rows that are current locked by other applications. For example:

```
SELECT *
FROM HRSCHEMA.EMP_PAY
SKIP LOCKED DATA;
```

To use SKIP LOCKED DATA the application must use either cursor stability (CS) or read stability (RS) isolation level. The SKIP LOCKED DATA clause is ignored if the isolation level is uncommitted read (UR) or repeatable read (RR).

How to Specify/Override Isolation Level

To specify an isolation level at bind time, use the ISOLATION keyword with the abbreviated form of the isolation level you want. For example:

```
ISOLATION(CS)
```

If you want to override an isolation level in a query, specify the override at the end of the query by using the WITH <isolation level abbreviation> clause. For example, to override the default isolation level of CS to use UR instead on a query, code the following and notice we've used WITH UR at the end of the query:

```
SELECT EMP_ID,
EMP_LAST_NAME,
EMP_FIRST_NAME
FROM EMPLOYEE
ORDER BY EMP_ID
WITH UR;
```

Bind Release Options

The RELEASE bind option determines when any acquired locks are released. The two options are DEALLOCATE and COMMIT. Specifying RELEASE(DEALLOCATE) means the acquired locks will be released when the application session ends. Specifying RELEASE(COMMIT) means locks are released at a commit point. Under TSO this means when a DB2 COMMIT statement is issued. Under IMS a commit occurs when a CHKP or SYNC IMS call is issued. Under CICS a commit occurs when a SYNCPOINT is issued.

As a practical matter, the best concurrency is achieved by using RELEASE(COMMIT) because locks are generally released sooner than the end of the application. However, assuming the program commits frequently, this will result in more processing time than if using RELEASE(DEALLOCATE). So you must weigh your objectives and decide accordingly.

Note: The RELEASE option is only applicable to static SQL statements, i.e., those bound before your program runs. Dynamic SQL statements release the locks at the next commit point.

COMMIT, ROLLBACK, and SAVEPOINTS

Central to understanding transaction management is the concept of a unit of work. A unit of work begins when a program is initiated. Multiple adds, changes and deletes may then take place during the same unit of work. The changes are not made permanent until a commit point is reached. A unit of work ends in one of three ways:

1. When a commit is issued.
2. When a rollback is issued.
3. When the program ends.

Let's look at each of these.

COMMIT

The COMMIT statement ends a transaction and makes the changes permanent and visible to other processes. Also, when a program ends, there is an implicit COMMIT. This is important to know; however an IBM recommended best practice is to do an explicit COMMIT at the end of the program.

Here are some other points about COMMIT to know and remember:

1. The DB2 COMMIT statement does not work in an IMS/DB2 or CICS/DB2 program because in those cases transaction management is performed by the IMS and CICS transaction managers. You won't receive an error for issuing the COMMIT statement, it simply will not work.

2. For an IMS/DB2 program, an IMS CHKP call causes a commit of both DB2 and IMS changes made during the unit of work. For CICS, an EXEC CICS SYNCPOINT call is made to commit DB2 data.

3. Autonomous procedures were introduced in DB2 11; these procedures run with their own units of work, separate from the calling program.

ROLLBACK

A ROLLBACK statement ends a transaction without making changes permanent – the changes are simply discarded. This is done either intentionally by the application when it determines there is a reason to ROLLBACK the changes and it issues a ROLLBACK explicitly, or because the system traps an error that requires it to do a ROLLBACK of changes. In both cases, the rolled back changes are those that have been made since the last COMMIT point. If no COMMITs have been issued, then all changes made in the session are rolled back.

You can also issue a ROLLBACK TO <savepoint> if you are using SAVEPOINTs. We'll take a look at that shortly.

Here are some other points about ROLLBACK to know and remember:

1. The abend of a process causes an implicit ROLLBACK.

2. Global variable contents are not affected by ROLLBACK.

SAVEPOINT

The SAVEPOINT statement creates a point within a unit of recovery to which you can roll back changes. This is similar to using ROLLBACK to back out changes since the last COMMIT point, except a SAVEPOINT gives you even more control because it allows a partial ROLLBACK between COMMIT points.

You might wonder what the point is of using a SAVEPOINT. Let's take an example. Suppose you have a program that does INSERT statements and you program logic to COMMIT every 500 inserts. If you issue a ROLLBACK, then all updates since the last COMMIT will be backed out. That's pretty straightforward.

But suppose you are updating information for vendors from a file of updates that is sorted by vendor, and if there is an error you want to roll back to where you started updating records for that vendor. And you want all other updates since the last COMMIT point to be applied to the database. This is different than rolling back to the last COMMIT point, and you can do it by setting a new savepoint each time the vendor changes. Issuing a SAVEPOINT enables you to execute several SQL statements as a single executable block between COMMIT statements. You can then undo changes back out to that savepoint by issuing a ROLLBACK TO SAVEPOINT statement.

Example

Let's do a simple example. First, create a new table and then add some records to the table. We'll create a copy of EMP_PAY.

```
CREATE TABLE HRSCHEMA.EMP_PAY_X
LIKE HRSCHEMA.EMP_PAY
IN TSHR;
```

Now let's add some records. We'll add one record, then create a SAVEPOINTT, add another record and then roll back to the SAVEPOINT. This should leave us with only the first record in the table.

```
INSERT INTO EMP_PAY_X
VALUES(1111,
45000.00,
1200.00);

SAVEPOINT A ON ROLLBACK RETAIN CURSORS;

INSERT INTO EMP_PAY_X
VALUES(2222,
55000.00,
1500.00);
```

```
ROLLBACK TO SAVEPOINT A;
```

We can verify that only the first record was added to the table:

```
SELECT * FROM HRSCHEMA.EMP_PAY_X;
---------+---------+---------+---------+---------+----
    EMP_ID  EMP_REGULAR_PAY  EMP_BONUS_PAY
---------+---------+---------+---------+---------+----
      1111          45000.00         1200.00
```

If you have multiple SAVEPOINTs and you ROLLBACK to one of them, then the ROLLBACK will include updates made after any later SAVEPOINTs. Let's illustrate this with an example. We'll set three SAVEPOINTs: A, B and C. We'll add a record, then issue savepoint and we'll do this three times. Then we'll ROLLBACK to the first SAVEPOINT which is A. What we're saying is that any updates made after A will be backed out, which includes the INSERTS made after SAVEPOINTs B and C. Let's try this:

```
INSERT INTO EMP_PAY_X
VALUES(2222,
55000.00,
1500.00);

SAVEPOINT A ON ROLLBACK RETAIN CURSORS;

INSERT INTO EMP_PAY_X
VALUES(3333,
65000.00,
2500.00);

SAVEPOINT B ON ROLLBACK RETAIN CURSORS;

INSERT INTO EMP_PAY_X
VALUES(4444,
75000.00,
2000.00);

SAVEPOINT C ON ROLLBACK RETAIN CURSORS;

ROLLBACK TO SAVEPOINT A;


SELECT * FROM HRSCHEMA.EMP_PAY_X;
---------+---------+---------+---------+---------
    EMP_ID  EMP_REGULAR_PAY  EMP_BONUS_PAY
---------+---------+---------+---------+---------
      1111          45000.00         1200.00
      2222          55000.00         1500.00
DSNE610I NUMBER OF ROWS DISPLAYED IS 2
```

190

Now as you can see, only the first record (2222) was inserted because we specified ROLLBACK all the way to SAVEPOINT A. Note that the 1111 record was already in the table. Here are a few more considerations for using SAVEPOINTs.

If you want to prevent a SAVEPOINT from being reused during the same unit of work, include the UNIQUE keyword when you define it.

When you issue a rollback, if you want to retain cursors, you must specify ON ROLLBACK RETAIN CURSORS. Similarly, if you want to retain any locks, you must specify ON ROLLBACK RETAIN LOCKS.

Units of Work

A unit of work is a set of database operations in an application that is ended by a commit, a rollback or the end of the application process. A commit or rollback operation applies only to the set of changes made within that unit of work. An application process can involve one or many units of work.

Once a commit action occurs, the database changes are permanent and visible to other application processes. Any locks obtained by the application process are held until the end of the unit of work. So if you update 10 records within one unit of work, the records are all locked until a commit point.

As explained elsewhere, in distributed environments where you update data stores on more than one system, a two-phase commit is performed. The two phase commit ensures that data is consistent between the two systems by either fully committing or fully rolling back the unit of work. The two phase commit consists of a commit-request phase and an actual commit phase.

Autonomous Transactions

Autonomous Transactions Basics

Autonomous transactions are native SQL procedures which run with their own units of work, separate from the calling program. If a calling program issues a ROLLBACK to back out its changes, the committed changes of the autonomous procedure are not affected.

You can call an autonomous procedures from application programs, other stored procedures, user-defined functions or triggers. Autonomous procedures can also invoke triggers, perform SQL statements, and execute commit and rollback statements.

Restrictions

There are some restrictions on use of an autonomous procedure. The only kind of procedure that can function as an autonomous procedure is a native SQL procedure. An autonomous procedure cannot call another autonomous procedure. Also, since autonomous procedures commit work separately from the calling program or procedure, the autonomous procedure cannot see uncommitted changes in that calling program or procedure.

Here's one other limitation to be aware of. Since autonomous procedures do not share locks with the calling program or procedure, it is possible to have lock contention between these entities. The developer must consider carefully what type of work is involved and understand the possible results if both the calling and called entity are doing updates on the same data.

Applications

Autonomous procedures are useful for logging information about error conditions encountered by an application program. Similarly they can be used for creating an audit trail of activity for transactions.

Checkpoint/Restart Processing

This section concerns the commit, rollback and recovery of an application or application program. We already covered the use of COMMIT, ROLLBACK and SAVEPOINTs in prior subsections. Here we'll apply the COMMIT and ROLLBACK in a DB2 program.

DB2 Program

For the DB2 program, we use the COMMIT statement at appropriate intervals. Let's use our update COBOL program and employ both the COMMIT and the ROLLBACK options. Let's say that we'll commit every 5 records. So we set up a commit counter called COMMIT-CTR and we'll increment it each time we update a record. Once the counter reaches 5 updates, we'll issue a COMMIT statement and reset our record counter to zero. If we perform an update that fails, we'll issue a ROLLBACK.

Note that we also added our generic SQL error handling routine. This will simplify our problem determination in case we encounter an error. Note that you must define the cursor WITH HOLD in order to keep it open when using COMMIT. Otherwise the COMMIT will close the cursor.

```
        IDENTIFICATION DIVISION.
        PROGRAM-ID. COBEMPC.

 ********************************************************
 *        PROGRAM DEMONSTRATING USE OF COMMIT AND      *
 *        ROLLBACK PROCESSING.                         *
```

```
*********************************************************

ENVIRONMENT DIVISION.
DATA DIVISION.
WORKING-STORAGE SECTION.

    EXEC SQL
      INCLUDE SQLCA
    END-EXEC.

    EXEC SQL
      INCLUDE EMPLOYEE
    END-EXEC.

    EXEC SQL
        DECLARE EMP-CURSOR CURSOR WITH HOLD FOR
        SELECT EMP_ID, EMP_LAST_NAME
        FROM HRSCHEMA.EMPLOYEE
        WHERE EMP_LAST_NAME <> UPPER(EMP_LAST_NAME)
        FOR UPDATE OF EMP_LAST_NAME
    END-EXEC.

01 COMMIT-CTR    PIC S9(9) USAGE COMP  VALUE 0.

01 ERR-REC.
   05 FILLER            PIC X(10) VALUE 'SQLCODE = '.
   05 SQLCODE-VIEW      PIC -999.
   05 FILLER            PIC X(005) VALUE SPACES.
   05 ERR-TAB           PIC X(016).
   05 ERR-PARA          PIC X(015).
   05 ERR-DETAIL        PIC X(040).

77 ERR-TXT-LGTH        PIC S9(9) USAGE COMP VALUE +72.

01 ERR-MSG.
   05 ERR-MSG-LGTH      PIC S9(04) COMP VALUE +864.
   05 ERR-MSG-TXT       PIC X(072) OCCURS 12 TIMES
                                   INDEXED BY ERR-NDX.

PROCEDURE DIVISION.

MAIN-PARA.
    DISPLAY "SAMPLE COBOL PROGRAM: UPDATE USING CURSOR".

    EXEC SQL
        OPEN EMP-CURSOR
    END-EXEC.

    IF SQLCODE NOT EQUAL 0
       PERFORM P9999-SQL-ERROR

    DISPLAY 'OPEN CURSOR SQLCODE: ' SQLCODE.
```

```
        PERFORM FETCH-CURSOR
          UNTIL SQLCODE NOT EQUAL 0.

        EXEC SQL
            CLOSE EMP-CURSOR
        END-EXEC.

        IF SQLCODE NOT EQUAL 0
           PERFORM P9999-SQL-ERROR

        DISPLAY 'CLOSE CURSOR SQLCODE: ' SQLCODE.

        STOP RUN.

    FETCH-CURSOR.

        EXEC SQL
            FETCH EMP-CURSOR INTO :EMP-ID, :EMP-LAST-NAME
        END-EXEC.

        IF SQLCODE = 0
           DISPLAY 'BEFORE CHANGE  ', EMP-LAST-NAME
           MOVE FUNCTION UPPER-CASE (EMP-LAST-NAME)
              TO EMP-LAST-NAME
           EXEC SQL
              UPDATE HRSCHEMA.EMPLOYEE
              SET EMP_LAST_NAME = :EMP-LAST-NAME
              WHERE CURRENT OF EMP-CURSOR
           END-EXEC

        END-IF.

        IF SQLCODE = 0
           DISPLAY 'AFTER CHANGE   ', EMP-LAST-NAME
           ADD +1 TO COMMIT-CTR
           IF COMMIT-CTR >= 5
              EXEC SQL
                  COMMIT
              END-EXEC
              MOVE ZERO TO COMMIT-CTR
           ELSE
              NEXT SENTENCE
           END-IF
        ELSE
           PERFORM P9999-SQL-ERROR
           EXEC SQL
              ROLLBACK
           END-EXEC
           GOBACK
        END-IF.

    P9999-SQL-ERROR.
```

```
        DISPLAY ERR-REC.

    CALL 'DSNTIAR' USING SQLCA,
                   ERR-MSG,
                   ERR-TXT-LGTH.

    IF RETURN-CODE IS EQUAL TO ZERO

       PERFORM P9999-DISP-ERR
          VARYING ERR-NDX FROM 1 BY 1
          UNTIL ERR-NDX > 12

    ELSE
       DISPLAY 'DSNTIAR ERROR CODE = ' RETURN-CODE
       STOP RUN.

P9999-DISP-ERR.

    DISPLAY ERR-MSG-TXT(ERR-NDX).

P9999-DISP-ERR-EXIT.
```

Here is the PLI version of the program.

```
    PLIEMPC: PROCEDURE OPTIONS(MAIN) REORDER;

/*********************************************************************
* PROGRAM NAME :   PLIEMPC - PROGRAM DEMONSTRATING USE OF          *
*                            COMMIT AND ROLLBACK PROCESSING.       *
*********************************************************************/

/*********************************************************************
*              E X T E R N A L   E N T R I E S                     *
*********************************************************************/

    DCL DSNTIAR ENTRY OPTIONS(ASM INTER RETCODE);

/*********************************************************************
/*             W O R K I N G   S T O R A G E                       *
*********************************************************************/

    DCL COMMIT_CTR              FIXED BIN(31) INIT(0);
    DCL RET_SQL_CODE            FIXED BIN(31) INIT(0);
    DCL RET_SQL_CODE_PIC        PIC 'S999999999' INIT (0);

    DCL 01 ERR_REC,
          05 FILLER1            CHAR(10) INIT ('SQLCODE = '),
          05 SQLCODE_VIEW       PIC '-999',
          05 ERR_EMPID          FIXED BIN (31) INIT (0),
          05 FILLER2            CHAR(01) INIT (' '),
          05 ERR_TAB            CHAR(08) INIT (' '),
```

```
           05 ERR_PARA             CHAR(15) INIT (' ');

     DCL 01 ERR_MSG AUTOMATIC,
           05 ERR_LGTH             FIXED BIN (31) INIT (864),
           05 ERR_TXT(10)          CHAR(72);

     DCL ERR_TXT_LGTH              FIXED BIN (15) INIT (72);
     DCL ERR_NDX                   FIXED BIN (31) INIT (0);


     EXEC SQL
       INCLUDE SQLCA;

     EXEC SQL
       INCLUDE EMPLOYEE;

     EXEC SQL
        DECLARE EMP_CURSOR CURSOR WITH HOLD FOR
        SELECT EMP_ID, EMP_LAST_NAME
        FROM HRSCHEMA.EMPLOYEE
        WHERE EMP_LAST_NAME <> UPPER(EMP_LAST_NAME)
        FOR UPDATE OF EMP_LAST_NAME;

/*******************************************************************
/*              P R O G R A M   M A I N L I N E                *
*******************************************************************/

     PUT SKIP LIST ('SAMPLE PLI PROGRAM: UPDATE USING CURSOR');

     EXEC SQL OPEN EMP_CURSOR;

     PUT SKIP LIST ('OPEN CURSOR SQLCODE: ' || SQLCODE);

     IF SQLCODE = 0 THEN
        DO UNTIL (SQLCODE ¬= 0);
           CALL P0100_FETCH_CURSOR;
        END;
     ELSE
        CALL P9999_SQL_ERROR;

     EXEC SQL CLOSE EMP_CURSOR;

     PUT SKIP LIST ('CLOSE CURSOR SQLCODE: ' || SQLCODE);

     IF SQLCODE ¬= 0 THEN
        DO;
           EXEC SQL
              GET DIAGNOSTICS CONDITION 1
              :RET_SQL_CODE  = DB2_RETURNED_SQLCODE;

           RET_SQL_CODE_PIC  = RET_SQL_CODE;
           PUT SKIP LIST (RET_SQL_CODE_PIC);
        END;
```

```
P0100_FETCH_CURSOR: PROC;

    DCLEMPLOYEE = '';

    EXEC SQL
        FETCH EMP_CURSOR INTO :EMP_ID, :EMP_LAST_NAME;

    IF SQLCODE = 0 THEN
        DO;
            PUT SKIP LIST ('BEFORE CHANGE  ' || EMP_LAST_NAME);
            EMP_LAST_NAME = UPPERCASE(EMP_LAST_NAME);
            EXEC SQL
                UPDATE HRSCHEMA.EMPLOYEE
                SET EMP_LAST_NAME = :EMP_LAST_NAME
                WHERE CURRENT OF EMP_CURSOR;

            IF SQLCODE = 0 THEN
                DO;
                    PUT SKIP LIST ('AFTER CHANGE  ' || EMP_LAST_NAME);
                    COMMIT_CTR = COMMIT_CTR + 1;
                    IF COMMIT_CTR >= 5 THEN
                        DO;
                            EXEC SQL COMMIT;
                            COMMIT_CTR = 0;
                        END;
                END;
            ELSE
                DO;
                    CALL P9999_SQL_ERROR;
                    EXEC SQL ROLLBACK;
                END;
        END;

    ELSE
        IF SQLCODE = +100 THEN
            PUT SKIP LIST ('*** NO MORE RECORDS TO PROCESS!!');
        ELSE
            CALL P9999_SQL_ERROR;

END P0100_FETCH_CURSOR;

P9999_SQL_ERROR: PROC;

    PUT SKIP LIST (ERR_REC);

    CALL DSNTIAR (SQLCA, ERR_MSG, ERR_TXT_LGTH);

    IF RETCODE = 0 THEN
        DO ERR_NDX = 1 TO 10;
            PUT SKIP DATA (ERR_TXT(ERR_NDX));
        END; /* DO */
    ELSE
```

```
              PUT SKIP LIST ('DSNTIAR ERROR CODE = ' || RETCODE);

        END P9999_SQL_ERROR;

        END PLIEMPC;
```

IMS Program

For the IMS program, you must issue the IMS CHKP call to commit both IMS and DB2 data. IMS programming is beyond the scope of this exam, but you do need to know a few things about use of the DB2 COMMIT statement in an IMS program:

1. In an IMS program, the DB2 COMMIT statement will not commit DB2 changes.

2. IMS/DB2 will not tell you that your DB2 COMMIT statement didn't work – it will not generate an error, the COMMIT statement will simply have no effect. You must use the IMS CHKP statement to commit both IMS and DB2 data.

3. Similarly, if you want to back out uncommitted DB2 changes, the ROLLBACK statement will not work. You must use the IMS ROLL or ROLB statements.

4. ROLB means that any changes are backed out to the last checkpoint, and then control is returned to the calling program which can continue processing. ROLL means that any changes are backed out to the last checkpoint, and then the program is terminated with abend code U0778.

Chapter Six Questions

1. To end a transaction without making the changes permanent, which DB2 statement should be issued?

    a. COMMIT

    b. BACKOUT

    c. ROLLBACK

    d. NO CHANGE

2. If you want to maximize data concurrency without seeing uncommitted data, which isolation level should you use?

    a. RR

    b. UR

    c. RS

    d. CS

3. Assume you have a long running process and you want to commit results after processing every 500 records, but still want the ability to undo any work that has taken place after the commit point. One mechanism that would allow you to do this is to issue a:

    a. SAVEPOINT

    b. COMMITPOINT

    c. BACKOUT

    d. None of the above

4. A procedure that commits transactions independent of the calling procedure is known as a/an:

    a. External procedure.

    b. SQL procedure.

    c. Autonomous procedure.

    d. Independent procedure.

5. To end a transaction and make the changes visible to other processes, which statement should be issued?

    a. ROLLBACK

    b. COMMIT

    c. APPLY

    d. CALL

6. Order the isolation levels, from greatest to least impact on performance.

    a. RR, RS, CS, UR

    b. UR, RR, RS, CS

    c. CS, UR, RR, RS

    d. RS, CS, UR, RR

7. Which isolation level is most appropriate when few or no updates are expected to a table?

    a. RR

    b. RS

    c. CS

    d. UR

8. In an IMS program that makes updates to DB2 tables, what call is required to make data changes permanent?

     a.   COMMIT

     b.   CHKP

     c.   UPDATE

     d.   REPL

Chapter Six Exercises

1. Code the concurrency bind option/value that ensures that no records which have been retrieved during a unit of work can be changed by other processes until the unit of work completes. However, it is ok for new records to be added to the table.

2. Write the COBOL code to end a unit of work and make the changes visible to other processes.

3. Write the COBOL code to end a unit of work and discard any updates that have been made since the last commit point.

CHAPTER SEVEN: TESTING & VALIDATING RESULTS

You obviously need to test and validate results for new and modified applications. This section is both a reminder to perform structured testing and some hints for how to go about it. If you have been an application developer for very long, most or all of this will not be new to you. Still, this is basic training and these are vitally important principles that must be followed to ensure high quality testing and validation.

Test Structures
You normally have a test environment which is typically a separate instance of DB2 and is used primarily or exclusively for testing. You or your DBA will create test objects (tables, indexes, views) in the test environment. The DDL is usually saved and then modified as necessary to recreate the same object in another DB2 instance, or to drop and create a new version in the same instance.

If you do both production support and new development activities in the same test environment (not recommended but it's the case in many shops), it is important to have a strategy for dealing with these work flows so they don't impact each other. For example if you add a column to a table in your test system and change a copybook, that may be fine for the development work. But if someone else is changing the same program (that obviously uses the same copybook) to resolve a production problem, they may inadvertently move something incorrect to production. So coordination is necessary and essential when sharing a test environment.

Test Data
It is vital to know the business rules of the application so that you select a robust set of test data for your application. To test successfully, all branches of your program or package must be tested, and then all components must be tested together (integration testing). It is especially important that in addition to testing new code and SQL, you also perform regression testing on existing code. Take the time to develop a good structured, comprehensive test plan that can be reused many times.

You can create brand new test data, or you can extract data from production and load it to test, or you can do both. Here are a few basic methods for loading test data.

1. Create the data in a flat file and write an application program to load it using INSERT statements.

2. Extract the data from production using a utility such as `DSNTIAUL`, then load it using an application program as in method 1.

3. Use the DB2 UNLOAD and LOAD utilities to extract data from production and load to test.

We'll go over details for this later in this section.

Testing SQL Statements

Before coding SQL statements in an application program, you should test them using SPUFI. If you have been using DB2 for z/OS for any length of time you are probably familiar with SPUFI. If you are not familiar, here is a sample query executed from SPUFI.

From the ISPF main menu select the DB2 option.

```
   Menu   Utilities   Compilers   Options   Status   Help
 _____
                        ISPF Primary Option Menu
 Option ===>

 0   Settings      Terminal and user parameters       User ID . : HRDEV1
 1   View          Display source data or listings     Time. . . : 21:19
 2   Edit          Create or change source data        Terminal. : 3278
 3   Utilities     Perform utility functions           Screen. . : 1
 4   Foreground    Interactive language processing     Language. : ENGLISH
 5   Batch         Submit job for language processing  Appl ID . : ISR
 6   Command       Enter TSO or Workstation commands   TSO logon : MATPROC
 7   Dialog Test   Perform dialog testing              TSO prefix: HRDEV1
 10  SCLM          SW Configuration Library Manager    System ID : MATE
 11  Workplace     ISPF Object/Action Workplace        MVS acct. : MT529
 12  DITTO         DITTO/ESA for MVS                   Release . : ISPF 6.0
 13  FMN           File Manager
 15  DB2           DB2 Primary Menu
 17  QMF           DB2 Query Management Facility
 S   SDSF          Spool Search and Display Facility

         Enter X to Terminate using log/list defaults
```

204

From the DB2 Interactive Primary Option menu, select option 1 (SPUFI).

```
                              DB2I PRIMARY OPTION MENU          SSID: DBAX
COMMAND ===>

Select one of the following DB2 functions and press ENTER.

    1  SPUFI                (Process SQL statements)
    2  DCLGEN               (Generate SQL and source language declarations)
    3  PROGRAM PREPARATION  (Prepare a DB2 application program to run)
    4  PRECOMPILE           (Invoke DB2 precompiler)
    5  BIND/REBIND/FREE     (BIND, REBIND, or FREE plans or packages)
    6  RUN                  (RUN an SQL program)
    7  DB2 COMMANDS         (Issue DB2 commands)
    8  UTILITIES            (Invoke DB2 utilities)
    D  DB2I DEFAULTS        (Set global parameters)
    Q  QMF                  (Query Management Facility
    X  EXIT                 (Leave DB2I)




    PRESS:                    END to exit      HELP for more information
```

Now enter the data set name where you will code and save your commands (DDL, DML or DCL), as well as the dataset to capture your output.

```
                         SPUFI                            SSID: DBAX
    ===>

    Enter the input data set name:        (Can be sequential or partitioned)
     1  DATA SET NAME ... ===> 'HRDEV1.SPUFI.CNTL(EXECSQL)'
     2  VOLUME SERIAL ... ===>          (Enter if not cataloged)
     3  DATA SET PASSWORD ===>          (Enter if password protected)

    Enter the output data set name:       (Must be a sequential data set)
     4  DATA SET NAME ... ===> 'HRDEV1.SPUFI.OUT'

    Specify processing options:
     5  CHANGE DEFAULTS   ===> NO       (Y/N - Display SPUFI defaults panel?)
     6  EDIT INPUT ...... ===> YES      (Y/N - Enter SQL statements?)
     7  EXECUTE ......... ===> YES      (Y/N - Execute SQL statements?)
     8  AUTOCOMMIT ...... ===> YES      (Y/N - Commit after successful run?)
     9  BROWSE OUTPUT ... ===> YES      (Y/N - Browse output data set?)

    For remote SQL processing:
    10  CONNECT LOCATION  ===>



    PRESS:  ENTER to process    END to exit          HELP for more information
```

205

When you press enter, you will be in EDIT mode with the input dataset you specified. In this case we will code a query to select all the EMPLOYEE records:

```
      File  Edit  Edit_Settings  Menu  Utilities  Compilers  Test  Help


 EDIT       HRDEV1.SPUFI.CNTL(EXECSQL) - 01.00          Columns 00001 00072
 Command ===>                                           Scroll ===> PAGE
 ****** **************************** Top of Data ****************************
 000001 SELECT * FROM EMPLOYEES;
 ****** *************************** Bottom of Data **************************
```

Press PF3 to save your code, then press ENTER to execute the query. Here are our results:

```
      Menu  Utilities  Compilers  Help


 BROWSE     HRDEV1.SPUFI.OUT                     Line 00000000 Col 001 080
 Command ===>                                           Scroll ===> PAGE
 ******************************* Top of Data *******************************
 ---------+---------+---------+---------+---------+---------+---------+-----
 SELECT * FROM EMPLOYEE;
 ---------+---------+---------+---------+---------+---------+---------+-----
      EMPNO   NAME
 ---------+---------+---------+---------+---------+---------+---------+-----
        100   SMITH
        200   JONES
 DSNE610I NUMBER OF ROWS DISPLAYED IS 2
 DSNE616I STATEMENT EXECUTION WAS SUCCESSFUL, SQLCODE IS 100
 ---------+---------+---------+---------+---------+---------+---------+---------+
 ---------+---------+---------+---------+---------+---------+---------+---------+
 DSNE617I COMMIT PERFORMED, SQLCODE IS 0
 DSNE616I STATEMENT EXECUTION WAS SUCCESSFUL, SQLCODE IS 0
 ---------+---------+---------+---------+---------+---------+---------+---------+
 DSNE601I SQL STATEMENTS ASSUMED TO BE BETWEEN COLUMNS 1 AND 72
 DSNE620I NUMBER OF SQL STATEMENTS PROCESSED IS 1
 DSNE621I NUMBER OF INPUT RECORDS READ IS 2
 DSNE622I NUMBER OF OUTPUT RECORDS WRITTEN IS 18
 ****************************** Bottom of Data *****************************
```

Debugging Programs

When you are getting unexpected results from your program, make sure to review these items from your compiler listing. I'd had many problems referred to me where the problem could clearly be found in the output, but the developer did not look closely enough.

Output from the precompiler – check for errors and warnings. Resolve any that appear. Sometimes a host variable will be undefined or improperly defined for the DB2 column you are trying to select into it. Suppose I specify host variable HV-ID in a select query but I forgot to actually define it? When that happens you will see something like this in the precompiler output:

```
DB2 SQL PRECOMPILER        MESSAGES
DSNH312I E     DSNHSMUD LINE 87 COL 21  UNDEFINED OR UNUSABLE HOST VARIABLE "HV-ID"
```

Output from the language compiler. If you receive any COBOL, PL/I or assembler errors or warnings, make sure to resolve them. These are typically the easiest to understand and correct because the compiler tells you the exact statement number and the error.

Suppose for example that I inadvertently defined a record counter variable REC-COUNT as PIC X(3). Then later in the program I try to increment it with the statement:

```
ADD +1 TO REC-COUNT.
```

This would cause the following compiler error:

```
PP 5655-S71 IBM Enterprise COBOL for z/OS  4.2.0              COBEMPZ   Date 0
LineID  Message code  Message text
  186  IGYPA3074-S   "REC-COUNT (ALPHANUMERIC)" was not numeric, but was a sender
in an arithmetic expression.  The statement was discarded.
```

Output from the linkage editor. If you are using standard compile JCL for your shop, linkage editor errors will be rare. However, do make sure you don't have any unresolved references. Suppose for example you are compiling the DB2 connection program DSNULI but in the linkage editor step it is misspelled as DSNULX. In this case you will get a linkage editor error as follows:

```
IEW2278I B352 INVOCATION PARAMETERS - MAP,XREF
IEW2322I 1220  1     INCLUDE SYSLIB(DSNULX)
IEW2303E 1030 MEMBER DSNULX OF THE DATA SET SPECIFIED BY SYSLIB COULD NOT BE FOUND.
```

Output from the bind process. Did you have any error messages? How about warning messages? Bind errors must be resolved or you will typically receive a -805 SQL code when you try to run the program. Here is a case where a bind is being attempted for a package that does not exist.

```
BIND   MEMBER   (COBEMPY)      PLAN      (COBEMPY)     ACTION   (REPLACE)
       VALIDATE  (BIND)            RELEASE  (COMMIT)     OWNER    (HRSCHEMA)
DSNT230I  -DBAX BIND DBRM-MEMBER-NAME ERROR
          USING HRSCHEMA AUTHORITY
          PLAN=COBEMPY
          MEMBER COBEMPY NOT FOUND IN PDS SEARCH ORDER
DSNT201I  -DBAX  BIND FOR PLAN COBEMPY  NOT SUCCESSFUL
```

In summary, when you encounter an error running a program, make sure you have thoroughly checked your outputs from the pre-compile, language compile, link-edit and bind steps. These almost always provide you with the information you need to diagnose the problem. Even if you end up asking for help, you should gather the available diagnostic information to show your colleague what you have looked at so far to resolve the problem.

Testing Connections and Stored Procedures

How to Set up a Data Source
Here are the basic instructions for how to set up a data source to use for testing.

.NET
For .NET you can set up a data source using any of three providers:

1. OLE DB
2. ODBC
3. IBM Data Server Provider for .NET

While you can use any of the three .NET providers above, IBM recommends using the IBM Data Server Provider for .NET.

OLE DB
A connection string sample for OLE DB written in C# for the HR database is as follows, as assume that :

```
OleDbConnection con = new OleDbConnection("Provider=IBMDADB2;" +
    "Data Source=DBHR;UID=HRUSER01;PWD=<your password>;" );
con.Open()
```

ODBC
The ODBC .NET provider uses the same connection parameters as the CLI interface (see example below under ODBC). Here is a sample connection in C# language for the HR database:

```
OdbcConnection con = new OdbcConnection("DSN=hrDSN;UID=HRUSER01;PWD=<your
password>;");
con.Open()
```

IBM Data Server Provider for .NET
To use the IBM Data Server Provider for .NET, you will need to create a connection string that includes the database and login credentials. Here is a sample connection string for the HR database.

```
String cs = "Database=DBHR;UID=HRUSER01;PWD=<your password>";
```

```
DB2Connection conn = new DB2Connection(connectString);
conn.Open();
return conn;
```

JAVA

For Java, you load the DB2 driver and then establish a connection using the get Connection method. Here is sample code to load the driver:

```java
try {
   // Load the IBM Data Server Driver for JDBC and SQLJ with DriverManager
   Class.forName("com.ibm.db2.jcc.DB2Driver");
} catch (ClassNotFoundException e) {
     e.printStackTrace();
}
```

And this code will establish the connection:

```java
String url = "jdbc:db2://HOUSTON1:5021/DBHR:" +
       "user=HRUSER01;password=PASS3454;";


Connection con = DriverManager.getConnection(url);
```

ODBC

You will need to install the IBM Data Server Driver for ODBC and CLI. From there you can specify configuration information in one of three methods:

1. Specify in the connect string when using the SQLDriverConnect function.
2. Store configuration parameters in the db2cli.ini file.
3. Store configuration parameters in the db2dsdriver.cfg file.

If you store the connection parameters in the db2dsdriver.cfg file, create an XML structure like this:

```xml
<configuration>
  <dsncollection>
      <dsn   alias="hrDSN"   name="hrConnect"   host="HRserver.domain.com"
port="446">
    </dsn>
  </dsncollection>
  <databases>
    <database name="DBHR" host=" HRserver.domain.com " port="446">
      <parameter name="CommProtocol" value="TCPIP"/>
      <parameter name="UID" value="HRUSER01"/>
    </database>
  </databases>
</configuration>
```

Now you can set pass the connection string in SQLDriverConnect() as:

```
DSN=hrDSN;PWD=<your password>:
```

How to Test a Connection

The CONNECT statement is used to connect a user or application to a DB2 database server. The basic syntax for the CONNECT statement is:

```
CONNECT TO <server-name> USER <user id> USING <password>
```

The server or the local DB2 subsystem checks the authorization ID and password to verify that the user is authorized to connect to the server.

Local Access

Local DB2 access (meaning you are logged onto the same machine where you bind your packages) is typically governed by local security. If you are logged onto TSO then you have already been authenticated by the z/OS security subsystem. If your TSO id is used as your primary DB2 authorization id (typically it is) then RACF checks to make sure you are authorized to access DB2. If you are, then a connection occurs.

Remote Access

A remote server can be either another instance of DB2 for z/OS or it can be an instance of some other product. The server name's location must be identified in the SYSIBM.LOCATIONS table on the local system. The LINKNAME in the SYSIBM.LOCATIONS table corresponds to LINKNAME in the SYSIBM.IPNAMES table which includes the IPADDR (IP address) of the remote system.

There are two ways to connect to a remote server:

1. Using an explicit CONNECT statement.
2. Using three part naming.

We'll look at examples of each.

Connecting Via Explicit CONNECT Statement

The application can connect to a server based on the location name in the CONNECT statement.

For example, suppose we want to run a select statement against an HREMP table owned by schema HRGROUP which resides on a server whose LOCATION value in the locations table is HOUSTON1. We also have a user id and password (HR001 and ACDVXZ84) that has authority to access the remote system. If our local id does not have access to the remote system, we can explicitly connect using these credentials. Our first example will do that.

To accomplish our task in an embedded SQL program, we would code the following:

```
EXEC SQL
    CONNECT TO HOUSTON1 USER HR001 USING ACDVXZ84;
    SELECT * FROM HRGROUP.HREMP
    WHERE EMP_ID = 3217;
```

Similarly you can call a stored procedure GET_EMPLOYEE (provided it is bound on the remote server) by coding the following:

```
EXEC SQL
  CONNECT TO HOUSTON1 USER HR001 USING ACDVXZ84;

EXEC SQL
  CALL GET_EMPLOYEE (3217);
```

Connection Via Three Part Names

A three-part name can be used consisting of a location that uniquely identifies the remote server, an authorization id that identifies the owner of the object, and the OBJECT name that identifies the object at the location that you want to access. When using three part naming an implicit CONNECT takes place provided the remote server is defined in the SYSIBM.LOCATIONS table, and that the user has security to connect to that remote server. Int his case we will assume the user does have the connect privilege on the remote server.

Let's use the same example of running a select statement against an HREMP table owned by schema HRGROUP which resides on a server whose LOCATION is HOUSTON1.

```
EXEC SQL
    SELECT * FROM HOUSTON1.HRGROUP.HREMP
    WHERE EMP_ID = 3217;
```

As you can see, you only need to add the location name in front of the schema/table name. The connect takes place implicitly.

Finally, you can create an ALIAS for the object using the three part name, and your SQL can then reference the ALIAS instead of the three part name. For example:

```
CREATE ALIAS EMPTBLH FOR HOUSTON1.HRGROUP.HREMP;
```

Now you can write your select as:

```
SELECT * FROM EMPTBLH;
```

Remember that to connect to a remote DB2 subsystem, the remote server must be listed in your local SYSIBM.LOCATIONS table. Once you connect to the remote sevrer, the location name of the remote server is placed in the CURRENT SERVER special register.

If your program logic needs to check which server you are connected to, you can do this by issuing a CONNECT without any parameters. When you do this, the current server name will be returned in the SQLERRP structure of the SQLCA.

How to Test a Stored Procedure

There are several ways you can test a stored procedure. Unfortunately SPUFI is not one of them. Here are some choices: Application Program, Rexx, QMF and Data Studio.

Application Program

You can put together a program to call the stored procedure. We did this in previous examples. Refer to the program listings above for COBEMP7 and COBEMP8 as examples.

Rexx

You can create a Rexx procedure such as the below to test a stored procedure. The load library names and subsystem name below must be changed to whatever the correct library names and subsystem name for your system.

```
/* REXX */
SUBSYS = "DBAX"
address TSO
  "FREE  FI(STEPLIBX) DA('DSNTST.SDSNLOAD')"
  "ALLOC FI(STEPLIBX) DA('DSNTST.SDSNLOAD') SHR REUSE"
  if rc <> 0
  then do
       say "DB2 SDSNLOAD library for SSID="ssid" is not available!"
       say "Check z/OS LINKLIST or allocate to STEPLIB in advance!"
       signal error
  end
ADDRESS TSO "SUBCOM DSNREXX" /* HOST CMD ENV AVAILABLE ? */
IF RC <> 0 THEN S_RC = RXSUBCOM('ADD','DSNREXX','DSNREXX')
say 'About to connect...'
ADDRESS DSNREXX "CONNECT" SUBSYS
IF SQLCODE <> 0 THEN CALL SQLCA
say 'About to call SP...'
ADDRESS DSNREXX
/* Identify Stored procedure, define host variables */
```

```
STOPRO = "HRSCHEMA.GETEMP"
EMP_ID = +3217
EMP_LAST_NAME = ''
EMP_FIRST_NAME = ''
/* call the stored procedure */
ADDRESS DSNREXX
"EXECSQL CALL :STOPRO(:EMP_ID,:EMP_LAST_NAME,:EMP_FIRST_NAME)"
IF SQLCODE <> 0 THEN CALL SQLCA
say SQLCODE
IF SQLCODE = 0 THEN
SAY "Stored Procedure: " GETEMP " was successful"
SAY "EMP_LAST_NAME= " EMP_LAST_NAME
SAY "EMP_FIRST_NAME= " EMP_FIRST_NAME
```

The output is displayed as follows:

```
Connected...
About to call SP...
0
Stored Procedure:  GETEMP  was successful
EMP_ID       =  3217
EMP_LAST_NAME=  JOHNSON
EMP_FIRST_NAME=  EDWARD
***
```

QMF

You can use QMF to run a stored procedure but it's use is limited as you cannot get any OUT variables displayed.

```
SQL QUERY                                    MODIFIED  LINE    1

CALL HRSCHEMA.GETEMP (&A01, &B01, &C01)




*** END ***


1=Help       2=Run        3=End        4=Print    5=Chart     6=Draw
7=Backward   8=Forward    9=Form       10=Insert  11=Delete   12=Report
OK, cursor positioned.
COMMAND ===>                                         SCROLL ===> PAGE
```

When you press the PF2 key to run the stored procedure you will be prompted for the parameter values. Enter the values and press enter.

```
SQL QUERY                                          MODIFIED  LINE    1
+-------------------------------------------------------------------------+
|                   RUN Command Prompt - Values of Variables              |
|                                                                         |
| Your RUN command runs a query or procedure with variables that need     |
| values. Fill in a value for each variable named below:                  |
|                                                         1  to 10 of 10  |
| &A01              3217                                                   |
| &B01              NULL                                                   |
| &C01              NULL                                                   |
|                                                                         |
|                                                                         |
|                                                                         |
|                                                                         |
|                                                                         |
+-------------------------------------------------------------------------+
| F1=Help  F3=End  F7=Backward  F8=Forward                                |
+-------------------------------------------------------------------------+


    Please give a value for each variable name.
```

Next we get a panel that says our stored procedure is successful. However, QMF cannot return the out parameters, so we have no output. This somewhat limits the usefulness of running stored procedures under QMF. You can however usefully execute queries under QMF where the output from the query is not needed, such as in update queries. We'll do an example of one on the next page.

```
QMF HOME PANEL                    Query      Management      Facility
Version 10 Release 1
                              ******    **    **      ********
Authorization ID                **    **   ***   ***       **
 HRSCHEMA                        **    **  ****  ****    *******
                          **    **  **  ** ** **      **
Connected to              **   *  **   **   ****  **    **
 LOCRGNA                  ******    **   ***   **  **
                               **
                                        http://www.ibm.com/qmf
Enter a command on the command line or press a function key.
For help, press the Help function key or enter the command HELP.

1=Help        2=List      3=End       4=Show      5=Chart      6=Query
7=Retrieve    8=Edit Table 9=Form     10=Proc     11=Profile   12=Report
OK, Your Stored Procedure has successfully completed.
COMMAND ===>
```

Let's create a stored procedure that updates the employee's years of service. Our IN parameters will be the employee id and the years of service:

```
CREATE PROCEDURE HRSCHEMA.UPDEMP
(IN EMP_NO INT, IN YRSSRV INT)

LANGUAGE SQL
MODIFIES SQL DATA

 BEGIN
    UPDATE HRSCHEMA.EMPLOYEE
    SET EMP_SERVICE_YEARS = YRSSRV
    WHERE EMP_ID = EMP_NO;
 END

---------+---------+---------+---------+---------+---------+-
DSNE616I STATEMENT EXECUTION WAS SUCCESSFUL, SQLCODE IS 0
```

Now let's move to QMF and run a query to see the current value of years of service for employee. And then we'll press PF2 to run the query.

```
SQL QUERY                                MODIFIED  LINE    1

SELECT EMP_ID, EMP_SERVICE_YEARS
FROM HRSCHEMA.EMPLOYEE
WHERE EMP_ID = 3217;




















*** END ***



1=Help      2=Run        3=End       4=Print     5=Chart      6=Draw
7=Backward  8=Forward    9=Form      10=Insert   11=Delete    12=Report
OK, cursor positioned.
COMMAND ===>                                          SCROLL ===> PAGE
```

Our query output will look like this:

```
REPORT                                           LINE 1      POS 1      79


                              EMP
                  EMP       SERVICE
                  ID         YEARS
               -----------  -----------
                   3217            4


      *** END ***




 1=Help         2=            3=End        4=Print      5=Chart      6=Query
 7=Backward     8=Forward    9=Form       10=Left      11=Right     12=
 OK, this is the REPORT from your RUN command.
 COMMAND ===>                                          SCROLL ===> PAGE
```

Then, let's press PF6 again to create a new query to call the UPDEMP stored procedure and we'll specify 5 years as the value we want to update for employee 3217. Since we are only using IN parameters, we can simply specify these values in parentheses.

Code the following and then press PF2 to execute.

```
SQL QUERY                                        MODIFIED  LINE   1

CALL HRSCHEMA.UPDEMP (3217, 5)










      *** END ***




 1=Help        2=Run       3=End        4=Print      5=Chart      6=Draw
 7=Backward    8=Forward   9=Form      10=Insert    11=Delete    12=Report
 OK, cursor positioned.
 COMMAND ===>                                         SCROLL ===> PAGE
```

You'll then see the main menu with the message that the procedure has successfully executed.

```
Licensed Materials - Property of IBM
5635-DB2, 5605-DB2 (C) Copyright IBM Corp. 1982, 2010
All Rights Reserved.
IBM is a registered trademark of International Business Machines


QMF HOME PANEL                 Query      Management    Facility
Version 10 Release 1
                             ******    **   **      ********
Authorization ID               **    **  ***  ***      **           ___
  HRSCHEMA                       **    **  ****  ****    *******      ___
                             **    **  ** ** ** **     **           ___
Connected to                 **   * **   **  ****  **    **       ___
  LOCRGNA                     ******    **   ***   **  **         ___
                               **   _____
                             http://www.ibm.com/qmf
Enter a command on the command line or press a function key.
For help, press the Help function key or enter the command HELP.


1=Help        2=List      3=End       4=Show      5=Chart     6=Query
7=Retrieve    8=Edit Table 9=Form     10=Proc     11=Profile  12=Report
OK, Your Stored Procedure has successfully completed.
COMMAND ===>
```

Finally, let's confirm that the years of service value is now 5 instead of 4. Press PF6 to get back to the query screen and enter this query:

```
SQL QUERY                              MODIFIED   LINE    1

SELECT EMP_ID, EMP_SERVICE_YEARS
FROM HRSCHEMA.EMPLOYEE
WHERE EMP_ID = 3217;













*** END ***




1=Help        2=Run       3=End       4=Print     5=Chart     6=Draw
7=Backward    8=Forward   9=Form      10=Insert   11=Delete   12=Report
OK, cursor positioned.
COMMAND ===>                                       SCROLL ===> PAGE
```

Now press PF2 to get the query result.

And our result shows that the stored procedure did in fact change the value of the years of service from 4 to 5.

```
REPORT                                          LINE 1       POS 1       79


                          EMP
            EMP         SERVICE
            ID           YEARS
        -----------   -----------
            3217             5


    *** END ***




    1=Help        2=          3=End      4=Print     5=Chart       6=Query
    7=Backward    8=Forward   9=Form     10=Left     11=Right      12=
    OK, this is the REPORT from your RUN command.
    COMMAND ===>                                        SCROLL ===> PAGE
```

So in some cases it is convenient to test stored procedures using QMF. Generally, as long as you don't use or need output parameters, you can test successfully with QMF.

Data Studio

Using data studio you can run the stored procedure by clicking Stored Procedures in the object tree, right clicking on the name of the stored procedure – in our case GETEMP – and then clicking on **RUN**. You'll have the opportunity to enter an EMP_NO. Then click **RUN**.

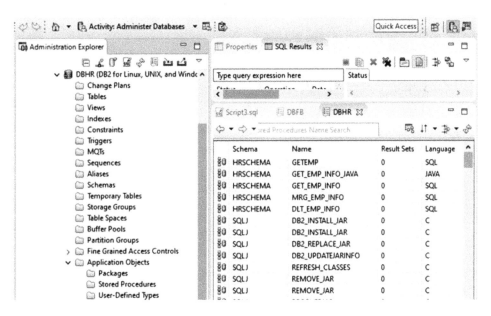

Here's the output.

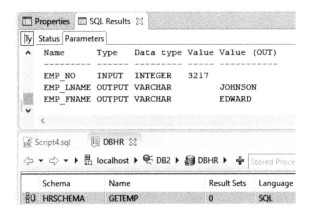

DB2 LOAD and UNLOAD utilities

UNLOAD

Use the unload utility to copy the contents of a table into a flat file. This example copies the EMP_PAY table to file HRSCHEMA.EMPPAY.UNLOAD.

```
UNLOAD DATA FROM TABLE HRSCHEMA.EMP_PAY
```

If you created the JCL from the online panels, you will see this DD for the output:

```
//DSNUPROC.SYSREC DD DSN=HRSCHEMA.EMPPAY.UNLOAD,
//       DISP=(MOD,CATLG),
//       SPACE=(16384,(20,20),,,ROUND),
```

If you are reusing JCL, you must add the above DD to your JCL.

You can keep the unload output in internal DB2 format by specifying FORMAT INTERNAL. If you want the output to be in another format you can specify EBCDIC, ASCII or UNICODE. Also if you want the output file to be delimited, you can specify DELIMIT.

If you want a subset of the data in the table, you can specify this using either the SAMPLE or WHEN clauses. The first example below unloads the first 100 records from EMP_PAY. The second example pulls all records for which the EMP_ID is greater than 3217.

```
UNLOAD DATA
FROM TABLE HRSCHEMA.EMP_PAY
SAMPLE 100

UNLOAD DATA
FROM TABLE HRSCHEMA.EMP_PAY
WHEN (EMP_ID > 3217)
```

LOAD

Use the LOAD utility when you want to load a DB2 table from an input file. This is useful when you are working in a test system and need to restore a baseline set of data. The input file can be in DB2 format or one of the other supported formats.

The load command can be taken from the SYSPUNCH file that was created when the table was unloaded. To take a simple example, let's use the file we unloaded from EMP_PAY and reload the EMP_PAY table with it.

The content of our SYSPUNCH file is:

```
LOAD DATA INDDN SYSREC   LOG NO   RESUME YES
 UNICODE CCSID(00367,01208,01200)
 INTO TABLE
 "HRSCHEMA".
 "EMP_PAY"
 WHEN(00001:00002) = X'012E'
```

```
NUMRECS                        5
( "EMP_ID"
  POSITION(  00003:00006) INTEGER
, "EMP_REGULAR_PAY"
  POSITION(  00007:00011) DECIMAL
, "EMP_BONUS_PAY"
  POSITION(  00013:00017) DECIMAL
                          NULLIF(00012)=X'FF'
)
```

Now we can substitute the SYSIN DD * in the load JCL with the name of the SYSPUNCH file and we are ready to run. Your output should look something like this:

```
DSNUGUTC - OUTPUT START FOR UTILITY, UTILID = TEMP
DSNUGTIS - PROCESSING SYSIN AS EBCDIC
DSNUGUTC -  LOAD DATA INDDN SYSREC LOG NO RESUME YES UNICODE CCSID(367, 1208, 12
.31 DSNURWI -  INTO TABLE "HRSCHEMA". "EMP_PAY" WHEN(1:2)=X'012E' NUMRECS 5
.31 DSNURWI -   ("EMP_ID" POSITION(3:6) INTEGER,
.31 DSNURWI -    "EMP_REGULAR_PAY" POSITION(7:11) DECIMAL,
.31 DSNURWI -    "EMP_BONUS_PAY" POSITION(13:17) DECIMAL NULLIF(12)=X'FF')
.73 DSNURWT - (RE)LOAD PHASE STATISTICS - NUMBER OF RECORDS=5 FOR TABLE HRSCHEMA.E
.73 DSNURWT - (RE)LOAD PHASE STATISTICS - TOTAL NUMBER OF RECORDS LOADED=5 FOR T

DSNURILD - (RE)LOAD PHASE STATISTICS - NUMBER OF INPUT RECORDS PROCESSED=5
DSNURILD - (RE)LOAD PHASE COMPLETE, ELAPSED TIME=00:00:00
.74 DSNUGSRX - TABLESPACE DBHR.TSHR IS IN COPY PENDING
```

Note that your tablespace is in COPY PENDING state. You can take a backup to clear this status, or you can use the REPAIR utility as follows:

```
REPAIR SET TABLESPACE DBHR.TSHR NOCHECKPEND
```

APPLICATION PERFORMANCE

As an application developer, you may or may not be asked to do performance troubleshooting. Some environments reply more on the DBA for this. Still it is important to develop with performance in mind. That being said, here are some recommendations.

Make sure your data concurrency settings are appropriate for your workload. If you are doing heavy read-only access against a static table, specify isolation level UR since it only locks those rows that are updated and the row the cursor is pointing at. Be careful not to use the RS or RR levels unless you have a good reason. Typically you should bind you application with ISOLATION(CS) and CURRENTDATA(NO) to prevent unnecessary locking.

It is important to commit your work regularly, which means often enough to avoid unnecessary locking, but not so often as to push unnecessary overhead. Ask your DBA for a recommendation on frequency, or experiment while you are still in development.

You'll also want to use the latest table statistics to ensure proper optimization. For example when a table is very small, DB2 will often select a table scan as the most efficient access method. If you never refresh the stats and rebind your packages, when the table grows large this will cause a performance problem. Ask your DBA to help keep an eye on performance, and do a periodic RUNSTATS and rebind.

Chapter Seven Questions

1. Suppose you have created a test version of a production table, and you want to to use the UNLOAD utility to extract the first 1,000 rows from the production table to load to the test version. Which keyword would you use in the UNLOAD statement?

    a. WHEN
    b. SELECT
    c. SAMPLE
    d. SUBSET

2. Which of the following is an SQL error code indicating a DB2 package is not found within the DB2 plan?

    a. -803
    b. -805
    c. -904
    d. -922

3. Which of the following will generate DB2 SQL data structures for a table or view that can be used in a PLI or COBOL program?

    a. DECLARE
    b. INCLUDE
    c. DCLGEN
    d. None of the above.

4. Which DB2 utility updates the statistics used by the DB2 Optimizer to choose a data access path?

    a. REORG

    b. RUNSTATS

    c. REBIND

    d. OPTIMIZE

5. When using static SQL, to enable parallel processing you must:

    a. Specify DEGREE(ANY) on the BIND or REBIND step.

    b. Issue SQL statement "SET CURRENT DEGREE='ANY'.

    c. Specify PARALLEL_PROC(YES) for the subsystem.

    d. None of the above would enable parallel processing for static SQL.

6. Which of the following is NOT a way you could test a DB2 SQL statement?

    a. Running the statement from the DB2 command line processor.

    b. Running the statement from the SPUFI utility.

    c. Running the statement from IBM Data Studio.

    d. All of the above are valid ways to test an SQL statement.

Chapter Seven Exercises:

1. Write an UNLOAD control statement to unload a sample of 5000 records from the HRSCHE-MA.EMP_PAY table for use in loading a test table.

2. Suppose that the HRSCHEMA.EMP_PAY table exists on a system whose location name is DENVER. Write a query that uses three part naming to implicitly connect to DENVER and then retrieve all information for EMP_ID 3217.

CHAPTER EIGHT: INTERMEDIATE TOPICS

STORED PROCEDURES

A stored procedure is a set of compiled statements that is stored on the DB2 server. The stored procedures typically include SQL statements to access data in a DB2 table. Stored procedures are similar to sub-programs in that they can be called by other programs. Specifically, stored procedures are invoked by the CALL statement as in:

```
CALL <stored procedure name><(parameters)>
```

Stored procedures can be called from an application program such as COBOL, from a Rexx exec, from QMF or from Data Studio. Stored procedures are created using the CREATE PROCEDURE statement. The details of the stored procedure depend on whether it is external or native. We'll look at examples of each.

Types of stored procedures

There are three types of stored procedures:

1. Native SQL Procedure
2. External stored procedure
3. External SQL Procedure

Native SQL procedures

A native SQL procedure is a procedure that consists exclusively of SQL statements, and is created entirely within the CREATE PROCEDURE statement. Native SQL procedures are not associated with an external program.

External stored procedures

An external stored procedure is one written in a programming language such as COBOL or Java.

External SQL procedures

An external SQL procedure is a procedure that is composed of SQL statements, and is created and implemented like an external stored procedure (including having an external program).

External Stored Procedure Programming Languages.

When you want to create an external stored procedure, the the following programming languages can be used:

- Assembler
- C
- C++
- COBOL
- REXX
- PL/I

Examples of Stored Procedures

Native SQL Stored Procedure

Let's start with a procedure that will return the first and last names of an employee, given an employee number. We will pass employee number as an IN parameter and receive the employee's first and last names as OUT parameters. Since we are only using SQL statements, we will specify the SQL language in the definition, and specify our intent to read data.

```
CREATE PROCEDURE GETEMP (IN EMP_NO INT,
  OUT EMP_LNAME VARCHAR(30),
  OUT EMP_FNAME VARCHAR(20))

LANGUAGE SQL
READS SQL DATA

 BEGIN
    SELECT EMP_LAST_NAME,
           EMP_FIRST_NAME
    INTO EMP_LNAME,
         EMP_FNAME
    FROM HRSCHEMA.EMPLOYEE
    WHERE EMP_ID = EMP_NO;
END
```

Now we need a program to call the stored procedure. Here is a COBOL program to do that.

```
 IDENTIFICATION DIVISION.
PROGRAM-ID. COBEMP6.

*******************************************************
*      PROGRAM USING DB2 CALL TO A NATIVE             *
*      STORED PROCEDURE.                              *
*******************************************************

ENVIRONMENT DIVISION.
DATA DIVISION.
WORKING-STORAGE SECTION.

01 HV-EMP-VARIABLES.
    10  HV-ID            PIC S9(9) USAGE COMP.
    10  HV-LAST-NAME     PIC X(30).
    10  HV-FIRST-NAME    PIC X(20).
```

228

```
01 ERR-REC.
   05 FILLER              PIC X(10) VALUE 'SQLCODE = '.
   05 SQLCODE-VIEW        PIC -999.
   05 FILLER              PIC X(005) VALUE SPACES.
   05 ERR-TAB             PIC X(016).
   05 ERR-PARA            PIC X(015).
   05 ERR-DETAIL          PIC X(040).

77 ERR-TXT-LGTH           PIC S9(9) USAGE COMP VALUE +72.

01 ERR-MSG.
   05 ERR-MSG-LGTH        PIC S9(04) COMP VALUE +864.
   05 ERR-MSG-TXT         PIC X(072) OCCURS 12 TIMES
                                     INDEXED BY ERR-NDX.

    EXEC SQL
      INCLUDE SQLCA
    END-EXEC.

    EXEC SQL
      INCLUDE EMPLOYEE
    END-EXEC.


PROCEDURE DIVISION.

MAIN-PARA.
     DISPLAY "SAMPLE COBOL PROGRAM: CALL STORED PROCEDURE".


*  SELECT AN EMPLOYEE

    MOVE 3217 TO HV-ID

    EXEC SQL
      CALL HRSCHEMA.GETEMP(:HV-ID,
                           :HV-LAST-NAME,
                           :HV-FIRST-NAME)
    END-EXEC.

    IF SQLCODE IS NOT EQUAL TO ZERO

       MOVE SQLCODE TO SQLCODE-VIEW
       MOVE 'GETEMP2 ' TO ERR-TAB
       MOVE 'MAIN'     TO ERR-PARA
       MOVE HV-ID      TO ERR-DETAIL
       PERFORM P9999-SQL-ERROR
    ELSE
       DISPLAY  'PROC CALL SUCCESSFULL ' HV-LAST-NAME
                HV-FIRST-NAME HV-ID
       DISPLAY SQLCODE

    END-IF


      P9999-SQL-ERROR.

    DISPLAY ERR-REC.
```

```
            CALL 'DSNTIAR' USING SQLCA,
                          ERR-MSG,
                          ERR-TXT-LGTH.

        IF RETURN-CODE IS EQUAL TO ZERO

            PERFORM P9999-DISP-ERR
               VARYING ERR-NDX FROM 1 BY 1
               UNTIL ERR-NDX > 12

        ELSE
            DISPLAY 'DSNTIAR ERROR CODE = ' RETURN-CODE
            STOP RUN.

    P9999-DISP-ERR.

        DISPLAY ERR-MSG-TXT(ERR-NDX).

    P9999-DISP-ERR-EXIT.
```

Now when we run the procedure we get the following results:

```
SAMPLE COBOL PROGRAM: CALL STORED PROCEDURE
PROC CALL SUCCESSFULL JOHNSON EDWARD 3217
```

The PLI version of the program is as follows:

```
PLIEMP6: PROCEDURE OPTIONS(MAIN) REORDER;
/*********************************************************************
*                                                                   *
* PROGRAM NAME :  PLIEMP6 - PROGRAM TO CALL A STORED PROCEDURE.     *
*                                                                   *
*********************************************************************/

/*********************************************************************
*              E X T E R N A L   E N T R I E S                      *
*********************************************************************/

   DCL DSNTIAR ENTRY OPTIONS(ASM INTER RETCODE);

/*********************************************************************
*              W O R K I N G   S T O R A G E                        *
*********************************************************************/

   DCL HV_ID             FIXED BIN (31) INIT (0);
   DCL HV_LAST_NAME      CHAR(30) INIT (' ');
   DCL HV_FIRST_NAME     CHAR(20) INIT (' ');

   DCL 01 ERR_REC,
          05 FILLER1            CHAR(10) INIT ('SQLCODE = '),
          05 SQLCODE_VIEW       PIC '-999',
          05 ERR_EMPID          FIXED BIN (31) INIT (0),
          05 FILLER2            CHAR(01) INIT (' '),
          05 ERR_TAB            CHAR(08) INIT (' '),
          05 ERR_PARA           CHAR(15) INIT (' ');
```

230

```
     DCL 01 ERR_MSG AUTOMATIC,
           05 ERR_LGTH              FIXED BIN (31) INIT (864),
           05 ERR_TXT(10)           CHAR(72);

     DCL ERR_TXT_LGTH              FIXED BIN (15) INIT (72);
     DCL ERR_NDX                   FIXED BIN (31) INIT (0);

     EXEC SQL
       INCLUDE SQLCA;

     EXEC SQL
       INCLUDE EMPLOYEE;

/*******************************************************************
/*               P R O G R A M   M A I N L I N E            *
*******************************************************************/

     PUT SKIP LIST ('SAMPLE PLI PROGRAM: CALL STORED PROCEDURE');

           DCLEMPLOYEE = '';

       /* SELECT AN EMPLOYEE */

           HV_ID = 3217;

           EXEC SQL
               CALL HRSCHEMA.GETEMP(:HV_ID,
                                    :HV_LAST_NAME,
                                    :HV_FIRST_NAME);

           IF SQLCODE ¬= 0 THEN
               DO;
                   SQLCODE_VIEW = SQLCODE;
                   ERR_TAB = 'EMPLOYEE';
                   ERR_PARA = 'MAIN';
                   ERR_EMPID = HV_ID;
                   CALL P9999_SQL_ERROR;
               END;

           ELSE
               PUT SKIP LIST ('PROC CALL SUCCESSFUL '
                       || TRIM(HV_LAST_NAME)
                       || ' ' || TRIM(HV_FIRST_NAME)
                       || ' ' || HV_ID);


P9999_SQL_ERROR: PROC;

     PUT SKIP LIST (ERR_REC);

     CALL DSNTIAR (SQLCA, ERR_MSG, ERR_TXT_LGTH);

     IF RETCODE = 0 THEN
        DO ERR_NDX = 1 TO 10;
            PUT SKIP DATA (ERR_TXT(ERR_NDX));
        END; /* DO */
     ELSE
        PUT SKIP LIST ('DSNTIAR ERROR CODE = ' || RETCODE);
```

231

```
        END P9999_SQL_ERROR;

        END PLIEMP6;
```

And here is the result of the run:

```
        SAMPLE PLI PROGRAM: CALL STORED PROCEDURE
        PROC CALL SUCCESSFUL JOHNSON EDWARD              3217
```

External Stored Procedure

Now let's do the same procedure but we'll make it an external procedure and use COBOL. First let's define the procedure and we'll call it GETEMP2. Note: it is important to specify the correct WLM environment. You might need to check with your DBA or system admin for this information.

```
        CREATE PROCEDURE HRSCHEMA.GETEMP2
        (IN EMP_NO INT,
         OUT EMP_LNAME VARCHAR(30),
         OUT EMP_FNAME VARCHAR(20))

        LANGUAGE COBOL
        READS SQL DATA
        EXTERNAL NAME "COBEMP7"
        COLLID HRSCHEMA
        ASUTIME NO LIMIT
        PARAMETER STYLE GENERAL
        STAY RESIDENT NO
        WLM ENVIRONMENT DBAGENV
        PROGRAM TYPE MAIN
        SECURITY DB2
        RESULT SETS 0
        COMMIT ON RETURN NO
```

Now we need to write the COBOL program. Here is one that will perform this task. Notice that we have moved the host variables to a Linkage section.

```
        IDENTIFICATION DIVISION.
        PROGRAM-ID. COBEMP7.

        *******************************************************
        *       PROGRAM USED AS A STORED PROCEDURE            *
        *******************************************************

        ENVIRONMENT DIVISION.
        DATA DIVISION.
        WORKING-STORAGE SECTION.


        01 ERR-REC.
           05 FILLER              PIC X(10) VALUE 'SQLCODE = '.
```

```
          05  SQLCODE-VIEW       PIC -999.
          05  FILLER             PIC X(005) VALUE SPACES.
          05  ERR-TAB            PIC X(016).
          05  ERR-PARA           PIC X(015).
          05  ERR-DETAIL         PIC X(040).

      77  ERR-TXT-LGTH           PIC S9(9) USAGE COMP VALUE +72.

      01  ERR-MSG.
          05  ERR-MSG-LGTH       PIC S9(04) COMP VALUE +864.
          05  ERR-MSG-TXT        PIC X(072) OCCURS 12 TIMES
                                            INDEXED BY ERR-NDX.
      77  LOGONID                PIC X(8)   VALUE 'HRSCHEMA'.
      77  PWORD                  PIC X(8)   VALUE 'RWUS'.

          EXEC SQL
            INCLUDE SQLCA
          END-EXEC.

          EXEC SQL
            INCLUDE EMPLOYEE
          END-EXEC.

      LINKAGE SECTION.
      ******************************************************
      *   DECLARE THE I/O PARAMETERS FOR THE PROCEDURE
      ******************************************************

      01  LK-EMP-VARIABLES.
          10  HV-ID              PIC S9(9) USAGE COMP.
          10  HV-LAST-NAME       PIC X(30).
          10  HV-FIRST-NAME      PIC X(20).

      PROCEDURE DIVISION.

      MAIN-PARA.
          DISPLAY "SAMPLE COBOL PROGRAM: STORED PROCEDURE".

      *   SELECT AN EMPLOYEE

          MOVE 3217 TO HV-ID

          EXEC SQL
            CALL HRSCHEMA.GETEMP2(:HV-ID,
                                  :HV-LAST-NAME,
                                  :HV-FIRST-NAME)
          END-EXEC.

          IF SQLCODE IS NOT EQUAL TO ZERO

             MOVE SQLCODE TO SQLCODE-VIEW
             MOVE 'GETEMP ' TO ERR-TAB
             MOVE 'MAIN'    TO ERR-PARA
             MOVE HV-ID     TO ERR-DETAIL
             PERFORM P9999-SQL-ERROR

          ELSE
             DISPLAY  'PROC CALL SUCCESFULL ' HV-LAST-NAME
                       HV-FIRST-NAME
                       HV-ID
```

```
        DISPLAY SQLCODE

    END-IF

    GOBACK.


P9999-SQL-ERROR.

    DISPLAY ERR-REC.

    CALL 'DSNTIAR' USING SQLCA,
                  ERR-MSG,
                  ERR-TXT-LGTH.

    IF RETURN-CODE IS EQUAL TO ZERO

        PERFORM P9999-DISP-ERR
          VARYING ERR-NDX FROM 1 BY 1
          UNTIL ERR-NDX > 12

    ELSE
        DISPLAY 'DSNTIAR ERROR CODE = ' RETURN-CODE
        STOP RUN.

P9999-DISP-ERR.

    DISPLAY ERR-MSG-TXT(ERR-NDX).

P9999-DISP-ERR-EXIT.
```

Now we need a program to call the external stored procedure. We can clone the one we used to call the native stored procedure. That was COBEMP6 and all we need to do is change the name of the procedure we are calling. The new program name is COBEMP8.

```
IDENTIFICATION DIVISION.
PROGRAM-ID. COBEMP8.

************************************************
*      PROGRAM USING DB2 CALL TO AN EXTERNAL     *
*      STORED PROCEDURE.                         *
************************************************

ENVIRONMENT DIVISION.
DATA DIVISION.
WORKING-STORAGE SECTION.

01 HV-EMP-VARIABLES.
    10  HV-ID          PIC S9(9) USAGE COMP.
    10  HV-LAST-NAME   PIC X(30).
    10  HV-FIRST-NAME  PIC X(20).

01 ERR-REC.
    05 FILLER          PIC X(10) VALUE 'SQLCODE = '.
    05 SQLCODE-VIEW    PIC -999.
    05 FILLER          PIC X(005) VALUE SPACES.
    05 ERR-TAB         PIC X(016).
```

```
    05 ERR-PARA            PIC X(015).
    05 ERR-DETAIL          PIC X(040).

77 ERR-TXT-LGTH           PIC S9(9) USAGE COMP VALUE +72.

01 ERR-MSG.
    05 ERR-MSG-LGTH        PIC S9(04) COMP VALUE +864.
    05 ERR-MSG-TXT         PIC X(072) OCCURS 12 TIMES
                                      INDEXED BY ERR-NDX.
77 LOGONID                PIC X(8)  VALUE 'HRSCHEMA'.
77 PWORD                  PIC X(8)  VALUE 'RWUS'.


    EXEC SQL
      INCLUDE SQLCA
    END-EXEC.

    EXEC SQL
      INCLUDE EMPLOYEE
    END-EXEC.


PROCEDURE DIVISION.

MAIN-PARA.
    DISPLAY "SAMPLE COBOL PROGRAM: CALL STORED PROCEDURE".


*   SELECT AN EMPLOYEE

    MOVE 3217 TO HV-ID

    EXEC SQL
       CALL HRSCHEMA.GETEMP2(:HV-ID,
                             :HV-LAST-NAME,
                             :HV-FIRST-NAME)
    END-EXEC.

    IF SQLCODE IS NOT EQUAL TO ZERO

       MOVE SQLCODE TO SQLCODE-VIEW
       MOVE 'GETEMP ' TO ERR-TAB
       MOVE 'MAIN'    TO ERR-PARA
       MOVE HV-ID     TO ERR-DETAIL
       PERFORM P9999-SQL-ERROR

    ELSE
       DISPLAY  'PROC CALL SUCCESFULL ' HV-LAST-NAME
                HV-FIRST-NAME
                HV-ID
       DISPLAY SQLCODE

    END-IF


P9999-SQL-ERROR.

    DISPLAY ERR-REC.

    CALL 'DSNTIAR' USING SQLCA,
```

```
                    ERR-MSG,
                    ERR-TXT-LGTH.

        IF RETURN-CODE IS EQUAL TO ZERO

            PERFORM P9999-DISP-ERR
                VARYING ERR-NDX FROM 1 BY 1
                UNTIL ERR-NDX > 12

        ELSE
            DISPLAY 'DSNTIAR ERROR CODE = ' RETURN-CODE
            STOP RUN.

    P9999-DISP-ERR.

        DISPLAY ERR-MSG-TXT(ERR-NDX).

    P9999-DISP-ERR-EXIT.
```

Now when we run this program, it will call the stored procedure and display these results:

```
    SAMPLE COBOL PROGRAM: CALL STORED PROCEDURE
    PROC CALL SUCCESSFULL JOHNSON EDWARD 3217
```

Finally, if you are following the examples but prefer to use PLI, we will implement a parallel stored procedure. We have to name it something else because we've already used GETEMP2 for the COBOL example. Let's add a P to the name and call is GETEMP2P. Not a very original naming convention, but it will work for our example.

Let's create the external stored procedure definition to be implemented with a PLI program. All we need to do is change the programming language.

```
    CREATE PROCEDURE HRSCHEMA.GETEMP2P
    (IN EMP_NO INT,
     OUT EMP_LNAME VARCHAR(30),
     OUT EMP_FNAME VARCHAR(20))

    LANGUAGE PLI
    READS SQL DATA
    EXTERNAL NAME "PLIEMP7"
    COLLID HRSCHEMA
    ASUTIME NO LIMIT
    PARAMETER STYLE GENERAL
    STAY RESIDENT NO
    WLM ENVIRONMENT DBAGENV1
    PROGRAM TYPE MAIN
    SECURITY DB2
    RESULT SETS 0
    COMMIT ON RETURN NO
```

Now we are ready to implement the stored procedure in the PLI language:

236

```
PLIEMP7: PROCEDURE (LK_EMP_VARIABLES);
/*********************************************************************
 *                                                                   *
 * PROGRAM NAME :   PLIEMP7 - PROGRAM USED AS A STORED PROCEDURE.    *
 *                                                                   *
 *********************************************************************/

/*********************************************************************
 *              E X T E R N A L   E N T R I E S                      *
 *********************************************************************/

   DCL DSNTIAR ENTRY OPTIONS(ASM INTER RETCODE);

/*********************************************************************
 *              W O R K I N G   S T O R A G E                        *
 *********************************************************************/

   DCL 01 LK_EMP_VARIABLES,
         05  HV_ID          FIXED BIN (31),
         05  HV_LAST_NAME   CHAR(30),
         05  HV_FIRST_NAME  CHAR(20);

   DCL 01 ERR_REC,
         05 FILLER1          CHAR(10) INIT ('SQLCODE = '),
         05 SQLCODE_VIEW     PIC '-999',
         05 ERR_EMPID        FIXED BIN (31) INIT (0),
         05 FILLER2          CHAR(01) INIT (' '),
         05 ERR_TAB          CHAR(08) INIT (' '),
         05 ERR_PARA         CHAR(15) INIT (' ');

   DCL 01 ERR_MSG AUTOMATIC,
         05 ERR_LGTH         FIXED BIN (31) INIT (864),
         05 ERR_TXT(10)      CHAR(72);

   DCL ERR_TXT_LGTH          FIXED BIN (15) INIT (72);
   DCL ERR_NDX               FIXED BIN (31) INIT (0);


   EXEC SQL
     INCLUDE SQLCA;

   EXEC SQL
     INCLUDE EMPLOYEE;

/*********************************************************************
/*              P R O G R A M   M A I N L I N E                      *
 *********************************************************************/

   PUT SKIP LIST ('SAMPLE PLI PROGRAM: CALLED STORED PROCEDURE');

         DCLEMPLOYEE = '';

     /* SELECT AN EMPLOYEE */

         EXEC SQL
            SELECT EMP_LAST_NAME,
                   EMP_FIRST_NAME
            INTO  :HV_LAST_NAME,
                  :HV_FIRST_NAME
```

237

```
                      FROM HRSCHEMA.EMPLOYEE
                      WHERE EMP_ID = :HV_ID;

             IF SQLCODE ¬= 0 THEN
                 DO;
                     SQLCODE_VIEW = SQLCODE;
                     ERR_TAB = 'EMPLOYEE';
                     ERR_PARA = 'MAIN';
                     ERR_EMPID = HV_ID;
                     CALL P9999_SQL_ERROR;
                 END;


       P9999_SQL_ERROR: PROC;

          PUT SKIP LIST (ERR_REC);

          CALL DSNTIAR (SQLCA, ERR_MSG, ERR_TXT_LGTH);

          IF RETCODE = 0 THEN
             DO ERR_NDX = 1 TO 10;
                 PUT SKIP DATA (ERR_TXT(ERR_NDX));
             END; /* DO */
          ELSE
             PUT SKIP LIST ('DSNTIAR ERROR CODE = ' || RETCODE);

       END P9999_SQL_ERROR;

    END PLIEMP7;
```

Next, here is the PLI program to call the stored procedure.

```
PLIEMP8: PROCEDURE OPTIONS(MAIN) REORDER;
/**********************************************************************
*                                                                    *
* PROGRAM NAME :    PLIEMP8 - PROGRAM TO CALL A STORED PROCEDURE.     *
*                                                                    *
**********************************************************************/

/**********************************************************************
*               E X T E R N A L   E N T R I E S                      *
**********************************************************************/

   DCL DSNTIAR ENTRY OPTIONS(ASM INTER RETCODE);

/**********************************************************************
*               W O R K I N G   S T O R A G E                        *
**********************************************************************/

   DCL HV_ID            FIXED BIN (31) INIT (0);
   DCL HV_LAST_NAME     CHAR(30) INIT (' ');
   DCL HV_FIRST_NAME    CHAR(20) INIT (' ');

   DCL 01 ERR_REC,
          05 FILLER1            CHAR(10) INIT ('SQLCODE = '),
          05 SQLCODE_VIEW       PIC '-999',
          05 ERR_EMPID          FIXED BIN (31) INIT (0),
          05 FILLER2            CHAR(01) INIT (' '),
```

```
               05 ERR_TAB            CHAR(08) INIT (' '),
               05 ERR_PARA           CHAR(15) INIT (' ');

       DCL 01 ERR_MSG AUTOMATIC,
               05 ERR_LGTH           FIXED BIN (31) INIT (864),
               05 ERR_TXT(10)        CHAR(72);

       DCL ERR_TXT_LGTH              FIXED BIN (15) INIT (72);
       DCL ERR_NDX                   FIXED BIN (31) INIT (0);

       EXEC SQL
         INCLUDE SQLCA;

       EXEC SQL
         INCLUDE EMPLOYEE;

   /*******************************************************************
   /*                P R O G R A M   M A I N L I N E              *
   ********************************************************************/

       PUT SKIP LIST ('SAMPLE PLI PROGRAM: CALL STORED PROCEDURE');

            DCLEMPLOYEE = '';

       /* SELECT AN EMPLOYEE */

            HV_ID = 3217;

            EXEC SQL
               CALL HRSCHEMA.GETEMP2P(:HV_ID,
                                      :HV_LAST_NAME,
                                      :HV_FIRST_NAME);

            IF SQLCODE ¬= 0 THEN
               DO;
                    SQLCODE_VIEW = SQLCODE;
                    ERR_TAB = 'EMPLOYEE';
                    ERR_PARA = 'MAIN';
                    ERR_EMPID  = HV_ID;
                    CALL P9999_SQL_ERROR;
               END;

            ELSE
               PUT SKIP LIST ('PROC CALL SUCCESSFUL '
                        || TRIM(HV_LAST_NAME)
                        || ' ' || TRIM(HV_FIRST_NAME)
                        || ' ' || HV_ID);


   P9999_SQL_ERROR: PROC;

       PUT SKIP LIST (ERR_REC);

       CALL DSNTIAR (SQLCA, ERR_MSG, ERR_TXT_LGTH);

       IF RETCODE = 0 THEN
          DO ERR_NDX = 1 TO 10;
             PUT SKIP DATA (ERR_TXT(ERR_NDX));
          END; /* DO */
       ELSE
```

```
                 PUT SKIP LIST ('DSNTIAR ERROR CODE = ' || RETCODE);

          END P9999_SQL_ERROR;

       END PLIEMP8;
```

And here is the result of the run:

```
     SAMPLE PLI PROGRAM: CALL STORED PROCEDURE
     PROC CALL SUCCESSFUL JOHNSON EDWARD              3217
```

Stored Procedure Error Handling

So far the stored procedures we've created did not encounter error conditions. Let's refine our GETEMP stored procedure to handle unexpected SQL codes. One especially good thing about native SQL procedures is that when you call them the SQL code is reflected in the SQLCA of the calling program. So you need only interrogate the SQLCODE as you normally would to detect an error.

Let's try running our COBEMP6 (which calls GETEMP) and specify a nonexistent employee id, for example 3218. If we run this, here is the output we'll receive:

```
     SAMPLE COBOL PROGRAM: CALL STORED PROCEDURE
     SQLCODE = -305     GETEMP          MAIN          000003218
      DSNT408I SQLCODE = -305, ERROR:  THE NULL VALUE CANNOT BE ASSIGNED TO
              OUTPUT HOST VARIABLE NUMBER 2 BECAUSE NO INDICATOR VARIABLE IS
              SPECIFIED
      DSNT418I SQLSTATE   = 22002 SQLSTATE RETURN CODE
      DSNT415I SQLERRP    = DSNXROHB SQL PROCEDURE DETECTING ERROR
      DSNT416I SQLERRD    = -115  0  0  -1  0  0 SQL DIAGNOSTIC INFORMATION
      DSNT416I SQLERRD    = X'FFFFFF8D'  X'00000000'  X'00000000'
              X'FFFFFFFF'  X'00000000'  X'00000000' SQL DIAGNOSTIC
              INFORMATION
```

This result indicates that our query in the GETEMP procedure did not return a value. The problem is that we didn't define indicator variables in our COBOL program and use them in the call to the stored procedure. Indicator variables are used to identify a situation where a NULL value was encountered in a query. This is important since a DB2 NULL value cannot be loaded into the specified COBOL host variable. Neither COBOL nor PLI know what a DB2 NULL value is, so you must add indicator variables to your query to prevent the -305 SQL result.

Once a query completes you can check the indicator variable and if its value is -1, that means a NULL was encountered for that column and the value in the host variable is a default value (typically zero for numeric variables and space for character variables). The query does not fail and you can decide what to do with the default result value (if anything).

240

Let's define indicator variables in our COBEMP6 program for the EMP_FIRST_NAME and EMP_LAST_NAME columns.

```
01 HV-INDICATOR-VARS.
   10  IND-HV-LAST-NAME  PIC S9(4) BINARY.
   10  IND-HV-FIRST-NAME PIC S9(4) BINARY.
```

Now these indicator variables must be used in the query. So our call to the GETEMP stored procedure becomes:

```
CALL HRSCHEMA.GETEMP(:HV-ID,
                     :HV-LAST-NAME:  IND-HV-LAST-NAME,
                     :HV-FIRST-NAME: IND-HV-FIRST-NAME)
```

Now when we call the stored procedure we will get a +100 SQLCODE which simply means the record for employee 3218 was not found.

```
SAMPLE COBOL PROGRAM: CALL STORED PROCEDURE
SQLCODE =  100      GETEMP          MAIN          000003218
 DSNT404I SQLCODE = 100, NOT FOUND:  ROW NOT FOUND FOR FETCH, UPDATE, OR
          DELETE, OR THE RESULT OF A QUERY IS AN EMPTY TABLE
 DSNT418I SQLSTATE  = 02000 SQLSTATE RETURN CODE
 DSNT415I SQLERRP   = DSNXRFF SQL PROCEDURE DETECTING ERROR
 DSNT416I SQLERRD   = -110  0  0  -1  0  0 SQL DIAGNOSTIC INFORMATION
 DSNT416I SQLERRD   = X'FFFFFF92'  X'00000000'  X'00000000'
          X'FFFFFFFF'  X'00000000'  X'00000000' SQL DIAGNOSTIC
          INFORMATION
```

Unlike native SQL procedures, when you call an external stored procedure you cannot use the calling program's SQLCODE value to determine the status of the procedure. However you can define additional OUT parameters to pass back information to the calling program. For example, in our COBEMP7 program we have a linkage section as follows, and a reference to it with PROCEDURE DIVISION USING LK-EMP-VARIABLES.

```
01 LK-EMP-VARIABLES.
   10  HV-ID             PIC S9(9) USAGE COMP.
   10  HV-LAST-NAME      PIC X(30).
   10  HV-FIRST-NAME     PIC X(20).

   PROCEDURE DIVISION USING LK-EMP-VARIABLES.
```

You can add some diagnostic variables to the stored procedure OUT parameter list, such as SQLCODE, SQLSTATE and message (the latter to send a customized message back to the calling program). Recall that program COBEMP7 is associated with stored procedure GETEMP2, so let's add the new variables to GETEMP2:

```
CREATE PROCEDURE HRSCHEMA.GETEMP2
(IN EMP_NO INT,
 OUT EMP_LNAME VARCHAR(30),
 OUT EMP_FNAME VARCHAR(20),
 OUT PRM_SQLCODE INT,
 OUT PRM_SQLSTATE CHAR(5),
 OUT PRM_MESSAGE  CHAR(80))
```

You would also need to add these variables to the program linkage variable list.

```
01 LK-EMP-VARIABLES.
    10  HV-ID             PIC S9(9) USAGE COMP.
    10  HV-LAST-NAME      PIC X(30).
    10  HV-FIRST-NAME     PIC X(20).
    10  PRM-SQLCODE       PIC X(5).
    10  PRM-SQLSTATE      PIC X(5).
    10  PRM-MESSAGE       PIC X(80).
```

Now if an error is encountered you can assign the diagnostic values to your parameter variables:

```
MOVE SQLCODE  TO PRM-SQLCODE
MOVE SQLSTATE TO PRM-SQLSTATE
MOVE 'ERROR IN PROC GETEMP2' TO PRM-MESSAGE
```

Since these variables are OUT parameters, they will be returned to the calling program and you can interrogate the values for diagnostic purposes.

More Stored Procedure Examples

Let's do a few more examples of stored procedures, and in this case we'll create some data access routines. Specifically we'll create stored procedures to retrieve information for an employee, to add or update an employee, and to delete an employee.

For retrieving employee data, we'll simply expand our GETEMP procedure to include all of the original fields we created the table with. We'll call the new procedure GET_EMP_INFO.

```
CREATE PROCEDURE HRSCHEMA.GET_EMP_INFO
(IN EMP_NO INT,
 OUT EMP_LNAME VARCHAR(30),
 OUT EMP_FNAME VARCHAR(20),
 OUT EMP_SRVC_YRS INT,
 OUT EMP_PROM_DATE DATE,
 OUT EMP_PROF XML,
 OUT EMP_SSN  CHAR(09))

LANGUAGE SQL
```

```
    READS SQL DATA

    BEGIN
       SELECT EMP_LAST_NAME,
                EMP_FIRST_NAME,
                EMP_SERVICE_YEARS,
                 EMP_SERVICE_YEARS,
                 EMP_PROMOTION_DATE,
                 EMP_PROFILE,
                 EMP_SSN
          INTO EMP_LNAME,
               EMP_FNAME,
               EMP_SRVC_YRS,
               EMP_PROM_DATE,
               EMP_PROF,
               EMP_SSN
          FROM HRSCHEMA.EMPLOYEE
          WHERE EMP_ID = EMP_NO;

    END #
```

Next, we'll create a procedure that merges the input data into the table, either adding it if it is a new record, or updating it if an old record.

```
CREATE PROCEDURE HRSCHEMA.MRG_EMP_INFO
(IN EMP_NO INT,
 IN EMP_LNAME VARCHAR(30),
 IN EMP_FNAME VARCHAR(20),
 IN EMP_SRVC_YRS INT,
 IN EMP_PROM_DATE DATE,
 IN EMP_PROF XML,
 IN EMP_SSN  CHAR(09))

LANGUAGE SQL
MODIFIES SQL DATA

BEGIN
   MERGE INTO HRSCHEMA.EMPLOYEE AS T
   USING
    (VALUES (EMP_NO,
    EMP_LNAME,
    EMP_FNAME,
    EMP_SRVC_YRS,
    EMP_PROM_DATE,
    EMP_PROF,
    EMP_SSN))
    AS S
    (EMP_ID,
     EMP_LAST_NAME,
     EMP_FIRST_NAME,
     EMP_SERVICE_YEARS,
     EMP_PROMOTION_DATE,
```

243

```
        EMP_PROFILE,
        EMP_SSN)
     ON S.EMP_ID = T.EMP_ID

     WHEN MATCHED
        THEN UPDATE
           SET EMP_ID              = S.EMP_ID,
               EMP_LAST_NAME       = S.EMP_LAST_NAME,
               EMP_FIRST_NAME      = S.EMP_FIRST_NAME,
               EMP_SERVICE_YEARS   = S.EMP_SERVICE_YEARS,
               EMP_PROMOTION_DATE  = S.EMP_PROMOTION_DATE,
               EMP_PROFILE         = S.EMP_PROFILE,
               EMP_SSN             = S.EMP_SSN

     WHEN NOT MATCHED
        THEN INSERT
           VALUES (S.EMP_ID,
           S.EMP_LAST_NAME,
           S.EMP_FIRST_NAME,
           S.EMP_SERVICE_YEARS,
           S.EMP_PROMOTION_DATE,
           S.EMP_PROFILE,
           S.EMP_SSN) ;

     END #
```

Finally, let's take care of the delete function.

```
     CREATE PROCEDURE HRSCHEMA.DLT_EMP_INFO
     (IN EMP_NO INT)

     LANGUAGE SQL
     MODIFIES SQL DATA
     BEGIN
        DELETE FROM HRSCHEMA.EMPLOYEE
        WHERE EMP_ID = EMP_NO;

     END #
```

Before we can use these procedures we must grant access to them. In our case we will grant to public, but normally you will grant access only to your developer and user groups.

```
     GRANT EXECUTE ON PROCEDURE HRSCHEMA.GET_EMP_INFO TO PUBLIC;

     GRANT EXECUTE ON PROCEDURE HRSCHEMA.MRG_EMP_INFO TO PUBLIC;

     GRANT EXECUTE ON PROCEDURE HRSCHEMA.DLT_EMP_INFO TO PUBLIC;
```

Next we need a COBOL program to test each of these stored procedures. Here is one that works:

```cobol
       IDENTIFICATION DIVISION.
       PROGRAM-ID. COBEMPH.

      ********************************************************
      *       PROGRAM USING DB2 CALL TO SEVERAL             *
      *       STORED PROCEDURES.                            *
      ********************************************************

       ENVIRONMENT DIVISION.
       DATA DIVISION.
       WORKING-STORAGE SECTION.

       01 HV-INDICATOR-VARS.
          10  IND-HV-LAST-NAME  PIC S9(4) BINARY VALUE 0.
          10  IND-HV-FIRST-NAME PIC S9(4) BINARY VALUE 0.
          10  IND-HV-SRVC-YEARS PIC S9(4) BINARY VALUE 0.
          10  IND-HV-PROM-DATE  PIC S9(4) BINARY VALUE 0.
          10  IND-HV-PROFILE    PIC S9(4) BINARY VALUE 0.
          10  IND-HV-SSN        PIC S9(4) BINARY VALUE 0.

       01 ERR-REC.
          05 FILLER             PIC X(10) VALUE 'SQLCODE = '.
          05 SQLCODE-VIEW        PIC -999.
          05 FILLER             PIC X(005) VALUE SPACES.
          05 ERR-TAB            PIC X(016).
          05 ERR-PARA           PIC X(015).
          05 ERR-DETAIL         PIC X(040).

       77 ERR-TXT-LGTH          PIC S9(9) USAGE COMP VALUE +72.

       01 ERR-MSG.
          05 ERR-MSG-LGTH        PIC S9(04) COMP VALUE +864.
          05 ERR-MSG-TXT         PIC X(072) OCCURS 12 TIMES
                                            INDEXED BY ERR-NDX.

          EXEC SQL
            INCLUDE SQLCA
          END-EXEC.

          EXEC SQL
            INCLUDE EMPLOYEE
          END-EXEC.


       PROCEDURE DIVISION.

       MAIN-PARA.
           DISPLAY "SAMPLE COBOL PROGRAM: CALL STORED PROCEDURES".

           DISPLAY 'MERGE EMPLOYEE INFORMATION'

           MOVE +7938     TO EMP-ID
           MOVE 'WINFIELD' TO EMP-LAST-NAME-TEXT
```

```
MOVE 'STANLEY'   TO EMP-FIRST-NAME-TEXT
MOVE +3          TO EMP-SERVICE-YEARS
MOVE SPACES      TO EMP-PROMOTION-DATE
MOVE -1          TO IND-HV-PROM-DATE
MOVE SPACES      TO EMP-PROFILE
MOVE -1          TO IND-HV-PROFILE
MOVE '382734509' TO EMP-SSN

EXEC SQL

    CALL HRSCHEMA.MRG_EMP_INFO
        (:EMP-ID,
         :EMP-LAST-NAME      :IND-HV-LAST-NAME,
         :EMP-FIRST-NAME     :IND-HV-FIRST-NAME,
         :EMP-SERVICE-YEARS  :IND-HV-SRVC-YEARS,
         :EMP-PROMOTION-DATE :IND-HV-PROM-DATE,
         :EMP-PROFILE        :IND-HV-PROFILE,
         :EMP-SSN            :IND-HV-SSN)

END-EXEC.

IF SQLCODE IS NOT EQUAL TO ZERO

    DISPLAY  'MERGE CALL FAILED ' EMP-ID
    MOVE SQLCODE TO SQLCODE-VIEW
    MOVE 'EMPLOYEE' TO ERR-TAB
    MOVE 'MAIN'    TO ERR-PARA
    MOVE EMP-ID    TO ERR-DETAIL
    PERFORM P9999-SQL-ERROR

ELSE
    DISPLAY  'MERGE CALL SUCCESSFUL ' EMP-ID
    DISPLAY  EMP-LAST-NAME
    DISPLAY  EMP-FIRST-NAME
    DISPLAY  EMP-SERVICE-YEARS
    DISPLAY  EMP-PROMOTION-DATE
    DISPLAY  EMP-SSN

END-IF

DISPLAY 'DISPLAY EMPLOYEE INFORMATION'

MOVE +7938      TO EMP-ID

EXEC SQL

    CALL HRSCHEMA.GET_EMP_INFO
        (:EMP-ID,
         :EMP-LAST-NAME      :IND-HV-LAST-NAME,
         :EMP-FIRST-NAME     :IND-HV-FIRST-NAME,
         :EMP-SERVICE-YEARS  :IND-HV-SRVC-YEARS,
         :EMP-PROMOTION-DATE :IND-HV-PROM-DATE,
         :EMP-PROFILE        :IND-HV-PROFILE,
```

```
                 :EMP-SSN                  :IND-HV-SSN)

        END-EXEC.

        IF SQLCODE IS NOT EQUAL TO ZERO

           DISPLAY  'GET CALL FAILED ' EMP-ID
           MOVE SQLCODE TO SQLCODE-VIEW
           MOVE 'EMPLOYEE' TO ERR-TAB
           MOVE 'MAIN'     TO ERR-PARA
           MOVE EMP-ID     TO ERR-DETAIL
           PERFORM P9999-SQL-ERROR

        ELSE
           DISPLAY  'GET CALL SUCCESSFUL ' EMP-ID
           DISPLAY  EMP-LAST-NAME
           DISPLAY  EMP-FIRST-NAME
           DISPLAY  EMP-SERVICE-YEARS
           DISPLAY  EMP-PROMOTION-DATE
           DISPLAY  EMP-SSN

        END-IF


        DISPLAY 'UPDATE EMPLOYEE INFORMATION'

        MOVE +7938      TO EMP-ID
        MOVE 'WINFIELD' TO EMP-LAST-NAME-TEXT
        MOVE 'SAMUEL '  TO EMP-FIRST-NAME-TEXT
        MOVE +2         TO EMP-SERVICE-YEARS
        MOVE '01/31/2017' TO EMP-PROMOTION-DATE
        MOVE 0          TO IND-HV-PROM-DATE
        MOVE SPACES     TO EMP-PROFILE
        MOVE -1         TO IND-HV-PROFILE
        MOVE '382734595' TO EMP-SSN

        EXEC SQL

           CALL HRSCHEMA.MRG_EMP_INFO
              (:EMP-ID,
               :EMP-LAST-NAME      :IND-HV-LAST-NAME,
               :EMP-FIRST-NAME     :IND-HV-FIRST-NAME,
               :EMP-SERVICE-YEARS  :IND-HV-SRVC-YEARS,
               :EMP-PROMOTION-DATE :IND-HV-PROM-DATE,
               :EMP-PROFILE        :IND-HV-PROFILE,
               :EMP-SSN            :IND-HV-SSN)

        END-EXEC.

        IF SQLCODE IS NOT EQUAL TO ZERO

           DISPLAY  'UPDATE MERGE CALL FAILED ' EMP-ID
           MOVE SQLCODE TO SQLCODE-VIEW
```

```
          MOVE 'EMPLOYEE' TO ERR-TAB
          MOVE 'MAIN'     TO ERR-PARA
          MOVE EMP-ID     TO ERR-DETAIL
          PERFORM P9999-SQL-ERROR

   ELSE
          DISPLAY  'UPDATE MERGE CALL SUCCESSFUL ' EMP-ID
          DISPLAY  EMP-LAST-NAME
          DISPLAY  EMP-FIRST-NAME
          DISPLAY  EMP-SERVICE-YEARS
          DISPLAY  EMP-PROMOTION-DATE
          DISPLAY  EMP-SSN

   END-IF


   DISPLAY 'DISPLAY UPDATED EMPLOYEE INFORMATION'

   MOVE +7938      TO EMP-ID

   EXEC SQL

          CALL HRSCHEMA.GET_EMP_INFO
             (:EMP-ID,
              :EMP-LAST-NAME       :IND-HV-LAST-NAME,
              :EMP-FIRST-NAME      :IND-HV-FIRST-NAME,
              :EMP-SERVICE-YEARS   :IND-HV-SRVC-YEARS,
              :EMP-PROMOTION-DATE  :IND-HV-PROM-DATE,
              :EMP-PROFILE         :IND-HV-PROFILE,
              :EMP-SSN             :IND-HV-SSN)

   END-EXEC.

   IF SQLCODE IS NOT EQUAL TO ZERO

          DISPLAY  'GET CALL FAILED ' EMP-ID
          MOVE SQLCODE TO SQLCODE-VIEW
          MOVE 'EMPLOYEE' TO ERR-TAB
          MOVE 'MAIN'     TO ERR-PARA
          MOVE EMP-ID     TO ERR-DETAIL
          PERFORM P9999-SQL-ERROR

   ELSE
          DISPLAY  'GET CALL SUCCESSFUL ' EMP-ID
          DISPLAY  EMP-LAST-NAME
          DISPLAY  EMP-FIRST-NAME
          DISPLAY  EMP-SERVICE-YEARS
          DISPLAY  EMP-PROMOTION-DATE
          DISPLAY  EMP-SSN

   END-IF
```

```
            DISPLAY 'DISPLAY DELETED EMPLOYEE INFORMATION'

            MOVE +7938      TO EMP-ID

            EXEC SQL

               CALL HRSCHEMA.DLT_EMP_INFO
                   (:EMP-ID)

            END-EXEC.

            IF SQLCODE IS NOT EQUAL TO ZERO

               DISPLAY  'DELETE CALL FAILED ' EMP-ID
               MOVE SQLCODE TO SQLCODE-VIEW
               MOVE 'EMPLOYEE' TO ERR-TAB
               MOVE 'MAIN'      TO ERR-PARA
               MOVE EMP-ID      TO ERR-DETAIL
               PERFORM P9999-SQL-ERROR

            ELSE
               DISPLAY  'DELETE CALL SUCCESSFUL ' EMP-ID

            END-IF


            GOBACK.

        P9999-SQL-ERROR.

            DISPLAY ERR-REC.

            CALL 'DSNTIAR' USING SQLCA,
                          ERR-MSG,
                          ERR-TXT-LGTH.

            IF RETURN-CODE IS EQUAL TO ZERO

               PERFORM P9999-DISP-ERR
                  VARYING ERR-NDX FROM 1 BY 1
                  UNTIL ERR-NDX > 12

            ELSE
               DISPLAY 'DSNTIAR ERROR CODE = ' RETURN-CODE
               STOP RUN.

        P9999-DISP-ERR.

            DISPLAY ERR-MSG-TXT(ERR-NDX).

        P9999-DISP-ERR-EXIT.
```

Finally, here is the output from the program run:

```
SAMPLE COBOL PROGRAM: CALL STORED PROCEDURES
MERGE EMPLOYEE INFORMATION
MERGE CALL SUCCESSFUL 000007938
  WINFIELD
  STANLEY
000000003

382734509
DISPLAY EMPLOYEE INFORMATION
GET CALL SUCCESSFUL 000007938
  WINFIELD
  STANLEY
000000003

382734509
UPDATE EMPLOYEE INFORMATION
UPDATE MERGE CALL SUCCESSFUL 000007938
  WINFIELD
  SAMUEL
000000002
01/31/2017
382734595

DISPLAY UPDATED EMPLOYEE INFORMATION
GET CALL SUCCESSFUL 000007938
  WINFIELD
  SAMUEL
000000002
2017-01-31
382734595

DISPLAY DELETED EMPLOYEE INFORMATION
DELETE CALL SUCCESSFUL 000007938
```

Last, here is our PLI version of the program to call the data access stored procedures.

```
PLIEMPH: PROCEDURE OPTIONS(MAIN) REORDER;

/******************************************************************
* PROGRAM NAME :   PLIEMPH - CALL SEVERAL STORED PROCEDURES      *
*                           FOR DATA ACCESS.                     *
******************************************************************/

/******************************************************************
*               E X T E R N A L   E N T R I E S                  *
******************************************************************/

   DCL DSNTIAR ENTRY OPTIONS(ASM INTER RETCODE);

/******************************************************************
/*               W O R K I N G   S T O R A G E                   *
```

```
        ***********************************************************************/
        DCL COMMIT_CTR              FIXED BIN(31) INIT(0);
        DCL RET_SQL_CODE            FIXED BIN(31) INIT(0);
        DCL RET_SQL_CODE_PIC        PIC 'S999999999' INIT (0);

        DCL 01 ERR_REC,
                05 FILLER1          CHAR(10) INIT ('SQLCODE = '),
                05 SQLCODE_VIEW     PIC '-999',
                05 ERR_EMPID        FIXED BIN (31) INIT (0),
                05 FILLER2          CHAR(01) INIT (' '),
                05 ERR_TAB          CHAR(08) INIT (' '),
                05 ERR_PARA         CHAR(15) INIT (' ');

        DCL 01 ERR_MSG AUTOMATIC,
                05 ERR_LGTH         FIXED BIN (31) INIT (864),
                05 ERR_TXT(10)      CHAR(72);

        DCL ERR_TXT_LGTH            FIXED BIN (15) INIT (72);
        DCL ERR_NDX                 FIXED BIN (31) INIT (0);



        DCL 01 HV_INDICATOR_VARS,
           10  IND_HV_LAST_NAME  FIXED BIN (15) INIT(0),
           10  IND_HV_FIRST_NAME FIXED BIN (15) INIT(0),
           10  IND_HV_SRVC_YEARS FIXED BIN (15) INIT(0),
           10  IND_HV_PROM_DATE  FIXED BIN (15) INIT(0),
           10  IND_HV_PROFILE    FIXED BIN (15) INIT(0),
           10  IND_HV_SSN        FIXED BIN (15) INIT(0);

        EXEC SQL
          INCLUDE SQLCA;

        EXEC SQL
          INCLUDE EMPLOYEE;

/*********************************************************************
/*              P R O G R A M   M A I N L I N E                    *
*********************************************************************/

        PUT SKIP LIST ('SAMPLE PLI PROGRAM: CALL SOME STORED PROCEDURE');

        PUT SKIP LIST ('DISPLAY MERGE EMPLOYEE INFORMATION');

        EMP_ID              = 7938;
        EMP_LAST_NAME       = 'WINFIELD';
        EMP_FIRST_NAME      = 'STANLEY';
        EMP_SERVICE_YEARS   = +3;
        EMP_PROMOTION_DATE  = ' ';
        IND_HV_PROM_DATE    = -1;
        EMP_PROFILE         = ' ';
        IND_HV_PROFILE      = -1;
```

```
                    EMP_SSN              = '382734509';

EXEC SQL

    CALL HRSCHEMA.MRG_EMP_INFO
        (:EMP_ID,
         :EMP_LAST_NAME        :IND_HV_LAST_NAME,
         :EMP_FIRST_NAME       :IND_HV_FIRST_NAME,
         :EMP_SERVICE_YEARS    :IND_HV_SRVC_YEARS,
         :EMP_PROMOTION_DATE   :IND_HV_PROM_DATE,
         :EMP_PROFILE          :IND_HV_PROFILE,
         :EMP_SSN              :IND_HV_SSN);

    IF SQLCODE ¬= 0 THEN
        DO;
            PUT SKIP LIST ('MERGE CALL FAILED ' || EMP_ID);
            SQLCODE_VIEW    =  SQLCODE;
            ERR_TAB         = 'EMPLOYEE';
            ERR_PARA        = 'MAIN';
            ERR_DETAIL      = EMP_ID;
            CALL P9999_SQL_ERROR;
        END;

    ELSE
        DO;
            PUT SKIP LIST ('MERGE CALL SUCCESSFUL ' || EMP_ID);
            PUT SKIP LIST (EMP_LAST_NAME);
            PUT SKIP LIST (EMP_FIRST_NAME);
            PUT SKIP LIST (EMP_SERVICE_YEARS);
            PUT SKIP LIST (EMP_PROMOTION_DATE);
            PUT SKIP LIST (EMP_SSN);
        END;

PUT SKIP LIST ('DISPLAY EMPLOYEE INFORMATION');

EMP_ID = 7938;

EXEC SQL

    CALL HRSCHEMA.GET_EMP_INFO
        (:EMP_ID,
         :EMP_LAST_NAME        :IND_HV_LAST_NAME,
         :EMP_FIRST_NAME       :IND_HV_FIRST_NAME,
         :EMP_SERVICE_YEARS    :IND_HV_SRVC_YEARS,
         :EMP_PROMOTION_DATE   :IND_HV_PROM_DATE,
         :EMP_PROFILE          :IND_HV_PROFILE,
         :EMP_SSN              :IND_HV_SSN);

    IF SQLCODE ¬= 0 THEN
        DO;
            PUT SKIP LIST ('GET CALL FAILED ' || EMP_ID);
            SQLCODE_VIEW    =  SQLCODE;
            ERR_TAB         = 'EMPLOYEE';
```

```
                    ERR_PARA          = 'MAIN';
                    ERR_DETAIL        = EMP_ID;
                    CALL P9999_SQL_ERROR;
                END;

        ELSE
            DO;
                PUT SKIP LIST ('GET CALL SUCCESSFUL ' || EMP_ID);
                PUT SKIP LIST (EMP_LAST_NAME);
                PUT SKIP LIST (EMP_FIRST_NAME);
                PUT SKIP LIST (EMP_SERVICE_YEARS);
                PUT SKIP LIST (EMP_PROMOTION_DATE);
                PUT SKIP LIST (EMP_SSN);
            END;


    PUT SKIP LIST ('UPDATE EMPLOYEE INFORMATION');

    EMP_ID               = 7938;
    EMP_LAST_NAME        = 'WINFIELD';
    EMP_FIRST_NAME       = 'SAMUEL';
    EMP_SERVICE_YEARS    = +2;
    EMP_PROMOTION_DATE   = ' ';
    IND_HV_PROM_DATE     = -1;
    EMP_PROFILE          = ' ';
    IND_HV_PROFILE       = -1;
    EMP_SSN              = '382734595';

    EXEC SQL

        CALL HRSCHEMA.MRG_EMP_INFO
            (:EMP_ID,
             :EMP_LAST_NAME        :IND_HV_LAST_NAME,
             :EMP_FIRST_NAME       :IND_HV_FIRST_NAME,
             :EMP_SERVICE_YEARS    :IND_HV_SRVC_YEARS,
             :EMP_PROMOTION_DATE   :IND_HV_PROM_DATE,
             :EMP_PROFILE          :IND_HV_PROFILE,
             :EMP_SSN              :IND_HV_SSN);

        IF SQLCODE ¬= 0 THEN
            DO;
                PUT SKIP LIST ('UPDATE MERGE CALL FAILED ' || EMP_ID);
                SQLCODE_VIEW      =  SQLCODE;
                ERR_TAB           = 'EMPLOYEE';
                ERR_PARA          = 'MAIN';
                ERR_DETAIL        = EMP_ID;
                CALL P9999_SQL_ERROR;
            END;

        ELSE
            DO;
                PUT SKIP LIST ('UPDATE MERGE CALL SUCCESSFUL ' || EMP_ID);
                PUT SKIP LIST (EMP_LAST_NAME);
```

```
                PUT SKIP LIST (EMP_FIRST_NAME);
                PUT SKIP LIST (EMP_SERVICE_YEARS);
                PUT SKIP LIST (EMP_PROMOTION_DATE);
                PUT SKIP LIST (EMP_SSN);
            END;

    PUT SKIP LIST ('DISPLAY UPDATED EMPLOYEE INFORMATION');

    EMP_ID = +7938;

    EXEC SQL

        CALL HRSCHEMA.GET_EMP_INFO
            (:EMP_ID,
             :EMP_LAST_NAME      :IND_HV_LAST_NAME,
             :EMP_FIRST_NAME     :IND_HV_FIRST_NAME,
             :EMP_SERVICE_YEARS  :IND_HV_SRVC_YEARS,
             :EMP_PROMOTION_DATE :IND_HV_PROM_DATE,
             :EMP_PROFILE        :IND_HV_PROFILE,
             :EMP_SSN            :IND_HV_SSN);

        IF SQLCODE ¬= 0 THEN
            DO;
                PUT SKIP LIST ('GET CALL FAILED ' || EMP_ID);
                SQLCODE_VIEW    =   SQLCODE;
                ERR_TAB         = 'EMPLOYEE';
                ERR_PARA        = 'MAIN';
                ERR_DETAIL      = EMP_ID;
                CALL P9999_SQL_ERROR;
            END;
        ELSE
            DO;
                PUT SKIP LIST ('GET CALL SUCCESSFUL ' || EMP_ID);
                PUT SKIP LIST (EMP_LAST_NAME);
                PUT SKIP LIST (EMP_FIRST_NAME);
                PUT SKIP LIST (EMP_SERVICE_YEARS);
                PUT SKIP LIST (EMP_PROMOTION_DATE);
                PUT SKIP LIST (EMP_SSN);
            END;

    PUT SKIP LIST ('DISPLAY DELETED EMPLOYEE INFORMATION');

    EMP_ID = 7938;

    EXEC SQL

        CALL HRSCHEMA.DLT_EMP_INFO
            (:EMP_ID);

        IF SQLCODE ¬= 0 THEN
            DO;
                PUT SKIP LIST ('DELETE CALL FAILED ' || EMP_ID);
                SQLCODE_VIEW    =   SQLCODE;
```

```
                 ERR_TAB        = 'EMPLOYEE';
                 ERR_PARA       = 'MAIN';
                 ERR_DETAIL     = EMP_ID;
                 CALL P9999_SQL_ERROR;
              END;

          ELSE
            DO;
                 PUT SKIP LIST ('DELETE CALL SUCCESSFUL ' || EMP_ID);
                 PUT SKIP LIST (EMP_LAST_NAME);
                 PUT SKIP LIST (EMP_FIRST_NAME);
                 PUT SKIP LIST (EMP_SERVICE_YEARS);
                 PUT SKIP LIST (EMP_PROMOTION_DATE);
                 PUT SKIP LIST (EMP_SSN);
            END;

    P9999_SQL_ERROR: PROC;

       PUT SKIP LIST (ERR_REC);

       CALL DSNTIAR (SQLCA, ERR_MSG, ERR_TXT_LGTH);

       IF RETCODE = 0 THEN
          DO ERR_NDX = 1 TO 10;
              PUT SKIP DATA (ERR_TXT(ERR_NDX));
          END; /* DO */
       ELSE
          PUT SKIP LIST ('DSNTIAR ERROR CODE = ' || RETCODE);

    END P9999_SQL_ERROR;

    END PLIEMPH;
```

And here is the output:

```
SAMPLE PLI PROGRAM: CALL SOME STORED PROCEDURE
DISPLAY MERGE EMPLOYEE INFORMATION
MERGE CALL SUCCESSFUL          7938
WINFIELD
STANLEY
              3

382734509

DISPLAY EMPLOYEE INFORMATION
GET CALL SUCCESSFUL            7938
WINFIELD
STANLEY
              3

382734509
```

```
UPDATE EMPLOYEE INFORMATION
UPDATE MERGE CALL SUCCESSFUL              7938
WINFIELD
SAMUEL
                2

382734595

DISPLAY UPDATED EMPLOYEE INFORMATION
GET CALL SUCCESSFUL              7938
WINFIELD
SAMUEL
                2

382734595

DISPLAY DELETED EMPLOYEE INFORMATION
DELETE CALL SUCCESSFUL              7938
WINFIELD
SAMUEL
                2

382734595
```

This concludes our discussion of stored procedures. As you can tell this is a very powerful technology that promotes reusability and can help minimize custom coding.

USER DEFINED FUNCTIONS

A user defined function (UDF) is one written by an application programmer or DBA, as opposed to those functions provided out of the box by DB2. UDFs extend DB2 functionality by allowing new functions to be created. As a function, a UDF always returns a value, and is called with the CALL statement.

```
CALL <UDF name><parameters>
```

Types of UDF

There are five varieties of UDFs as follows:

1. SQL Scalar Function
2. SQL Table Function
3. External Scalar Function
4. External Table Function
5. Sourced Function

Examples of UDFs

SQL Scalar Function

An SQL scalar function will return a single value using only SQL statements. There is no external program. You may recall earlier we established a business rule that an employee's "level" was based on their years of service. We used an SQL with a CASE statement to return a value of JUNIOR, ADVANCED or SENIOR. Here's the SQL we used earlier:

```
SELECT EMP_ID,
EMP_LAST_NAME,
EMP_FIRST_NAME,
CASE
   WHEN EMP_SERVICE_YEARS  < 1 THEN 'ENTRY'
   WHEN EMP_SERVICE_YEARS  < 5 THEN 'ADVANCED'
   ELSE 'SENIOR'
END CASE
FROM HRSCHEMA.EMPLOYEE
---------+---------+---------+---------+---------+-----
    EMP_ID  EMP_LAST_NAME        EMP_FIRST_NAME       CASE
---------+---------+---------+---------+---------+-----
      3217  JOHNSON              EDWARD               ADVANCED
      7459  STEWART              BETTY                SENIOR
      9134  FRANKLIN             BRIANNA              ENTRY
      4175  TURNBULL             FRED                 ADVANCED
      4720  SCHULTZ              TIM                  SENIOR
      6288  WILLARD              JOE                  SENIOR
DSNE610I NUMBER OF ROWS DISPLAYED IS 6
```

257

Now let's say we have several programs that need to generate these values. We could copy the same SQL to each program, but what if the logic changes in the future? Either the cutoff years or the named literals could change. In that case it would be convenient to only have to make the change in one place. A UDF can accomplish that objective.

We'll create a UDF that accepts an integer which is the years of service, and then it will return the literal value that represents the employee's level of service in the company. First, we must define the UDF to DB2. We need to specify at least:

- The name of the function
- Input parameter type
- Return parameter type

Now let's code the UDF:

```
CREATE FUNCTION HRSCHEMA.EMP_LEVEL (YRS_SRVC INT)
    RETURNS VARCHAR(10)
    READS SQL DATA
    RETURN
   (SELECT
    CASE
       WHEN YRS_SRVC  < 1 THEN 'ENTRY      '
       WHEN YRS_SRVC  < 5 THEN 'ADVANCED  '
       ELSE 'SENIOR    '
    END CASE
    FROM SYSIBM.SYSDUMMY1)
```

Finally, we can run a query against the new UDF:

```
SELECT HRSCHEMA.EMP_LEVEL(7)
AS EMP_LVL
FROM SYSIBM.SYSDUMMY1;

---------+---------+---------+---------+----
EMP_LVL
---------+---------+---------+---------+----
SENIOR

DSNE610I NUMBER OF ROWS DISPLAYED IS 1
```

The above is a very simple example, and the SQL in this case does not actually access a table. Let's do one more that will access a table. How about a UDF that will return the full name of an employee given the employee's id number?

258

```
CREATE FUNCTION HRSCHEMA.EMP_FULLNAME (EMP_NO INT)
    RETURNS VARCHAR(40)
    READS SQL DATA
    RETURN
    SELECT
    EMP_FIRST_NAME || ' ' || EMP_LAST_NAME AS FULL_NAME
    FROM HRSCHEMA.EMPLOYEE
    WHERE EMP_ID  = EMP_NO;
```

Now let's run the query to use this UDF:

```
SELECT HRSCHEMA.EMP_FULLNAME(3217) AS FULLNAME
FROM SYSIBM.SYSDUMMY1;

---------+---------+---------+---------+----
FULLNAME
---------+---------+---------+---------+----

EDWARD JOHNSON

DSNE610I NUMBER OF ROWS DISPLAYED IS 1
```

SQL Table Function

An SQL table function returns a table of values. Let's again replace the common table expression we used earlier. Remember it goes like this:

```
WITH EMP_PAY_SUM (EMP_ID, EMP_PAY_TOTAL) AS
(SELECT EMP_ID,
SUM(EMP_PAY_AMT)
AS EMP_PAY_TOTAL
FROM EMP_PAY_HIST
GROUP BY EMP_ID)

SELECT EMP_ID,
EMP_PAY_TOTAL
FROM EMP_PAY_SUM;

---------+---------+---------+---------+----
    EMP_ID       EMP_PAY_TOTAL
---------+---------+---------+---------+----
     3217              9166.64
     7459             13333.32
     9134             13333.32
DSNE610I NUMBER OF ROWS DISPLAYED IS 3
```

Now let's define the UDF:

```
CREATE FUNCTION HRSCHEMA.EMP_PAY_SUM ()
    RETURNS TABLE (EMP_ID   INTEGER,
                   EMP_PAY_TOTAL DECIMAL (9,2))
```

259

```
READS SQL DATA
RETURN
    SELECT EMP_ID,
    SUM(EMP_PAY_AMT)
    AS EMP_PAY_TOTAL
    FROM EMP_PAY_HIST
    GROUP BY EMP_ID
```

And then we'll call it using SPUFI. Notice that we invoke the TABLE function to return the values generated by the EMP_PAY_SUM UDF.

```
SELECT * FROM TABLE(HRSCHEMA.EMP_PAY_SUM()) AS EPS
---------+---------+---------+---------+---------+---
    EMP_ID  EMP_PAY_TOTAL
---------+---------+---------+---------+---------+---
    3217      9166.64
    7459     13333.32
    9134     13333.32
DSNE610I NUMBER OF ROWS DISPLAYED IS 3
```

External Scalar Function

An external scalar function is one that returns a single scalar value, usually based on some parameter value that is passed in. The function is implemented using a program, hence the designation as an "external" function.

You may recall earlier we created a UDF that returned a string value for an employee "level" based on the years of service. We could create a similar external UDF as follows:

```
CREATE FUNCTION HRSCHEMA.EMP_LEVEL2 (INT)
RETURNS VARCHAR(10)
EXTERNAL NAME 'EMPLEVEL'
LANGUAGE COBOL
NOSQL
FENCED
PARAMETER STYLE SQL

---------+---------+---------+---------+---------+-------
DSNE616I STATEMENT EXECUTION WAS SUCCESSFUL, SQLCODE IS 0
```

Now we need to implement this procedure by way of an external program named EMPLEV-EL (the name of the external program must match what we specified above in the EXTERNAL NAME clause). Although in this case we will use COBOL, the external portion of a UDF can be written in any of these languages:

- ASSEMBLER
- C or C++
- COBOL

260

- JAVA
- PL/I

We'll need a linkage section in our COBOL program that accepts the integer number of years and returns the employee level literal. Here's our program:

```
IDENTIFICATION DIVISION.
PROGRAM-ID. EMPLEVEL.

*******************************************************
*       PROGRAM USED AS A USER DEFINED FUNCTION       *
*******************************************************

ENVIRONMENT DIVISION.
DATA DIVISION.
WORKING-STORAGE SECTION.

LINKAGE SECTION.
*****************************************************
*    DECLARE THE I/O PARAMETERS FOR THE PROCEDURE   *
*****************************************************

01 LK-EMP-VARIABLES.
   10  LK-YEARS          PIC S9(9) USAGE COMP.
   10  LK-EMP-LEVEL      PIC X(10).

PROCEDURE DIVISION.

MAIN-PARA.
    DISPLAY "SAMPLE COBOL PROGRAM: USER DEFINED FUNCTION".

*   DETERMINE AN EMPLOYEE SERVICE LEVEL BASED ON YEARS OF SERVICE

    EVALUATE LK-YEARS
        WHEN 0          MOVE 'ENTRY     ' TO LK-EMP-LEVEL
        WHEN 1 THRU 5   MOVE 'ADVANCED  ' TO LK-EMP-LEVEL
        WHEN OTHER      MOVE 'SENIOR    ' TO LK-EMP-LEVEL
    END-EVALUATE.

    GOBACK.
```

Now we can call this function from another program or even from SPUFI:

```
SELECT HRSCHEMA.EMP_LEVEL2(0) AS EMP_LVL
FROM SYSIBM.SYSDUMMY1;
---------+---------+---------+---------+----
EMP_LVL
---------+---------+---------+---------+----

ENTRY
```

```
SELECT HRSCHEMA.EMP_LEVEL(2) AS EMP_LVL
FROM SYSIBM.SYSDUMMY1;
---------+---------+---------+---------+----
EMP_LVL
---------+---------+---------+---------+----

ADVANCED


SELECT HRSCHEMA.EMP_LEVEL(7) AS EMP_LVL
FROM SYSIBM.SYSDUMMY1;
---------+---------+---------+---------+----
EMP_LVL
---------+---------+---------+---------+----

SENIOR
```

To create the PLI version of our function, we will create EMP_LEVEL2P.

```
CREATE FUNCTION HRSCHEMA.EMP_LEVEL2P (INT)
RETURNS VARCHAR(10)
EXTERNAL NAME 'EMPLEVEP'
LANGUAGE PLI
NOSQL
FENCED
PARAMETER STYLE SQL

---------+---------+---------+---------+---------+-------
DSNE616I STATEMENT EXECUTION WAS SUCCESSFUL, SQLCODE IS 0
```

Here is the PLI program code.

```
EMPLEVEP: PROCEDURE (LK_EMP_VARIABLES);

/********************************************************************
* PROGRAM NAME :   EMPLEVEP - PROGRAM USED AS A USER DEFINED      *
*                             FUNCTION.                           *
********************************************************************/

/********************************************************************
*              E X T E R N A L   E N T R I E S                     *
********************************************************************/

   DCL DSNTIAR ENTRY OPTIONS(ASM INTER RETCODE);

/********************************************************************
/*              W O R K I N G   S T O R A G E                      *
********************************************************************/

   DCL 01 LK_EMP_VARIABLES,
```

```
               10   LK_YEARS           FIXED BIN(31),
               10   LK_EMP_LEVEL       CHAR(10);


 /*****************************************************************
 /*                P R O G R A M   M A I N L I N E               *
 *****************************************************************/

    PUT SKIP LIST ('SAMPLE PLI PROGRAM: USER DEFINED FUNCTION');

   /* DETERMINE AN EMPLOYEE SERVICE LEVEL BASED ON YEARS OF SERVICE */

      SELECT(LK_YEARS);

         WHEN (0)        LK_EMP_LEVEL = 'ENTRY';
         WHEN (1,2,3,4)  LK_EMP_LEVEL = 'ADVANCED';
         OTHERWISE       LK_EMP_LEVEL = 'SENIOR';

      END; /* SELECT */


  END EMPLEVEP;
```

External Table Function

An external table function returns a table of values. Here we could use such a function as a replacement for the common table expression we used earlier in this study guide. Let's first return to that.

```
WITH EMP_PAY_SUM (EMP_ID, EMP_PAY_TOTAL) AS
(SELECT EMP_ID,
SUM(EMP_PAY_AMT)
AS EMP_PAY_TOTAL
FROM EMP_PAY_HIST
GROUP BY EMP_ID)

SELECT EMP_ID,
EMP_PAY_TOTAL
FROM EMP_PAY_SUM;

---------+---------+---------+---------+----
     EMP_ID          EMP_PAY_TOTAL
---------+---------+---------+---------+----
       3217             9166.64
       7459            13333.32
       9134            13333.32
DSNE610I NUMBER OF ROWS DISPLAYED IS 3
```

Normally common table expressions are used with complex SQL to simplify things. Ours is not very complex, but we could simplify even further by using a UDF instead of the common table expression. To do this, let's define the UDF:

263

```
CREATE FUNCTION HRSCHEMA.EMP_PAY_SUM2 ()
RETURNS TABLE (EMP_ID   INTEGER,
              EMP_PAY_TOTAL DECIMAL (8,2))
EXTERNAL NAME 'EMPPAYTL'
LANGUAGE COBOL
PARAMETER STYLE DB2SQL
READS SQL DATA
RESULTS SETS 1
FENCED
```

Now let's create our COBOL program that implements the UDF. This can be done by defining a cursor to return a result set to the calling program.

```
IDENTIFICATION DIVISION.
PROGRAM-ID. EMPPAYTL

**********************************************************
*       EXTERNAL TABLE FUNCTION FOR EMP_PAY TABLE        *
*                                                        *
**********************************************************

ENVIRONMENT DIVISION.
DATA DIVISION.
WORKING-STORAGE SECTION.

    EXEC SQL
      INCLUDE SQLCA
    END-EXEC.

    EXEC SQL
      INCLUDE EMPPAYTL
    END-EXEC.

    EXEC SQL

        DECLARE EMP-PAY-CSR CURSOR WITH RETURN FOR
          SELECT EMP_ID,
          SUM(EMP_PAY_AMT)
          AS EMP_PAY_TOTAL
          FROM HRSCHEMA.EMP_PAY_HIST
          GROUP BY EMP_ID

    END-EXEC.


PROCEDURE DIVISION.

MAIN-PARA.
    DISPLAY "SAMPLE COBOL PROGRAM: EXTERNAL TABLE FUNCTION".

    EXEC SQL
        OPEN EMP-PAY-CSR
```

```
        END-EXEC.

        MOVE SQLCODE TO OUT-CODE

        DISPLAY 'OPEN CURSOR SQLCODE: ' SQLCODE.

        STOP RUN.
```

Finally, let's construct a program to call the UDF:

```
    IDENTIFICATION DIVISION.
    PROGRAM-ID. COBEMPA.

    ******************************************************
    *       PROGRAM CALLING EXTERNAL TABLE FUNCTION      *
    *                                                    *
    ******************************************************

    ENVIRONMENT DIVISION.
    DATA DIVISION.
    WORKING-STORAGE SECTION.

        EXEC SQL
          INCLUDE SQLCA
        END-EXEC.

        EXEC SQL
          INCLUDE EMPPAYTL
        END-EXEC.

    01  EMP-ID-PIC              PIC ZZZZZ9999.
    01  EMP-PAY-TTL             PIC S9(6)V9(2) USAGE COMP-3.
    01  EMP-PAY-TTL-PIC         PIC 999999.99.
    01  I                      PIC S9(9) USAGE COMP.

    *   DEFINE CURSOR TO ITERATE THE RESULTS OF THE TABLE

        EXEC SQL
            DECLARE CRSR-EMPPAYTL CURSOR FOR
            SELECT EMP_ID, EMP_PAY_TOTAL
            FROM TABLE(HRSCHEMA.EMP_PAY_SUM2()) AS EPS
            FOR READ ONLY
        END-EXEC.

    PROCEDURE DIVISION.

    MAIN-PARA.
        DISPLAY "SAMPLE COBOL PROGRAM: CALL EXTERNAL TABLE FUNCTION".

    * OPEN THE CURSOR

        EXEC SQL
          OPEN CRSR-EMPPAYTL
        END-EXEC.

        IF SQLCODE NOT EQUAL ZERO THEN
           DISPLAY 'BAD RC = ' SQLCODE
           STOP RUN
```

```
        END-IF.

        PERFORM RETRIEVE-DATA
           VARYING I FROM 1 BY 1
              UNTIL SQLCODE EQUAL TO +100.

    RETRIEVE-DATA.

        EXEC SQL
           FETCH CRSR-EMPPAYTL INTO :EMP-ID,
                         :EMP-PAY-TTL
        END-EXEC.

        IF SQLCODE = 0
           MOVE EMP-ID      TO EMP-ID-PIC
           MOVE EMP-PAY-TTL TO EMP-PAY-TTL-PIC
           DISPLAY EMP-ID-PIC  ' ' EMP-PAY-TTL-PIC
        ELSE
           DISPLAY 'SQL CODE = ' SQLCODE
           STOP RUN
        END-IF.
```

The output from the program is as follows:

```
    SAMPLE COBOL PROGRAM: EXTERNAL TABLE FUNCTION
         3217    9166.64
         7459   13333.32
         9134   13333.32
```

The PLI version of the UDF and the implementing and calling programs follows:

```
    CREATE FUNCTION HRSCHEMA.EMP_PAY_SUMP ()
    RETURNS TABLE (EMP_ID  INTEGER,
                   EMP_PAY_TOTAL DECIMAL (9,2) )
    EXTERNAL NAME EMPPAYTP
    LANGUAGE PLI
    PARAMETER STYLE DB2SQL
    READS SQL DATA
    RESULTS SETS 1
    FENCED
```

The implementing program is:

```
    EMPPAYTP: PROCEDURE (MAIN);
    /****************************************************************
    * PROGRAM NAME :   EMPPAYTP - EXTERNAL TABLEFUNCTION FOR EMP_PAY.  *
    ****************************************************************/


    /****************************************************************
    *              E X T E R N A L   E N T R I E S            *
    ****************************************************************/

        DCL DSNTIAR ENTRY OPTIONS(ASM INTER RETCODE);
```

```
/********************************************************************
/*              W O R K I N G    S T O R A G E                   *
********************************************************************/

   EXEC SQL
     INCLUDE SQLCA;

   EXEC SQL
     INCLUDE EMPPAYTL;

   EXEC SQL
     DECLARE EMP_PAY_CSR CURSOR WITH RETURN FOR
     SELECT EMP_ID,
     SUM(EMP_PAY_AMT)
     AS EMP_PAY_TOTAL
     FROM HRSCHEMA.EMP_PAY_HIST
     GROUP BY EMP_ID;

/********************************************************************
/*              P R O G R A M    M A I N L I N E                 *
********************************************************************/

   PUT SKIP LIST ('SAMPLE PLI PROGRAM: EXTERNAL TABLE FUNCTION');

   EXEC SQL OPEN EMP_PAY_CSR;

   PUT SKIP LIST ('OPEN CURSOR SQLCODE: ' || SQLCODE);

END EMPPAYTP;
```

And we could call the UDF either in SPUFI or with a program such as the following.

```
PLIEMPA: PROCEDURE OPTIONS(MAIN);
/********************************************************************
* PROGRAM NAME :   PLIEMPA - PROGRAM TO CALL EMP_PAY_SUM UDF.    *
********************************************************************/

/********************************************************************
*              E X T E R N A L    E N T R I E S                 *
********************************************************************/
   DCL DSNTIAR ENTRY OPTIONS(ASM INTER RETCODE);

/********************************************************************
/*              W O R K I N G    S T O R A G E                   *
********************************************************************/
   DCL COMMIT_CTR            FIXED BIN(31) INIT(0);
   DCL RET_SQL_CODE          FIXED BIN(31) INIT(0);
   DCL RET_SQL_CODE_PIC      PIC 'S999999999' INIT (0);

   DCL 01 ERR_REC,
        05 FILLER1           CHAR(10) INIT ('SQLCODE = '),
        05 SQLCODE_VIEW      PIC '-999',
        05 ERR_EMPID         FIXED BIN (31) INIT (0),
        05 FILLER2           CHAR(01) INIT (' '),
        05 ERR_TAB           CHAR(08) INIT (' '),
        05 ERR_PARA          CHAR(15) INIT (' ');
```

```
   DCL 01 ERR_MSG AUTOMATIC,
         05 ERR_LGTH            FIXED BIN (31) INIT (864),
         05 ERR_TXT(10)         CHAR(72);

   DCL ERR_TXT_LGTH            FIXED BIN (15) INIT (72);
   DCL ERR_NDX                 FIXED BIN (31) INIT (0);

   DCL EMP_ID_PIC              PIC 'ZZZZ9999';
   DCL EMP_PAY_TTL             FIXED DEC (8,2);
   DCL EMP_PAY_TTL_PIC         PIC '999999.99';

   EXEC SQL
     INCLUDE SQLCA;

   EXEC SQL
     INCLUDE EMPPAYTL;

   EXEC SQL
       DECLARE CRSR_EMPPAYTL CURSOR FOR
       SELECT EMP_ID, EMP_PAY_TOTAL
       FROM TABLE(HRSCHEMA.EMP_PAY_SUMP()) AS EPS
       FOR READ ONLY;

/********************************************************************
/*              P R O G R A M   M A I N L I N E                 *
********************************************************************/

   PUT SKIP LIST ('SAMPLE PLI PROGRAM: CALL EXTERNAL TABLE FUNCTION');

   EXEC SQL OPEN CRSR_EMPPAYTL;

   IF SQLCODE = 0 THEN
      DO UNTIL (SQLCODE ¬= 0);
         CALL P0100_FETCH_CURSOR;
      END;
   ELSE
      PUT SKIP LIST ('BAD SQLCODE ON CURSOR OPEN = ' || SQLCODE);
   EXEC SQL CLOSE CRSR_EMPPAYTL;

   PUT SKIP LIST ('CLOSE CURSOR SQLCODE: ' || SQLCODE);

   IF SQLCODE ¬= 0 THEN
      PUT SKIP LIST ('BAD SQLCODE ON CLOSE CURSOR ' || SQLCODE);

P0100_FETCH_CURSOR: PROC;

   EXEC SQL
       FETCH CRSR_EMPPAYTL
        INTO
        :EMP_ID,
        :EMP_PAY_TTL;

   IF SQLCODE = 0 THEN
      DO;
         EMP_ID_PIC      = EMP_ID;
         EMP_PAY_TTL_PIC = EMP_PAY_TTL;
         PUT SKIP LIST (EMP_ID_PIC ||  ' ' || EMP_PAY_TTL_PIC);
      END;
   ELSE
      IF SQLCODE = +100 THEN
```

```
            PUT SKIP LIST ('*** NO MORE RECORDS TO PROCESS!!');
        ELSE
            PUT SKIP LIST ('BAD SQLCODE = ' || SQLCODE);

    END P0100_FETCH_CURSOR;

    END PLIEMPA;
```

And here are the results

```
SAMPLE PLI PROGRAM: CALL EXTERNAL TABLE FUNCTION
        3217    9166.64
        7459   13333.32
        9134   13333.32
*** NO MORE RECORDS TO PROCESS!!
CLOSE CURSOR SQLCODE:                0
```

Sourced Function

A sourced function redefines or extends an existing DB2 function. It is typically written to enable the processing of user defined data types in a function. For example, suppose you define a Canadian dollar type as follows:

```
CREATE DISTINCT TYPE HRSCHEMA.CANADIAN_DOLLAR AS DECIMAL (9,2);
```

Now create a table using this type:

```
CREATE TABLE HRSCHEMA.CAN_PAY_TBL
  (EMP_ID INT,
   PAY_DATE DATE,
   PAY_AMT CANADIAN_DOLLAR)
   IN TSHR;
```

Now assume we've loaded 4 rows into the table, and we want to query a sum of the PAY_AMT rows:

```
    SELECT * FROM HRSCHEMA.CAN_PAY_TBL;

    ---------+---------+---------+---------
      EMP_ID  PAY_DATE          PAY_AMT
    ---------+---------+---------+---------
        3217  2017-01-01         5500.50
        3217  2017-02-01         5500.50
        3217  2017-03-01         5500.50
        3217  2017-04-01         5500.50
    DSNE610I NUMBER OF ROWS DISPLAYED IS 4

  SELECT SUM(PAY_AMT) FROM HRSCHEMA.CAN_PAY_TBL;
---------+---------+---------+---------+---------+---------+---------+-
DSNT408I SQLCODE = -440, ERROR:  NO AUTHORIZED FUNCTION NAMED SUM HAVING COMPATIBLE
ARGUMENTS WAS FOUND
DSNT418I SQLSTATE   = 42884 SQLSTATE RETURN CODE
DSNT415I SQLERRP    = DSNXORFN SQL PROCEDURE DETECTING ERROR
```

```
DSNT416I SQLERRD    = -100 0  0  -1  0  0 SQL DIAGNOSTIC INFORMATION
DSNT416I SQLERRD    = X'FFFFFF9C'  X'00000000'  X'00000000'  X'FFFFFFFF'
           X'00000000'  X'00000000' SQL DIAGNOSTIC INFORMATION
```

Unfortunately we get an error because the SUM function in DB2 does not know about a CANADIAN_DOLLAR type of input parameter, so the value we passed is an "incompatible argument". To fix this we must extend the SUM function to work with CANADIAN_DOLLAR input type by creating a user defined function based on the SUM function but accepting a CANADIAN_DOLLAR argument. Try this one:

```
CREATE FUNCTION SUM(CANADIAN_DOLLAR)
RETURNS DECIMAL (9,2)
SOURCE SYSIBM.SUM(DECIMAL)
---------+---------+---------+---------+---------+---------+-----
DSNE616I STATEMENT EXECUTION WAS SUCCESSFUL, SQLCODE IS 0
```

Now you have a SUM function for which CANADIAN_DOLLAR is an input parameter. When DB2 processes the query it will use the new user defined version of the SUM function because that's the one that matches your query arguments. Your SUM query will work now.

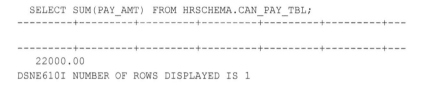

```
    SELECT SUM(PAY_AMT) FROM HRSCHEMA.CAN_PAY_TBL;
---------+---------+---------+---------+---------+---------+---

---------+---------+---------+---------+---------+---------+---
    22000.00
DSNE610I NUMBER OF ROWS DISPLAYED IS 1
```

TRIGGERS

A trigger performs a set of actions when an INSERT, UPDATE or DELETE takes place. Triggers are stored in the database which is a significant advantage of using them instead of application logic.

The CREATE TRIGGER statement defines a trigger and builds a trigger package at the current server. Advantages of using a trigger include:

- Ability to write to other tables for audit trail.
- Ability to read other tables for validation.
- Ability to compare data before and after update operations.

Types of triggers
There are three types of triggers:

1. INSERT
2. UPDATE
3. DELETE

A MERGE action also fires INSERT and UPDATE triggers (if they exist) depending on whether the MERGE causes an INSERT or UPDATE.

Timings of triggers

There are three timings of triggers as well:

1. BEFORE
2. AFTER
3. INSTEAD OF

A BEFORE trigger performs its action before the SQL operation (INSERT, UPDATE or DELETE) that fired the trigger. An AFTER trigger performs its action after the SQL operation (INSERT, UPDATE or DELETE) that fired the trigger. An INSTEAD OF trigger is completely different – it enables ADD, UPDATE or DELETE operation through what would normally be a read-only view. We'll explain that more when we get to the INSTEAD of example below.

The basic syntax of the CREATE TRIGGER statement is:

```
CREATE TRIGGER <trigger name>
<AFTER / BEFORE / INSTEAD OF>
ON <table name>
REFERENCING <see examples>
FOR EACH ROW
<action to take>
```

Examples of Triggers

Sample After Trigger

One common use of triggers is to automatically add records to a history table when there is a change to the records in a base table. In this case we will create a history table to store previous versions of pay rates in the EMP_PAY table. We can create the history table like this:

```
CREATE TABLE HRSCHEMA.EMP_PAY_HST
LIKE HRSCHEMA.EMP_PAY;
```

And then we'll add an additional column to the history table to keep track of when the record was added:

```
ALTER TABLE HRSCHEMA.EMP_PAY_HST
ADD AUDIT_DATE TIMESTAMP DEFAULT CURRENT TIMESTAMP;
```

Now we will create a trigger so that when a change is made to an EMP_PAY record, we will write the old version of the record to the history table. The trigger knows about the old and new versions of the record we are modifying so we specify the OLD version of the record and the fields to be added to the history table.

```
CREATE TRIGGER HRSCHEMA.TRG_EMP_PAY
AFTER UPDATE ON HRSCHEMA.EMP_PAY_X
REFERENCING OLD AS oldcol NEW AS newcol
FOR EACH ROW MODE DB2SQL
        INSERT INTO HRSCHEMA.EMP_PAY_HST(
        EMP_ID,
        EMP_REGULAR_PAY,
        EMP_BONUS_PAY,
        AUDIT_DATE)
        VALUES
        (oldcol.EMP_ID,
        oldcol.EMP_REGULAR_PAY,
        oldcol.EMP_BONUS_PAY,
        CURRENT TIMESTAMP)
```

Now let's look at an EMP_PAY record, modify it, and then see if the old version get's added to the history table:

```
SELECT * FROM HRSCHEMA.EMP_PAY
WHERE EMP_ID = 3217;
-------+---------+---------+---------+------
   EMP_ID   EMP_REGULAR_PAY   EMP_BONUS_PAY
-------+---------+---------+---------+------
    3217         55000.00         5500.00
NE610I NUMBER OF ROWS DISPLAYED IS 1
```

Let's change the EMP_REGULAR_PAY to 57000.

```
UPDATE HRSCHEMA.EMP_PAY
SET EMP_REGULAR_PAY = 57000
WHERE EMP_ID = 3217;
```

Now if we select from the history table, we see the previous version of the record and it was added today:

```
SELECT * FROM HRSCHEMA.EMP_PAY_HST
WHERE EMP_ID = 3217;
```

```
---------+---------+---------+---------+---------+---------+-----
    EMP_ID  EMP_REGULAR_PAY  EMP_BONUS_PAY  AUDIT_DATE
---------+---------+---------+---------+---------+---------+-----
    3217          55000.00        5500.00  2017-02-24-07.08.39.
DSNE610I NUMBER OF ROWS DISPLAYED IS 1
```

Note: the temporal tables introduced in DB2 10 provides more functionality for storing record history for system time enabled tables. Keep this in mind when designing your tables. But the trigger technique described above is still a very reliable way of automating the capture of record history.

Sample BEFORE Trigger

For this example, assume two tables:

1. DEPTMENT which has department codes and descriptions.
2. EMP_DATA_X which has an employee id, first and last names, and a department code.

Let's say we have a business rule that the department column in EMP_DAT_X can only have values that exist in the DEPTMENT table. Of course we could create a referential constraint with a foreign key, but let's say we prefer to implement this rule as a trigger instead. The trigger should prevent invalid updates and return an error message if a user tries to update a EMP_DAT_X record using a deprtment code that is not in the DEPTMENT table.

This trigger would accomplish this job:

```
CREATE TRIGGER HRSCHEMA.BLOCK_DEPT_UPDATE
    NO CASCADE BEFORE UPDATE OF
    EMP_DEPT ON HRSCHEMA.EMP_DATA_X
    REFERENCING NEW AS N
    FOR EACH ROW MODE DB2SQL
    WHEN (N.EMP_DEPT
        NOT IN (SELECT DEPT_CODE FROM DEPTMENT))
        BEGIN ATOMIC
            SIGNAL SQLSTATE '85101' ('Invalid department code');
        END
```

Currently the data in these tables looks like this:

```
SELECT * FROM HRSCHEMA.DEPTMENT;
---------+---------+---------+---------+
DEPT_CODE  DEPT_NAME
---------+---------+---------+---------+
DPTA       DEPARTMENT A
DPTB       DEPARTMENT B
DSNE610I NUMBER OF ROWS DISPLAYED IS 2
```

```
SELECT * FROM EMP_DATA_X

---------+---------+---------+---------+---------+---------+-----
    EMP_ID  EMP_LNAME           EMP_FNAME              EMP_DEPT
---------+---------+---------+---------+---------+---------+-----
    8888  JONES               WILLIAM                DPTA
DSNE610I NUMBER OF ROWS DISPLAYED IS 1
```

If we try this SQL it will fail because department code "DPTC" does not exist in the DEPT-MENT table. And the result is as we expected, plus the error text is what we defined in the trigger:

```
    UPDATE HRSCHEMA.EMP_DATA_X
    SET EMP_DEPT = 'DPTC'
    WHERE EMP_ID = 8888;
---------+---------+---------+---------+---------+---------+---------+----
DSNT408I SQLCODE = -438, ERROR:  APPLICATION RAISED ERROR WITH DIAGNOSTIC
         TEXT: Invalid department code
DSNT418I SQLSTATE  = 85101 SQLSTATE RETURN CODE
DSNT415I SQLERRP   = DSNXRTYP SQL PROCEDURE DETECTING ERROR
DSNT416I SQLERRD   = 1 0  0  -1  0  0 SQL DIAGNOSTIC INFORMATION
DSNT416I SQLERRD   = X'00000001'  X'00000000'  X'00000000'  X'FFFFFFFF'
         X'00000000'  X'00000000' SQL DIAGNOSTIC INFORMATION
```

Sample INSTEAD OF Trigger

An INSTEAD OF trigger is different than all other types of triggers. The purpose of an IN-STEAD OF trigger is to allow updates to take place from what is normally a read-only view. You may know that a view that includes more than one table is read only. Let's look at an example of creating ansd updating data using a view with an INSTEAD OF trigger.

We'll start with a query that joins certain columns in the EMPLOYEE table with the EMP_PAY table.

```
    SELECT
    A.EMP_ID,
    A.EMP_LAST_NAME,
    B.EMP_REGULAR_PAY
    FROM HRSCHEMA.EMPLOYEE A, HRSCHEMA.EMP_PAY B
    WHERE A.EMP_ID = B.EMP_ID;
---------+---------+---------+---------+---------+--
    EMP_ID  EMP_LAST_NAME       EMP_REGULAR_PAY
---------+---------+---------+---------+---------+--
    3217  JOHNSON                 55000.00
    7459  STEWART                 80000.00
    9134  FRANKLIN                80000.00
    4720  SCHULTZ                 80000.00
    6288  WILLARD                 70000.00
DSNE610I NUMBER OF ROWS DISPLAYED IS 5
```

Now let's create a view based on this query:

```
CREATE VIEW HRSCHEMA.EMP_PROFILE_PAY
AS
SELECT
A.EMP_ID,
A.EMP_LAST_NAME,
B.EMP_REGULAR_PAY
FROM HRSCHEMA.EMPLOYEE A, HRSCHEMA.EMP_PAY B
WHERE A.EMP_ID = B.EMP_ID;
---------+---------+---------+---------+---------+--------
DSNE616I STATEMENT EXECUTION WAS SUCCESSFUL, SQLCODE IS 0
---------+---------+---------+---------+---------+--------
```

And now we can query the data using the view:

```
SELECT * FROM HRSCHEMA.EMP_PROFILE_PAY

---------+---------+---------+---------+---------+-
    EMP_ID  EMP_LAST_NAME        EMP_REGULAR_PAY
---------+---------+---------+---------+---------+-
      3217  JOHNSON                     55000.00
      7459  STEWART                     80000.00
      9134  FRANKLIN                    80000.00
      4720  SCHULTZ                     80000.00
      6288  WILLARD                     70000.00
DSNE610I NUMBER OF ROWS DISPLAYED IS 5
```

Now suppose we want to use this view to update the EMP_REGULAR_PAY column. Let's try and see what happens:

```
UPDATE HRSCHEMA.EMP_PROFILE_PAY
SET EMP_REGULAR_PAY = 65000
WHERE EMP_ID = 3217;

---------+---------+---------+---------+---------+---------+---------+------
DSNT408I SQLCODE = -151, ERROR:  THE UPDATE OPERATION IS INVALID BECAUSE THE
         CATALOG DESCRIPTION OF COLUMN HRSCHEMA.EMP_PROFILE_PAY.EMP_REGULAR_PAY
         INDICATES THAT IT CANNOT BE UPDATED
DSNT418I SQLSTATE   = 42808 SQLSTATE RETURN CODE
DSNT415I SQLERRP    = DSNXOST SQL PROCEDURE DETECTING ERROR
DSNT416I SQLERRD    = -400 0  0  -1  0  0 SQL DIAGNOSTIC INFORMATION
DSNT416I SQLERRD    = X'FFFFFE70'  X'00000000'  X'00000000'  X'FFFFFFFF'
           X'00000000'  X'00000000' SQL DIAGNOSTIC INFORMATION
```

As you can see, we are not allowed to perform updates using this view. However, we can perform the updates through this view if we create an INSTEAD OF trigger on the view. The DDL looks like this:

```
CREATE TRIGGER HRSCHEMA.EMP_PROF_PAY_UPDATE
INSTEAD OF UPDATE ON HRSCHEMA.EMP_PROFILE_PAY
   REFERENCING NEW AS NEWEMP OLD AS OLDEMP
     FOR EACH ROW
     MODE DB2SQL
       BEGIN ATOMIC
         UPDATE HRSCHEMA.EMP_PAY AS E
           SET (EMP_REGULAR_PAY)
             = (NEWEMP.EMP_REGULAR_PAY)
         WHERE NEWEMP.EMP_ID = E.EMP_ID ;
       END
```

The trigger is intercepting the UPDATE request from the `EMP_PROFILE_PAY` view and performing a direct update to the `EMP_PAY` table.

Now let's try our update:

```
UPDATE HRSCHEMA.EMP_PROFILE_PAY
SET EMP_REGULAR_PAY = 65000
WHERE EMP_ID = 3217;
```

Finally let's select the row we just changed using the view:

```
SELECT * FROM HRSCHEMA.EMP_PROFILE_PAY
WHERE EMP_ID = 3217;

EMP_ID        EMP_LAST_NAME        EMP_REGULAR_PAY
------        -------------        ---------------
  3217        JOHNSON                  65000.00
```

And as we can see, the `EMP_REGULAR_PAY` did get changed.

Of course when all is said and done, you could simply have updated the base table to begin with. However, views can give you more control over what users and/or programmers are allowed to see and change in a table. The point of the INSTEAD OF triggers is to allow you to use a view as the interface for all adds, changes and deletes.

SPECIAL TABLES

Temporal and Archive Tables

Temporal Tables

Temporal tables were introduced to DB2 in version 10. Briefly, a temporal table is one that keeps track of "versions" of data over time and allows you to query data according to the time frame. It is important to understand what problems you can solve with the technologies, such as automatically preventing overlapping rows for business time. We'll get to that in the examples.

Some benefits of DB2's built in support for managing temporal data include:

- Reduces application logic
- Can automatically maintain a history of table changes
- Ensures consistent handling of time related events

Now let's look at the two varieties of time travel in DB2, which are business time (sometimes referred to as application time) and system time.

Business Time

An employee's pay typically changes over time. Besides wanting to know the current salary, there may be many scenarios under which an HR department or supervisor might need to know what pay rate was in effect for an employee at some time in the past. We might also need to allow for cases where the employee terminated for some period of time and then returned. Or maybe they took a non-paid leave of absence. This is the concept of business time and it can be fairly complex depending on the business rules required by the application. It basically means a period of time in which the data is accurate. You could think of it as a data value an effective date and discontinue date.

A table can only have one business time period. When a BUSINESS_TIME period is defined for a table, DB2 generates a check constraint in which the end column value must be greater than the begin column value. Once a table is version enabled, the following clauses allow you to pull data for a particular business time period:

```
FOR BUSINESS_TIME FROM ... TO ...
FOR BUSINESS_TIME BETWEEN... AND...
```

For example:

```
SELECT * FROM HRSCHEMA.EMP_PAY
FOR BUSINESS_TIME BEWTWEEN
'2017-01-01' AND '2017-02-01'
ORDER BY EMP_ID;
```

System Time

System time simply means the time during which a piece of data is in the database, i.e., when the data was added, changed or deleted. Sometimes it is important to know this. For example a user might enter an employee's salary change on a certain date but the effective date of the salary change might be earlier or later than the date it was actually entered into the system. An audit trail table often has a timestamp that can be considered system time at which a transaction occurred.

Like with business time, once a table is version-enabled for system time, the following clauses allow you to pull data for a particular system period:

```
FOR SYSTEM_TIME FROM ... TO ...
FOR SYSTEM_TIME BETWEEN... AND...
```

For example, maybe we want to know see several series of EMPLOYEE table records that were changed over a period of a month. Assuming a system version enabled table, this would work:

```
SELECT * FROM HRSCHEMA.EMPLOYEE
FOR SYSTEM_TIME BEWTWEEN '2017-01-01' AND '2017-02-01'
ORDER BY EMP_ID;
```

Bitemporal Support

In some cases you may need to support both business and system time in the same table. DB2 supports this and it is called bitemporal support. Now let's move on to some examples of all three types of temporal tables!

Business Time Example

You create a temporal table by adding columns for the start and ending period for which the data is valid. Let's do an example. We could modify our existing EMP_PAY table and we'll do that, but first let's look at how we would have defined it if we originally made it a temporal table.

Our original DDL for creating EMP_PAY looks like this:

```
CREATE TABLE HRSCHEMA.EMP_PAY(
EMP_ID INT NOT NULL,
EMP_REGULAR_PAY DECIMAL (8,2) NOT NULL,
```

```
EMP_BONUS_PAY DECIMAL    (8,2))
PRIMARY KEY (EMP_ID)) IN TSHR;
```

To create this table as a temporal table, we could have used this DDL instead and our new table name is `EMP_PAYX`:

```
CREATE TABLE HRSCHEMA.EMP_PAYX(
EMP_ID INT NOT NULL,
EMP_REGULAR_PAY DECIMAL (8,2) NOT NULL,
EMP_BONUS_PAY DECIMAL    (8,2)),
BUS_START    DATE  NOT NULL,
BUS_END      DATE  NOT NULL,

PERIOD BUSINESS_TIME(BUS_START, BUS_END),

PRIMARY KEY (EMP_ID, BUSINESS_TIME WITHOUT OVERLAPS))
        IN TSHR;
```

Now let's insert a few rows into the table. Keep in mind that we now have a start and end date for which the information is valid. That could pose a problem if our end date is really "until further notice". Some applications solve that problem by establishing a date in the distant future as the standard end date for current data. We'll use 12/31/2099 for this example. For convenience we can use the existing `EMP_PAY` table to load `EMP_PAYX` using a query:

```
INSERT INTO HRSCHEMA.EMP_PAYX
SELECT EMP_ID,
EMP_REGULAR_PAY,
EMP_BONUS_PAY,
'2017-01-01',
'2099-12-31'
FROM HRSCHEMA.EMP_PAY;
```

Here's our resulting data:

```
SELECT * FROM HRSCHEMA.EMP_PAYX;

EMP_ID   EMP_REGULAR_PAY      EMP_BONUS_PAY  BUS_START    BUS_END
------   ---------------      -------------  ----------   ----------
  3217          55000.00           5500.00  2017-01-01   2099-12-31
  7481          80000.00           4500.00  2017-01-01   2099-12-31
  9134          80000.00           2500.00  2017-01-01   2099-12-31
```

Now let's suppose employee 3217 has been given a raise to 60K per year effective 2/1/2017. First we need to set the end business date on the existing record.

```
UPDATE HRSCHEMA.EMP_PAYX
SET BUS_END      = '2017-02-01'
WHERE EMP_ID = 3217;
```

IMPORTANT: both system and business time are inclusive of start date and exclusive of end date. That means when you set an end date, you'll usually want to add a day to the true end date and use that as the end date. For example, to set an employee salary effective January 1, 2017 and ending at midnight on January 31, 2017 you would use start date 2017-01-01. But you would use end date 2017-02-01. Otherwise January 31 will not be included when you do your query.

If the above is a little confusing, it is because generally date related evaluations do not work this way (if you say BETWEEN two dates, it means inclusive at both ends), but this one does work this way. So be sure that you get this! For setting business and system time, the start date is inclusive but the end date is exclusive. Now let's add the new row:

```
INSERT INTO HRSCHEMA.EMP_PAYX
VALUES (3217,
60000.00,
5500.00,
'2017-02-01',
'2099-12-31')
```

Here's the result:

```
SELECT * FROM HRSCHEMA.EMP_PAYX ORDER BY EMP_ID;
```

EMP_ID	EMP_REGULAR_PAY	EMP_BONUS_PAY	BUS_START	BUS_END
3217	55000.00	5500.00	2017-01-01	2017-02-01
3217	60000.00	5500.00	2017-02-01	2099-12-31
7459	80000.00	4500.00	2017-01-01	2099-12-31
9134	80000.00	2500.00	2017-01-01	2099-12-31

Note that there are now two records for employee 3217. If you were to query this data as of 2/1/2017, you would get a different result than if you queried it for business time 1/15/2017. Recall that querying data in temporal tables is supported by specific temporal clauses, including:

```
AS OF
FROM
BETWEEN

SELECT * FROM HRSCHEMA.EMP_PAYX
FOR BUSINESS_TIME AS OF '2017-02-01'
ORDER BY EMP_ID;
```

EMP_ID	EMP_REGULAR_PAY	EMP_BONUS_PAY	BUS_START	BUS_END
3217	60000.00	5500.00	2017-02-01	2099-12-31
7459	80000.00	4500.00	2017-01-01	2099-12-31
9134	80000.00	2500.00	2017-01-01	2099-12-31

```
SELECT * FROM HRSCHEMA.EMP_PAYX
FOR BUSINESS_TIME AS OF '2017-01-15'
ORDER BY EMP_ID;

EMP_ID        EMP_REGULAR_PAY   EMP_BONUS_PAY   BUS_START    BUS_END
------        ---------------   -------------   ----------   ----------
  3217              55000.00          5500.00   2017-01-01   2017-02-01
  7459              80000.00          4500.00   2017-01-01   2099-12-31
  9134              80000.00          2500.00   2017-01-01   2099-12-31
```

Since you defined the primary key with non-overlapping business times, DB2 will not allow you to enter any overlapping start and end dates. That saves some coding and solves one of the most pervasive and time-consuming application design errors I've observed over the years.

System Time Example

When you want to capture actions taken on a table at a particular time, use system time. Suppose you want to keep a snapshot of every record BEFORE it is changed. DB2's temporal table functionality also includes automated copying of a "before" image of each record to a history table. This feature can be used in lieu of using triggers which are also often used to store a history of each version of a record.

Let's take the example of our EMPLOYEE table. For business audit purposes, we want to capture all changes made to it. To do this is pretty easy. Follow these steps:

1. Add system time fields to the base table
2. Create a history table
3. Version-enable the base table

Adding system time to the table is as simple as adding the time fields needed to track system time.

```
ALTER TABLE HRSCHEMA.EMPLOYEE
ADD COLUMN SYS_START TIMESTAMP(12)
GENERATED ALWAYS AS ROW BEGIN NOT NULL;

ALTER TABLE HRSCHEMA.EMPLOYEE
ADD COLUMN SYS_END TIMESTAMP(12)
GENERATED ALWAYS AS ROW END NOT NULL;

ALTER TABLE HRSCHEMA.EMPLOYEE
ADD COLUMN TRANS_ID TIMESTAMP(12) NOT NULL GENERATED
ALWAYS AS TRANSACTION START ID;

ALTER TABLE HRSCHEMA.EMPLOYEE
ADD PERIOD SYSTEM_TIME (SYS_START, SYS_END);
```

Now let's explore one more temporal table feature – the history table. There may be cases in which you want to maintain a record of all changes made to table. You can do this automatically by defining a history table and enabling your base table for versioning. Let's create a history table EMPLOYEE_HISTORY and we'll make it identical to EMPLOYEE.

```
CREATE TABLE EMPLOYEE_HISTORY LIKE EMPLOYEE;
```

Now we can enable versioning in the EMPLOYEE table like this:

```
ALTER TABLE EMPLOYEE
ADD VERSIONING
USE HISTORY TABLE EMPLOYEE_HISTORY;
```

At this point we can make a change to one of the EMPLOYEE records and we expect to see the old version of the record in the history table.

```
UPDATE HRSCHEMA.EMPLOYEE
SET EMP_FIRST_NAME = 'FREDERICK'
WHERE EMP_ID = 4175;
```

Assume that today is January 30, 2017 so that's when we changed our data. When you query with a specified system time, DB2 implicitly joins the base table and the history table. For example, let's pull data for employee 4175 as of 1/15/2017:

```
SELECT EMP_ID, EMP_FIRST_NAME, SYS_START, SYS_END
FROM HRSCHEMA.EMPLOYEE
FOR SYSTEM_TIME AS OF '2017-01-15'
WHERE EMP_ID = 4175;

EMP_ID EMP_FIRST_NAME        SYS_START            SYS_END
------ --------------        ---------------------  --------------------------
 4175  FRED                  0001-01-01 00:00:00.0 2017-01-30 17:29:38.608073
```

Notice that the previous version of the record is pulled up (FRED instead of FREDERICK) because we specified system time 1/15/2017, so that means we want the record that was present in the table on 1/15/2017.

Now let's perform the same query for system time as of February 1, 2017.

```
SELECT EMP_ID, EMP_FIRST_NAME, SYS_START, SYS_END
FROM HRSCHEMA.EMPLOYEE
FOR SYSTEM_TIME AS OF '2017-02-01'
WHERE EMP_ID = 4175;
```

EMP_ID	EMP_FIRST_NAME	SYS_START	SYS_END
4175	FREDERICK	2017-01-30 17:29:38.608073	9999-12-30 00:00:00.0

Now you've got the most current record with the modified name FREDERICK. That is pretty cool feature and most if it happens automatically once you set it up. It can really help save time when researching particular values that were in the table sometime in the past.

NOTE: You can only use a history table with a system time enabled table.

Bi-Temporal Example

Finally, let's do an example where you need both business time and system time enabled for the same table. Let's go back go our EMP_PAY table and create yet another version called EMP_PAYY:

```
CREATE TABLE HRSCHEMA.EMP_PAYY(
EMP_ID INT NOT NULL,
EMP_REGULAR_PAY DECIMAL (8,2) NOT NULL,
EMP_BONUS_PAY DECIMAL   (8,2)),
BUS_START   DATE  NOT NULL,
BUS_END     DATE  NOT NULL,
SYS_START   TIMESTAMP(12)
GENERATED ALWAYS AS ROW BEGIN NOT NULL,
SYS_END     TIMESTAMP(12)
GENERATED ALWAYS AS ROW END NOT NULL,
     TRANS_ID TIMESTAMP(12) NOT NULL GENERATED
ALWAYS AS TRANSACTION START ID;

PERIOD BUSINESS_TIME(BUS_START, BUS_END),
PERIOD SYSTEM_TIME (SYS_START, SYS_END);

PRIMARY KEY (EMP_ID, BUSINESS_TIME WITHOUT OVERLAPS))
   IN TSHR;
```

You'll still need to create the history table and version enable EMP_PAYY.

```
CREATE TABLE EMP_PAYY_HISTORY LIKE EMP_PAYY;
```

Now we can enable versioning in the EMP_PAYY table like this:

```
ALTER TABLE EMP_PAYY
ADD VERSIONING
USE HISTORY TABLE EMP_PAYY_HISTORY;
```

This concludes our discussion of DB2's support for temporal tables and time travel queries. This is a very powerful technology and I encourage you to learn it not just to pass the exam, but to take advantage of it's features that improve your client's access to actionable business information. It can also ease the application development and production support efforts!

Archive Tables

Archive tables are similar to history tables, but are unrelated to temporal tables. We provided an example of a archive table back in the first section of this study guide. We'll echo it here for convenience.

An archive table is a table that stores data that was deleted from another table called an archive-enabled table. When a row is deleted from the archive-enabled table, DB2 automatically adds the row to the archive table. When you query the archive-enabled table, you can specify whether or not to include archived records or not. We'll look at these features in an example.

Assume we want to delete some records from our EMPLOYEE table and we want to automatically archive the deleted records to a new table EMPLOYEE_ARCHIVE. Assume that the new table is already set up and defined correctly, i.e., with the same column definitions as EMPLOYEE.

To enable archiving of deleted records from table EMPLOYEE you would execute the following:

```
ALTER TABLE EMPLOYEE ENABLE ARCHIVE USE EMPLOYEE_ARCHIVE;
```

To automatically archive records, set the global variable SYSIBMADM.MOVE_TO_ARCHIVE to Y or E. MOVE_TO_ARCHIVE indicates whether deleting a record from an archive-enabled table should store a copy of the deleted record in the archive table. The values are:

Y - store a copy of the deleted record, and also make any attempted insert/update operation against the archive table an error.

E - store a copy of the deleted record.

N- do not store a copy of the deleted record.

In the future when you query the EMPLOYEE you can choose to include or exclude the archived records in a given session. To do this, your package must first be bound with the ARCHIVE-SENSITIVE(YES) bind option. Then the package/program should set the GET_ARCHIVE global variable to Y (the default is N). At this point, any query against the archive-enabled table during this session will automatically include data from both the archive-enabled table and its corresponding archive table.

In our EMPLOYEE example, suppose we have a package EMP001 that is bound with ARCHIVE-

`SENSITIVE(YES)`. Suppose further that the program issues this SQL:

```
SET SYSIBMADM.GET_ARCHIVE = 'Y';
```

At this point any query we issue during this session against `EMPLOYEE` will automatically return any qualifying rows from both `EMPLOYEE` and `EMPLOYEE_ARCHIVE`. For example:

```
SELECT EMP_ID, EMP_LAST_NAME, EMPL_FIRST_NAME
FROM EMPLOYEE
ORDER BY EMP_ID;
```

If the package needs to revert to only picking up data from the `EMPLOYEE` table, it can simply issue the SQL:

```
SET SYSIBMADM.GET_ARCHIVE = 'N';
```

When you use an archive table there are some design advantages. The first and most obvious is that your historical data is managed automatically. You don't have to have a custom process for moving older data to a separate table. Second, you can control whether the archived data is included in a query by setting a global variable – you don't need to change the actual SQL statement. Finally, you can realize a cost advantage because the archived rows could be stored on a cheaper device than the current data. These are all advantages to consider when you make your design decisions.

Materialized Query Tables

A materialized query table (MQT) basically stores the result set of a query. It is used to store aggregate results from one or more other tables. MQTs are often used to improve performance for certain aggregation queries by providing pre-computed results. Consequently, MQTs are most often used in analytic or data warehousing environments.

MQTs are either system-maintained or user maintained. For a system maintained table, the data can be updated using the `REFRESH TABLE` statement. A user-maintained MQT can be updated using the LOAD utility, and also the UPDATE, INSERT, and DELETE SQL statements.

Let's do an example of an MQT that summarizes monthly payroll. Assume we have a source table named `EMP_PAY_HIST` which will be a history of each employee's salary for each paycheck. The table is defined as follows:

Column Name	Definition
EMP_ID	Numeric
EMP_PAY_DATE	Date
EMP_PAY_AMT	Decimal(8,2)

The DDL for the table is as follows:

```
CREATE TABLE HRSCHEMA.EMP_PAY_HIST(
EMP_ID              INT NOT NULL,
EMP_PAY_DATE        DATE NOT NULL,
EMP_PAY_AMT         DECIMAL (8,2) NOT NULL)
IN TSHR;
```

Now let's assume the data in the table is the twice-monthly pay amount for each employee for the first two months of 2017. Perhaps you have a payroll program that loads the table each pay period, possibly using a query like this where the date changes with the payroll period:

```
INSERT INTO HRSCHEMA.EMP_PAY_HIST
   SELECT EMP_ID,
   '01/15/2017',
   EMP_SEMIMTH_PAY
   FROM HRSCHEMA.EMP_PAY_CHECK;
```

Assume that the data is as follows:

```
    SELECT * FROM EMP_PAY_HIST ORDER BY EMP_PAY_DATE, EMP_ID;
---------+---------+---------+---------+---------+---------
    EMP_ID  EMP_PAY_DATE  EMP_PAY_AMT
---------+---------+---------+---------+---------+---------
      3217  2017-01-15       2291.66
      7459  2017-01-15       3333.33
      9134  2017-01-15       3333.33
      3217  2017-01-31       2291.66
      7459  2017-01-31       3333.33
      9134  2017-01-31       3333.33
      3217  2017-02-15       2291.66
      7459  2017-02-15       3333.33
      9134  2017-02-15       3333.33
      3217  2017-02-28       2291.66
      7459  2017-02-28       3333.33
      9134  2017-02-28       3333.33
DSNE610I NUMBER OF ROWS DISPLAYED IS 12
```

Finally, let's assume we regularly need an aggregated total of each employee's year to date pay. We could do this with a materialized query table. Let's build the query that will summarize the employee pay from the beginning of the year to current date:

```
SELECT EMP_ID, SUM(EMP_PAY_AMT) AS EMP_PAY_YTD
FROM HRSCHEMA.EMP_PAY_HIST
GROUP BY EMP_ID
ORDER BY EMP_ID;
---------+---------+---------+---------+---------
    EMP_ID              EMP_PAY_YTD
---------+---------+---------+---------+---------
      3217                9166.64
      7459               13333.32
      9134               13333.32
DSNE610I NUMBER OF ROWS DISPLAYED IS 3
```

Now let's create the MQT using this query and we'll make it a system managed table:

```
CREATE TABLE EMP_PAY_TOT (EMP_ID, EMP_PAY_YTD) AS
(SELECT EMP_ID, SUM(EMP_PAY_AMT) AS EMP_PAY_YTD
FROM HRSCHEMA.EMP_PAY_HIST
GROUP BY EMP_ID)
DATA INITIALLY DEFERRED
REFRESH DEFERRED
MAINTAINED BY SYSTEM
ENABLE QUERY OPTIMIZATION;
```

We can now populate the table by issuing the REFRESH TABLE statement as follows:

```
REFRESH TABLE HRSCHEMA.EMP_PAY_TOT;
```

Finally we can query the MQT as follows:

```
SELECT * FROM HRSCHEMA.EMP_PAY_TOT;

---------+---------+---------+---------+---------+--------
    EMP_ID              EMP_PAY_YTD
---------+---------+---------+---------+---------+--------
      3217                9166.64
      7459               13333.32
      9134               13333.32
DSNE610I NUMBER OF ROWS DISPLAYED IS 3
```

Temporary Tables

Sometimes you may need to create a DB2 table for the duration of a session but no longer than that. For example you may have a programming situation where it is convenient to have a temporary table which you can load for these operations:

- To join the data in the temporary table with another table
- To store intermediate results that you can query later in the program
- To load data from a flat file into a relational format

Let's assume that you only need the temporary table for the duration of a session or iteration of a program because temporary tables are dropped automatically as soon as the session ends.

Temporary tables are created using either the CREATE statement or the DECLARE statement. The differences will be explored in the Application Design section of this book. For now we will just look at an example of creating a table called EMP_INFO using both methods:

```
CREATE GLOBAL TEMPORARY TABLE
EMP_INFO(EMP_ID    INT,
EMP_LNAME   VARCHAR(30),
EMP_FNAME   VARCHAR(30));

DECLARE GLOBAL TEMPORARY TABLE
EMP_INFO(EMP_ID    INT,
EMP_LNAME   VARCHAR(30),
EMP_FNAME   VARCHAR(30));
```

When using the LIKE clause to create a temporary table, the implicit table definition includes only the column name, data type and nullability characteristic of each of the columns of the source table, and any column defaults. The temporary table does NOT have any unique constraints, foreign key constraints, triggers, indexes, table partitioning keys, or distribution keys.

CREATED Temporary Tables
Created temporary tables:

- Have an entry in the system catalog (SYSIBM.SYSTABLES)
- Cannot have indexes
- Their columns cannot use default values (except NULL)
- Cannot have constraints
- Cannot be used with DB2 utilities
- Cannot be used with the UPDATE statement
- If DELETE is used at all, it will delete all rows from the table
- Do not provide for locking or logging

DECLARED Temporary Tables
A declared temporary table offers some advantages over created temporary tables.

- Can have indexes and check constraints
- Can use the UPDATE statement
- Can do positioned deletes

So declared temporary tables offer more flexibility than created temporary tables. However, when a session ends, DB2 will automatically delete both the rows in the table and the table definition. So if you want a table definition that persists in the DB2 catalog for future use, you would need to use a created temporary table.

Things to remember about temporary tables:

- Use temporary tables when you need the data only for the duration of the session.
- Created temporary tables can provide excellent performance because they do not use locking or logging.
- Declared temporary tables can also be very efficient because you can choose not to log, and they only allow limited locking.
- The schema for a temporary table is always SESSION.
- If you create a temporary table and you wish to replace any existing temporary table that has the same name, use the WITH REPLACE clause.
- If you create a temporary table from another table using the LIKE clause, the temporary table will NOT have any unique constraints, foreign key constraints, triggers, indexes, table partitioning keys, or distribution keys from the original table.

Auxiliary Tables

An auxiliary table is used to store Large Object (LOB) data that is linked to another table. To fully understand auxiliary tables, it is necessary to know how DB2 handles large object data. Let's review LOB basics and then we'll do a programming example.

Basic LOB Concepts

A large object (LOB) is a data type for large, unstructured data such as photographs, audio or video files, large character data files, etc. There are three types of LOB:

CLOB is a character large object. CLOBs are used to store single byte character type files up to 2 GB in size. This includes large documents and other text files.

BLOB is a binary large object. BLOBs are used to store binary unstructured data, often multimedia files such as photos, music or video files up to 2 GB in size.

DBCLOB is a double byte character large object. It is used for storing up to 1 GB of double byte character data. It is often used for storing text files in languages that require two bytes per character.

LOB Example

To store and retrieve LOB data, you follow these steps:

1. Add an LOB column to a table.
2. Create an auxiliary LOB tablespace (if one doesn't already exist for your purpose).
3. Create an auxiliary table to store the actual LOB value and to tie it to the column from the base table.
4. Create an index on the LOB table.

For an example, let's add an employee photo column to the EMPLOYEE table. Since photo data is large binary data, we will define our employee photo column as a BLOB column of up to 5 MB. We also need to define a ROWID column which will be used to locate the actual BLOB value in the auxiliary table:

```
ALTER TABLE EMPLOYEE
ADD ROW_ID ROWID NOT NULL GENERATED ALWAYS;
```

Now let's add the LOB photo column.

```
ALTER TABLE EMPLOYEE
ADD EMP_PHOTO BLOB(5M);
```

Next, if we do not already have an LOB table space, we can create one as follows:

```
CREATE LOB TABLESPACE
EMP_PHOTO_TS
IN HRDB
LOG NO;
```

While not mandatory, it is good practice to NOT log the LOB data, as this can slow performance considerably when dealing with large amounts of LOB data. Of course if the data is mission or time critical you may need to log it for recovery purposes.

Now we need to create the auxiliary table. We have to specify that the table be created in the new LOB tablespace, and that it will store column EMP_PHOTO from table EMPLOYEE. And we need a unique index on the auxiliary table. Here's the DDL for these operations.

```
CREATE AUX TABLE EMP_PHOTOS_TAB
IN EMP_PHOTO_TS
STORES EMPLOYEE
COLUMN (EMP_PHOTO);

CREATE UNIQUE INDEX XEMP_PHOTO
ON EMP_PHOTOS_TAB;
```

Now we would need to rerun the DCLGEN on the EMPLOYEE table. You'll notice that the DCLGEN now specifies the EMP_PHOTO as a BLOB type.

```
SQL TYPE is BLOB (5M) EMP_PHOTO;
```

Our update program can now load the photo data by defining a host variable into which you load the binary photo data. The host variable PHOTO-DATA must be defined as usage SQL and type as BLOB(5M). This is the COBOL declaration for the SQL host variable:

```
01 EMP-PHOTO USAGE IS SQL TYPE IS BLOB(5M).
```

Here it gets a little different from how we use other host variables. DB2 will generate an appropriate host language variable for you based on the SQL variable. When referring to the host variable in SQL you must use the name you declared (EMP_PHOTO). However, when you refer to that host variable in the host language (in this case COBOL), you'll need to use the variable name that DB2 generates (EMP-PHOTO-DATA).

```
01  EMP-PHOTO.
   49 EMP-PHOTO-LENGTH                PIC S9(9) COMP-5.
   49 EMP-PHOTO-DATA                  PIC X(5242880).
 *01 EMP-PHOTO USAGE IS SQL TYPE IS BLOB(5M).
```

You can now retrieve an LOB value into your host variable just like any other variable:

```
SELECT EMP_PHOTO
INTO   :PHOTO-DATA
WHERE EMP_ID = :EMP-ID;
```

If your program modifies the PHOTO-DATA, you can then update the stored BLOB value by updating the length and data portions of the DB2-generated variable, and then issuing an UPDATE using the SQL host variable. Assuming you have read a binary photo file into EMP-PHOTO-DATA and then set the EMP-PHOTO-LENGTH to the actual length of the file, you can now do the update.

```
MOVE <length of the file> to EMP-PHOTO-LENGTH

EXEC SQL
         UPDATE EMPLOYEE SET EMP_PHOTO = :PHOTO-DATA
   WHERE EMP_ID = :EMP-ID;
END-EXEC.
```

The above is a fairly inefficient way of retrieving or updating photo data if the data is acquired from an external file system. Materializing an LOB value inside a program space is usually not the best way to go because it takes a lot of overhead in the program space, and there are other alternatives. First let's mention LOB locator variables, and then we'll look at file reference variables. Finally we'll consider inline LOBs where a portion of the LOB value is actually stored in the base table.

LOB Locators

In the previous example, we materialized the LOB data when we read it into the host variable `PHOTO-DATA`. By materialized, we mean the data was copied from the LOB record to the host variable in the program. In many cases you may wish to work with LOBs where you simply locate the value without actually materializing it. In that case, you can use locator host variables.

A locator variable is a locator to the actual LOB data in the auxiliary table. So if you execute a query in which you read an LOB column into a locator host variable, only the locator information is contained in the host variable. That saves a lot of space.

We could define a locator host variable for the example as follows:

```
77 PHOTO-DATA-LOC USAGE IS SQL TYPE IS BLOB LOCATOR.
```

Now if you issue a query against this, only the locator value will be returned in the query.

```
SELECT EMP_PHOTO
INTO  :PHOTO-DATA-LOC
WHERE EMP_ID = :EMP-ID;
```

Then if your program logic determines that it really needs to materialize the BLOB, you could do so by reading the BLOB column into the BLOB host variable rather than into the locator variable. That's what we did in the first example a few pages back.

File Reference Variables

Sometimes you need to load a value into a LOB column using the content of an external file. In other cases you may need to unload an LOB value from DB2 into an external file. In these cases, you can avoid having to allocate program storage for the LOB value by using file reference variables. With file reference variables, you define a file as the source of an LOB value, and you can then perform an insert or update to the DB2 table without materializing the LOB inside the program. In this way the I/O takes place strictly between DB2 and the file system. This saves a lot of overhead because the program does not need to materialize the LOB value.

Here's an example of defining a file reference and using it to load a photo to the `EMP_PHOTO` table for employee 3217. Assume we have a binary file named `EMP3217.PHOTO` that is sized 1.786835 MB.

```cobol
       IDENTIFICATION DIVISION.
       PROGRAM-ID. COBEMPB.

      ******************************************************
      *        PROGRAM USING DB2 FOR LOB FILE VARIABLE DEC. *
      ******************************************************

       ENVIRONMENT DIVISION.
       DATA DIVISION.
       WORKING-STORAGE SECTION.


       01 ERR-REC.
          05 FILLER               PIC X(10) VALUE 'SQLCODE = '.
          05 SQLCODE-VIEW          PIC -999.
          05 FILLER               PIC X(005) VALUE SPACES.
          05 ERR-TAB              PIC X(016).
          05 ERR-PARA             PIC X(015).
          05 ERR-DETAIL           PIC X(040).

       77 ERR-TXT-LGTH            PIC S9(9) USAGE COMP VALUE +72.

       01 ERR-MSG.
          05 ERR-MSG-LGTH          PIC S9(04) COMP VALUE +864.
          05 ERR-MSG-TXT           PIC X(072) OCCURS 12 TIMES
                                               INDEXED BY ERR-NDX.

       01 EMP-PHOTO-FILE USAGE IS SQL TYPE IS BLOB-FILE.

           EXEC SQL
             INCLUDE SQLCA
           END-EXEC.


       PROCEDURE DIVISION.

       MAIN-PARA.
           DISPLAY "SAMPLE COBOL PROGRAM: LOB WITH FILE REF VAR".

           MOVE 13 TO EMP-PHOTO-FILE-NAME-LENGTH
           MOVE 1786835 TO EMP-PHOTO-FILE-DATA-LENGTH
           MOVE 1 TO EMP-PHOTO-FILE-FILE-OPTION
           MOVE 'EMP3217.PHOTO' TO EMP-PHOTO-FILE-NAME


           EXEC SQL
             UPDATE HRSCHEMA.EMPLOYEE
             SET EMP_PHOTO = :EMP-PHOTO-FILE
             WHERE EMP_ID = 3217
           END-EXEC.

           IF SQLCODE IS NOT EQUAL TO ZERO
```

```
            MOVE SQLCODE TO SQLCODE-VIEW
            MOVE 'EMPLOYEE' TO ERR-TAB
            MOVE 'MAIN'     TO ERR-PARA
            MOVE 3217       TO ERR-DETAIL
            PERFORM P9999-SQL-ERROR

        ELSE
            DISPLAY  'UPDATE CALL SUCCESFULL ' HV-ID

        END-IF

        STOP RUN.

    P9999-SQL-ERROR.

        DISPLAY ERR-REC.

        CALL 'DSNTIAR' USING SQLCA,
                        ERR-MSG,
                        ERR-TXT-LGTH.

        IF RETURN-CODE IS EQUAL TO ZERO

            PERFORM P9999-DISP-ERR
                VARYING ERR-NDX FROM 1 BY 1
                UNTIL ERR-NDX > 12

        ELSE
            DISPLAY 'DSNTIAR ERROR CODE = ' RETURN-CODE
            STOP RUN.

    P9999-DISP-ERR.

        DISPLAY ERR-MSG-TXT(ERR-NDX).

    P9999-DISP-ERR-EXIT.
```

The above is a very simple example of working with LOBs and file locator variables. If you had more file names and file sizes, you could set up a loop to process the photo files. You'd need a way of passing the multiple file names and file sizes to the program, perhaps by storing these in a text file. There are a lot of possibilities, but I think you know the basics now.

Here is the PLI version of the program.

```
PLIEMPB: PROCEDURE OPTIONS(MAIN) REORDER;
/*******************************************************************
* PROGRAM NAME :   PLIEMPB - LOB FILE VARIABLE DECLARATION/USAGE   * ``
*******************************************************************/

/*******************************************************************
*                 E X T E R N A L   E N T R I E S                 *
```

```
  ********************************************************************/
     DCL DSNTIAR ENTRY OPTIONS(ASM INTER RETCODE);

  /*******************************************************************
  /*               W O R K I N G   S T O R A G E               *
  *******************************************************************/

     DCL 01  HV_ID                FIXED BIN(31);

     DCL EMP_PHOTO_FILE USAGE IS SQL TYPE IS BLOB_FILE;

     DCL RET_SQL_CODE             FIXED BIN(31) INIT(0);
     DCL RET_SQL_CODE_PIC         PIC 'S999999999' INIT (0);

     DCL 01 ERR_REC,
          05 FILLER1              CHAR(10) INIT ('SQLCODE = '),
          05 SQLCODE_VIEW         PIC '-999',
          05 ERR_EMPID            FIXED BIN (31) INIT (0),
          05 FILLER2              CHAR(01) INIT (' '),
          05 ERR_TAB              CHAR(08) INIT (' '),
          05 ERR_PARA             CHAR(15) INIT (' ');

     DCL 01 ERR_MSG AUTOMATIC,
          05 ERR_LGTH             FIXED BIN (31) INIT (864),
          05 ERR_TXT(10)          CHAR(72);

     DCL ERR_TXT_LGTH             FIXED BIN (15) INIT (72);
     DCL ERR_NDX                  FIXED BIN (31) INIT (0);

     EXEC SQL
       INCLUDE SQLCA;


  /*******************************************************************
  /*               P R O G R A M   M A I N L I N E               *
  *******************************************************************/

     PUT SKIP LIST ('SAMPLE PLI PROGRAM: LOB WITH FILE REF VAR');

        EMP_PHOTO_FILE_NAME_LENGTH = 12;
        EMP_PHOTO_FILE_DATA_LENGTH = 1786835;
        EMP_PHOTO_FILE_FILE_OPTION = 1;
        EMP_PHOTO_FILE_NAME        = 'HRSCHEMA.PHOTO';

        EXEC SQL

           UPDATE HRSCHEMA.EMP_PHOTO
           SET EMP_PHOTO = :EMP_PHOTO_FILE
           WHERE EMP_ID = 3217;

        IF SQLCODE ¬= 0 THEN
           DO;
              SQLCODE_VIEW = SQLCODE;
```

```
                    ERR_TAB = 'EMPLOYEE';
                    ERR_PARA = 'MAIN';
                    ERR_EMPID = HV_ID;
                    CALL P9999_SQL_ERROR;
               END;
            ELSE
               PUT SKIP LIST ('UPDATE CALL SUCCESFULL ' || HV_ID);


     P9999_SQL_ERROR: PROC;

        PUT SKIP LIST (ERR_REC);

        CALL DSNTIAR (SQLCA, ERR_MSG, ERR_TXT_LGTH);

        IF RETCODE = 0 THEN
           DO ERR_NDX = 1 TO 10;
              PUT SKIP DATA (ERR_TXT(ERR_NDX));
           END; /* DO */
        ELSE
           PUT SKIP LIST ('DSNTIAR ERROR CODE = ' || RETCODE);

     END P9999_SQL_ERROR;

     END PLIEMPB;
```

LOB Inline

You can store part or all of a LOB inline which means that part or all of the LOB value can be stored in the base table. That way some part of the data is available without materializing the entire LOB. This has some advantages, especially when you are using CLOBs where a given query may only need to reference data at the beginning of the CLOB record.

You define how much of the LOB will be stored in the base table using the INLINE LENGTH clause. So in the case of a CLOB named EMP_RECOG_TEXT you might define it as follows:

```
CREATE TABLE HRSCHEMA.EMP_RECOG_HIST
(EMP_ID INT NOT NULL,
 EMP_RECOG_TEXT CLOB(1M) INLINE LENGTH 5000)
 IN TSHR;
```

Now any value in the EMP_RECOG_TEXT field up to 5000 bytes will be stored in the base table. You still need to define the auxiliary table for the LOB, just as we did in the earlier examples. However, defining your LOB with an inline length means you avoid the additional I/O of bringing in the CLOB from the LOB tablespace any time the data you need is within the first 5000 bytes of the CLOB. That can be quite an advantage.

XML DATA

XML is a highly used standard for exchanging self-describing data files or documents. Even if you work in a shop that does not use the DB2 XML data type or XML functions, it is good to know how to use these. You will not be expected to have mastered advanced XML concepts for the exam, but you will need to know the basics of how to use XML in DB2 in order to answer the XML-related DB2 questions.

A complete tutorial on XML is well beyond the scope of this book, but we'll review some XML basics. If you have little or no experience with XML, I strongly suggest that you purchase some books to acquire this knowledge. The following are a few that can help fill in the basics:

> XML in a Nutshell, Third Edition 3rd Edition by Elliotte Rusty Harold (ISBN 978-0596007645)
>
> XSLT 2.0 and XPath 2.0 Programmer's Reference by Michael Kay (ISBN: 978-0470192740)
>
> XQuery: Search Across a Variety of XML Data by Priscilla Walmsley
> (ISBN: ISBN-13: 978-1491915103)

Basic XML Concepts

You may know that XML stands for Extensible Markup Language. XML technology is cross-platform and independent of machine and software. It provides a structure that consists of both data and data element tags, and so it describes the data in both human readable and machine readable format. The tag names for the elements are defined by the developer/user of the data.

XML Structure

XML has a tree type structure that is required to begin with a root element and then it expands to the branches. To continue our discussion of the EMPLOYEE domain, let's take a simple XML example with an employee profile as the root. We'll include the employee id, the address and birth date. The XML document might look like this:

```
<?xml version="1.0" encoding="UTF-8"?>
<EMP_PROFILE>
      <EMP_ID>4175</EMP_ID>
      <EMP_ADDRESS>
<STREET>6161 MARGARET LANE</STREET>
<CITY>ERINDALE</CITY>
<STATE>AR</STATE>
<ZIP_CODE>72653</ZIP_CODE>
</EMP_ADDRESS>
<BIRTH_DATE>07/14/1991</BIRTH_DATE>
</EMP_PROFILE>
```

XML documents frequently begin with a declaration which includes the XML version and the encoding scheme of the document. In our example, we are using XML version 1.0 which is still very common. This declaration is optional but it's a best practice to include it.

Notice after the version specification that we continue with the tag name `EMP_PROFILE` enclosed by the <> symbols. The employee profile element ends with `/EMP_PROFILE` enclosed by the <> symbols. Similarly each sub-element is tagged and enclosed and the value (if any) appears between the opening and closing of the element.

XML documents must have a single root element, i.e., one element that is the root of all other elements. If you want more than one `EMP_PROFILE` in a document, then you would need a higher level element to contain the profiles. For example you could have a `DEPARTMENT` element that contains employee profiles, and a `COMPANY` element that contains `DEPARTMENTS`.

All elements must have a closing tag. Elements that are not populated can be represented by an opening and closing with nothing in between. For example, if an employee's birthday is not know, it can be represented by `<BIRTH_DATE></BIRTH_DATE>` or you can use the short hand form `<BIRTH_DATE/>`.

The example document includes elements such as the employee id, address and birth date. The address is broken down into a street name, city, state and zip code. Comments can be included in an XML document by following the following format:

```
<!-- This is a sample comment -->
```

By default, white space is preserved in XML documents.

Ok, so we've given you a drive-thru version of XML. We'll provide more information later in the Application Design section, but for now we have almost enough to move on to how to manipulate XML data in DB2. Before we get to that, let's first look at two XML-related technologies that we will need.

XML Related Technologies

XPath
The extensible path language (XPath) is used to locate and extract information from an XML document using "path" expressions through the XML nodes. For example, in the case of the employee XML document we created earlier, you could locate and return a zip code value by specifying the path.

Recall this structure:

```
<EMP_PROFILE>
        <EMP_ID>4175</EMP_ID>
        <EMP_ADDRESS>
<STREET>6161 MARGARET LANE</STREET>
<CITY>ERINDALE</CITY>
<STATE>AR</STATE>
<ZIP_CODE>72653</ZIP_CODE>
</EMP_ADDRESS>
<BIRTH_DATE>07/14/1991</BIRTH_DATE>
</EMP_PROFILE>
```

In this example, the employee profile nodes with zip code 72653 can be identified using the following path:

```
/EMP_PROFILE/ADDRESS[ZIP_CODE=72653]
```

The XPath expression for all employees who live in Texas as follows:

```
/EMP_PROFILE/ADDRESS[STATE="TX"]
```

XQuery

XQuery enables us to query XML data using XPath expressions. It is similar to how we query relational data using SQL, but of course the syntax is different. Here's an example of pulling the employee id of every employee who lives at a zip code greater than 90000 from an XML document named employees.xml.

```
for $x in doc("employees.xml")employee/profile/address/zipcode
where $x/zipcode>90000
order by $x/zipcode
return $x/empid
```

In DB2 you run an XQuery using the built-in function XMLQUERY. We'll show you some examples using XMLQUERY shortly.

XML Schema Validation

DB2 does a basic check to ensure that the data you use to populate an XML column is well formed. We saw an example of this check back in section 1. As long as the XML is well formed, DB2 will apply it to the XML column.

In addition to ensuring well formed XML, you can also validate the XML against an XML schema. XML schema help you ensure that the XML content meets the rules you define. Again, if you are not very familiar with these concepts, I encourage you to read the recommended XML books. Let's create an example to go with the EMP_PROFILE column of the EMPLOYEE table.

First, let's review the XML column and some sample content.

```
<?xml version="1.0" encoding="UTF-8"?>
<EMP_PROFILE>
<EMP_ID>4175</EMP_ID>
<EMP_ADDRESS>
<STREET>6161 MARGARET LANE</STREET>
<CITY>ERINDALE</CITY>
<STATE>AR</STATE>
<ZIP_CODE>72653</ZIP_CODE>
</EMP_ADDRESS>
<BIRTH_DATE>1991-07-14</BIRTH_DATE>
</EMP_PROFILE>
```

Now let's establish some rules for the content of the EMP_PROFILE structure:

- EMP_ID is required and must be an integer greater than zero.
- STREET, CITY, STATE are required and must be string values.
- ZIP_CODE is required and must be an integer greater than zero.
- BIRTH_DATE is optional, but if entered must be a valid date.

An XML schema for this structure might look like this:

```
<?xml version="1.0" encoding="UTF-8" ?>
<xs:schema xmlns:xs="http://www.w3.org/2001/XMLSchema">
<xs:element name="EMP_PROFILE">
   <xs:complexType>
     <xs:sequence>
        <xs:element name="EMP_ID" type="xs:positiveInteger" />
        <xs:element name="EMP_ADDRESS">
        <xs:complexType>
        <xs:sequence>
           <xs:element name="STREET" type="xs:string" />
           <xs:element name="CITY" type="xs:string" />
           <xs:element name="STATE" type="xs:string" />
<xs:element name="ZIP_CODE" type="xs:positiveInteger"/>
        </xs:sequence>
        </xs:complexType>
        </xs:element>
     <xs:element name="BIRTH_DATE" minOccurs="0"
       type="xs:date" />
       </xs:sequence>
     </xs:complexType>
</xs:element>
</xs:schema>
```

300

Now we need to know how to define the XML schema to DB2. The schema must be added to the XML Schema Repository (XSR) before it can be used to validate XML docs. The XSR is a repository for all XML schemas that are required to validate and process the XML documents that are stored in XML columns. DB2 creates the XSR tables during installation or migration.

You can register an XML schema by calling these DB2-supplied stored procedures:

- SYSPROC.XSR_REGISTER - Begins registration of an XML schema. You call this stored procedure when you add the first XML schema document to an XML schema.

- SYSPROC.XSR_ADDSCHEMADOC - Adds additional XML schema documents to an XML schema that you are in the process of registering. You can call SYSPROC. XSR_ADDSCHEMADOC only for an existing XML schema that is not yet complete.

- SYSPROC.XSR_COMPLETE - Completes the registration of an XML schema.

The stored procedures must be called either from an application program (such as a COBOL program), from Rexx or from Data Studio. Once registers, we can validate against the specified schema. Let try inserting an XML column with an invalid birth date:

```
UPDATE HRSCHEMA.EMPLOYEE
SET EMP_PROFILE
 = DSN_XMLVALIDATE (
 XMLPARSE(
 DOCUMENT(
 '<EMP_PROFILE>
  <EMP_ID>3217</EMP_ID>
  <EMP_ADDRESS>
      <STREET>2913 PATE DR</STREET>
      <CITY>FORT WORTH</CITY>
      <STATE>TX</STATE>
      <ZIP_CODE>76105</ZIP_CODE>
      </EMP_ADDRESS>
      <BIRTH_DATE>1952-02-30</BIRTH_DATE>
      </EMP_PROFILE>')) ACCORDING TO XMLSCHEMA ID HRSCHEMA.EMP_PROFILE )
WHERE EMP_ID = 3217;

SQLCODE=-16105, SQLSTATE=2200M

Incorrect XML data. Expected data of type "dateTime" and found value "1952-
02-30" which is not a valid value for that type..
```

Now let's correct the birth date. We'll change it from February 30 to February 28, and we'll see that it now executes correctly:

```
UPDATE HRSCHEMA.EMPLOYEE
SET EMP_PROFILE
 = DSN_XMLVALIDATE (
 XMLPARSE(
 DOCUMENT(
 '<EMP_PROFILE>
  <EMP_ID>3217</EMP_ID>
  <EMP_ADDRESS>
      <STREET>2913 PATE DR</STREET>
      <CITY>FORT WORTH</CITY>
      <STATE>TX</STATE>
      <ZIP_CODE>76105</ZIP_CODE>
      </EMP_ADDRESS>
      <BIRTH_DATE>1952-02-28</BIRTH_DATE>
      </EMP_PROFILE>')) ACCORDING TO XMLSCHEMA ID HRSCHEMA.EMP_PROFILE )
WHERE EMP_ID = 3217;

Updated 1 rows.
```

Finally, let's look at how we could change the EMP_PROFILE column in the EMPLOYEE table to automatically do the XML validation instead of us having to code it using the DSN_ XMLVALIDATE routine. Assume we have created the XML schema named EMP_PROFILE. We can tie it to our EMP_PROFILE column as follows:

```
ALTER TABLE HRSCHEMA.EMPLOYEE
ALTER EMP_PROFILE
SET DATA TYPE XML(XMLSCHEMA ID HRSCHEMA.EMP_PROFILE);
```

Now when we try to add a value to an XML column that violates these rules, we will get an error. For example, let's try to add this structure using the same value we tried earlier, with an invalid birth date:

```
UPDATE HRSCHEMA.EMPLOYEE
SET EMP_PROFILE
 = XMLPARSE(
 DOCUMENT(
 '<EMP_PROFILE>
  <EMP_ID>3217</EMP_ID>
  <EMP_ADDRESS>
      <STREET>2913 PATE DR</STREET>
      <CITY>FORT WORTH</CITY>
      <STATE>TX</STATE>
      <ZIP_CODE>76105</ZIP_CODE>
      </EMP_ADDRESS>
      <BIRTH_DATE>1952-02-30</BIRTH_DATE>
      </EMP_PROFILE>'))
WHERE EMP_ID = 3217;
```

```
SQLCODE=-16105, SQLSTATE=2200M

Incorrect XML data. Expected data of type "dateTime" and found value "1952-
02-30" which is not a valid value for that type.
```

Again, we get an error because the birth date value is not a valid date and the XML schema requires it to be. From now on, any record we try to add to the EMPLOYEE table will fail if it includes an EMP_PROFILE value that does not conform to the schema we set up.

NOTE: To use the XSR, you must first set it up. This is an installation task and is beyond the scope of study for this text book. The procedure is available in the DB2 product documentation.

PERFORMANCE

It's vital to design your DB2 applications with optimal performance in mind. Resolving existing performance issues can also be part of your job when enhanced functionality or larger data volumes begin to cause performance problems. This chapter looks at several areas you should be familiar with to develop and tune your applications.

Creating and Using Explain Data

The EXPLAIN statement helps you to gather information about the access paths DB2 uses when retrieving or updating data. This in turn can help you to diagnose performance related issues, such as excessively long running queries.

Creating Plan Tables

If you bind a plan using the EXPLAIN(YES) option, then appropriate explain tables will be created for you automatically using your login id as the schema (provided you have access to the appropriate tablespace). At a minimum the PLAN_TABLE will be created and this is usually what you will query to get information about the access paths DB2 has chosen.

If you simply want to determine the access path for a query, and explain tables do not already exist, you must create them. To create the PLAN_TABLE you can modify the sample CREATE TABLE statements in the DSNTESC member of the SDSNSAMP library. You may need to ask your system admin which library these samples are stored on your local system. On my system the file name for the SDSNSAMP PDS is DSNxxxx.SDSNSAMP where the xxxx is the DB2 instance name.

You only need the PLAN_TABLE to enable the basic EXPLAIN function. If you need the other tables (enumerated below), you can create those as well.

Here is the query I used to create my PLAN_TABLE in my tablespace TSHR (naturally you must use whatever tablespace name is appropriate for your system).

```
CREATE TABLE PLAN_TABLE
(QUERYNO              INTEGER        NOT NULL,
 QBLOCKNO             SMALLINT       NOT NULL,
 APPLNAME             CHAR(8)        NOT NULL,
 PROGNAME             CHAR(8)        NOT NULL,
 PLANNO               SMALLINT       NOT NULL,
 METHOD               SMALLINT       NOT NULL,
 CREATOR              CHAR(8)        NOT NULL,
 TNAME                CHAR(18)       NOT NULL,
 TABNO                SMALLINT       NOT NULL,
 ACCESSTYPE           CHAR(2)        NOT NULL,
 MATCHCOLS            SMALLINT       NOT NULL,
 ACCESSCREATOR        CHAR(8)        NOT NULL,
 ACCESSNAME           CHAR(18)       NOT NULL,
 INDEXONLY            CHAR(1)        NOT NULL,
 SORTN_UNIQ           CHAR(1)        NOT NULL,
 SORTN_JOIN           CHAR(1)        NOT NULL,
 SORTN_ORDERBY        CHAR(1)        NOT NULL,
 SORTN_GROUPBY        CHAR(1)        NOT NULL,
 SORTC_UNIQ           CHAR(1)        NOT NULL,
 SORTC_JOIN           CHAR(1)        NOT NULL,
 SORTC_ORDERBY        CHAR(1)        NOT NULL,
 SORTC_GROUPBY        CHAR(1)        NOT NULL,
 TSLOCKMODE           CHAR(3)        NOT NULL,
 TIMESTAMP            CHAR(16)       NOT NULL,
 REMARKS              VARCHAR(254)   NOT NULL,
 PREFETCH             CHAR(1)        NOT NULL,
 COLUMN_FN_EVAL       CHAR(1)        NOT NULL,
 MIXOPSEQ             SMALLINT       NOT NULL,
 VERSION              VARCHAR(64)    NOT NULL,
 COLLID               CHAR(18)       NOT NULL,
 ACCESS_DEGREE        SMALLINT,
 ACCESS_PGROUP_ID     SMALLINT,
 JOIN_DEGREE          SMALLINT,
 JOIN_PGROUP_ID       SMALLINT,
 SORTC_PGROUP_ID      SMALLINT,
 SORTN_PGROUP_ID      SMALLINT,
 PARALLELISM_MODE     CHAR(1),
 MERGE_JOIN_COLS      SMALLINT,
 CORRELATION_NAME     CHAR(18),
 PAGE_RANGE           CHAR(1)        NOT NULL WITH DEFAULT,
 JOIN_TYPE            CHAR(1)        NOT NULL WITH DEFAULT,
 GROUP_MEMBER         CHAR(8)        NOT NULL WITH DEFAULT,
 IBM_SERVICE_DATA     VARCHAR(254)   NOT NULL WITH DEFAULT,
 WHEN_OPTIMIZE        CHAR(1)        NOT NULL WITH DEFAULT,  -- V5
 QBLOCK_TYPE          CHAR(6)        NOT NULL WITH DEFAULT,  -- V5
 BIND_TIME            TIMESTAMP      NOT NULL WITH DEFAULT,  -- V5
 OPTHINT              CHAR(8)        NOT NULL WITH DEFAULT,  -- V6
 HINT_USED            CHAR(8)        NOT NULL WITH DEFAULT,  -- V6
 PRIMARY_ACCESSTYPE   CHAR(1)        NOT NULL WITH DEFAULT,  -- V6
 PARENT_QBLOCKNO      SMALLINT       NOT NULL WITH DEFAULT,  -- V7
 TABLE_TYPE           CHAR(1)                             ,  -- V7
 TABLE_ENCODE         CHAR(1)        NOT NULL WITH DEFAULT,  -- V8
 TABLE_SCCSID         SMALLINT       NOT NULL WITH DEFAULT,  -- V8
 TABLE_MCCSID         SMALLINT       NOT NULL WITH DEFAULT,  -- V8
 TABLE_DCCSID         SMALLINT       NOT NULL WITH DEFAULT,  -- V8
```

```
ROUTINE_ID       INTEGER     NOT NULL WITH DEFAULT, -- V8
CTEREF           SMALLINT    NOT NULL WITH DEFAULT, -- V8
STMTTOKEN        VARCHAR(240))                      -- V8
IN TSHR;
```

The EXPLAIN Statement

The EXPLAIN statement generates explain data that can be analyzed to determine access paths the DB2 Optimizer has chosen for a query or plan. We'll look first at the EXPLAIN syntax, generate some data into the PLAN_TABLE and then query it. Later we'll look at the EXPLAIN bind option and how it adds data to the PLAN_TABLE. Finally we'll look at using the Visual Explain component of IBM's Data Studio to see a visual representation of the access path associated with a query.

EXPLAIN Data with Queries

With the explain statement you can get information about packages, plans and queries. Let's start with a very simple example. This is just to get us somewhat familiar with the PLAN_TABLE. Here is the query:

```
EXPLAIN PLAN SET QUERYNO = 1
   FOR SELECT EMP_ID, EMP_LAST_NAME
      FROM HRSCHEMA.EMPLOYEE
         WHERE EMP_ID IN (3217, 9134)
         ORDER BY EMP_ID;
```

The above generates explain data into the PLAN_TABLE. Now we can select some of the fields from the table to determine what access path the query is taking. Here's our first query:

```
SELECT TNAME,
       ACCESSTYPE,
       MATCHCOLS,
       ACCESSNAME
       FROM HRSCHEMA.PLAN_TABLE
       WHERE QUERYNO = 1;
```

```
---------+---------+---------+---------+---------+---------+-
TNAME              ACCESSTYPE  MATCHCOLS  ACCESSNAME
---------+---------+---------+---------+---------+---------+-
EMPLOYEE           N                   1  NDX_EMPLOYEE
```

The result from the PLAN_TABLE indicates that the dynamic query we explained will use an index -- specifically the NDX_EMPLOYEE index -- to access the data. We'll be looking at all the access types in a few minutes, but for now just be aware that access type N means an index call based on an "IN" predicate in the SQL.

Now recall that earlier we defined NDX_EMPLOYEE as follows:

```
CREATE UNIQUE INDEX NDX_EMPLOYEE
      ON EMPLOYEE (EMP_ID);
```

This is good because our EXPLAIN data tells us an index exists and is being used to locate the data rows needed by the query. That typically means we can expect pretty good performance.

Now let's take a different scenario where we are trying to solve a performance issue. Let's assume we are pulling data from the EMP_PAY_CHECK table and the query is running very slow. Here is the query:

```
SELECT EMP_ID, EMP_REGULAR_PAY
FROM HRSCHEMA.EMP_PAY_CHECK
WHERE (EMP_ID = 3217 OR EMP_ID = 9134);
```

Let's create an EXPLAIN statement for this as follows:

```
EXPLAIN PLAN SET QUERYNO = 2
    FOR SELECT EMP_ID, EMP_REGULAR_PAY
        FROM HRSCHEMA.EMP_PAY_CHECK
        WHERE (EMP_ID = 3217 OR EMP_ID = 9134);
```

Now we can run this query to determine what access path is being used.

```
SELECT TNAME,ACCESSTYPE,
       PREFETCH,MATCHCOLS,
       ACCESSNAME
       FROM HRSCHEMA.PLAN_TABLE
       WHERE QUERYNO = 2;
---------+---------+---------+---------+---------+---------+---------+--------
TNAME                ACCESSTYPE  PREFETCH  MATCHCOLS  ACCESSNAME
---------+---------+---------+---------+---------+---------+----
EMP_PAY_CHECK        R           S                    0
```

A brief look at the result tells us what our problem is. DB2 is using access type R which means a table scan. We are walking through the entire table record-by-record to find the qualifying rows. For a very small table this may be ok, but for tables that have any significant amount of data, this is the slowest way to access the data.

Let's try to solve this problem by creating an index on EMP_ID and then see the result.

```
CREATE UNIQUE INDEX HRSCHEMA.EMP_PC_NDX
ON HRSCHEMA.EMP_PAY_CHECK (EMP_ID);
```

Now we can rerun the explain statement:

```
EXPLAIN PLAN SET QUERYNO = 2
   FOR SELECT EMP_ID, EMP_REGULAR_PAY
      FROM HRSCHEMA.EMP_PAY_CHECK
         WHERE (EMP_ID = 3217 OR EMP_ID = 9134);
```

Finally let's requery the PLAN_TABLE and see the results.

```
SELECT TNAME,
       ACCESSTYPE,
       MATCHCOLS,
       ACCESSNAME
       FROM HRSCHEMA.PLAN_TABLE
       WHERE QUERYNO = 2;
```

TNAME	ACCESSTYPE	MATCHCOLS	ACCESSNAME
EMP_PAY_CHECK	N	1	EMP_PC_NDX

Ok, we're in business now. Our access type is N which means an index. Specifically ACCESSNAME column tells us DB2 will use the index EMP_PC_NDX that we just created. We are matching on one column, the EMP_ID. This is good. Again, using an index should mean fairly good performance.

Now let's do a third example. Suppose we have a new requirement to order the results of our previous query by regular pay in descending order. And this time we want all the employees (not a specific one). What effect will that have? Let's run the EXPLAIN statement again, changing the SQL and also the QUERYNO so that it is unique.

```
EXPLAIN PLAN SET QUERYNO = 3
   FOR SELECT EMP_ID, EMP_REGULAR_PAY
      FROM HRSCHEMA.EMP_PAY_CHECK
         ORDER BY EMP_REGULAR_PAY DESC;
```

Now let's run our query against PLAN_TABLE and see what we have.

```
SELECT TNAME,
       ACCESSTYPE,
       MATCHCOLS,
       ACCESSNAME,
       SORTC_ORDERBY
       FROM HRSCHEMA.PLAN_TABLE
       WHERE QUERYNO = 3;
```

TNAME	ACCESSTYPE	MATCHCOLS	ACCESSNAME	SORTC_ORDERBY
EMP_PAY_CHECK	R	0		N
		0		Y

Now we see there are two entries in the table, which means there are two steps to satisfy the query. We are first doing a table scan (since we are reading all the records we don't need the

`EMP_ID` index). Second we are doing a sort on the data. The sort is not necessarily so good. Once again, if the table contents is fairly small then the SORT step is not likely to be a problem. But if there are many rows in the table we may take a performance hit for having to do the sort to satisfy the ORDER BY clause.

One way to resolve the issue could be to create another index that includes both the employee id and the regular pay column. We'll do that momentarily. First I want to pause to state that adding new indexes is not always the best approach to resolving a performance issue. There are tradeoffs between the overhead cost of additional indexes versus the cost of a long running query. Moreover there are other things to look into besides indexing, such as how the SQL statement is structured to begin with and whether it is using stage 1 or stage 2 predicates.

Having issued the above caveat, let's assume that we decide to create the new index and then run the EXPLAIN statement again. Here is the DDL for the new index which will be organized by `EMP_REGULAR_PAY`.

```
CREATE INDEX HRSCHEMA.EMP_PC_RP_NDX
ON HRSCHEMA.EMP_PAY_CHECK
(EMP_REGULAR_PAY DESC, EMP_ID ASC);
```

Here's the EXPLAIN statement for our query:

```
EXPLAIN PLAN SET QUERYNO = 4
    FOR SELECT EMP_REGULAR_PAY, EMP_ID
        FROM HRSCHEMA.EMP_PAY_CHECK
            ORDER BY EMP_REGULAR_PAY DESC;
```

And let's retrieve the information from the `PLAN_TABLE`:

```
SELECT TNAME,
       ACCESSTYPE,
       ACCESSNAME,
       INDEXONLY,
       SORTC_ORDERBY
       FROM HRSCHEMA.PLAN_TABLE
       WHERE QUERYNO = 4;
```

TNAME	ACCESSTYPE	ACCESSNAME	INDEXONLY	SORTC_ORDERBY
EMP_PAY_CHECK	I	EMP_PC_RP_NDX	Y	N

This access path looks a lot better. We've eliminated the sort step because we have an index that is available to order the results. Notice also that we are doing an index-only scan (ACCESSTYPE is I) with the new index EMP_PC_RP_NDX. Since all the columns we are requesting are available in the index itself, we don't even need to touch the base table. This should be a very efficient scan!

Ok, that fairly well wraps up EXPLAIN statement basics. The above examples, while trivial, should give us a basic understanding of how to use the PLAN_TABLE with the EXPLAIN statement. To conclude, here is a table of all the various access types you might encounter in the EXPLAIN table and what they mean.

Access Types

The various access types and their meaning is as follows:

Value	Meaning
`A`	The query is sent to an accelerator server.
`DI` DOCID list	By an intersection of multiple DOCID lists to return the final
`DU` list	By a union of multiple DOCID lists to return the final DOCID
`DX` to	By an XML index scan on the index that is named in ACCESSNAME return a DOCID list
`E`	By direct row access using a row change timestamp column.
`H` overflow used.	By hash access. IF an overflow condition occurs, the hash index that is identified by ACCESSCREATOR and ACCESSNAME is
`HN` DB2 overflow used.	By hash access using an IN predicate, or an IN predicate that generates. If a hash overflow condition occurs, the hash ndex that is identified in ACCESSCREATOR and ACCESSNAME is
`I`	By an index (identified in ACCESSCREATOR and ACCESSNAME)
`IN` predicate	By an index scan when the matching predicate contains an IN and the IN-list is accessed through an in-memory table.
`I1`	By a one-fetch index scan
`M` be	By a multiple index scan. A row that contains this value might followed by a row that contains one of the following values:

```
'DI'
'DU'
'MH'
'MI'
'MU'
'MX'
```

'MH'
contains

By the hash overflow index named in ACCESSNAME. A row that this value always follows a row that contains M.

'MI'
this

By an intersection of multiple indexes. A row that contains value always follows a row that contains M.

'MU'
always

By a union of multiple indexes. A row that contains this value follows a row that contains M.

'MX'
access

is

returned

follows a

By an index scan on the index named in ACCESSNAME. When the ethod MX follows the access method DX, DI, or DU, the table accessed by the DOCID index by using the DOCID list that is by DX, DI, or DU. A row that contains this value always row that contains M.

'N'

One of the following types:

- By an index scan when the matching predicate contains the IN keyword
- By an index scan when DB2 rewrites a query using the IN keyword

'O'

By a work file scan, as a result of a correlated subquery.

'NR'

Range list access.

'P'

By a dynamic pair-wise index scan

'R'

By a table space scan

'RW'
table function

By a work file scan of the result of a materialized user-defined

'V'

By buffers for an INSERT statement within a SELECT

Blank

Not applicable to the current row

EXPLAIN Bind Option

If you bind your application plan with `EXPLAIN(YES)` then the bind process automatically adds info to the `PLAN_TABLE` For example let's go back to program `COBEMP2` which was our update program. We'll rebind it with `EXPLAIN(YES)`. Now let's look at the explain table results.

```
SELECT
TNAME,
QBLOCK_TYPE,
ACCESSTYPE,
MATCHCOLS,
ACCESSNAME,
SORTC_ORDERBY
FROM HRSCHEMA.PLAN_TABLE
WHERE PROGNAME = 'COBEMP2'
```

TNAME	QBLOCK_TYPE	ACCESSTYPE	MATCHCOLS	ACCESSNAME
EMPLOYEE	SELUPD	R	0	
EMPLOYEE	UPDCUR		0	

We can see that there are two queries in the program. One is a cursor to SELECT for UP-DATE, and the second is to perform the update (again via the cursor). The access type for the retrieval is R which means a table scan. If we look at the query, this makes sense because there is no index on `EMP_LAST_NAME`.

```
EXEC SQL
    DECLARE EMP-CURSOR CURSOR FOR
    SELECT EMP_ID, EMP_LAST_NAME
    FROM HRSCHEMA.EMPLOYEE
    WHERE EMP_LAST_NAME <> UPPER(EMP_LAST_NAME)
    FOR UPDATE OF EMP_LAST_NAME
END-EXEC.
```

The second query (UPDCUR) does not have an accesstype because it is based on a positional update. So the record is already acquired.

So besides explaining individual queries, you can use the EXPLAIN statement to generate and review access paths for an entire program. It is worthwhile to do this before you implement a program, and also periodically afterwards, especially if data volumes increase.

Visual Explain Using Data Studio
You can also use Data Studio to evaluate the EXPLAIN statement results and it will give you a visual result. Let's run through a couple of queries just to see how we would do it.

Suppose again we run this SQL and that we discover it is a very long running query:

311

```
SELECT * FROM HRSCHEMA.EMP_PAY_CHECK
WHERE EMP_ID = 3217;
```

To check why we might be having a performance issue, we can use visual explain with Data Studio to check the access path chosen by the DB2 Optimizer. Simply open Data Studio, select the RUN SQL perspective, type the query in and select it, right click and select Open Visual Explain. You can accept the defaults on the configuration panels and then click Finish. You will see this screen:

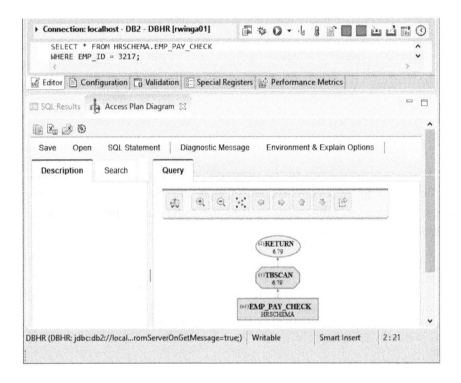

Note the TBSCAN in the middle of the diagram. This indicates you are doing a table scan, which means you are not using an index. Unless your table is very small, doing a table scan can definitely create a performance problem.

Now let's go back and try to solve our performance problem by creating an index.

```
CREATE UNIQUE INDEX HRSCHEMA.EMP_PC_NDX
ON HRSCHEMA.EMP_PAY_CHECK (EMP_ID);
```

And now retry the explain table with our query and check the result.

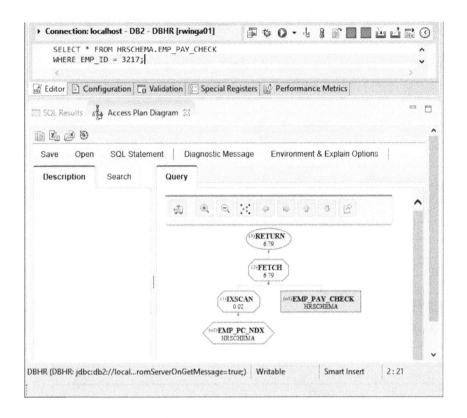

And now we can see the optimizer chose our new index – note the path is to use an index scan (IXSCAN) using index EMP_PC_NDX. This should increase the performance considerably. You could use Visual Explain for all the queries we looked at earlier. Some people prefer the raw data from the PLAN_TABLE and some like the visualization of the results you get with Visual Explain.

Stage 1 versus Stage 2 Predicates

In terms of both development standards and resolving performance issues, focus upon preferring stage 1 predicates over stage 2 predicates. By predicates I am referring to the WHERE clause as well as HAVING and ON clauses of the SELECT statement. When you retrieve rows from a table it is done through two stages. Some predicates can be applied during the first stage, and other predicates must wait until the second. You can improve performance by employing stage 1 predicates instead of stage 2 predicates.

The following is the order in which predicates are applied:

1. Indexable predicates are applied when DB2 accesses the index to match on key columns. This is a first level of selection.
2. Stage 1 predicates are applied to determine the data rows to be returned.

3. Stage 2 predicates are applied to the rows returned by stage 1.

Stage 1 and Stage 2 predicates are enumerated below and on the IBM product documentation web site: [1]

Indexable and Stage 1 Predicates
COL = value
COL = noncol expr
COL IS NULL
COL op value
COL op noncol expr
value BETWEEN COL1 AND COL2
COL BETWEEN value1 AND value2
COL BETWEEN noncol expr 1 AND noncol expr
COL BETWEEN expr-1 AND expr-2
COL LIKE 'pattern'
COL IN (list)
COL IS NOT NULL
COL LIKE host variable
COL LIKE UPPER ('pattern')
COL LIKE UPPER (host-variable)
COL LIKE UPPER (SQL-variable)
COL LIKE UPPER (global-variable)
COL LIKE UPPER (CAST ('pattern' AS data-type))
COL LIKE UPPER (CAST (host-variable AS data-type))
COL LIKE UPPER (CAST (SQL-variable AS data-type))
COL LIKE UPPER (CAST (global-variable AS data-type))
T1.COL = T2.COL
T1.COL op T2.COL
T1.COL = T2 col expr
T1.COL op T2 col expr
COL = (noncor subq)
COL op (noncor subq)
COL = ANY (noncor subq)
(COL1,...COLn) IN (noncor subq)
COL = ANY (cor subq)
COL IS NOT DISTINCT FROM value
COL IS NOT DISTINCT FROM noncol expr

---

1 https://www.ibm.com/support/knowledgecenter/en/SSEPEK_11.0.0/perf/src/tpc/db2z_summarypredicateprocessing.html

T1.COL1 IS NOT DISTINCT FROM T2.COL2
T1.COL1 IS NOT DISTINCT FROM T2 col expr
COL IS NOT DISTINCT FROM (noncor subq)
SUBSTR(COL,1,n) = value
SUBSTR(COL,1,n) op value
DATE(COL) = value
DATE(COL) op value
YEAR(COL) = value
YEAR(COL) op value
Stage 1 not indexable predicates – these might be evaluated during stage 1 processing, during index screening, or after data page access.
COL <> value
COL <> noncol expr
COL NOT BETWEEN value1 AND value2
COL NOT IN (list)
COL NOT LIKE ' char'
COL LIKE '%char'
COL LIKE '_char'
T1.COL <> T2 col expr
COL op ANY (noncor subq)
COL op ALL (noncor subq)
COL IS DISTINCT FROM value
COL IS DISTINCT FROM (noncor subq)
STAGE 2 Predicates – these must be processed during stage 2, after the data is returned.
COL BETWEEN COL1 AND COL2
value NOT BETWEEN COL1 AND COL2
value BETWEEN col expr and col expr
T1.COL <> T2.COL
T1.COL1 = T1.COL2
T1.COL1 op T1.COL2
T1.COL1 <> T1.COL2
COL = ALL (noncor subq)
COL <> (noncor subq)
COL <> ALL (noncor subq)
COL NOT IN (noncor subq)
COL = (cor subq)
COL = ALL (cor subq)

COL op (cor subq)
COL op ANY (cor subq)
COL op ALL (cor subq)
COL <> (cor subq)
COL <> ANY (cor subq)
(COL1,...COLn) IN (cor subq)
COL NOT IN (cor subq)
(COL1,...COLn) NOT IN (cor subq)
T1.COL1 IS DISTINCT FROM T2.COL2
T1.COL1 IS DISTINCT FROM T2 col expr
COL IS NOT DISTINCT FROM (cor subq)
EXISTS (subq)
expression = value
expression <> value
expression op value
expression op (subq)
NOT XMLEXISTS
CASE expression WHEN expression ELSE expression END = value
Indexable but not stage 1 predicates can be processed during index access, but cannot be processed during stage 1.
XMLEXISTS

Basic Query Optimization:

Always prefer stage 1 predicates over stage 2 if you have a choice. Stage 1 are more efficient because they eliminate rows earlier and thereby reduce the processing to be done at stage 2.

Write your queries such that the most restrictive predicates are evaluated first. For example if you have a nation-wide company and you run a query to return all male employees who live in the state of Texas, the query is more efficient if written as:

```
WHERE EMP_ADDRESS_STATE = 'TX' AND EMP_SEX = 'M'
```

instead of:

```
WHERE EMP_SEX = 'M' AND EMP_ADDRESS_STATE = 'TX'
```

It likely that there are many more employees who are male than the number of employees who live in Texas. By specifying the state of residence as the first predicate you automatically eliminate all the employees living anywhere else, hence you restrict the initial selection to a smaller number of rows than if you specified all male employees.

316

Final Considerations on Performance

As an application developer, you may or may not be asked to do performance troubleshooting. Some environments rely more on the DBA for this. Still it is important to develop with performance in mind. That being said, here are some recommendations.

Make sure your data concurrency settings are appropriate for your workload. If you are doing heavy read-only access against a static table, specify isolation level UR since it only locks those rows that are updated and the row the cursor is pointing at. Be careful not to use the RS or RR levels unless you have a good reason. Typically you should bind you application with `ISOLATION(CS)` and `CURRENTDATA(NO)` to prevent unnecessary locking.

It is important to commit your work regularly, which means often enough to avoid unnecessary locking, but not so often as to push unnecessary overhead. Ask your DBA for a recommendation on frequency, or experiment while you are still in development.

You'll also want to use the latest table statistics to ensure proper optimization. For example when a table is very small, DB2 will often select a table scan as the most efficient access method. If you never refresh the stats and rebind your packages, when the table grows large this will cause a performance problem. Ask your DBA to help keep an eye on performance, and do a periodic RUNSTATS and rebind.

If you have designed your queries efficiently and still encounter issues, you can also perform the following actions to resolve specific problems.

1. Enable queries to be re-optimized at run time (the REOPT bind option).

2. Specify optimization parameters at the statement level.

3. Specify an access path at the statement level.

4. Specify an access path in a `PLAN_TABLE` instance.

DB2 Trace

When you are trying to solve a problem it helps a lot to have accurate information about what DB2 is doing. One way of obtaining useful information is to use the DB2 trace feature. There are several trace types to investigate different kinds of problems.

Trace Types

The following table summarizes the valid DB2 trace types and what they are used for. The only one you will be tested on is the accounting trace, but it is good to know the full trace capabilities of DB2.

Trace Type	Description
Accounting trace	The accounting trace records transaction-level data that is written when the processing for a transaction is completed. It provides data that enables you to conduct DB2 capacity planning and to tune application programs.
Audit trace	The audit trace collects information about DB2 security controls and can be used to ensure that data access is allowed only for authorized purposes.
Monitor trace	The monitor trace enables attached monitor programs to access DB2 trace data through calls to the instrumentation facility interface (IFI). Monitor programs can access the trace data asynchronously through an OPx buffer by issuing READA requests, or synchronously in the monitor return area by issuing READS requests.
Performance trace	The performance trace is intended for performance analysis and tuning. This trace includes records of specific events in the system, including events related to distributed data processing. The data can be used for program, resource, user, and subsystem-related tuning.
Statistics trace	The statistics trace captures information about DB2 system and database services. You would use this when you want to do capacity planning.

Accounting Trace Basics

The accounting trace collects processing data that is written when a transaction completes. The monitor trace permits attached monitor programs to access DB2 trace data via calls to the instrumentation facility interface (IFI). A statistics trace provides data about how much the DB2 system and database services are used.

DB2 Trace Commands

START TRACE

To initiate a DB2 accounting trace, you would issue this abbreviated command:

```
STA TRA (ACCTG)
```

You could also issue START TRACE(ACCTG) which has the same meaning.

318

If you want to limit the trace to a particular DB2 plan, you can specify it. For example:

```
STA TRACE(ACCTG) PLAN(COBEMP4)
```

In fact you can get even more specific with your trace. Here's an example of capturing only class xyz for package COBEMP4 and userid HRUSER07:

```
STA TRACE(ACCTG) CLASS(1,2,3) PKGPROG(COBEMP4)  USERID(HRUSER07)
```

DISPLAY TRACE

The DISPLAY TRACE command displays a list of active traces.

```
DISPLAY TRACE (*)
```

You can also limit the display to a particular plan, user or class.

```
DISPLAY TRACE(ACCTG) PLAN(COBEMP6) USERID(HRUSER02)
```

MODIFY TRACE

You can change an active trace by issuing a MODIFY TRACE command. Typically you will need to know the trace number to modify a specific trace. For example, suppose we have issued an accounting trace for plan COBEMP4 and the trace number (the TNO) is 5. Now we decide to change the trace to only report class 1 or 2 events. We could change it as follows:

```
MOD TRA(ACCTG)  PLAN (COBEMP4) TNO(5)  CLASS(1,2)
```

STOP TRACE

The STOP TRACE command terminates an active trace. To stop all trace activity, issue:

```
STO TRA(*)
```

To stop an accounting trace, issue:

```
STO TRA (ACCTG)
```

To stop the accounting trace on plan COBEMP4, issue:

```
STO TRA (ACCTG) PLAN (COBEMP4)
```

The DB2 accounting trace provides the following types of information:

- Start and stop times
- Number of commits and aborts
- The number of times certain SQL statements are issued
- Number of buffer pool requests
- Counts of certain locking events
- Processor resources consumed
- Thread wait times for various events
- RID pool processing
- Distributed processing
- Resource limit facility statistics

DB2 trace begins collecting these items when a thread is successfully allocated to DB2. DB2 trace writes a completed record when the thread terminates or when the authorization ID changes.

Chapter Eight Questions

1. Consider the following stored procedure:

```
CREATE PROCEDURE GET_PATIENTS
(IN intHosp INTEGER)
DYNAMIC RESULT SETS 1
LANGUAGE SQL
P1: BEGIN

DECLARE cursor1 CURSOR
WITH RETURN FOR
SELECT PATIENT_ID,
LNAME,
FNAME
FROM PATIENT
WHERE PATIENT_HOSP = intHosp
ORDER BY PATIENT_ID ASC;

OPEN cursor1;
END P1
```

Answer this question: How many parameters are used in this stored procedure?

    a. 0

    b. 1

    c. 2

    d. 3

2. When you want to create an external stored procedure, which of the following programming languages can NOT be used?

    a. COBOL

    b. REXX

    c. Fortran

    d. C++

3. In order to invoke a stored procedure, which keyword would you use?

    a. RUN

    b. CALL

    c. OPEN

    d. TRIGGER

4. Which of the following is NOT a valid return type for a User Defined Function?

    a. Scalar

    b. Aggregate

    c. Column

    d. Row

5. Which of the following is NOT a valid type of user-defined function (UDF)?

    a. External sourced

    b. SQL sourced

    c. External table

    d. SQL table

6. Assume the following trigger DDL:

```
CREATE TRIGGER SAVE_EMPL
AFTER UPDATE ON EMPL
FOR EACH ROW
INSERT INTO EMPLOYEE_HISTORY
VALUES (EMPLOYEE_NUMBER,
EMPLOYEE_STATUS,
CURRENT TIMESTAMP)
```

What will the result of this DDL be, provided the tables and field names are correctly defined?

    a.   The DDL will create the trigger successfully and it will work as intended.

    b.   The DDL will fail because you cannot use an INSERT with a trigger.

    c.   The DDL will fail because the syntax of this statement is incorrect.

    d.   The DDL will create the trigger successfully but it will fail when executed.

7. Which ONE of the following actions will NOT cause a trigger to fire?

    a.   INSERT

    b.   LOAD

    c.   DELETE

    d.   MERGE

8. If you use the "FOR EACH STATEMENT" granularity clause in a trigger, what type of timing can you use?

    a.   BEFORE

    b.   AFTER

    c.   INSTEAD OF

    d.   All of the above.

9. What is the schema for a declared GLOBAL TEMPORARY table?

    a.   SESSION

    b.   DB2ADMIN

    c.   TEMP1

    d.   USERTEMP

10. If you create a temporary table and you wish to replace any existing temporary table that has the same name, what clause would you use?

    a.   WITH REPLACE

    b.   OVERLAY DATA ROWS

    c.   REPLACE EXISTING

d. None of the above.

11. What happens to the rows of a temporary table when the session that created it ends?

    a. The rows are deleted when the session ends.

    b. The rows are preserved in memory until the instance is restarted.

    c. The rows are held in the temp table space.

    d. None of the above.

12. Which is true of temporary tables declared within a SAVEPOINT after a ROLLBACK TO SAVEPOINT command has been issued?

    a. Temporary tables declared within the savepoint are still in the system catalog.

    b. Temporary tables declared within the savepoint are dropped and no longer accessible.

    c. Temporary tables declared within the savepoint are still accessible.

    d. None of the above.

13. Which of the following clauses DOES NOT allow you to pull data for a particular period from a version enabled table?

    a. FOR BUSINESS_TIME UP UNTIL

    b. FOR BUSINESS_TIME FROM ... TO ...

    c. FOR BUSINESS_TIME BETWEEN... AND...

    d. All of the above enable you to pull data for a particular period.

14. Assume you have an application that needs to aggregate and summarize data from several tables multiple times per day. One way to improve performance of that application would be to use a:

    a. Materialized query table

    b. View

    c. Temporary table

    d. Range clustered table

15. Assume you want to track employees in your company over time. Review the following DDL:

```
CREATE TABLE HRSCHEMA.EMPLOYZZ(
EMP_ID INT NOT NULL,
EMP_LAST_NAME VARCHAR(30) NOT NULL,
EMP_FIRST_NAME VARCHAR(20) NOT NULL,
EMP_SERVICE_YEARS INT
NOT NULL WITH DEFAULT 0,
EMP_PROMOTION_DATE DATE,
BUS_START    DATE  NOT NULL,
BUS_END      DATE  NOT NULL,

PERIOD BUSINESS_TIME(BUS_START, BUS_END),
PRIMARY KEY (EMP_ID, BUSINESS_TIME WITHOUT OVERLAPS));
```

What will happen when you execute this DDL?

    a. It will fail because you cannot specify WITHOUT OVERLAPS in the primary key – the WITHOUT OVERLAPS clause belongs in the BUSINESS_TIME definition.

    b. It will fail because you must specify SYSTEM_TIME instead of BUSINESS_TIME.

    c. It will fail because the BUS_START has a syntax error.

    d. It will execute successfully.

16. Given the previous question, assume there is a table named EMPLOYEE_HIST defined just like EMPLOYEE. What will happen when you execute the following DDL?

```
ALTER TABLE EMPLOYEE
ADD VERSIONING
USE HISTORY TABLE EMPLOYEE_HIST
```

    a. The DDL will execute successfully and updates to EMPLOYEE will generate records in the EMPLOYEE_HIST table.

    b. The DDL will succeed but you must still enable the history table.

    c. The DDL will generate an error – only SYSTEM time enabled tables can use a history table.

    d. The DDL will generate an error – only BUSINESS time enabled tables can use a history table.

17. For a system managed Materialized Query Table (MQT) named EMPMQT, how does the data get updated so that it becomes current?

a. Issuing INSERT, UPDATE and DELETE commands against EMPMQT.

b. Issuing the statement REFRESH TABLE EMPMQT.

c. Issuing the statement MATERIALIZE TABLE EMPMQT.

d. None of the above.

18. Which of the following is TRUE about SQLJ applications that need to handle XML data?

a. You cannot select or update XML data as textual XML data.

b. For update of data in XML columns, xmlFormat does the appropriate formatting.

c. You can store an entire XML document into an XML column using a single UPDATE, INSERT or MERGE statement.

d. External encoding for Java applications cannot use Unicode encoding.

19. Which of the following is NOT true about XML validation using an XML type modifier?

a. An XML type modifier associates the type with an XML schema.

b. The XML type modifier can identify a single XML schema only.

c. An XML type modifier is defined in a CREATE TABLE or ALTER TABLE statement as part of an XML column definition.

d. You can use an ALTER TABLE statement to remove an XML schema from the column XML type definition.

20. An XML index can be created on what column types?

a. VARCHAR and XML.

b. CLOB AND XML.

c. XML only.

d. Any of the above.

21. Which of the following can be used to validate an XML value according to a schema?

a. Defining a column as type XML.

b. Manually running the DSN_XMLVALIDATE.

c. Both of the above.

d. Neither of the above.

22. To determine whether an XML document has been validated, which function could you use?

  a. XMLXSROBJECTID.

  b. XMLDOCUMENT.

  c. XMLPARSE.

  d. None of the above.

23. Which bind option would you use to enable parallel processing to improve performance of a query?

  a. DEGREE(1)

  b. DEGREE(2)

  c. DEGREE(ANY)

  d. DEGREE(PARALLEL)

24. To improve performance for read-only queries against remote sites, which DBPROTOCOL value should be used when binding applications?

  a. DRDACBF

  b. DRDA

  c. PRIVATE

  d. DRDABCF

25. Which of the following is a Stage 2 predicate?

  a. COL IS NULL

  b. SUBSTR(COL,1,n) = value

  c. EXISTS(subquery)

  d. COL LIKE pattern

26. Which of the following would probably NOT improve query performance?

  a. Use indexable predicates in your queries.

  b. Execute the RUNSTATS utility and rebind application programs.

  c. Use the EXISTS clause instead of COL IN (value list).

d. All of the above could improve application performance.

27. Which of the following trace types could be used to collect information about which users tried to access DB2 objects and were denied due to inadequate authorization?

    a. ACCTG

    b. MONITOR

    c. AUDIT

    d. STATISTICS

28. Which of the following is NOT a valid value for the SMFACCT subsystem parameter?

    a. YES

    b. NO

    c. $

    d. *

29. Which of the following EXPLAIN tables includes information about the access path that will be used to return data?

    a. PLAN_TABLE

    b. DSN_QUERY_TABLE

    c. DSN_STATEMENT_TABLE

    d. None of the above.

30. If you find out that your application query is doing a table space scan, what changes could you make to improve the scan efficiency?

    a. Create one or more indexes on the query search columns.

    b. Load the data to a temporary table and query that table instead of the base table.

    c. If the table is partitioned, change it to a non-partitioned table.

    d. All of the above could improve the scan efficiency.

CHAPTER NINE: FINAL PROJECT

I want to finish out the text book with a project that applies some of the skills and knowledge we've learned, but in a different problem domain. Let's switch from the HR domain to a simple frequent buyer domain (also known these days as loyalty systems). We'll provide a skeleton set of requirements, work through creating tables, indexes, stored procedures and so forth.

Project Requirements

At its most basic a frequent buyer system includes members, deposits and rewards. Let's use FB as an acronym for our frequent buyer program. Besides creating a new FB database and tablespace, we will also be creating a Members table, a Deposit table, and a Rewards table to track the various transactions in our Frequent Buyer system – let's call it FB for an acronym. In addition, we should be thinking about referential integrity. So let's plan on creating a Deposits Type table and a Rewards Type table.

Here are the requirements for the aforementioned tables:

Member Table

Field	Type	Constraints
Member Number	Integer	NOT NULL, autogenerated
Last Name	Character up to 20	NOT NULL
First Name	Character up to 15	NOT NULL
Street	Character up to 30	NOT NULL
City	Character up to 20	NOT NULL
State	Character 2	NOT NULL
Zip Code	Big Integer	NOT NULL
Telephone	Big Integer	
Points Balance	Integer	NOT NULL

Deposits Table

Field	Type	Constraints
Member Number	Integer	NOT NULL, must exist on MEMBER table
Activity Date	Date	NOT NULL
Deposit Type	Character 3	NOT NULL, must exist in Deposit Type table
Deposit Amount	Integer	NOT NULL
Deposit Posted Date	Date	NOT NULL

Rewards Table

Field	Type	Constraints
Member Number	Integer	NOT NULL, must exist on MEMBER table
Reward Date	Date	NOT NULL
Reward Type	Char 3	NOT NULL, must exist in REWARD TYPE table
Reward Amount	Integer	NOT NULL

Deposit Type Table

Field	Type	Constraints
Deposit Type Code	Char 3	NOT NULL
Deposit Type Description	Char up to 20	NOT NULL
Maintenance Date	Date	NOT NULL

Reward Type Table

Field	Type	Constraints
Reward Type Code	Char 3	NOT NULL
Reward Type Description	Char up to 20	NOT NULL
Maintenance Date	Date	NOT NULL

We've made a few assumptions to keep things simple, such as that the credited points are always whole numbers (so we defined them as integers). Similarly the choice of DATE versus TIMESTAMP is somewhat arbitrary, and in a real production situation you could have reasons for choosing one over the other. TIMESTAMP of course is more precise but we'll stick with DATE.

Project DDL

Create the Tables

Now let's start to work on our DB2 system. Let's build the DDL to create the database, tablespace and a schema. Also since the member number is to be generated, we will create a sequence. Here's our DDL:

```
CREATE DATABASE DBFB
STOGROUP SGFB
BUFFERPOOL BPFB
INDEXBP IBPFB
CCSID UNICODE;
```

```
CREATE TABLESPACE TSFB
    IN DBFB
    USING STOGROUP SGHR
      PRIQTY 50
      SECQTY 20
    LOCKSIZE PAGE
    BUFFERPOOL BPFB;


CREATE SCHEMA FBSCHEMA
AUTHORIZATION DBA001;  <--  This should be your DB2 id, whatever it is.
```

Now let's create the sequence object. We specified it should be auto-numbered beginning with 100100. Here is our sequence DDL:

```
CREATE SEQUENCE FBSCHEMA.MBRSEQ
START WITH 100100
INCREMENT BY 1
NO CYCLE;
```

Finally, let's create the DDL for our tables.

```
CREATE TABLE FBSCHEMA.MEMBER(
MBR_NBR         INT NOT NULL,
MBR_LAST_NAME   VARCHAR(20) NOT NULL,
MBR_FIRST_NAME  VARCHAR(15) NOT NULL,
MBR_ADDRESS     VARCHAR(30) NOT NULL,
MBR_CITY        VARCHAR(20) NOT NULL,
MBR_STATE       CHAR(02)    NOT NULL,
MBR_ZIP         BIGINT      NOT NULL,
MBR_PHONE       BIGINT      NOT NULL,
MBR_BALANCE     INTEGER     NOT NULL,
    PRIMARY KEY(MBR_NBR))
        IN TSFB;

CREATE UNIQUE INDEX FBSCHEMA.NDX_MEMBER
        ON FBSCHEMA.MEMBER (MBR_NBR);

CREATE TABLE FBSCHEMA.DEPOSITS(
DEP_MBR_NBR    INT        NOT NULL,
DEP_ACT_DATE   DATE       NOT NULL,
DEP_TYPE       CHAR(03)   NOT NULL,
DEP_AMOUNT     INTEGER    NOT NULL,
DEP_POST_DATE  DATE       NOT NULL)
    IN TSFB;


CREATE TABLE FBSCHEMA.REWARDS(
RWD_MBR_NBR    INT        NOT NULL,
RWD_ACT_DATE   DATE       NOT NULL,
```

```
RWD_TYPE       CHAR(03)    NOT NULL,
RWD_AMOUNT     INTEGER     NOT NULL)
    IN TSFB;


CREATE TABLE FBSCHEMA.DEPOSIT_TYPE(
DEP_TYPE       CHAR(03)    NOT NULL,
DEP_DESC       VARCHAR(20) NOT NULL,
DEP_MAINT_DATE DATE        NOT NULL,
    PRIMARY KEY(DEP_TYPE))
    IN TSFB;


CREATE UNIQUE INDEX FBSCHEMA.NDX_DEP_TYPE
      ON FBSCHEMA.DEPOSIT_TYPE (DEP_TYPE);


CREATE TABLE FBSCHEMA.REWARD_TYPE(
REW_TYPE       CHAR(03)    NOT NULL,
REW_DESC       VARCHAR(20) NOT NULL,
REW_MAINT_DATE DATE        NOT NULL,
    PRIMARY KEY(REW_TYPE))
    IN TSFB;

CREATE UNIQUE INDEX FBSCHEMA.NDX_REW_TYPE
      ON FBSCHEMA.REWARD_TYPE (REW_TYPE);
```

Ok, now that we've created the tables and indexes, let's do the referential constraints. We'll need several. First, we need to make sure that no record can be added to the DEPOSITS or REWARDS tables if the type on the record does not have an entry in the DEPOSIT_TYPE or REWARD_TYPE table respectively. So here is the DDL for that:

```
ALTER TABLE FBSCHEMA.DEPOSITS
   FOREIGN KEY FK_DEP_TYPE (DEP_TYPE)
      REFERENCES FBSCHEMA.DEPOSIT_TYPE (DEP_TYPE)
         ON DELETE RESTRICT;

ALTER TABLE FBSCHEMA.REWARDS
   FOREIGN KEY FK_REW_TYPE (RWD_TYPE)
      REFERENCES FBSCHEMA.REWARD_TYPE (REW_TYPE)
         ON DELETE RESTRICT;
```

Next, we need to ensure that any member number entered on the DEPOSITS and REWARDS table actually exists in the MEMBER table. Here's the DDL for that.

```
ALTER TABLE FBSCHEMA.DEPOSITS
   FOREIGN KEY FK_DEP_MBR (DEP_MBR_NBR)
      REFERENCES FBSCHEMA.MEMBER (MBR_NBR)
         ON DELETE RESTRICT;
```

```
ALTER TABLE FBSCHEMA.REWARDS
    FOREIGN KEY FK_REW_MBR (RWD_MBR_NBR)
        REFERENCES FBSCHEMA.MEMBER (MBR_NBR)
            ON DELETE RESTRICT;
```

Ok that takes care of referential constraints. You could also add some check constraints if you wanted to restrict the value or format of certain fields. I'll leave that to your imagination and business requirements, and we'll just use what we have.

Initial Testing

We'll do some testing to ensure our tables, indexes and so forth have been set up and function correctly. Due to our referential constraints, let's first populate the DEPOSIT_TYPE and REWARD_TYPE tables. Let us say we have these entries, and we'll always use the current date as the maintenance date when we add or change a value.

Deposit Type Entries

DEP_TYPE	DEP_DESC
PUR	MEMBER PURCHASE
BON	BONUS POINTS
MGR	MANAGER DISCRETION

Reward Type Entries

REW_TYPE	REW_DESC
DEB	DEBITED DOLLAR AMOUNT REWARD
PRM	FREE PROMOTIONAL REWARD

Let's go ahead and add these entries and then verify them. First the DEPOSIT_TYPE entries:

```
INSERT INTO FBSCHEMA.DEPOSIT_TYPE
VALUES('PUR',
'MEMBER PURCHASE',
CURRENT DATE);

INSERT INTO FBSCHEMA.DEPOSIT_TYPE
VALUES('BON',
'BONUS POINTS',
CURRENT DATE);

INSERT INTO FBSCHEMA.DEPOSIT_TYPE
VALUES('MGR',
'MANAGER DISCRETION',
CURRENT DATE);
```

```
SELECT *
FROM FBSCHEMA.DEPOSIT_TYPE;
---------+---------+---------+---------+---------+
DEP_TYPE  DEP_DESC             DEP_MAINT_DATE
---------+---------+---------+---------+---------+
PUR       MEMBER PURCHASE      2017-09-28
BON       BONUS POINTS         2017-09-28
MGR       MANAGER DISCRETION   2017-09-28
DSNE610I NUMBER OF ROWS DISPLAYED IS 3
```

And now the REWARD_TYPE entries:

```
INSERT INTO FBSCHEMA.REWARD_TYPE
VALUES('DEB',
'DOLLAR AMT REWARD',
CURRENT DATE);

INSERT INTO FBSCHEMA.REWARD_TYPE
VALUES('PRM',
'FREE PROMOTIONAL REW',
CURRENT DATE);

  SELECT *
  FROM FBSCHEMA.REWARD_TYPE;
---------+---------+---------+---------+---------+-
REW_TYPE  REW_DESC             REW_MAINT_DATE
---------+---------+---------+---------+---------+-
DEB       DOLLAR AMT REWARD    2017-09-28
PRM       FREE PROMOTIONAL REW 2017-09-28
DSNE610I NUMBER OF ROWS DISPLAYED IS 2
```

Ok, we have our control tables populated. Now let's add a member to the table, and then add the first deposit and withdrawal. Here's the DDL to add the first member:

```
INSERT INTO FBSCHEMA.MEMBER
(MBR_NBR,
 MBR_LAST_NAME,
 MBR_FIRST_NAME,
 MBR_ADDRESS,
 MBR_CITY,
 MBR_STATE,
 MBR_ZIP,
 MBR_PHONE,
 MBR_BALANCE)
 VALUES
 (NEXT VALUE FOR FBSCHEMA.MBRSEQ,
  'JEFFERSON',
  'RICHARD',
  '2497 MYRTLE LANE',
  'HOUSTON',
```

```
       'TX',
        77099,
       '2815683572',
        0);
       --------+---------+---------+---------+---------+------
       DSNE615I NUMBER OF ROWS AFFECTED IS 1


      SELECT * FROM FBSCHEMA.MEMBER;
      --------+---------+---------+---------+---------+---------+---------+---------+---------+
       MBR_NBR  MBR_LAST_NAME        MBR_FIRST_NAME  MBR_ADDRESS           MBR_CI
      --------+---------+---------+---------+---------+---------+---------+---------+---------+
        100100  JEFFERSON            RICHARD         2497 MYRTLE LANE      HOUSTO
      DSNE610I NUMBER OF ROWS DISPLAYED IS 1
```

Ok now let's test our referential constraints on the deposits and awards table. We'll try adding a deposit for which the member number does not exist and for which the deposit type does not exist. We should get SQL errors indicating violation of the constraints.

```
        INSERT INTO FBSCHEMA.DEPOSITS
        (DEP_MBR_NBR,
         DEP_ACT_DATE,
         DEP_TYPE,
         DEP_AMOUNT,
         DEP_POST_DATE)
         VALUES
         (100222,
          '08/01/2017',
          'ZZZ',
          15,
          CURRENT DATE);
       --------+---------+---------+---------+---------+---------+---------+---------+---------+
       DSNT408I SQLCODE = -530, ERROR:  THE INSERT OR UPDATE VALUE OF FOREIGN KEY
                FK_DEP_MBR IS INVALID
       DSNT418I SQLSTATE   = 23503 SQLSTATE RETURN CODE
       DSNT415I SQLERRP    = DSNXRINS SQL PROCEDURE DETECTING ERROR
       DSNT416I SQLERRD    = -110 13172774  0  -1  0  0 SQL DIAGNOSTIC INFORMATION
       DSNT416I SQLERRD    = X'FFFFFF92'  X'00C90026'  X'00000000'  X'FFFFFFFF'
                X'00000000'  X'00000000' SQL DIAGNOSTIC INFORMATION
```

And as you can see there is a violation of the FK_DEP_MBR constraint. Let's fix this and try an invalid deposit type.

```
        INSERT INTO FBSCHEMA.DEPOSITS
        (DEP_MBR_NBR,
         DEP_ACT_DATE,
         DEP_TYPE,
         DEP_AMOUNT,
         DEP_POST_DATE)
         VALUES
         (100100,
          '08/01/2017',
          'ZZZ',
          15,
          CURRENT DATE);
```

```
---------+---------+---------+---------+---------+---------+---------+---------+
DSNT408I SQLCODE = -530, ERROR:  THE INSERT OR UPDATE VALUE OF FOREIGN KEY
          FK_DEP_TYPE IS INVALID
DSNT418I SQLSTATE   = 23503 SQLSTATE RETURN CODE
DSNT415I SQLERRP    = DSNXRINS SQL PROCEDURE DETECTING ERROR
DSNT416I SQLERRD    = -110 13172774  0  -1  0  0 SQL DIAGNOSTIC INFORMATION
DSNT416I SQLERRD    = X'FFFFFF92'  X'00C90026'  X'00000000'  X'FFFFFFFF'
          X'00000000'  X'00000000' SQL DIAGNOSTIC INFORMATION
```

Ok good, this is what we were expecting. Out insert failed with invalid foreign key in the deposit type field. Let's clean that up and do a good insert.

```
INSERT INTO FBSCHEMA.DEPOSITS
(DEP_MBR_NBR,
 DEP_ACT_DATE,
 DEP_TYPE,
 DEP_AMOUNT,
 DEP_POST_DATE)
 VALUES
 (100100,
  '08/01/2017',
  'PUR',
  15,
  CURRENT DATE);
---------+---------+---------+---------+---------+---------+---------+---------+
DSNE615I NUMBER OF ROWS AFFECTED IS 1
```

And we can verify our result by querying the DEPOSITS table.

```
SELECT * FROM FBSCHEMA.DEPOSITS;
---------+---------+---------+---------+---------+---------+-----
DEP_MBR_NBR  DEP_ACT_DATE  DEP_TYPE   DEP_AMOUNT  DEP_POST_DATE
---------+---------+---------+---------+---------+---------+-----
     100100  2017-08-01    PUR               15  2017-09-28
DSNE610I NUMBER OF ROWS DISPLAYED IS 1
```

Now let's check the REWARDS table for referential constraints.

```
INSERT INTO FBSCHEMA.REWARDS
(RWD_MBR_NBR,
 RWD_ACT_DATE,
 RWD_TYPE,
 RWD_AMOUNT)
 VALUES
 (100199,
  '09/01/2017',
  'XXX',
  10);
---------+---------+---------+---------+---------+---------+---------+---------+
DSNT408I SQLCODE = -530, ERROR:  THE INSERT OR UPDATE VALUE OF FOREIGN KEY
          FK_REW_MBR IS INVALID
DSNT418I SQLSTATE   = 23503 SQLSTATE RETURN CODE
DSNT415I SQLERRP    = DSNXRINS SQL PROCEDURE DETECTING ERROR
DSNT416I SQLERRD    = -110 13172774  0  -1  0  0 SQL DIAGNOSTIC INFORMATION
```

```
DSNT416I SQLERRD    = X'FFFFFF92'  X'00C90026'  X'00000000'  X'FFFFFFFF'
           X'00000000'  X'00000000' SQL DIAGNOSTIC INFORMATION
```

Let's fix the member and try again.

```
    INSERT INTO FBSCHEMA.REWARDS
    (RWD_MBR_NBR,
     RWD_ACT_DATE,
     RWD_TYPE,
     RWD_AMOUNT)
     VALUES
     (100100,
      '09/01/2017',
      'XXX',
      10);
---------+---------+---------+---------+---------+---------+---------+---------+
DSNT408I SQLCODE = -530, ERROR:  THE INSERT OR UPDATE VALUE OF FOREIGN KEY
         FK_REW_TYPE IS INVALID
DSNT418I SQLSTATE   = 23503 SQLSTATE RETURN CODE
DSNT415I SQLERRP    = DSNXRINS SQL PROCEDURE DETECTING ERROR
DSNT416I SQLERRD    = -110 13172774  0  -1  0  0 SQL DIAGNOSTIC INFORMATION
DSNT416I SQLERRD    = X'FFFFFF92'  X'00C90026'  X'00000000'  X'FFFFFFFF'
```

Finally, let's go ahead and do a good insert, and we see it works fine.

```
      INSERT INTO FBSCHEMA.REWARDS
      (RWD_MBR_NBR,
       RWD_ACT_DATE,
       RWD_TYPE,
       RWD_AMOUNT)
       VALUES
       (100100,
        '09/01/2017',
        'DEB',
        10);
    ---------+---------+---------+---------+--------
    DSNE615I NUMBER OF ROWS AFFECTED IS 1


    SELECT * FROM FBSCHEMA.REWARDS;
    ---------+---------+---------+---------+---------+----
    RWD_MBR_NBR  RWD_ACT_DATE  RWD_TYPE   RWD_AMOUNT
    ---------+---------+---------+---------+---------+----
        100100  2017-09-01    DEB              10
    DSNE610I NUMBER OF ROWS DISPLAYED IS 1
```

We should do additional testing, of course. Such as with 5-digit zip codes versus 9-digit. Also we should test incoming data to see what happens if someone sends a phone number with non-numeric values, such as punctuation. I'll leave these tasks to you to complete as an exercise, and we'll move on to loading and accessing data.

Stored Procedures and Programs for Data Access

Here we are going to create four stored procedures, all of which pertain to the MEMBER table. One procedure will be to retrieve data from the table. The second will be to add data to the table. The third will be to update data on the table. The fourth will be to delete data from the table. In all four cases we will use native SQL procedures, and I recommend that you do so whenever possible.

Stored Procedure to SELECT

Let's begin by defining the retrieval procedure which we will name GETMEM. Here is the DDL.

```
CREATE PROCEDURE FBSCHEMA.GETMEM
(IN   M_NBR          INTEGER,
 OUT M_LAST_NAME   VARCHAR(20),
 OUT M_FIRST_NAME  VARCHAR(15),
 OUT M_ADDRESS     VARCHAR(30),
 OUT M_CITY        VARCHAR(20),
 OUT M_STATE       CHAR(02),
 OUT M_ZIP         INTEGER,
 OUT M_PHONE       BIGINT,
 OUT M_BALANCE     BIGINT)

LANGUAGE SQL
READS SQL DATA

BEGIN
    SELECT MBR_LAST_NAME,
           MBR_FIRST_NAME,
           MBR_ADDRESS,
           MBR_CITY,
           MBR_STATE,
           MBR_ZIP,
           MBR_PHONE,
           MBR_BALANCE
       INTO M_LAST_NAME,
           M_FIRST_NAME,
           M_ADDRESS,
           M_CITY,
           M_STATE,
           M_ZIP,
           M_PHONE,
           M_BALANCE
    FROM FBSCHEMA.MEMBER
    WHERE M_NBR  = MBR_NBR ;

END
```

You'll also need to grant security on your stored procedure as follows (grant it to your id, to whichever group you belong to, or in this case I am granting to PUBLIC).

338

```
GRANT EXECUTE ON PROCEDURE FBSCHEMA.GETMEM TO PUBLIC;
```

Now let's test our stored procedure. We'll create a COBOL program for this. The code should look very similar to the previous programs earlier in the text book. Notice we are including indicator variables for all columns to allow for the possibility the record does not exist.

```
IDENTIFICATION DIVISION.
PROGRAM-ID. COBMEM1.

*********************************************************
*     PROGRAM USING DB2 CALL TO SEVERAL FREQUENT     *
*     BUYER STORED PROCEDURES.                       *
*********************************************************
ENVIRONMENT DIVISION.
DATA DIVISION.
WORKING-STORAGE SECTION.

01 INDICATOR-VARS.
   10 IND-MBR-LAST-NAME      PIC S9(4) BINARY VALUE 0.
   10 IND-MBR-FIRST-NAME     PIC S9(4) BINARY VALUE 0.
   10 IND-MBR-ADDRESS        PIC S9(4) BINARY VALUE 0.
   10 IND-MBR-CITY           PIC S9(4) BINARY VALUE 0.
   10 IND-MBR-STATE          PIC S9(4) BINARY VALUE 0.
   10 IND-MBR-ZIP            PIC S9(4) BINARY VALUE 0.
   10 IND-MBR-PHONE          PIC S9(4) BINARY VALUE 0.
   10 IND-MBR-BALANCE        PIC S9(4) BINARY VALUE 0.

01 ERR-REC.
   05 FILLER               PIC X(10) VALUE 'SQLCODE = '.
   05 SQLCODE-VIEW         PIC -999.
   05 FILLER               PIC X(005) VALUE SPACES.
   05 ERR-TAB              PIC X(016).
   05 ERR-PARA             PIC X(015).
   05 ERR-DETAIL           PIC X(040).

77 ERR-TXT-LGTH           PIC S9(9) USAGE COMP VALUE +72.

01 ERR-MSG.
   05 ERR-MSG-LGTH         PIC S9(04) COMP VALUE +864.
   05 ERR-MSG-TXT          PIC X(072) OCCURS 12 TIMES
                                      INDEXED BY ERR-NDX.
   EXEC SQL
     INCLUDE SQLCA
   END-EXEC.

   EXEC SQL
     INCLUDE MEMBER
   END-EXEC.

PROCEDURE DIVISION.

MAIN-PARA.
```

339

```
           DISPLAY "SAMPLE COBOL PROGRAM: CALL STORED PROCEDURES".

           DISPLAY 'DISPLAY MEMBER INFORMATION'

           MOVE +100100     TO MBR-NBR

           EXEC SQL

               CALL FBSCHEMA.GETMEM
                   (:MBR-NBR,
                    :MBR-LAST-NAME   :IND-MBR-LAST-NAME,
                    :MBR-FIRST-NAME  :IND-MBR-FIRST-NAME,
                    :MBR-ADDRESS     :IND-MBR-ADDRESS,
                    :MBR-CITY        :IND-MBR-CITY,
                    :MBR-STATE       :IND-MBR-STATE,
                    :MBR-ZIP         :IND-MBR-ZIP,
                    :MBR-PHONE       :IND-MBR-PHONE,
                    :MBR-BALANCE     :IND-MBR-BALANCE)

           END-EXEC.

           IF SQLCODE IS NOT EQUAL TO ZERO

               DISPLAY  'GET CALL FAILED ' MBR-NBR
               MOVE SQLCODE TO SQLCODE-VIEW
               MOVE 'MEMBER'   TO ERR-TAB
               MOVE 'MAIN'     TO ERR-PARA
               MOVE MBR-NBR    TO ERR-DETAIL
               PERFORM P9999-SQL-ERROR

           ELSE
               DISPLAY  'GET CALL SUCCESSFUL ' MBR-NBR
               DISPLAY 'MBR-NBR         = ' MBR-NBR
               DISPLAY 'MBR-LAST-NAME   = ' MBR-LAST-NAME
               DISPLAY 'MBR-FIRST-NAME  = ' MBR-FIRST-NAME
               DISPLAY 'MBR-ADDRESS     = ' MBR-ADDRESS
               DISPLAY 'MBR-CITY        = ' MBR-CITY
               DISPLAY 'MBR-ZIP         = ' MBR-ZIP
               DISPLAY 'MBR-PHONE       = ' MBR-PHONE
               DISPLAY 'MBR-BALANCE     = ' MBR-BALANCE

           END-IF

           GOBACK.

       P9999-SQL-ERROR.

           DISPLAY ERR-REC.

           CALL 'DSNTIAR' USING SQLCA,
                        ERR-MSG,
                        ERR-TXT-LGTH.
```

```
          IF RETURN-CODE IS EQUAL TO ZERO

             PERFORM P9999-DISP-ERR
                VARYING ERR-NDX FROM 1 BY 1
                UNTIL ERR-NDX > 12

          ELSE
             DISPLAY 'DSNTIAR ERROR CODE = ' RETURN-CODE
             STOP RUN.

      P9999-DISP-ERR.

          DISPLAY ERR-MSG-TXT(ERR-NDX).

      P9999-DISP-ERR-EXIT.
```

And here is the output from our program run:

```
      SAMPLE COBOL PROGRAM: CALL STORED PROCEDURES
      DISPLAY MEMBER INFORMATION
      GET CALL SUCCESSFUL 000100100
      MBR-NBR         = 000100100
      MBR-LAST-NAME   =   JEFFERSON
      MBR-FIRST-NAME  =   RICHARD
      MBR-ADDRESS     =   2497 MYRTLE LANE
      MBR-CITY        =   HOUSTON
      MBR-ZIP         = 00000000000077099
      MBR-PHONE       = 000000002815683572
      MBR-BALANCE     = 000000000
```

Finally, let's change the searched member number to 100101 which we know does not yet exist in the table, and then rerun. Here is the result, and of course we get an SQLCODE +100 meaning the record is not found.

```
      SAMPLE COBOL PROGRAM: CALL STORED PROCEDURES
      DISPLAY MEMBER INFORMATION
      GET CALL FAILED 000100101
      SQLCODE =  100      MEMBER        MAIN            000100101
       DSNT404I SQLCODE = 100, NOT FOUND:  ROW NOT FOUND FOR FETCH, UPDATE, OR
                DELETE, OR THE RESULT OF A QUERY IS AN EMPTY TABLE
       DSNT418I SQLSTATE   = 02000 SQLSTATE RETURN CODE
       DSNT415I SQLERRP    = DSNXRFF SQL PROCEDURE DETECTING ERROR
       DSNT416I SQLERRD    = -110  0  0  -1  0  0 SQL DIAGNOSTIC INFORMATION
       DSNT416I SQLERRD    = X'FFFFFF92'  X'00000000'  X'00000000'
                X'FFFFFFFF'  X'00000000'  X'00000000' SQL DIAGNOSTIC
                INFORMATION
```

Ok, let's take a short break and then come back and add the calls for add, insert and delete.

Stored Procedure to INSERT

Alright, I'm back – hope you are too. Let's create and test an INSERT stored procedure. You can use any earlier example in the HR system as a model. Give it a try on your own and then you can compare your DDL to mine.

Alright, here is my DDL. Notice there is a single OUT parameter which will be used to return the value of the generated MBR_NBR. Your calling program will likely need that number – otherwise it won't know what account number was generated for the new member.

```
CREATE PROCEDURE FBSCHEMA.ADD_MEM_INFO
(OUT M_NBR        INTEGER,
 IN M_LAST_NAME   VARCHAR(20),
 IN M_FIRST_NAME  VARCHAR(15),
 IN M_ADDRESS     VARCHAR(30),
 IN M_CITY        VARCHAR(20),
 IN M_STATE       CHAR(02),
 IN M_ZIP         INTEGER,
 IN M_PHONE       BIGINT,
 IN M_BALANCE     BIGINT)

LANGUAGE SQL
MODIFIES SQL DATA

BEGIN
    INSERT INTO FBSCHEMA.MEMBER
    (MBR_NBR,
     MBR_LAST_NAME,
     MBR_FIRST_NAME,
      MBR_FIRST_NAME,
      MBR_ADDRESS,
      MBR_CITY,
      MBR_STATE,
      MBR_ZIP,
      MBR_PHONE,
      MBR_BALANCE)
    VALUES
    (NEXT VALUE FOR FBSCHEMA.MBRSEQ,
     M_LAST_NAME,
     M_FIRST_NAME,
     M_ADDRESS,
     M_CITY,
     M_STATE,
     M_ZIP,
     M_PHONE,
     M_BALANCE);

    SET M_NBR = PREVIOUS VALUE FOR FBSCHEMA.MBRSEQ;

    END #
```

Now we must grant security on the stored procedure.

```
GRANT EXECUTE ON PROCEDURE FBSCHEMA.ADD_MEM_INFO TO PUBLIC;
```

And finally let's look at our COBOL program to call the stored procedure.

```
IDENTIFICATION DIVISION.
PROGRAM-ID. COBMEM2.

*********************************************************
*      PROGRAM USING DB2 CALL TO STORED PROCEDURE    *
*      TO ADD NEW MEMBERS                             *
*********************************************************

ENVIRONMENT DIVISION.
DATA DIVISION.
WORKING-STORAGE SECTION.


01 ERR-REC.
   05 FILLER                PIC X(10) VALUE 'SQLCODE = '.
   05 SQLCODE-VIEW          PIC -999.
   05 FILLER                PIC X(005) VALUE SPACES.
   05 ERR-TAB               PIC X(016).
   05 ERR-PARA              PIC X(015).
   05 ERR-DETAIL            PIC X(040).

77 ERR-TXT-LGTH            PIC S9(9) USAGE COMP VALUE +72.

01 ERR-MSG.
   05 ERR-MSG-LGTH          PIC S9(04) COMP VALUE +864.
   05 ERR-MSG-TXT           PIC X(072) OCCURS 12 TIMES
                                       INDEXED BY ERR-NDX.

   EXEC SQL
     INCLUDE SQLCA
   END-EXEC.

   EXEC SQL
     INCLUDE MEMBER
   END-EXEC.

PROCEDURE DIVISION.

MAIN-PARA.
   DISPLAY "SAMPLE COBOL PROGRAM: CALL STORED PROCEDURES".


   DISPLAY 'ADD NEW MEMBER INFORMATION'

   MOVE ZERO           TO MBR-NBR
   MOVE 'BROWN'        TO MBR-LAST-NAME-TEXT
   MOVE 'OSCAR'        TO MBR-FIRST-NAME-TEXT
```

343

```
MOVE '5162 HUNTINGTON RD'
                        TO MBR-ADDRESS-TEXT
MOVE 'FRIENDSWOOD'  TO MBR-CITY-TEXT

MOVE LENGTH OF MBR-LAST-NAME-TEXT   TO MBR-LAST-NAME-LEN
MOVE LENGTH OF MBR-FIRST-NAME-TEXT  TO MBR-FIRST-NAME-LEN
MOVE LENGTH OF MBR-ADDRESS-TEXT     TO MBR-ADDRESS-LEN
MOVE LENGTH OF MBR-CITY-TEXT        TO MBR-CITY-LEN

MOVE 'TX'            TO MBR-STATE
MOVE 770822154       TO MBR-ZIP
MOVE 7139873472      TO MBR-PHONE
MOVE ZERO            TO MBR-BALANCE

EXEC SQL

    CALL FBSCHEMA.ADD_MEM_INFO
        (:MBR-NBR,
         :MBR-LAST-NAME,
         :MBR-FIRST-NAME,
         :MBR-ADDRESS,
         :MBR-CITY,
         :MBR-STATE,
         :MBR-ZIP,
         :MBR-PHONE,
         :MBR-BALANCE)

END-EXEC.

IF SQLCODE IS NOT EQUAL TO ZERO

    DISPLAY  'ADD CALL FAILED ' MBR-NBR
    MOVE SQLCODE TO SQLCODE-VIEW
    MOVE 'MEMBER'   TO ERR-TAB
    MOVE 'MAIN'     TO ERR-PARA
    MOVE MBR-NBR    TO ERR-DETAIL
    PERFORM P9999-SQL-ERROR
    DISPLAY 'MBR-NBR         = ' MBR-NBR
    DISPLAY 'MBR-LAST-NAME   = ' MBR-LAST-NAME
    DISPLAY 'MBR-FIRST-NAME  = ' MBR-FIRST-NAME
    DISPLAY 'MBR-ADDRESS     = ' MBR-ADDRESS
    DISPLAY 'MBR-CITY        = ' MBR-CITY
    DISPLAY 'MBR-ZIP         = ' MBR-ZIP
    DISPLAY 'MBR-PHONE       = ' MBR-PHONE
    DISPLAY 'MBR-BALANCE     = ' MBR-BALANCE

ELSE
    DISPLAY  'ADD CALL SUCCESSFUL ' MBR-NBR
    DISPLAY 'MBR-NBR         = ' MBR-NBR
    DISPLAY 'MBR-LAST-NAME   = ' MBR-LAST-NAME
    DISPLAY 'MBR-FIRST-NAME  = ' MBR-FIRST-NAME
    DISPLAY 'MBR-ADDRESS     = ' MBR-ADDRESS
    DISPLAY 'MBR-CITY        = ' MBR-CITY
```

```
                DISPLAY 'MBR-ZIP        = ' MBR-ZIP
                DISPLAY 'MBR-PHONE      = ' MBR-PHONE
                DISPLAY 'MBR-BALANCE    = ' MBR-BALANCE

         END-IF

         GOBACK.

    P9999-SQL-ERROR.

         DISPLAY ERR-REC.

         CALL 'DSNTIAR' USING SQLCA,
                       ERR-MSG,
                       ERR-TXT-LGTH.

         IF RETURN-CODE IS EQUAL TO ZERO

            PERFORM P9999-DISP-ERR
               VARYING ERR-NDX FROM 1 BY 1
               UNTIL ERR-NDX > 12

         ELSE
            DISPLAY 'DSNTIAR ERROR CODE = ' RETURN-CODE
            STOP RUN.

    P9999-DISP-ERR.

         DISPLAY ERR-MSG-TXT(ERR-NDX).

    P9999-DISP-ERR-EXIT.
```

And here is the result of our run:

```
SAMPLE COBOL PROGRAM: CALL STORED PROCEDURES
ADD NEW MEMBER INFORMATION
ADD CALL SUCCESSFUL 000100101
MBR-NBR          = 000100101
MBR-LAST-NAME  =    BROWN
MBR-FIRST-NAME =    OSCAR
MBR-ADDRESS    =    5162 HUNTINGTON RD
MBR-CITY       =    FRIENDSWOOD
MBR-ZIP          = 000000000770822154
MBR-PHONE        = 000000007139873472
MBR-BALANCE      = 000000000
```

The UPDATE and DELETE stored procedures follow the examples given earlier in the text. It is best if you work on these yourself first, and then compare to the code examples. Take some now to do that.

Stored Procedure to UPDATE

Here is the DDL to create the stored procedure to update the MEMBER table.

```
CREATE PROCEDURE FBSCHEMA.UPD_MEM_INFO
(IN M_NBR         INTEGER,
 IN M_LAST_NAME   VARCHAR(20),
 IN M_FIRST_NAME  VARCHAR(15),
 IN M_ADDRESS     VARCHAR(30),
 IN M_CITY        VARCHAR(20),
 IN M_STATE       CHAR(02),
 IN M_ZIP         INTEGER,
 IN M_PHONE       BIGINT,
 IN M_BALANCE     BIGINT)

LANGUAGE SQL
MODIFIES SQL DATA

BEGIN
   UPDATE FBSCHEMA.MEMBER
   SET MBR_NBR          = M_NBR,
       MBR_LAST_NAME    = M_LAST_NAME,
       MBR_FIRST_NAME   = M_FIRST_NAME,
       MBR_ADDRESS      = M_ADDRESS,
       MBR_ADDRESS      = M_ADDRESS,
       MBR_CITY         = M_CITY,
       MBR_STATE        = M_STATE,
       MBR_ZIP          = M_ZIP,
       MBR_PHONE        = M_PHONE,
       MBR_BALANCE      = M_BALANCE
   WHERE MBR_NBR = M_NBR;

END #
```

Don't forget to grant security on the procedure:

```
GRANT EXECUTE ON PROCEDURE FBSCHEMA.UPD_MEM_INFO TO PUBLIC;
```

Now here's a program to run the stored procedure. We'll just change the first name on the second record (100101) from Oscar to Osborne. You can change more fields if you like. Also, we could have read the record into the host variables first and then not had to reassign all the values for the call. That is more typical, but you can do it either way.

```
IDENTIFICATION DIVISION.
PROGRAM-ID. COBMEM3.
********************************************************
*      PROGRAM USING DB2 CALL TO STORED PROCEDURE     *
*      TO MODIFY MEMBER DATA                           *
********************************************************
ENVIRONMENT DIVISION.
DATA DIVISION.
```

```
WORKING-STORAGE SECTION.

01 INDICATOR-VARS.
   10 IND-MBR-NBR          PIC S9(4) BINARY VALUE 0.
   10 IND-MBR-LAST-NAME    PIC S9(4) BINARY VALUE 0.
   10 IND-MBR-FIRST-NAME   PIC S9(4) BINARY VALUE 0.
   10 IND-MBR-ADDRESS      PIC S9(4) BINARY VALUE 0.
   10 IND-MBR-CITY         PIC S9(4) BINARY VALUE 0.
   10 IND-MBR-STATE        PIC S9(4) BINARY VALUE 0.
   10 IND-MBR-ZIP          PIC S9(4) BINARY VALUE 0.
   10 IND-MBR-PHONE        PIC S9(4) BINARY VALUE 0.
   10 IND-MBR-BALANCE      PIC S9(4) BINARY VALUE 0.

01 ERR-REC.
   05 FILLER               PIC X(10) VALUE 'SQLCODE = '.
   05 SQLCODE-VIEW         PIC -999.
   05 FILLER               PIC X(005) VALUE SPACES.
   05 ERR-TAB              PIC X(016).
   05 ERR-PARA             PIC X(015).
   05 ERR-DETAIL           PIC X(040).

77 ERR-TXT-LGTH           PIC S9(9) USAGE COMP VALUE +72.

01 ERR-MSG.
   05 ERR-MSG-LGTH         PIC S9(04) COMP VALUE +864.
   05 ERR-MSG-TXT          PIC X(072) OCCURS 12 TIMES
                                      INDEXED BY ERR-NDX.

   EXEC SQL
     INCLUDE SQLCA
   END-EXEC.

   EXEC SQL
     INCLUDE MEMBER
   END-EXEC.


PROCEDURE DIVISION.

MAIN-PARA.
    DISPLAY "SAMPLE COBOL PROGRAM: CALL STORED PROCEDURES".
    DISPLAY 'UPDATE NEW MEMBER INFORMATION'

    MOVE 100101        TO MBR-NBR
    MOVE 'BROWN'       TO MBR-LAST-NAME-TEXT
    MOVE 'OSBORNE'     TO MBR-FIRST-NAME-TEXT
    MOVE '5162 HUNTINGTON RD'
                       TO MBR-ADDRESS-TEXT
    MOVE 'FRIENDSWOOD' TO MBR-CITY-TEXT

    MOVE LENGTH OF MBR-LAST-NAME-TEXT  TO MBR-LAST-NAME-LEN
    MOVE LENGTH OF MBR-FIRST-NAME-TEXT TO MBR-FIRST-NAME-LEN
    MOVE LENGTH OF MBR-ADDRESS-TEXT    TO MBR-ADDRESS-LEN
    MOVE LENGTH OF MBR-CITY-TEXT       TO MBR-CITY-LEN
```

```
MOVE 'TX'          TO MBR-STATE
MOVE 770822154     TO MBR-ZIP
MOVE 7139873472    TO MBR-PHONE
MOVE ZERO          TO MBR-BALANCE

EXEC SQL

    CALL FBSCHEMA.UPD_MEM_INFO
        (:MBR-NBR,
         :MBR-LAST-NAME,
         :MBR-FIRST-NAME,
         :MBR-ADDRESS,
         :MBR-CITY,
         :MBR-STATE,
         :MBR-ZIP,
         :MBR-PHONE,
         :MBR-BALANCE)

END-EXEC.

IF SQLCODE IS NOT EQUAL TO ZERO

    DISPLAY  'UPD CALL FAILED ' MBR-NBR
    MOVE SQLCODE TO SQLCODE-VIEW
    MOVE 'MEMBER'   TO ERR-TAB
    MOVE 'MAIN'     TO ERR-PARA
    MOVE MBR-NBR    TO ERR-DETAIL
    PERFORM P9999-SQL-ERROR
    DISPLAY 'MBR-NBR         = ' MBR-NBR
    DISPLAY 'MBR-LAST-NAME   = ' MBR-LAST-NAME
    DISPLAY 'MBR-FIRST-NAME  = ' MBR-FIRST-NAME
    DISPLAY 'MBR-ADDRESS     = ' MBR-ADDRESS
    DISPLAY 'MBR-CITY        = ' MBR-CITY
    DISPLAY 'MBR-ZIP         = ' MBR-ZIP
    DISPLAY 'MBR-PHONE       = ' MBR-PHONE
    DISPLAY 'MBR-BALANCE     = ' MBR-BALANCE

ELSE
    DISPLAY  'ADD CALL SUCCESSFUL ' MBR-NBR
    DISPLAY 'MBR-NBR         = ' MBR-NBR
    DISPLAY 'MBR-LAST-NAME   = ' MBR-LAST-NAME
    DISPLAY 'MBR-FIRST-NAME  = ' MBR-FIRST-NAME
    DISPLAY 'MBR-ADDRESS     = ' MBR-ADDRESS
    DISPLAY 'MBR-CITY        = ' MBR-CITY
    DISPLAY 'MBR-ZIP         = ' MBR-ZIP
    DISPLAY 'MBR-PHONE       = ' MBR-PHONE
    DISPLAY 'MBR-BALANCE     = ' MBR-BALANCE

END-IF

GOBACK.
```

```
P9999-SQL-ERROR.

    DISPLAY ERR-REC.

    CALL 'DSNTIAR' USING SQLCA,
                    ERR-MSG,
                    ERR-TXT-LGTH.

    IF RETURN-CODE IS EQUAL TO ZERO

       PERFORM P9999-DISP-ERR
          VARYING ERR-NDX FROM 1 BY 1
          UNTIL ERR-NDX > 12

    ELSE
       DISPLAY 'DSNTIAR ERROR CODE = ' RETURN-CODE
       STOP RUN.

P9999-DISP-ERR.

    DISPLAY ERR-MSG-TXT(ERR-NDX).

P9999-DISP-ERR-EXIT.
```

And here are the results.

```
SAMPLE COBOL PROGRAM: CALL STORED PROCEDURES
UPDATE NEW MEMBER INFORMATION
ADD CALL SUCCESSFUL 000100101
MBR-NBR         = 000100101
MBR-LAST-NAME   =   BROWN
MBR-FIRST-NAME  =   OSBORNE
MBR-ADDRESS     =   5162 HUNTINGTON RD
MBR-CITY        =   FRIENDSWOOD
MBR-ZIP         = 000000000770822154
MBR-PHONE       = 000000007139873472
MBR-BALANCE     = 000000000
```

Stored Procedure to DELETE

Finally, let's create the delete stored procedure and program. The stored procedure is easy:

```
CREATE PROCEDURE FBSCHEMA.DLT_MEM_INFO
(IN M_NBR INT)

 LANGUAGE SQL
 MODIFIES SQL DATA

 BEGIN
    DELETE FROM FBSCHEMA.MEMBER
    WHERE MBR_NBR = M_NBR;

 END #
```

349

And again we will grant access to use the procedure:

```
GRANT EXECUTE ON PROCEDURE FBSCHEMA.DLT_MEM_INFO TO PUBLIC;
```

Now for variety, instead of writing another COBOL program, let's test the delete using a Rexx script. Here is mine:

```
/* REXX */
SUBSYS = "DBAG"
address TSO
/*  set steplib   */
  "FREE  FI(STEPLIBX) DA('DSNA10.SDSNLOAD')"
  "ALLOC FI(STEPLIBX) DA('DSNA10.SDSNLOAD') SHR REUSE"
  if rc <> 0
  then do
        say "DB2 SDSNLOAD library for SSID="ssid" is not available!"
        say "Check z/OS LINKLIST or allocate to STEPLIB in advance!"
        signal error
  end
ADDRESS TSO "SUBCOM DSNREXX" /* HOST CMD ENV AVAILABLE ? */
IF RC <> 0 THEN S_RC = RXSUBCOM('ADD','DSNREXX','DSNREXX')
say 'About to connect...'
ADDRESS DSNREXX "CONNECT" SUBSYS
IF SQLCODE =  0 THEN say 'Connected...'
IF SQLCODE <> 0 THEN CALL SQLCA
say 'About to call SP...'
/* Identify Stored procedure, define host variables */
STOPRO = 'FBSCHEMA.DLT_MEM_INFO'
MBR_NBR = +100101
/* call the stored procedure  */
ADDRESS DSNREXX
"EXECSQL CALL :STOPRO(:MBR_NBR)"
IF SQLCODE <> 0 THEN CALL SQLCA
say SQLCODE
IF SQLCODE = 0 THEN
SAY "Stored Procedure: " DLT_MEM_INFO " was successful"
SAY "MBR_NBR        = " MBR_NBR
```

And here is the result:

```
About to call SP...
0
Stored Procedure:  DLT_MEM_INFO  was successful
MBR_NBR        =   100101
***
```

And we can verify that the record 100101 was deleted by listing the content of the MEMBER table:

350

```
SELECT MBR_NBR,
MBR_LAST_NAME,
MBR_FIRST_NAME
FROM FBSCHEMA.MEMBER;

  SELECT MBR_NBR,
  MBR_LAST_NAME,
  MBR_FIRST_NAME
  FROM FBSCHEMA.MEMBER;
---------+---------+---------+---------+---------+-------
   MBR_NBR   MBR_LAST_NAME          MBR_FIRST_NAME
---------+---------+---------+---------+---------+-------
    100100   JEFFERSON              RICHARD
DSNE610I NUMBER OF ROWS DISPLAYED IS 1
```

Special Project Wrap-up

There are many other things you could do with this project. Lacking a real project, I encourage you to use your imagination. For example you might need a UDF to extract all member activity (deposits and rewards) for an online display on a web page.

Here are just a few more ideas you can consider. How about setting up archive tables for the DEPOSIT_TYPE and REWARD_TYPE tables – the archive records will come in handy when someone asked when these tables changed and what the previous entries were. Similarly you could set up an archive table for the MEMBER table. This way whenever a MEMBER record changes you will always have a copy of the previous version. Set up DEPOSITS and REWARDS as temporal tables to enable time travel queries to show activity such as BALANCE as of a certain period of time. The possibilities are endless but the necessities will depend on your actual project requirements.

We've come to the end of this text book, so let me close with a sincere "best of luck". It's been a pleasure walking you through intermediate level DB2 concepts. I truly hope you do exceptionally well as a DB2 for z/OS developer, and that you have every success!

Robert Wingate

APPENDIXES

Answers for Chapter Questions and Exercises

Chapter Two Questions and Answers

1. Which of the following is NOT a valid data type for use as an identity column?

    a. INTEGER
    b. REAL
    c. DECIMAL
    d. SMALLINT

    The correct answer is B. A REAL type cannot be used as an identity field because it is considered an approximation of a number rather than an exact value. Only numeric types that have an exact value can be used as an identity field. INTEGER, DECIMAL, and SMALLINT are all incorrect here because they CAN be used as identity fields.

2. You need to store numeric integer values of up to 5,000,000,000. What data type is appropriate for this?

    a. INTEGER
    b. BIGINT
    c. LARGEINT
    d. DOUBLE

    The correct answer is B. BIGINT is an integer that can hold up to 9,223,372,036,854,775,807. INTEGER is not correct because an INTEGER can only hold up to 2,147,483,647. LARGEINT is an invalid type. DOUBLE could be used but since we are dealing with integer data, the double precision is not needed.

3. Which of the following is NOT a LOB (Large Object) data type?

    a. CLOB
    b. BLOB
    c. DBCLOB
    d. DBBLOB

The correct answer is **D**. There is no **DBBLOB** datatype in DB2. The other data types are valid. **CLOB** is a character large object with maximum length 2,147,483,647 bytes. A **BLOB** stores binary data and has a maximum size of 2,147,483,647. A **DB-CLOB** stores double character data and has a maximum length of 1,073,741,824.

4. If you want to add an XML column VAR1 to table TBL1, which of the following would accomplish that?

    a. ALTER TABLE TBL1 ADD VAR1 XML
    b. ALTER TABLE TBL1 ADD COLUMN VAR1 XML
    c. ALTER TABLE TBL1 ADD COLUMN VAR1 (XML)
    d. ALTER TABLE TBL1 ADD XML COLUMN VAR1

The correct answer is **B**. The correct syntax is:

```
ALTER TABLE TBL1
ADD COLUMN VAR1 XML;
```

The other choices would result in a syntax error.

5. If you want rows that have similar key values to be stored physically close to each other, what keyword should you specify when you create an index?

    a. UNIQUE
    b. ASC
    c. INCLUDE
    d. CLUSTER

The correct answer is **D - CLUSTER**. Specifying a **CLUSTER** type index means that DB2 will attempt to physically store rows with similar keys close together. This is used for performance reasons when sequential type processing is needed according to the index. **UNIQUE** is incorrect because this keyword simply guarantees that there can be no more than one row with the same index key. **ASC** is incorrect because it has to do with the sort order for the index, and does not affect the physical storage of rows. **INCLUDE** specifies that a non-key field or fields will be stored with the index.

6. To ensure all records inserted into a view of a table are consistent with the view definition, you would need to include which of the following keywords when defining the view?

    a. UNIQUE
    b. WITH CHECK OPTION
    c. VALUES
    d. ALIAS

The correct answer is B. The WITH CHECK OPTION ensures that a record inserted via a view is consistent with the view definition. UNIQUE is a type of index and is unrelated to views. VALUES is part of an INSERT DML statement, but it does not ensure that the record is consistent with a view definition. An ALIAS is another name for a table that allows the table to be referenced without regard to the owning schema for that table.

7. If you want to determine various characteristics of a set of tables such as type (table or view), owner and status, which system catalog view would you query?

    a. SYSCAT.SYSTABLES
    b. SYSIBM.SYSTABLES
    c. SYSCAT.OBJECTS
    d. SYSIBM.OBJECTS

The correct answer is B. Query the SYSIBM.SYSTABLES view to get characteristics of the table such as table type (table or view), owner and status.

Chapter Two Exercises

1. Write a DDL statement to create a base table named EMP_DEPENDENTS owned by schema HRSCHEMA and in tablespace TSHR. The columns should be named as follows and have the specified attributes. There is no primary key.

Field Name	Type	Attributes
EMP_ID	INTEGER	NOT NULL, PRIMARY KEY
EMP_DEP_LAST_NAME	VARCHAR(30)	NOT NULL
EMP_DEP_FIRST_NAME	VARCHAR(20)	NOT NULL
EMP_RELATIONSHIP	VARCHAR(15)	NOT NULL

```
CREATE TABLE HRSCHEMA.EMP_DEPENDENT
(EMP_ID INT NOT NULL,
EMP_DEP_LAST_NAME     VARCHAR(30) NOT NULL,
EMP_DEP_FIRST_NAME    VARCHAR(20) NOT NULL,
EMP_DEP_RELATIONSHIP VARCHAR(15) NOT NULL)
IN TSHR;
```

You can add data to the table and retrieve it as follows:

```
INSERT INTO HRSCHEMA.EMP_DEPENDENT
VALUES(3217,'JOHNSON','ELENA','WIFE');


  SELECT * FROM HRSCHEMA.EMP_DEPENDENT;
---------+---------+---------+---------+---------+---------+---------+---
    EMP_ID  EMP_DEP_LAST_NAME   EMP_DEP_FIRST_NAME   EMP_DEP_RELATIONSHIP
---------+---------+---------+---------+---------+---------+---------+---
      3217  JOHNSON             ELENA                WIFE
DSNE610I NUMBER OF ROWS DISPLAYED IS 1
```

2. Create a statement to create a referential constraint on table EMP_DEPENDENTS such that only employee ids which exist on the HRSCHEMA.EMPLOYEE table can have an entry in EMP_DEPENDENTS. If there is an attempt to delete an EMPLOYEE record that has EMP_DE-PENDENT records associated with it, then do not allow the delete to take place.

```
ALTER TABLE HRSCHEMA.EMP_DEPENDENT
   FOREIGN KEY FK_EMP_ID_DEP (EMP_ID)
      REFERENCES HRSCHEMA.EMPLOYEE(EMP_ID) ;

OR

ALTER TABLE HRSCHEMA.EMP_DEPENDENT
   FOREIGN KEY FK_EMP_ID_DEP (EMP_ID)
      REFERENCES HRSCHEMA.EMPLOYEE(EMP_ID)
         ON DELETE RESTRICT;
```

Both of the above have the same effect which is to prevent a parent record (EMPLOYEE) from being deleted if it has a related child record (in EMP_DEPENDENT).

Chapter Three Questions and Answers

1. Assume you are doing a multi-row INSERT and have specified NOT ATOMIC CONTINUE ON SQLEXCEPTION. On the INSERT of one of the rows, a -803 is returned. What will the result be for this transaction?

    a. The row causing the -803 will not be inserted, and the other inserted rows will be backed out.
    b. The rows are all inserted but the row causing the -803 is also placed in an error table.
    c. The rows up until the -803 are all inserted but none after that and the program will continue with the next statement.
    d. The row causing the -803 will not be inserted but the other rows will be inserted.

The correct answer is D. When the NOT ATOMIC CONTINUE ON SQLEXCEPTION clause is specified in the INSERT statement, any row causing a SQL exception will not be inserted but all the other rows are still inserted.

2. Suppose you issue this INSERT statement:

```
UPDATE HRSCHEMA.EMPLOYEE
SET EMP_PROFILE
= (
'<?xml version="1.0"?>
<EMP_PROFILE>
<EMP_ID>4175</EMP_ID>
<EMP_ADDRESS>
<STREET>6161 MARGARET LANE</STREET>
<CITY>ERINDALE</CITY>
<STATE>AR</STATE>
<ZIP_CODE>72653</ZIP_CODE>
</EMP_ADDRESS>
<BIRTH_DATE>07/14/1991</BIRTH_DATE>
<EMP_PROFILE>
' )
WHERE EMP_ID = 4175;
```

3. What will the result be?

    a. An error – the specified XML version is incorrect
    b. An error – the document is not well formed
    c. The record will be inserted with a warning that it has not been validated
    d. The record will be inserted successfully

The correct answer is B. The XML document is not well formed – the last tag should be `</EMP_PROFILE>` **rather than** `<EMP_PROFILE>`.

4. Which of the following is NOT a valid expression to use with the `XMLMODIFY` function?

      a. Insert expressions.
      b. Delete expressions.
      c. Update expressions.
      d. Replace expressions.

The correct answer is C. There is no update expression for `XMLMODIFY`. Three expressions are available for `XMLMODIFY`: insert, delete and replace.

5. Which of the following is NOT a special register in DB2 11?

      a. CURRENT DEGREE
      b. CURRENT RULES
      c. CURRENT HINT
      d. All of the above are valid DB2 special registers.

The correct answer is C. There is no `CURRENT HINT` special register in DB2, although there is a `CURRENT OPTIMIZATION HINT` special register. `CURRENT OPTIMIZATION HINT` refers to the user-defined optimization hint that DB2 will use to generate an access path for dynamic SQL statements. `CURRENT DEGREE` indicates whether or not parallelism will be used for executing dynamic queries. `CURRENT RULES` specifies whether SQL statements are executed according to SQL standard rules or according to DB2 for z/OS rules.

6. Which built-in routine returns the value of the first non-null expression?

      a. COALESCE
      b. ABS
      c. CEILING
      d. MIN

The correct answer is A. The `COALESCE` function returns the value of the first non-null expression. The `ABS` function returns the absolute value of a number. The `CEILING` function returns the smallest integer value that is greater than or equal to an expression. The `MIN` function returns the smallest value in a set of values in a group.

For example:

```
SELECT COALESCE(SALARY,0)
```

Here, if the SALARY is not null then the COALESCE function returns the value of SALARY. Otherwise it returns the value zero and zero is included in the aggregation.

7. If you want the aggregate total for a set of values, which function would you use?

    a. COUNT
    b. SUM
    c. ABS
    d. CEIL

The correct answer is B - SUM. SUM returns the total of a set of numeric values. COUNT returns the number of records that meet the search criteria. ABS returns the absolute value of a numeric column. CEILING returns the smallest integer that is greater than or equal to an expression or value, e.g. CEILING(3.5) = 4.0.

8. If you want to return the first 3 characters of a 10-character column, which function would you use?

    a. SUBSTR
    b. LTRIM
    c. DIGITS
    d. ABS

The correct answer is A. SUBSTR returns a subset of the source string. The syntax is SUBSTR(X,Y, Z) where X is the source column, Y is the starting position, and Z is the length of the sub-string. Assuming a 10-character column FLD1, you would get the first three positions by coding SUBSTR(FLD1, 1,3).

The other answers are incorrect. LTRIM removes all leading blanks from a value, e.g., LTRIM(LASTNAME) would return the LASTNAME value minus any leading spaces. DIGITS returns a character representation of a numeric value. ABS returns the absolute value of a number and is unrelated to partial string values.

9. Assuming all referenced objects are valid, what will the result of this statement be?

`DELETE FROM EMPLOYEE;`

    a. The statement will fail because there is no WHERE clause.
    b. The statement will fail because you must specify DELETE * .
    c. The statement will succeed and all rows in the table will be deleted.
    d. The statement will run but no rows in the table will be deleted.

The correct answer is C. Assuming all referenced objects are valid, running the `DELETE FROM EMPLOYEE` **statement will succeed and all rows in the table will be deleted.**

Chapter Three Exercises

1. Write a query to display the last and first names of all employees in the EMPLOYEE table. Display the names in alphabetic order by EMP_LAST_NAME.

```
SELECT EMP_LAST_NAME, EMP_FIRST_NAME
FROM HRSCHEMA.EMPLOYEE
ORDER BY EMP_LAST_NAME;
```

2. Write a query to change the first name of Edward Johnson (employee 3217) to Eddie.

```
UPDATE HRSCHEMA.EMPLOYEE
SET EMP_FIRST_NAME = 'EDDIE'
WHERE EMP_ID = 3217;
```

3. Write a query to produce the number of employees in the EMPLOYEE table.

```
SELECT COUNT(*)
FROM HRSCHEMA.EMPLOYEE;
```

Chapter Four Questions and Answers

1. Assume a table where certain columns contain sensitive data and you don't want all users to see these columns. Some other columns in the table must be made accessible to all users. What type of object could you create to solve this problem?

    a. INDEX
    b. SEQUENCE
    c. VIEW
    d. TRIGGER

The correct answer is C. A view is a virtual table based upon a SELECT query that can include a subset of the columns in a table. So you can create multiple views against the same base table, and control access to the views based upon userid or group.

The other answers do not address the problem of limiting access to specific columns. An INDEX is an object that stores the physical location of records and is used to improve performance and enforce uniqueness. A SEQUENCE allows for the automatic generation of sequential values, and has nothing to do with limiting access to columns in a table. A TRIGGER is an object that performs some predefined action when it is activated. A trigger is only activated by an INSERT, UPDATE or DELETE of a record in a particular table.

2. To grant a privilege to all users of the database, grant the privilege to whom?

    a. ALL
    b. PUBLIC
    c. ANY
    d. DOMAIN

The correct answer is B. PUBLIC is a special "pseudo" group that means all users of the database. The other answers ALL, ANY, and DOMAIN are incorrect because they are not valid recipients of a grant statement.

3. Tara wants to grant CONTROL of table TBL1 to Bill, and also allow Bill to grant the same privilege to other users. What clause should Tara use on the GRANT statement?

    a. WITH CONTROL OPTION
    b. WITH GRANT OPTION

c. WITH USE OPTION

d. WITH REVOKE OPTION

The correct answer is B. Using the `WITH GRANT OPTION` **permits the recipient of the grant to also grant this privilege to other users. The other choices** `WITH CONTROL OPTION,` `WITH USE OPTION,` **and** `WITH REVOKE OPTION` **are incorrect because they are not valid clauses on a GRANT statement.**

4. Assume USER01 was granted the UPDATE privilege on table TABLE01 and it was issued WITH GRANT OPTION. If you want to revoke user USER01's UPDATE access on TABLE01, and you also want to revoke the UPDATE access of any other users that were granted this permission by USER01, what clause would you include in the REVOKE statement?

    a. CASCADE

    b. EXTEND

    c. ALL GRANTED

    d. No other clause is required, DB2 automatically revokes the access from all users that received their grant from the designated user specified on the REVOKE command.

The correct answer is A. The CASCADE option revokes the specified permission from the designated user, and also revokes the access from all users that received their grant from the designated user. If CASCADE is not specified, DB2 will only revoke the permission from the specified USER on the REVOKE command. EXTEND and ALL GRANTED are not valid DB2 commands.

Chapter Four Exercises

1. Write a DCL statement to grant SELECT access on table HRSCHEMA.EMPLOYEE to users HR001 and HR002.

    ```
    GRANT SELECT ON HRSCHEMA.EMPLOYEE
    TO HR001, HR002;
    ```

2. Write a DCL statement to revoke SELECT access on table HRSCHEMA.EMPLOYEE from user HR002.

    ```
    REVOKE SELECT ON HRSCHEMA.EMPLOYEE
    FROM HR002;
    ```

3. Write a DCL statement to grant SELECT, INSERT, UPDATE and DELETE access on table HRSCHEMA.EMP_PAY to user HRMGR01.

    ```
    GRANT SELECT, INSERT, UPDATE, DELETE
    ON HRSCHEMA.EMP_PAY
    TO HRMGR01;
    ```

Chapter Five Questions and Answers

1. Assume you are doing a multi-row INSERT and have specified `NOT ATOMIC CONTINUE ON SQLEXCEPTION`. On the INSERT of one of the rows, a -803 is returned. What will the result be for this transaction?

    a. The row causing the -803 will not be inserted, and the other inserted rows will be backed out.
    b. The rows are all inserted but the row causing the -803 is also placed in an error table.
    c. The rows up until the -803 are all inserted but none after that and the program will continue with the next statement.
    d. The row causing the -803 will not be inserted but the other rows will be inserted.

    The correct answer is D. When the `NOT ATOMIC CONTINUE ON SQLEXCEPTION` clause is specified in the INSERT statement, any row causing a SQL exception will not be inserted but all the other rows are still inserted.

2. Which of the following will generate DB2 SQL data structures for a table or view that can be used in a PLI or COBOL program?

    a. DECLARE
    b. INCLUDE
    c. DCLGEN
    d. None of the above.

    The correct answer is C. DCLGEN is an IBM utility that generates SQL data structures (table definition and host variables) for a table or view, stores it in a PDS and then that PDS member can be included in a PL/1 or COBOL program. DECLARE is a verb used to define a temporary table or cursor. INCLUDE can be used to embed the generated structure into the program. Assuming the structure is in member MEMBER1 of the PDS, the statement `EXEC SQL INCLUDE MEMBER1` will include it in the program.

3. As part of the program preparation process, SQL in a program must be pre-processed. Which of the following CANNOT be used to accomplish the SQL pre-processing to prepare a program for execution?

a. DB2 Precompiler.
b. DB2 Bind Package.
c. DB2 Coprocessor.
d. All of the above are valid for doing SQL preprocessing of an application program.

The correct answer is B. The bind package step does not pre-process SQL. The SQL can be processed by either the DB2 precompiler or by the compiler's DB2 coprocessor. The bind package step occurs after the SQL is processed and a Database Request Module (DBRM) is created.

4. Assuming you are using a DB2 precompiler, which of the following orders the DB2 program preparation steps correctly?

   a. Precompile SQL, Bind Package, Bind Plan.
   b. Precompile SQL, Bind Plan, Bind Package.
   c. Bind Package, Precompile SQL, Bind Plan.
   d. Bind Plan, Precompile SQL, Bind Package.

The correct answer is A. The DB2 related steps for program preparation are:

   · **Precompile SQL which produces a DBRM**
   · **Bind package using the DBRM**
   · **Bind plan specifying the package(s)**

5. Assume you have a COBOL DB2 program and you have defined an error message area as follows:

```
ERR-MSG.
02  ERR-LEN   PIC S9(4)   COMP VALUE +1320.
ERR-TEXT  PIC X(132) OCCURS 10 TIMES
INDEXED BY ERR-INDEX.
77  ERR-TEXT-LEN      PIC S9(9)   COMP VALUE +132.
```

What is the correct syntax to use DSNTIAR to retrieve an error message after an SQL statement?

   a. CALL 'DSNTIAR' USING ERR-MSG ERR-TEXT-LEN SQLCA.
   b. CALL 'DSNTIAR' USING SQLCA ERR-TEXT-LEN ERR-MSG.
   c. CALL 'DSNTIAR' USING SQLCA ERR-MSG ERR-TEXT-LEN.
   d. All of the above are invalid and will fail.

The correct answer is C. The syntax for retrieving the error message using **DSNTIAR is:**

```
CALL 'DSNTIAR' USING SQLCA ERR-MSG ERR-TEXT-LEN
```

6. If you want to still reference data using a cursor after you issue a COMMIT, which clause would you use when you declare the cursor?

    a. WITH HOLD
    b. WITH RETAIN
    c. WITH STAY
    d. WITH REOPEN

The correct answer is A. The WITH HOLD clause causes a commit to leave the cursor open and avoid releasing locks necessary to maintain the cursor's positioning. The other answers are invalid clauses.

Chapter Five Exercises

1. Write a program that creates a cursor to select all employees who have 5 years or more of service from the HRSCHEMA.EMPLOYEE table. Include logic to fetch any rows that are returned. Display the employee number, last name and first name of these employees.

```
IDENTIFICATION DIVISION.
PROGRAM-ID. COBEMPE.

***********************************************************
*       PROGRAM USING DB2 CURSOR HANDLING         *
*                                                 *
***********************************************************

ENVIRONMENT DIVISION.
DATA DIVISION.
WORKING-STORAGE SECTION.

    EXEC SQL
      INCLUDE SQLCA
    END-EXEC.

    EXEC SQL
      INCLUDE EMPLOYEE
    END-EXEC.

    EXEC SQL
        DECLARE EMP-CURSOR CURSOR FOR
        SELECT EMP_ID, EMP_LAST_NAME, EMP_FIRST_NAME
        FROM HRSCHEMA.EMPLOYEE
        WHERE EMP_SERVICE_YEARS >= 5
        FOR READ ONLY
    END-EXEC.

01 WS-EMPNO          PIC ZZZZZZZ9.

PROCEDURE DIVISION.

MAIN-PARA.
    DISPLAY "SAMPLE COBOL PROGRAM: READ ONLY USING CURSOR".

    EXEC SQL
        OPEN EMP-CURSOR
    END-EXEC.

    DISPLAY 'OPEN CURSOR SQLCODE: ' SQLCODE.

    PERFORM FETCH-CURSOR
      UNTIL SQLCODE NOT EQUAL 0.

    EXEC SQL
        CLOSE EMP-CURSOR
    END-EXEC.

    DISPLAY 'CLOSE CURSOR SQLCODE: ' SQLCODE.

    STOP RUN.
```

```
FETCH-CURSOR.

    INITIALIZE DCLEMPLOYEE
    EXEC SQL
        FETCH EMP-CURSOR INTO :EMP-ID,
                              :EMP-LAST-NAME,
                              :EMP-FIRST-NAME
    END-EXEC.

    IF SQLCODE = 0
       MOVE EMP-ID TO WS-EMPNO
       DISPLAY WS-EMPNO EMP-LAST-NAME EMP-FIRST-NAME
    END-IF.
```

OUTPUT FROM PROGRAM:

```
SAMPLE COBOL PROGRAM: READ ONLY USING CURSOR
OPEN CURSOR SQLCODE: 0000000000
    3217   JOHNSON                  EDWARD
    7459   STEWART                  BETTY
    4720   SCHULTZ                  TIM
    6288   WILLARD                  JOE
    3333   FORD                     JAMES
CLOSE CURSOR SQLCODE: 0000000000
```

2. Write a program that tries to insert a record that already exists into the HRSCHEMA.EM-PLOYEE table. Your program should capture the error, and your error routine should detail the cause of the error.

```
IDENTIFICATION DIVISION.
PROGRAM-ID. COBEMPF.

****************************************************
*      PROGRAM USING DB2 SELECT WITH ERROR TO      *
*      DEMONSTRATE TRYING TO ADD A RECORD THAT      *
*      ALREADY EXISTS TO THE EMPLOYEE TABLE.        *
****************************************************

ENVIRONMENT DIVISION.
DATA DIVISION.
WORKING-STORAGE SECTION.

01 HV-EMP-VARIABLES.
    10  HV-ID            PIC S9(9) USAGE COMP.
    10  HV-LAST-NAME     PIC X(30).
    10  HV-FIRST-NAME    PIC X(20).
    10  HV-SERVICE-YEARS PIC S9(9) USAGE COMP.
    10  HV-PROMOTION-DATE PIC X(10).


01 ERR-REC.
    05 FILLER            PIC X(10) VALUE 'SQLCODE = '.
```

```
           05 SQLCODE-VIEW      PIC -999.
           05 FILLER           PIC X(005) VALUE SPACES.
           05 ERR-TAB          PIC X(016).
           05 ERR-PARA         PIC X(015).
           05 ERR-DETAIL       PIC X(040).

       77 ERR-TXT-LGTH         PIC S9(9) USAGE COMP VALUE +72.

       01 ERR-MSG.
           05 ERR-MSG-LGTH     PIC S9(04) COMP VALUE +864.
           05 ERR-MSG-TXT      PIC X(072) OCCURS 12 TIMES
                                          INDEXED BY ERR-NDX.

           EXEC SQL
             INCLUDE SQLCA
           END-EXEC.

           EXEC SQL
             INCLUDE EMPLOYEE
           END-EXEC.

       PROCEDURE DIVISION.

       MAIN-PARA.
           DISPLAY "SAMPLE COBOL PROGRAM: HANDLE INVALID INSERT".

           MOVE +3217          TO HV-ID
           MOVE 'WHEELER'       TO HV-LAST-NAME
           MOVE 'RITA'          TO HV-FIRST-NAME
           MOVE +4             TO HV-SERVICE-YEARS
           MOVE '01/01/2016'    TO HV-PROMOTION-DATE


       *   INSERT AN EMPLOYEE

           EXEC SQL
             INSERT
             INTO HRSCHEMA.EMPLOYEE
             (EMP_ID,
              EMP_LAST_NAME,
              EMP_FIRST_NAME,
              EMP_SERVICE_YEARS,
              EMP_PROMOTION_DATE)

             VALUES(:HV-ID,
                    :HV-LAST-NAME,
                    :HV-FIRST-NAME,
                    :HV-SERVICE-YEARS,
                    :HV-PROMOTION-DATE)

           END-EXEC.

           IF SQLCODE IS NOT EQUAL TO ZERO

              MOVE SQLCODE TO SQLCODE-VIEW
              MOVE 'EMPLOYEE' TO ERR-TAB
              MOVE 'MAIN'     TO ERR-PARA
              MOVE EMP-ID     TO ERR-DETAIL
              PERFORM P9999-SQL-ERROR.
```

```
                STOP RUN.

          P9999-SQL-ERROR.

              DISPLAY ERR-REC.

              CALL 'DSNTIAR' USING SQLCA,
                              ERR-MSG,
                              ERR-TXT-LGTH.

              IF RETURN-CODE IS EQUAL TO ZERO

                 PERFORM P9999-DISP-ERR
                    VARYING ERR-NDX FROM 1 BY 1
                    UNTIL ERR-NDX > 12

              ELSE
                 DISPLAY 'DSNTIAR ERROR CODE = ' RETURN-CODE
                 STOP RUN.

          P9999-DISP-ERR.

              DISPLAY ERR-MSG-TXT(ERR-NDX).

          P9999-DISP-ERR-EXIT.
```

OUTPUT FROM PROGRAM

```
SAMPLE COBOL PROGRAM: HANDLE INVALID INSERT
SQLCODE = -803      EMPLOYEE        MAIN            000000000
 DSNT408I SQLCODE = -803, ERROR: AN INSERTED OR UPDATED VALUE IS
          INVALID BECAUSE INDEX IN INDEX SPACE NDXREMPL CONSTRAINS
          COLUMNS OF THE TABLE SO NO TWO ROWS CAN CONTAIN DUPLICATE
          VALUES IN THOSE COLUMNS.
          RID OF EXISTING ROW IS X'0000000201'.
 DSNT418I SQLSTATE   = 23505 SQLSTATE RETURN CODE
 DSNT415I SQLERRP    = DSNXRINS SQL PROCEDURE DETECTING ERROR
 DSNT416I SQLERRD    = -110  13172739  0  13817814  -490143744  0 SQL
          DIAGNOSTIC INFORMATION
 DSNT416I SQLERRD    = X'FFFFFF92'  X'00C90003'  X'00000000'
          X'00D2D7D6'  X'E2C90000'  X'00000000' SQL DIAGNOSTIC
          INFORMATION
```

Chapter Six Questions and Answers

1. To end a transaction without making the changes permanent, which DB2 statement should be issued?

    a. COMMIT
    b. BACKOUT
    c. ROLLBACK
    d. NO CHANGE

The correct answer is C. Issuing a ROLLBACK statement will end a transaction without making the changes permanent.

2. If you want to maximize data concurrency without seeing uncommitted data, which isolation level should you use?

    a. RR
    b. UR
    c. RS
    d. CS

The correct answer is D (Cursor Stability). CURSOR STABILITY (CS) only locks the row where the cursor is placed, thus maximizing concurrency compared to RR or RS. REPEATABLE READ (RR) ensures that a query issued multiple times within the same unit of work will produce the exact same results. It does this by locking ALL rows that could affect the result, and does not permit any changes to the table that could affect the result. With READ STABILITY(RS), all rows that are returned by the query are locked. UNCOMMITTED READ (UR) is incorrect because it permits reading of uncommitted data and the question specifically disallows that.

3. Assume you have a long running process and you want to commit results after processing every 500 records, but still want the ability to undo any work that has taken place after the commit point. One mechanism that would allow you to do this is to issue a:

    a. SAVEPOINT
    b. COMMITPOINT
    c. BACKOUT
    d. None of the above

The correct answer is A. Issuing a SAVEPOINT enables you to execute several SQL statements as a single executable block. You can then undo changes back out to that savepoint by issuing a ROLLBACK TO SAVEPOINT statement.

4. A procedure that commits transactions independent of the calling procedure is known as a/an:
   a. External procedure.
   b. SQL procedure.
   c. Autonomous procedure.
   d. Independent procedure.

The correct answer is C. Autonomous procedures run with their own units of work, separate from the calling program. Autonomous procedures were introduced in DB2 11.

External procedures are written in a host language. They can contain SQL statements. SQL procedures are written entirely in SQL statements. There is no "independent" type of procedure.

5. To end a transaction and make the changes visible to other processes, which statement should be issued?

   a. ROLLBACK
   b. COMMIT
   c. APPLY
   d. CALL

The correct answer is B. The COMMIT statement ends a transaction and makes the changes visible to other processes.

6. Order the isolation levels, from greatest to least impact on performance.

   a. RR, RS, CS, UR
   b. UR, RR, RS, CS
   c. CS, UR, RR, RS
   d. RS, CS, UR, RR

The correct answer is A - RR, RS, CS, UR. Repeatable Read has the greatest impact on performance because it incurs the most overhead and locks the most rows. It ensures that a query issued multiple times within the same unit of work will pro-

duce the exact same results. It does this by locking all rows that could affect the result, and does not permit any adds/changes/deletes to the table that could affect the result. Next, READ STABILITY locks for the duration of the transaction those rows that are returned by a query, but it allows additional rows to be added to the table. CURSOR STABILITY only locks the row that the cursor is placed on (and any rows it has updated during the unit of work). UNCOMMITTED READ permits reading of uncommitted changes which may never be applied to the database and does not lock any rows at all unless the row(s) is updated during the unit of work.

7. Which isolation level is most appropriate when few or no updates are expected to a table?

    a. RR
    b. RS
    c. CS
    d. UR

The correct answer is D. UR - Uncommitted Read uses less overhead than the other isolation levels and is most appropriate for read-only access of tables. The other isolation levels acquire locks that are unnecessary in a read-only environment. Repeatable Read is required to obtain locks to ensure that a query issued multiple times within the same unit of work will produce the exact same results. With READ STABILITY any rows that are returned by the query are locked. CURSOR STABILITY locks the row that the cursor is placed on, which is not necessary in a primarily read-only environment.

8. In an IMS program that makes updates to DB2 tables, what call is required to make data changes permanent?

    a. COMMIT
    b. CHKP
    c. UPDATE
    d. REPL

The correct answer is B. The checkpoint call CHKP is required to make DB2 data changes permanent. If you issue a DB2 COMMIT statement it will have no effect in an IMS program, so COMMIT is incorrect. The UPDATE call makes DB2 updates but they do not become permanent until a CHKP is issued (or when another commit point occurs such as when the program ends). A REPL call updates an IMS data segment, not DB2 data.

Chapter Six Exercises

1. Code the concurrency bind option/value that ensures that no records which have been retrieved during a unit of work can be changed by other processes until the unit of work completes. However, it is ok for new records to be added to the table.

```
ISOLATION(RS)
```

2. Write the COBOL code to end a unit of work and make the changes visible to other processes.

```
EXEC SQL
COMMIT
END-EXEC
```

OR

```
EXEC SQL
    COMMIT WORK
END-EXEC
```

3. Write the COBOL code to end a unit of work and discard any updates that have been made since the last commit point.

```
EXEC SQL
    ROLLBACK
END-EXEC
```

Chapter Seven Questions and Answers

1. Suppose you have created a test version of a production table, and you want to to use the UNLOAD utility to extract the first 1,000 rows from the production table to load to the test version. Which keyword would you use in the UNLOAD statement?

    a. WHEN
    b. SELECT
    c. SAMPLE
    d. SUBSET

    The correct answer is C. You can specify SAMPLE n where n is the number of rows to unload. For example you can limit the unloaded rows to the first 5,000 by specifying:

    ```
    SAMPLE 1000
    ```

    WHEN is used to specify rows that meet a criteria such as: WHEN (EMP_ SALARY < 90000).

    SELECT and SUBSET are invalid clauses and would cause an error.

2. Which of the following is an SQL error code indicating a DB2 package is not found within the DB2 plan?

    a. -803
    b. -805
    c. -904
    d. -922

    The correct answer is B. The -805 SQLCODE indicates that the specified package was not found in the DB2 plan (or the named package with the correct timestamp could not be found). Typically this requires a BIND PACKAGE action to resolve.

    The -803 SQLCODE means a violation of a unique index. A -904 SQLCODE means an unavailable resource such as a tablespace. A -922 is a security violation such as when an unauthorized user tries to access a DB2 plan (usually this requires a GRANT action to correct the problem).

3. Which of the following will generate DB2 SQL data structures for a table or view that can be used in a PLI or COBOL program?

    a. DECLARE
    b. INCLUDE
    c. DCLGEN
    d. None of the above.

The correct answer is C. DCLGEN is an IBM utility that generates SQL data structures (table definition and host variables) for a table or view, stores it in a PDS and then that PDS member can be included in a PL/1 or COBOL program. DECLARE is a verb used to define a temporary table or cursor. INCLUDE can be used to embed the generated structure into the program. Assuming the structure is in member MEMBER1 of the PDS, the statement EXEC SQL INCLUDE MEMBER1 will include it in the program.

4. Which DB2 utility updates the statistics used by the DB2 Optimizer to choose a data access path?

    a. REORG
    b. RUNSTATS
    c. REBIND
    d. OPTIMIZE

The correct answer is B. Executing RUNSTATS provides the DB2 Optimizer with the latest information on the tables and could improve the access path chosen for the DB2 plan. Of course after RUNSTATS is executed, the related application packages need to be rebound in order for the DB2 Optimizer to use this new information.

5. When using static SQL, to enable parallel processing you must:

    a. Specify DEGREE(ANY) on the BIND or REBIND step.
    b. Issue SQL statement "SET CURRENT DEGREE='ANY'.
    c. Specify PARALLEL_PROC(YES) for the subsystem.
    d. None of the above would enable parallel processing for static SQL.

The correct answer is A. When using static SQL you can enable parallel process-

ing by including the **DEGREE(ANY)** bind option.

Issuing SQL statement SET CURRENT DEGREE='ANY' would only affect dynamic SQL statements, not static SQL. There is no PARALLEL_PROC() register or variable.

6. Which of the following is NOT a way you could test a DB2 SQL statement?

    a. Running the statement from the DB2 command line processor.
    b. Running the statement from the SPUFI utility.
    c. Running the statement from IBM Data Studio.
    d. All of the above are valid ways to test an SQL statement.

The correct answer is D. Any of these three methods could be used to test a DB2 SQL statement.

Chapter Seven Exercises:

1. Write an UNLOAD control statement to unload a sample of 5000 records from the HRSCHE-MA.EMP_PAY table for use in loading a test table.

```
UNLOAD DATA
FROM TABLE HRSCHEMA.EMP_PAY
SAMPLE 5000
```

2. Suppose that the HRSCHEMA.EMPLOYEE table exists on a system whose location name is DENVER. Write a query that uses three part naming to implicitly connect to DENVER and then retrieve all information for EMP_ID 3217.

```
SELECT *
FROM DENVER.HRSCHEMA.EMPLOYEE
WHERE EMP_ID = 3217;
```

Chapter Eight Questions and Answers

1. Consider the following stored procedure:

    ```
    CREATE PROCEDURE GET_PATIENTS
    (IN intHosp INTEGER)
    DYNAMIC RESULT SETS 1
    LANGUAGE SQL
    P1: BEGIN

    DECLARE cursor1 CURSOR
    WITH RETURN FOR
    SELECT PATIENT_ID,
    LNAME,
    FNAME
    FROM PATIENT
    WHERE PATIENT_HOSP = intHosp
    ORDER BY PATIENT_ID ASC;

    OPEN cursor1;
    END P1
    ```

    Answer this question: How many parameters are used in this stored procedure?

    a. 0
    b. 1
    c. 2
    d. 3

    The correct answer is B (1). intHosp is accepted as an IN parameter that is used in the query. Parameters can be IN (they pass a value to the stored procedure), OUT (they return a value from a stored procedure), or INOUT (they pass a value to and return a value from a stored procedure). The answers 0, 2, and 3 are incorrect because exactly 1 parameter is used in this stored procedure.

2. When you want to create an external stored procedure, which of the following programming languages can NOT be used?

    a. COBOL
    b. REXX
    c. Fortran
    d. C++

    The correct answer is C. You cannot use Fortran to create an external stored procedure. The valid programming languages for creating an external stored

procedure are:

- **Assembler**
- **C**
- **C++**
- **COBOL**
- **REXX**
- **PL/I**

3. In order to invoke a stored procedure, which keyword would you use?

    a.   RUN
    b.   CALL
    c.   OPEN
    d.   TRIGGER

The correct answer is B. CALL is the correct statement to invoke a stored procedure. The syntax is CALL <procedure-name>. RUN is not a valid DB2 statement or command unless you are issuing the command to RUN(DSN). The OPEN statement opens a cursor in an embedded SQL program. A TRIGGER is an object that performs some predefined action when it is activated by an INSERT, UPDATE or DELETE of a record in a particular table.

4. Which of the following is NOT a valid return type for a User Defined Function?

    a. Scalar
    b. Aggregate
    c. Column
    d. Row

The correct answer is C. There is no "column" return type for a UDF. A user-defined function can be any of the following which returns the specific data type:

- **A scalar function, which returns a single value each time it is called.**
- **An aggregate function, which is passed a set of like values and returns a single value for the set.**
- **A row function, which returns one row.**
- **A table function, which returns a table.**

5. Which of the following is NOT a valid type of user-defined function (UDF)?

    a. External sourced
    b. SQL sourced
    c. External table
    d. SQL table

The correct answer is B. There is no SQL sourced user-defined function type. Valid types of user defined functions include:

- **External scalar**
- **External table**
- **External sourced**
- **SQL scalar**
- **SQL table**

An external scalar function is written in a programming language and returns a scalar value. An external table function is written in a programming language and returns a table to the subselect from which it was started. A sourced function is implemented by starting another function that exists at the server. An SQL scalar function is written exclusively in SQL statements and returns a scalar value. An SQL table function is written exclusively as an SQL RETURN statement and returns a set of rows.

6. Assume the following trigger DDL:

```
CREATE TRIGGER SAVE_EMPL
AFTER UPDATE ON EMPL
FOR EACH ROW
INSERT INTO EMPLOYEE_HISTORY
VALUES (EMPLOYEE_NUMBER,
EMPLOYEE_STATUS,
CURRENT TIMESTAMP)
```

What will the result of this DDL be, provided the tables and field names are correctly defined?

    a. The DDL will create the trigger successfully and it will work as intended.
    b. The DDL will fail because you cannot use an INSERT with a trigger.
    c. The DDL will fail because the syntax of this statement is incorrect.
    d. The DDL will create the trigger successfully but it will fail when executed.

The correct answer is A. The DDL is syntactically correct and will sucessfully create a trigger that will work as intended.

7. Which ONE of the following actions will NOT cause a trigger to fire?

    a. INSERT
    b. LOAD
    c. DELETE
    d. MERGE

The correct answer is B. The LOAD action does not (by default) causes triggers to fire. The INSERT, DELETE and MERGE do cause INSERT, UPDATE and DELETE triggers to fire.

8. If you use the "FOR EACH STATEMENT" granularity clause in a trigger, what type of timing can you use?

    a. BEFORE
    b. AFTER
    c. INSTEAD OF
    d. All of the above.

The correct answer is B. You cannot use a FOR EACH STATEMENT with BEFORE or INSTEAD OF timing. FOR EACH STATEMENT means your trigger logic is to be applied only once after the triggering statement finishes processing the affected rows.

9. What is the schema for a declared GLOBAL TEMPORARY table?

    a. SESSION
    b. DB2ADMIN
    c. TEMP1
    d. USERTEMP

The correct answer is A. The schema for a GLOBAL TEMPORARY table is always SESSION. The schema for a GLOBAL TEMPORARY table cannot be DB2ADMIN, TEMP1, or USERTEMP.

10. If you create a temporary table and you wish to replace any existing temporary table that has the same name, what clause would you use?

    a. WITH REPLACE
    b. OVERLAY DATA ROWS
    c. REPLACE EXISTING
    d. None of the above.

The correct answer is A. If you create a temporary table and you wish to replace any existing temporary table that has the same name, use the WITH REPLACE clause. OVERLAY DATA ROWS and REPLACE EXISTING are fictitious clauses that would result in an error.

11. What happens to the rows of a temporary table when the session that created it ends?

    a. The rows are deleted when the session ends.
    b. The rows are preserved in memory until the instance is restarted.
    c. The rows are held in the temp table space.
    d. None of the above.

The correct answer is A. When the session that created a temporary table ends, any rows in the table are deleted, along with the table and table definition.

12. Which is true of temporary tables declared within a SAVEPOINT after a ROLLBACK TO SAVEPOINT command has been issued?

    a. Temporary tables declared within the savepoint are still in the system catalog.
    b. Temporary tables declared within the savepoint are dropped and no longer accessible.
    c. Temporary tables declared within the savepoint are still accessible.
    d. None of the above.

The correct answer is B, temporary tables declared within the savepoint are dropped and no longer accessible after a ROLLBACK TO SAVEPOINT. Issuing a SAVEPOINT enables you to execute several SQL statements as a single executable block. You can then undo changes back out to that savepoint by issuing a ROLLBACK TO SAVEPOINT statement. The DECLARE GLOBAL TEMPO-

RARY TABLE statement defines a temporary table for the current session. The declared temporary table description does not appear in the system catalog.

13. Which of the following clauses DOES NOT allow you to pull data for a particular period from a version enabled table?

    a. FOR BUSINESS_TIME UP UNTIL
    b. FOR BUSINESS_TIME FROM ... TO ...
    c. FOR BUSINESS_TIME BETWEEN... AND...
    d. All of the above enable you to pull data for a particular period.

The correct answer is A. There is no UP UNTIL clause in DB2 temporal data management. The other two clauses may be used to specify the time period on a query against a version enabled table.

14. Assume you have an application that needs to aggregate and summarize data from several tables multiple times per day. One way to improve performance of that application would be to use a:

    a. Materialized query table
    b. View
    c. Temporary table
    d. Range clustered table

The correct answer is A, a materialized query table (MQT) is a table whose definition is based upon the result of a query, similar to a view. The difference is that the query on which a view is based must generate the resultset each time the view is referenced. In contrast, an MQT stores the query results as table data, and you can work with the data that is in the MQT instead of incurring the overhead of running a query to generate the data each time you run it. An MQT can thereby significantly improve performance for applications that need summarized, aggregated data.

15. Assume you want to track employees in your company over time. Review the following DDL:

```
CREATE TABLE HRSCHEMA.EMPLOYZZ(
EMP_ID INT NOT NULL,
EMP_LAST_NAME VARCHAR(30) NOT NULL,
EMP_FIRST_NAME VARCHAR(20) NOT NULL,
EMP_SERVICE_YEARS INT
NOT NULL WITH DEFAULT 0,
EMP_PROMOTION_DATE DATE,
BUS_START    DATE  NOT NULL,
BUS_END      DATE  NOT NULL,

PERIOD BUSINESS_TIME(BUS_START, BUS_END),

PRIMARY KEY (EMP_ID, BUSINESS_TIME WITHOUT OVERLAPS));
```

What will happen when you execute this DDL?

    a. It will fail because you cannot specify `WITHOUT OVERLAPS` in the primary key – the `WITHOUT OVERLAPS` clause belongs in the `BUSINESS_TIME` definition.
    b. It will fail because you must specify `SYSTEM_TIME` instead of `BUSINESS_TIME`.
    c. It will fail because the BUS_START has a syntax error.
    d. It will execute successfully.

The correct answer is D. It will execute successfully.

16. Given the previous question, assume there is a table named EMPLOYEE_HIST defined just like EMPLOYEE. What will happen when you execute the following DDL?

```
ALTER TABLE EMPLOYEE
ADD VERSIONING
USE HISTORY TABLE EMPLOYEE_HIST
```

    a. The DDL will execute successfully and updates to EMPLOYEE will generate records in the EMPLOYEE_HIST table.
    b. The DDL will succeed but you must still enable the history table.
    c. The DDL will generate an error – only SYSTEM time enabled tables can use a history table.
    d. The DDL will generate an error – only BUSINESS time enabled tables can use a history table.

The correct answer is C. Only SYSTEM time enabled tables can use a history table.

17. For a system managed Materialized Query Table (MQT) named EMPMQT, how does the data get updated so that it becomes current?

    a. Issuing INSERT, UPDATE and DELETE commands against EMPMQT.
    b. Issuing the statement REFRESH TABLE EMPMQT.
    c. Issuing the statement MATERIALIZE TABLE EMPMQT.
    d. None of the above.

The correct answer is B. The REFRESH TABLE statement refreshes the data in a materialized query table. This is the only way to refresh a system-managed MQT. For example:

```
REFRESH TABLE EMPMQT;
```

For a user defined MQT you can use INSERT, UPDATE, DELETE, TRUN-CATE, MERGE or LOAD to make the data current. There is no MATERIALIZE TABLE statement.

18. Which of the following is TRUE about SQLJ applications that need to handle XML data?

    a. You cannot select or update XML data as textual XML data.
    b. For update of data in XML columns, xmlFormat does the appropriate formatting.
    c. You can store an entire XML document into an XML column using a single UPDATE, INSERT or MERGE statement.
    d. External encoding for Java applications cannot use Unicode encoding.

The correct answer is C. You can store an entire XML document into an XML column using a single UPDATE, INSERT or MERGE statement. The other statements are false. You can select or update XML data as textual XML data (or as binary XML data). For update of data in XML columns, xmlFormat has no effect. External encoding for Java applications is always Unicode encoding.

19. Which of the following is NOT true about XML validation using an XML type modifier?

    a. An XML type modifier associates the type with an XML schema.
    b. The XML type modifier can identify a single XML schema only.
    c. An XML type modifier is defined in a CREATE TABLE or ALTER TABLE statement as part of an XML column definition.
    d. You can use an ALTER TABLE statement to remove an XML schema from the column XML type definition.

The correct answer is B. It is not true that you can only specify one schema in the XML type modifier. In fact, the XML type modifier can identify more than one XML schema. For example:

```
CREATE TABLE EMPLOYEE(
ID INT NOT NULL,
CONTENT XML(XMLSCHEMA ID SYSXSR.ID01,
ID SYSXSR.ID02))
```

The other statements are true. An XML type modifier associates the type with an XML schema. An XML type modifier is defined in a CREATE TABLE or ALTER TABLE statement as part of an XML column definition. You can use an ALTER TABLE statement to remove an XML schema from the column XML type definition. An example of removing any XML schema modifiers could be:

```
ALTER TABLE EMPLOYEE
ALTER CONTENT
SET DATA TYPE XML
```

20. An XML index can be created on what column types?

    a. VARCHAR and XML.
    b. CLOB AND XML.
    c. XML only.
    d. Any of the above.

The correct answer is C. An XML index can be created only on an XML type column.

21. Which of the following can be used to validate an XML value according to a schema?

    a. Defining a column as type XML.
    b. Manually running the DSN_XMLVALIDATE.
    c. Both of the above.
    d. Neither of the above.

The correct answer is C. There are two ways to validate an XML value. Defining a column with the XML type modifier ensures that all XML documents stored in an XML column are validated according to a specified XML schema. You can also manually do the validation using the DSN_XMLVALIDATE function. DSN_ XMLVALIDATE returns an XML value that is the result of applying XML schema validation to the first argument of the function.

22. To determine whether an XML document has been validated, which function could you use?

    a. XMLXSROBJECTID.
    b. XMLDOCUMENT.
    c. XMLPARSE.
    d. None of the above.

The correct answer is A. The XMLXSROBJECTID function returns the XSR object identifier of the XML schema that was used to validate the specified XML document. If the value returned is zero, then the document was not validated.

The XMLDOCUMENT function returns an XML value with a single document node and its children nodes (if any). The XMLPARSE function parses an argument as an XML document and returns an XML value.

23. Which bind option would you use to enable parallel processing to improve performance of a query?

    a. DEGREE(1)
    b. DEGREE(2)
    c. DEGREE(ANY)
    d. DEGREE(PARALLEL)

The correct answer is C. The DEGREE option determines whether to attempt to run a query using parallel processing to maximize performance. Specifying DEGREE(1) prohibits parallel processing, while DEGREE(ANY) enables parallel processing. The values 2 and PARALLEL are invalid.

24. To improve performance for read-only queries against remote sites, which DBPROTOCOL value should be used when binding applications?

    a. DRDACBF
    b. DRDA
    c. PRIVATE
    d. DRDABCF

The correct answer is A. Binding applications with the new **DBPROTOCOL (DRDACBF)** option results in package-based continuous block fetch. Package-based continuous block fetch provides a performance advantage for an application that generates large read-only result sets for remote sites.

DRDA protocol is the default and is a standard architecture for accessing distributed databases. PRIVATE is no longer supported as a DBPROTOCOL value in DB2 10 and later. DRDABCF is an invalid value for DBPROTOCOL.

25. Which of the following is a Stage 2 predicate?

    a. COL IS NULL
    b. SUBSTR(COL,1,n) = value
    c. EXISTS(subquery)
    d. COL LIKE pattern

The correct answer is C. EXISTS(subquery) is a stage two predicate. The other choices are stage 1.

26. Which of the following would probably NOT improve query performance?

    a. Use indexable predicates in your queries.
    b. Execute the RUNSTATS utility and rebind application programs.

391

c. Use the EXISTS clause instead of COL IN (value list).

d. All of the above could improve application performance.

The correct answer is C. EXISTS is a stage 2 predicate, whereas COL IN (value list) is stage 1. Stage 2 predicates are always processed after Stage 1, thereby slowing performance. The other choices could all potentially improve performance in an application. All indexable predicates are stage one and refer to table indexes (both of which could improve performance). Executing RUNSTATS and rebinding application programs uses the latest information on the tables and could improve the access path chosen in the DB2 plan.

27. Which of the following trace types could be used to collect information about which users tried to access DB2 objects and were denied due to inadequate authorization?

    a. ACCTG

    b. MONITOR

    c. AUDIT

    d. STATISTICS

The correct answer is C. An audit trace gathers information about DB2 security controls. Class 1 for this trace gathers information about which users tried to access DB2 objects and were denied due to inadequate authorization.

The accounting trace collects processing data that is written when a transaction completes. The monitor trace permits attached monitor programs to access DB2 trace data via calls to the instrumentation facility interface (IFI). A statistics trace provides data about how much the DB2 system and database services are used.

28. Which of the following is NOT a valid value for the SMFACCT subsystem parameter?

    a. YES

    b. NO

    c. $

    d. *

The correct answer is C. $ is not a valid value for SMFACCT. The SMFACCT subsystem parameter indicates whether DB2 will send accounting data to SMF

automatically when DB2 is started. The four valid values are:

- YES
- NO
- A list of classes separated by commas
- * (starts all classes)

29. Which of the following EXPLAIN tables includes information about the access path that will be used to return data?

    a. PLAN_TABLE
    b. DSN_QUERY_TABLE
    c. DSN_STATEMENT_TABLE
    d. None of the above.

The correct answer is A. The PLAN_TABLE includes information about access paths that is derived from the explain statements.

The DSN_QUERY_TABLE includes information about a SQL statement both before and after transformation. The DSN_STATEMENT_TABLE contains information about the estimated cost of specified SQL statements.

30. If you find out that your application query is doing a table space scan, what changes could you make to improve the scan efficiency?

    a. Create one or more indexes on the query search columns.
    b. Load the data to a temporary table and query that table instead of the base table.
    c. If the table is partitioned, change it to a non-partitioned table.
    d. All of the above could improve the scan efficiency.

The correct answer is A. You could create one or more indexes on the search columns so that an index scan would occur instead of the tablespace scan. The other choices would not improve scan efficiency. Temporary tables do not allow for indexes and so a full table scan would still occur. It would not make sense to change partitioned tables to non-partitioned if you were trying to improve scan efficiency. Partitioned tables have some advantage over non-partitioned if the table is partitioned by one of the fields being searched on. In that case the search could be automatically limited to only certain partitions instead of the entire ta-

ble. Also, partitioned tables enable other performance improving techniques such as parallel processing.

Index

Other Titles by Robert Wingate

COBOL Basic Training Using VSAM, IMS, DB2 and CICS

ISBN-13: 978-1734584721

This book will teach you the basic information and skills you need to develop applications with the COBOL programming language on IBM mainframe computers running z/OS. The instruction, examples and sample programs in this book are a fast track to becoming productive with COBOL as quickly as possible. The coverage includes COBOL with VSAM, IMS, DB2 and CICS. The content of this book is easy to read and digest, well organized and focused on honing real job skills. Acquiring these skills is a key step in mastering COBOL application development so you'll be ready to perform effectively on an application development team.

ISBN-13: 978-1734584714

This book will help you learn the basic and intermediate skills you need to write applications with Db2 11 for Linux, UNIX and Windows. The instruction, examples and questions/answers in this book are a fast track to becoming productive as quickly as possible. The content is easy to read and digest, well organized and focused on honing real job skills. Demonstration programs are given in both the Java and c# .NET languages. Db2 11 for LUW Developer Training and Reference Guide is a key step in the direction of mastering Db2 application development so you'll be ready to perform on a technical development team.

IBM Mainframe Developer

Training and Reference Guide

JCL, MVS Utilities, COBOL, VSAM, IMS, DB2, CICS

Robert Wingate

ISBN-13: 978-1734584738

This book will teach you the basic information and skills you need to develop applications on IBM mainframe computers running z/OS. The instruction, examples and sample programs in this book are a fast track to becoming productive as a developer in the IBM mainframe environment as quickly as possible. The coverage includes JCL, MVS Utilities, COBOL, VSAM, IMS, DB2 and CICS. The content of this book is easy to read and digest, well organized and focused on honing real job skills. Acquiring these skills is a key step in mastering IBM application development so you'll be ready to perform effectively on an application development team.

COBOL Basic Training Using VSAM, IMS and DB2

ISBN-13: 978-1720820710

This book will teach you the basic information and skills you need to develop applications with COBOL on IBM mainframes running z/OS. The instruction, examples and sample programs in this book are a fast track to becoming productive as quickly using COBOL. The content is easy to read and digest, well organized and focused on honing real job skills.

CICS Basic Training for Application Developers Using DB2 and VSAM

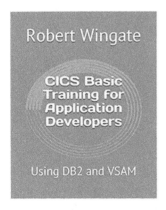

ISBN-13: 978-1794325067

This book will teach you the basic information and skills you need to develop applications with CICS on IBM mainframe computers running z/OS. The instruction, examples and sample programs in this book are a fast track to becoming productive as quickly as possible using CICS with the COBOL programming language. The content is easy to read and digest, well organized and focused on honing real job skills.

Quick Start Training for IBM z/OS Application Developers, Volume 1

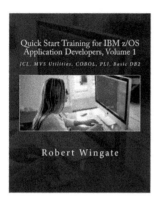

ISBN-13: 978-1986039840

This book will teach you the basic information and skills you need to develop applications on IBM mainframes running z/OS. The instruction, examples and sample programs in this book are a fast track to becoming productive as quickly as possible in JCL, MVS Utilities, COBOL, PLI and DB2. The content is easy to read and digest, well organized and focused on honing real job skills. IBM z/OS Quick Start Training for Application Developers is a key step in the direction of mastering IBM application development so you'll be ready to join a technical team.

Quick Start Training for IBM z/OS Application Developers, Volume 2

ISBN-13: 978-1717284594

This book will teach you the basic information and skills you need to develop applications on IBM mainframes running z/OS. The instruction, examples and sample programs in this book are a fast track to becoming productive as quickly as possible in VSAM, IMS and DB2. The content is easy to read and digest, well organized and focused on honing real job skills. IBM z/OS Quick Start Training for Application Developers is a key step in the direction of mastering IBM application development so you'll be ready to join a technical team.

Teradata Basic Training for Application Developers

ISBN-13: 978-1082748882

This book will help you learn the basic information and skills you need to develop applications with Teradata. The instruction, examples and questions/answers in this book are a fast track to becoming productive as quickly as possible. The content is easy to read and digest, well organized and focused on honing real job skills. Programming examples are coded in both Java and C# .NET. Teradata Basic Training for Application Developers is a key step in the direction of mastering Teradata application development so you'll be ready to join a technical team.

IMS Basic Training for Application Developers

ISBN-13: 978-1793440433

This book will teach you the basic information and skills you need to develop applications with IMS on IBM mainframe computers running z/OS. The instruction, examples and sample programs in this book are a fast track to becoming productive as quickly as possible using IMS with COBOL and PLI. The content is easy to read and digest, well organized and focused on honing real job skills.

DB2 Exam C2090-313 Preparation Guide

ISBN 13: 978-1548463052

This book will help you pass IBM Exam C2090-313 and become an IBM Certified Application Developer - DB2 11 for z/OS. The instruction, examples and questions/answers in the book offer you a significant advantage by helping you to gauge your readiness for the exam, to better understand the objectives being tested, and to get a broad exposure to the DB2 11 knowledge you'll be tested on.

DB2 Exam C2090-313 Practice Questions

ISBN 13: 978-1534992467

This book will help you pass IBM Exam C2090-313 and become an IBM Certified Application Developer - DB2 11 for z/OS. The 180 questions and answers in the book (three full practice exams) offer you a significant advantage by helping you to gauge your readiness for the exam, to better understand the objectives being tested, and to get a broad exposure to the DB2 11 knowledge you'll be tested on.

DB2 Exam C2090-320 Preparation Guide

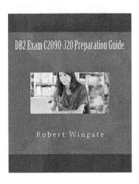

ISBN 13: 978-1544852096

This book will help you pass IBM Exam C2090-320 and become an IBM Certified Database Associate - DB2 11 Fundamentals for z/OS. The instruction, examples and questions/answers in the book offer you a significant advantage by helping you to gauge your readiness for the exam, to better understand the objectives being tested, and to get a broad exposure to the DB2 11 knowledge you'll be tested on. The book is also a fine introduction to DB2 for z/OS!

DB2 Exam C2090-320 Practice Questions

ISBN-13: 978-1539715405

This book will help you pass IBM Exam C2090-320 and become an IBM Certified Database Associate - DB2 11 Fundamentals for z/OS. The 189 questions and answers in the book (three full practice exams) offer you a significant advantage by helping you to gauge your readiness for the exam, to better understand the objectives being tested, and to get a broad exposure to the DB2 11 knowledge you'll be tested on.

About the Author

Robert Wingate is a computer services professional with over 30 years of IBM mainframe and distributed programming experience. He holds several IBM certifications, including IBM Certified Application Developer - DB2 11 for z/OS, and IBM Certified Database Administrator for LUW.